THE
APOCRYPHA

OF THE

OLD TESTAMENT

REVISED STANDARD VERSION

TRANSLATED FROM THE GREEK AND LATIN TONGUES
BEING THE VERSION SET FORTH A.D. 1611
REVISED A.D. 1894
COMPARED WITH THE MOST ANCIENT AUTHORITIES
AND REVISED A.D. 1957

NELSON

THOMAS NELSON AND SONS LTD

36 Park Street London W1
P.O. Box 336 Apapa Lagos
P.O. Box 25012 Nairobi
77 Coffee Street San Fernando Trinidad

THOMAS NELSON (AUSTRALIA) LTD
597 Little Collins Street Melbourne

THOMAS NELSON & SONS (SOUTH AFRICA) (PROPRIETARY) LTD
P.O. Box 9881 Johannesburg

THOMAS NELSON AND SONS (CANADA) LTD
81 Curlew Drive Don Mills Ontario

THOMAS NELSON AND SONS
Copewood and Davis Streets Camden 3, N.J.

First published in this edition February 1958
Third impression 1965
Fourth impression 1967

Printed in Great Britain by
Thomas Nelson (Printers) Ltd, London and Edinburgh

PREFACE

In response to the request of the General Convention of the Protestant Episcopal Church, October, 1952, the Division of Christian Education of the National Council of the Churches of Christ in the U.S.A. organized a committee of scholars to undertake revision of the English translation of the Apocrypha; and its publication was authorized by the General Board, NCCCUSA, December 12, 1952. The scholars accepting this assignment were Millar Burrows, Winkley Professor of Biblical Theology, Yale University; Henry J. Cadbury, Hollis Professor of Divinity, Harvard University; Clarence T. Craig, Dean and Professor of New Testament, Drew Theological Seminary; Floyd V. Filson, Dean and Professor of New Testament Literature and History, McCormick Theological Seminary; Frederick C. Grant, Professor of Biblical Theology, Union Theological Seminary; Bruce M. Metzger, Professor of New Testament, Princeton Theological Seminary; Robert H. Pfeiffer, Hancock Professor of Hebrew and other Oriental Languages, Harvard University; Allen P. Wikgren, Professor of New Testament, University of Chicago; and Luther A. Weigle, Sterling Professor of Religious Education and Dean of the Divinity School, Emeritus, Yale University, who was appointed chairman of the Committee. A great loss was sustained in the death, August 20, 1953, of Dean Craig. In 1954, J. Carter Swaim, Professor of New Testament at Western Theological Seminary, Pittsburgh, became Executive Director, Department of the English Bible, in the Division of Christian Education, NCCCUSA, and was added to the membership of the Committee. Roy G. Ross, General Secretary of the National Council of the Churches of Christ in the U.S.A., and Paul C. Payne, Chairman, and Gerald E. Knoff, Executive Secretary, of its Division of Christian Education, have been members of the Committee ex officio.

The work has involved the preparation and circulation of mimeographed drafts of translation, the discussion and resolution of all disputed points in face-to-face conference, the circulation of new drafts embodying the decisions reached in conference, and a final review of each book in the light of written agenda proposed by the members of the Committee and of the Advisory Board made up of representatives appointed by denominations which accepted the invitation to review the drafts. This procedure is similar to that followed by the Committee which prepared the Revised Standard Version of the Bible, containing the Old and New Testaments; and, in general, similar principles of translation have been followed.

Meetings of the Committee were held at the Yale University Divinity School, January 30–31, June 22 to July 3, and December 18–23, in 1953; and December 7–9, 1956. Most of the conferences, however, were held at the Hotel Northfield, East Northfield, Massachusetts, where the Committee was in session over the following periods: August 17–29, 1953; June 14–26 and August 16–28, 1954; June 13–25 and August 15–27, 1955; and June 11–23, 1956.

The Apocrypha here translated are those books and portions of books which appear in the Latin Vulgate, either as part of the Old Testament or as an appendix, but are not in the Hebrew Bible. With the exception of 2 Esdras these books appear in the Greek version of the Old Testament which is known as the Septuagint, but they are not included in the Hebrew Canon of Holy Scripture.

Because of their inclusion in the Latin Vulgate, the Church throughout the medieval period looked upon these books as belonging to the Scriptures, though not unaware of their lack of canonical status among the Jews. In 1546, the Council of Trent decreed that the Canon of the Old Testament includes them (except the Prayer of Manasseh and 1 and 2 Esdras), and condemned any one who "does not accept these entire books, with all their parts, as they have customarily been read in the Catholic Church and are found in the ancient editions of the Latin Vulgate, as sacred and canonical."

In Luther's German translation of the Bible (1534) the Apocrypha stand between the Old Testament and the New Testament, with the title: "Apocrypha, that is, books which are not held equal to the sacred Scriptures, and nevertheless are useful and good to read." Coverdale's English translation of the Bible (1535) gave them the same position, with the title: "Apocrypha. The books and treatises which among the fathers of old are not reckoned to be of like authority with the other books of the Bible, neither are they found in the Canon of the Hebrew."

The Apocrypha had a place in all the sixteenth century English translations of the Bible, and in the King James Version (1611). The Thirty-nine Articles of the Church of England say concerning the Apocrypha: "And the other books (as Jerome saith) the Church doth read for example of life, and instruction of manners; but yet doth it not apply them to establish any doctrine." The Puritans opposed every use of them that would suggest that they possessed any authority; and the Westminster Confession (1648) declares: "The books commonly called Apocrypha, not being of divine inspiration, are no part of the Canon of Scripture; and therefore are of no authority in the Church of God, nor to be otherwise approved, or made use of, than other human writings."

The basic Greek text of the books of the Apocrypha from which the present translation was made is the edition of the Septuagint prepared by Alfred Rahlfs, published by the Württemberg Bible Society, Stuttgart, 1935. This text is based mainly upon the Codex Vaticanus (4th century A.D.), the Codex Sinaiticus (4th century), and the Codex Alexandrinus (5th century). For the book of Tobit the Greek text found in the codices Vaticanus and Alexandrinus was followed; and for the Additions to Daniel (namely, Susanna, the Prayer of Azariah and the Song of the Three Young Men, and Bel and the Dragon) the translators used the Greek version of Theodotion. In both these cases the Committee's procedure was in accord with general usage.

The basic text followed in the case of 2 Esdras is the Old Latin version edited by Robert L. Bensly. This was supplemented by consulting the Latin text edited by Bruno Violet, as well as the several Oriental versions of 2 Esdras, namely, the Syriac, Ethiopic, Arabic (two forms, referred to as Arabic 1 and Arabic 2), Armenian, and Georgian versions. In addition, account was taken of a few verses of the fifteenth chapter of 2 Esdras which have been preserved in Greek (Oxyrhynchus Papyrus number 1010).

In the translation of Sirach, constant reference was made to the medieval Hebrew fragments of a large part of this book, which were discovered at the end of the nineteenth century. Throughout the work of translating the books of the Apocrypha consideration was given to variant readings, including those in the *apparatus criticus* of Rahlfs as well as those in other editions of the Septuagint or of single books of the Apocrypha. Likewise, a search was made for all portions of the Apocrypha preserved in the Greek papyri from Egypt, and the text of these fragments was collated with that of Rahlfs.

No attempt has been made to provide introductions to the various books of the Apocrypha, as here translated. The scholar will not need them, and for the general reader there are admirable recent books on the Apocrypha by Charles C. Torrey, Edgar J. Goodspeed, Robert H. Pfeiffer, and Bruce M. Metzger.

We gladly acknowledge our debt, not only to the scholars who throughout the centuries have made competent studies of these books, but also to the former English translations, especially the King James Version of 1611, the English Revised Version of 1894, and Goodspeed's translation of 1938.

The quarrels over the authority of the Apocrypha are now largely matters of the past. A generation that has witnessed the discovery of the Dead Sea Scrolls will probably agree with the statement by Professor Frank C. Porter, in Hastings' Dictionary of the Bible (1901), that "modern historical interest, on the other hand, is putting the Apocrypha in their true place as significant documents of a most important era in religious history."

THE NAMES AND ORDER

OF THE

BOOKS CALLED APOCRYPHA

1 Josiah kept the passover to his Lord in Jerusalem; he killed the passover lamb on the fourteenth day of the first month, ² having placed the priests according to their divisions, arrayed in their garments, in the temple of the Lord. ³ And he told the Levites, the temple servants of Israel, that they should sanctify themselves to the Lord and put the holy ark of the Lord in the house which Solomon the king, the son of David, had built; ⁴ and he said, "You need no longer carry it upon your shoulders. Now worship the Lord your God and serve his people Israel; and prepare yourselves by your families and kindred, ⁵ in accordance with the directions of David king of Israel and the magnificence of Solomon his son. Stand in order in the temple according to the grouping of the fathers' houses of you Levites, who minister before your brethren the sons of Israel, ⁶ and kill the passover lamb and prepare the sacrifices for your brethren, and keep the passover according to the commandment of the Lord which was given to Moses."

7 And Josiah gave to the people who were present thirty thousand lambs and kids, and three thousand calves; these were given from the king's possessions, as he promised, to the people and the priests and Levites. ⁸ And Hilkiah, Zechariah, and Jehiel,ᵃ the chief officers of the temple, gave to the priests for the passover two thousand six hundred sheep and three hundred calves. ⁹ And Jeconiah and Shemaiah and Nethanel his brother, and Hashabiah and Ochiel and Joram, captains over thousands, gave the Levites for the passover five thousand sheep and seven hundred calves.

10 And this is what took place.

ᵃ Gk *Esyelus*

The priests and the Levites. properly arrayed and having the unleavened bread, stood according to kindred ¹¹ and the grouping of the fathers' houses, before the people, to make the offering to the Lord as it is written in the book of Moses; this they did in the morning. ¹² They roasted the passover lamb with fire, as required; and they boiled the sacrifices in brass pots and cauldrons, with a pleasing odour, ¹³ and carried them to all the people. Afterward they prepared the passover for themselves and for their brethren the priests, the sons of Aaron, ¹⁴ because the priests were offering the fat until night; so the Levites prepared it for themselves and for their brethren the priests, the sons of Aaron. ¹⁵ And the temple singers, the sons of Asaph, were in their place according to the arrangement made by David, and also Asaph, Zechariah, and Eddinus, who represented the king. ¹⁶ The gatekeepers were at each gate; no one needed to depart from his duties, for their brethren the Levites prepared the passover for them.

17 So the things that had to do with the sacrifices to the Lord were accomplished that day: the passover was kept ¹⁸ and the sacrifices were offered on the altar of the Lord, according to the command of King Josiah. ¹⁹ And the people of Israel who were present at that time kept the passover and the feast of unleavened bread seven days. ²⁰ No passover like it had been kept in Israel since the times of Samuel the prophet; ²¹ none of the kings of Israel had kept such a passover as was kept by Josiah and the priests and the Levites and the men of Judah and all of Israel who were dwelling in Jerusalem. ²² In the eighteenth

year of the reign of Josiah this pass-over was kept. 23 And the deeds of Josiah were upright in the sight of his Lord, for his heart was full of godliness. 24 The events of his reign have been recorded in the past, con-cerning those who sinned and acted wickedly toward the Lord beyond any other people or kingdom, and how they grieved the Lord *b* deeply, so that the words of the Lord rose up against Israel.

25 After all these acts of Josiah, it happened that Pharaoh, king of Egypt, went to make war at Car-chemish on the Euphrates, and Josiah went out against him. 26 And the king of Egypt sent word to him saying, "What have we to do with each other, king of Judea? 27 I was not sent against you by the Lord God, for my war is at the Euphrates. And now the Lord is with me! The Lord is with me, urging me on! Stand aside, and do not oppose the Lord."

28 But Josiah did not turn back to his chariot, but tried to fight with him, and did not heed the words of Jeremiah the prophet from the mouth of the Lord. 29 He joined battle with him in the plain of Megiddo, and the commanders came down against King Josiah. 30 And the king said to his servants, "Take me away from the battle, for I am very weak." And immediately his servants took him out of the line of battle. 31 And he got into his second chariot; and after he was brought back to Jerusalem he died, and was buried in the tomb of his fathers. 32 And in all Judea they mourned for Josiah. Jeremiah the prophet lamented for Josiah, and the prin-cipal men, with the women,*c* have made lamentation for him to this day: it was ordained that this should always be done throughout the whole nation of Israel. 33 These things are written in the book of the histories of the kings of Judea; and every one of the acts of Josiah, and his splen-

dour, and his understanding of the law of the Lord, and the things that he had done before and these that are now told, are recorded in the book of the kings of Israel and Judah.

34 And the men of the nation took Jeconiah the son of Josiah, who was twenty-three years old, and made him king in succession to Josiah his father. 35 And he reigned three months in Judah and Jerusalem. Then the king of Egypt deposed him from reigning in Jerusalem, 36 and fined the nation a hundred talents of silver and a talent of gold. 37 And the king of Egypt made Jehoiakim his brother king of Judea and Jeru-salem. 38 Jehoiakim put the nobles in prison, and seized his brother Zarius and brought him up out of Egypt.

39 Jehoiakim was twenty-five years old when he began to reign in Judea and Jerusalem, and he did what was evil in the sight of the Lord. 40 And Nebuchadnezzar king of Babylon came up against him, and bound him with a chain of brass and took him away to Babylon. 41 Nebuchadnezzar also took some of the holy vessels of the Lord, and carried them away, and stored them in his temple in Babylon. 42 But the things that are reported about Jehoiakim *d* and his uncleanness and impiety are written in the chronicles of the kings.

43 Jehoiachin *e* his son became king in his stead; when he was made king he was eighteen years old, 44 and he reigned three months and ten days in Jerusalem. He did what was evil in the sight of the Lord. 45 So after a year Nebuchadnezzar sent and re-moved him to Babylon, with the holy vessels of the Lord, 46 and made Zedekiah king of Judea and Jeru-salem.

Zedekiah was twenty-one years old, and he reigned eleven years. 47 He also did what was evil in the sight of the Lord, and did not heed the words that were spoken by Jere-

b Gk *him*   *c* Or, *their wives*   *d* Gk *him*   *e* Gk *Jehoiakim* miah the prophet from the mouth of the Lord. ⁴⁸ And though King Nebuchadnezzar had made him swear by the name of the Lord, he broke his oath and rebelled; and he stiffened his neck and hardened his heart and transgressed the laws of the Lord, the God of Israel. ⁴⁹ Even the leaders of the people and of the priests committed many acts of sacrilege and lawlessness beyond all the unclean deeds of all the nations, and polluted the temple of the Lord which had been hallowed in Jerusalem. ⁵⁰ So the God of their fathers sent by his messenger to call them back, because he would have spared them and his dwelling place. ⁵¹ But they mocked his messengers, and whenever the Lord spoke, they scoffed at his prophets, ⁵² until in his anger against his people because of their ungodly acts he gave command to bring against them the kings of the Chaldeans. ⁵³ These slew their young men with the sword around their holy temple, and did not spare young man or virgin, old man or child, for he gave them all into their hands. ⁵⁴ And all the holy vessels of the Lord, great and small, and the treasure chests of the Lord, and the royal stores, they took and carried away to Babylon. ⁵⁵ And they burned the house of the Lord and broke down the walls of Jerusalem and burned their towers with fire, ⁵⁶ and utterly destroyed all its glorious things. The survivors he led away to Babylon with the sword, ⁵⁷ and they were servants to him and to his sons until the Persians began to reign, in fulfilment of the word of the Lord by the mouth of Jeremiah: ⁵⁸ "Until the land has enjoyed its sabbaths, it shall keep sabbath all the time of its desolation until the completion of seventy years."

2 In the first year of Cyrus as king of the Persians, that the word of the Lord by the mouth of

^f Gk *Sanabassarus*

Jeremiah might be accomplished, ² the Lord stirred up the spirit of Cyrus king of the Persians, and he made a proclamation throughout all his kingdom and also put it in writing: ³ "Thus says Cyrus king of the Persians: The Lord of Israel, the Lord Most High, has made me king of the world, ⁴ and he has commanded me to build him a house at Jerusalem, which is in Judea. ⁵ If any one of you, therefore, is of his people, may his Lord be with him, and let him go up to Jerusalem, which is in Judea, and build the house of the Lord of Israel—he is the Lord who dwells in Jerusalem; ⁶ and let each man, wherever he may live, be helped by the men of his place with gold and silver, ⁷ with gifts, and with horses and cattle, besides the other things added as votive offerings for the temple of the Lord which is in Jerusalem."

8 Then arose the heads of families of the tribes of Judah and Benjamin, and the priests and the Levites, and all whose spirit the Lord had stirred to go up to build the house in Jerusalem for the Lord; ⁹ and their neighbours helped them with everything, with silver and gold, with horses and cattle, and with a very great number of votive offerings from many whose hearts were stirred.

10 Cyrus the king also brought out the holy vessels of the Lord which Nebuchadnezzar had carried away from Jerusalem and stored in his temple of idols. ¹¹ When Cyrus king of the Persians brought these out, he gave them to Mithridates his treasurer, ¹² and by him they were given to Sheshbazzar ^f the governor of Judea. ¹³ The number of these was: a thousand gold cups, a thousand silver cups, twenty-nine silver censers, thirty gold bowls, two thousand four hundred and ten silver bowls, and a thousand other vessels. ¹⁴ All the vessels were handed over, gold and silver, five thousand four hundred and sixty-nine, ¹⁵ and they were carried back

by Sheshbazzar[1] with the returning exiles from Babylon to Jerusalem.

16 But in the time of Artaxerxes king of the Persians, Bishlam, Mithridates, Tabeel, Rehum, Beltethmus, Shimshai the scribe, and the rest of their associates, living in Samaria and other places, wrote him the following letter, against those who were living in Judea and Jerusalem:

17 "To King Artaxerxes our lord, Your servants Rehum the recorder and Shimshai the scribe and the other judges of their council in Coelesyria and Phoenicia: 18 Now be it known to our lord the king that the Jews who came up from you to us have gone to Jerusalem and are building that rebellious and wicked city, repairing its market places and walls and laying the foundations for a temple. 19 Now if this city is built and the walls finished, they will not only refuse to pay tribute but will even resist kings. 20 And since the building of the temple is now going on, we think it best not to neglect such a matter, 21 but to speak to our lord the king, in order that, if it seems good to you, search may be made in the records of your fathers. 22 You will find in the chronicles what has been written about them, and will learn that this city was rebellious, troubling both kings and other cities, 23 and that the Jews were rebels and kept setting up blockades in it from of old. That is why this city was laid waste. 24 Therefore we now make known to you, O lord and king, that if this city is built and its walls finished, you will no longer have access to Coelesyria and Phoenicia."

25 Then the king, in reply to Rehum the recorder and Beltethmus and Shimshai the scribe and the others associated with them and living in Samaria and Syria and Phoenicia, wrote as follows:

26 "I have read the letter which you sent me. So I ordered search to be made, and it has been found that

this city from of old has fought against kings, 27 and that the men in it were given to rebellion and war, and that mighty and cruel kings ruled in Jerusalem and exacted tribute from Coelesyria and Phoenicia. 28 Therefore I have now issued orders to prevent these men from building the city and to take care that nothing more be done 29 and that such wicked proceedings go no further to the annoyance of kings."

30 Then, when the letter from King Artaxerxes was read, Rehum and Shimshai the scribe and their associates went in haste to Jerusalem, with horsemen and a multitude in battle array, and began to hinder the builders. And the building of the temple in Jerusalem ceased until the second year of the reign of Darius king of the Persians.

3 Now King Darius gave a great banquet for all that were under him and all that were born in his house and all the nobles of Media and Persia 2 and all the satraps and generals and governors that were under him in the hundred and twenty-seven satrapies from India to Ethiopia. 3 They ate and drank, and when they were satisfied they departed; and Darius the king went to his bedroom, and went to sleep, and then awoke.

4 Then the three young men of the bodyguard, who kept guard over the person of the king, said to one another, 5 "Let each of us state what one thing is strongest; and to him whose statement seems wisest, Darius the king will give rich gifts and great honours of victory. 6 He shall be clothed in purple, and drink from gold cups, and sleep on a gold bed, and have a chariot with gold bridles, and a turban of fine linen, and a necklace about his neck; 7 and because of his wisdom he shall sit next to Darius and shall be called kinsman of Darius."

8 Then each wrote his own statement, and they sealed them and put

them under the pillow of Darius the king, ⁹ and said, "When the king wakes, they will give him the writing; and to the one whose statement the king and the three nobles of Persia judge to be wisest the victory shall be given according to what is written." ¹⁰ The first wrote, "Wine is strongest." ¹¹ The second wrote, "The king is strongest." ¹² The third wrote, "Women are strongest, but truth is victor over all things."

13 When the king awoke, they took the writing and gave it to him, and he read it. ¹⁴ Then he sent and summoned all the nobles of Persia and Media and the satraps and generals and governors and prefects, ¹⁵ and he took his seat in the council chamber, and the writing was read in their presence. ¹⁶ And he said, "Call the young men, and they shall explain their statements." So they were summoned, and came in. ¹⁷ And they said to them, "Explain to us what you have written."

Then the first, who had spoken of the strength of wine, began and said: ¹⁸ "Gentlemen, how is wine the strongest? It leads astray the minds of all who drink it. ¹⁹ It makes equal the mind of the king and the orphan, of the slave and the free, of the poor and the rich. ²⁰ It turns every thought to feasting and mirth, and forgets all sorrow and debt. ²¹ It makes all hearts feel rich, forgets kings and satraps, and makes every one talk in millions.ᵍ ²² When men drink they forget to be friendly with friends and brothers, and before long they draw their swords; ²³ And when they recover from the wine, they do not remember what they have done. ²⁴ Gentlemen, is not wine the strongest, since it forces men to do these things?" When he had said this, he stopped speaking.

4 Then the second, who had spoken of the strength of the king, began to speak: ² "Gentlemen, are not men strongest, who rule over

ᵍ Gk *talents*

land and sea and all that is in them? ³ But the king is stronger; he is their lord and master, and whatever he says to them they obey. ⁴ If he tells them to make war on one another, they do it; and if he sends them out against the enemy, they go, and conquer mountains, walls, and towers. ⁵ They kill and are killed, and do not disobey the king's command; if they win the victory, they bring everything to the king—whatever spoil they take and everything else. ⁶ Likewise those who do not serve in the army or make war but till the soil, whenever they sow, reap the harvest and bring some to the king; and they compel one another to pay taxes to the king. ⁷ And yet he is only one man! If he tells them to kill, they kill; if he tells them to release, they release; ⁸ if he tells them to attack, they attack; if he tells them to lay waste, they lay waste; if he tells them to build, they build; ⁹ if he tells them to cut down, they cut down; if he tells them to plant, they plant. ¹⁰ All his people and his armies obey him. Moreover, he reclines, he eats and drinks and sleeps, ¹¹ but they keep watch around him and no one may go away to attend to his own affairs, nor do they disobey him. ¹² Gentlemen, why is not the king the strongest, since he is to be obeyed in this fashion?" And he stopped speaking.

13 Then the third, that is Zerubbabel, who had spoken of women and truth, began to speak: ¹⁴ "Gentlemen, is not the king great, and are not men many, and is not wine strong? Who then is their master, or who is their lord? Is it not women? ¹⁵ Women gave birth to the king and to every people that rules over sea and land. ¹⁶ From women they came; and women brought up the very men who plant the vineyards from which comes wine. ¹⁷ Women make men's clothes; they bring men glory; men cannot exist without women. ¹⁸ If men gather gold and silver or any

5

other beautiful thing, and then see a woman lovely in appearance and beauty, 19 they let all those things go, and gape at her, and with open mouths stare at her, and all prefer her to gold or silver or any other beautiful thing. 20 A man leaves his own father, who brought him up, and his own country, and cleaves to his wife. 21 With his wife he ends his days, with no thought of his father or his mother or his country. 22 Hence you must realize that women rule over you!

"Do you not labour and toil, and bring everything and give it to women? 23 A man takes his sword, and goes out to travel and rob and steal and to sail the sea and rivers; 24 he faces lions, and he walks in darkness, and when he steals and robs and plunders, he brings it back to the woman he loves. 25 A man loves his wife more than his father or his mother. 26 Many men have lost their minds because of women, and have become slaves because of them. 27 Many have perished, or stumbled, or sinned, because of women. 28 And now do you not believe me?

"Is not the king great in his power? Do not all lands fear to touch him? 29 Yet I have seen him with Apame, the king's concubine, the daughter of the illustrious Bartacus; she would sit at the king's right hand 30 and take the crown from the king's head and put it on her own, and slap the king with her left hand. 31 At this the king would gaze at her with mouth agape. If she smiles at him, he laughs; if she loses her temper with him, he flatters her, that she may be reconciled to him. 32 Gentlemen, why are not women strong, since they do such things?"

33 Then the king and the nobles looked at one another; and he began to speak about truth: 34 "Gentlemen, are not women strong? The earth is vast, and heaven is high, and the sun is swift in its course, for it makes the circuit of the heavens and returns to its place in one day. 35 Is he not great who does these things? But truth is great, and stronger than all things. 36 The whole earth calls upon truth, and heaven blesses her. All God's *h* works quake and tremble, and with him there is nothing unrighteous. 37 Wine is unrighteous, the king is unrighteous, women are unrighteous, all the sons of men are unrighteous, all their works are unrighteous, and all such things. There is no truth in them and in their unrighteousness they will perish. 38 But truth endures and is strong for ever, and lives and prevails for ever and ever. 39 With her there is no partiality or preference, but she does what is righteous instead of anything that is unrighteous or wicked. All men approve her deeds, 40 and there is nothing unrighteous in her judgment. To her belongs the strength and the kingship and the power and the majesty of all the ages. Blessed be the God of truth!" 41 He ceased speaking; then all the people shouted, and said, "Great is truth, and strongest of all!"

42 Then the king said to him, "Ask what you wish, even beyond what is written, and we will give it to you, for you have been found to be the wisest. And you shall sit next to me, and be called my kinsman." 43 Then he said to the king, "Remember the vow which you made to build Jerusalem, in the day when you became king, 44 and to send back all the vessels that were taken from Jerusalem, which Cyrus set apart when he began *i* to destroy Babylon, and vowed to send them back there. 45 You also vowed to build the temple, which the Edomites burned when Judea was laid waste by the Chaldeans. 46 And now, O lord the king, this is what I ask and request of you, and this befits your greatness. I pray therefore that you fulfil the vow whose fulfilment you vowed to the King of heaven with your own lips."

47 Then Darius the king rose, and

h Gk *All the works*   *i* Cn: Gk *vowed*

6

kissed him, and wrote letters for him to all the treasurers and governors and generals and satraps, that they should give escort to him and all who were going up with him to build Jerusalem. ⁴⁸ And he wrote letters to all the governors in Coelesyria and Phoenicia and to those in Lebanon, to bring cedar timber from Lebanon to Jerusalem, and to help him build the city. ⁴⁹ And he wrote for all the Jews who were going up from his kingdom to Judea, in the interest of their freedom, that no officer or satrap or governor or treasurer should forcibly enter their doors; ⁵⁰ that all the country which they would occupy should be theirs without tribute; that the Idumeans should give up the villages of the Jews which they held; ⁵¹ that twenty talents a year should be given for the building of the temple until it was completed, ⁵² and an additional ten talents a year for burnt offerings to be offered on the altar every day, in accordance with the commandment to make seventeen offerings; ⁵³ and that all who came from Babylonia to build the city should have their freedom, they and their children and all the priests who came. ⁵⁴ He wrote also concerning their support and the priests' garments in which ʲ they were to minister. ⁵⁵ He wrote that the support for the Levites should be provided until the day when the temple should be finished and Jerusalem built. ⁵⁶ He wrote that land and wages should be provided for all who guarded the city. ⁵⁷ And he sent back from Babylon all the vessels which Cyrus had set apart; everything that Cyrus had ordered to be done, he also commanded to be done and to be sent to Jerusalem.

⁵⁸ When the young man went out, he lifted up his face to heaven toward Jerusalem, and praised the King of heaven, saying, ⁵⁹ "From thee is the victory; from thee is wisdom; and thine is the glory. I am thy servant. ⁶⁰ Blessed art thou, who hast given me wisdom; I give thee thanks, O Lord of our fathers."

61 So he took the letters, and went to Babylon and told this to all his brethren. ⁶² And they praised the God of their fathers, because he had given them release and permission ⁶³ to go up and build Jerusalem and the temple which is called by his name; and they feasted, with music and rejoicing, for seven days.

5 After this the heads of fathers' houses were chosen to go up, according to their tribes, with their wives and sons and daughters, and their menservants and maidservants, and their cattle. ² And Darius sent with them a thousand horsemen to take them back to Jerusalem in safety, with the music of drums and flutes; ³ and all their brethren were making merry. And he made them go up with them.

4 These are the names of the men who went up, according to their fathers' houses in the tribes, over their groups: ⁵ the priests, the sons of Phinehas, son of Aaron; Jeshua the son of Jozadak, son of Seraiah, and Joakim the son of Zerubbabel, son of Shealtiel, of the house of David, of the lineage of Phares, of the tribe of Judah, ⁶ who spoke wise words before Darius the king of the Persians, in the second year of his reign, in the month of Nisan, the first month.

7 These are the men of Judea who came up out of their sojourn in captivity, whom Nebuchadnezzar king of Babylon had carried away to Babylon ⁸ and who returned to Jerusalem and the rest of Judea, each to his own town. They came with Zerubbabel and Jeshua, Nehemiah, Seraiah, Resaiah, Bigvai,ᵏ Mordecai, Bilshan,ˡ Mispar,ᵐ Reeliah, Rehum, and Baanah, their leaders.

9 The number of the men of the nation and their leaders: the sons of Parosh, two thousand one hun-

ʲ Gk *in what priestly garments*   ᵏ Gk *Eneneus*   ˡ Gk *Beelsarus*   ᵐ Gk *Aspharasus*

dred and seventy-two. The sons of Shephatiah, four hundred and seventy-two. [10] The sons of Arah, seven hundred and fifty-six. [11] The sons of Pahathmoab, of the sons of Jeshua and Joab, two thousand eight hundred and twelve. [12] The sons of Elam, one thousand two hundred and fifty-four. The sons of Zattu, nine hundred and forty-five. The sons of Chorbe, seven hundred and five. The sons of Bani, six hundred and forty-eight. [13] The sons of Bebai, six hundred and twenty-three. The sons of Azgad, one thousand three hundred and twenty-two. [14] The sons of Adonikam, six hundred and sixty-seven. The sons of Bigvai, two thousand and sixty-six. The sons of Adin, four hundred and fifty-four. [15] The sons of Ater, namely of Hezekiah, ninety-two. The sons of Kilan and Azetas, sixty-seven. The sons of Azaru, four hundred and thirty-two. [16] The sons of Annias, one hundred and one. The sons of Arom. The sons of Bezai, three hundred and twenty-three. The sons of Jorah,[n] one hundred and twelve. [17] The sons of Baiterus, three thousand and five. The sons of Bethlehem,[o] one hundred and twenty-three. [18] The men of Netophah, fifty-five. The men of Anathoth, one hundred and fifty-eight. The men of Bethasmoth, forty-two. [19] The men of Kiriatharim, twenty-five. The men of Chephirah and Beeroth, seven hundred and forty-three. [20] The Chadiasans and Ammidians, four hundred and twenty-two. The men of Ramah[p] and Geba, six hundred and twenty-one. [21] The men of Michmas,[q] one hundred and twenty-two. The men of Bethel,[r] fifty-two. The sons of Magbish,[s] one hundred and fifty-six. [22] The sons of the other Elam[t] and Ono, seven hundred and twenty-five. The sons of Jericho,

three hundred and forty-five. [23] The sons of Senaah, three thousand three hundred and thirty.

24 The priests: the sons of Jedaiah the son of Jeshua, of the sons of Anasib, nine hundred and seventy-two. The sons of Immer, one thousand and fifty-two. [25] The sons of Pashhur, one thousand two hundred and forty-seven. The sons of Harim, one thousand and seventeen.

26 The Levites: the sons of Jeshua and Kadmiel and Bannas and Sudias, seventy-four. [27] The temple singers: the sons of Asaph, one hundred and twenty-eight. [28] The gatekeepers: the sons of Shallum, the sons of Ater, the sons of Talmon, the sons of Akkub, the sons of Hatita, the sons of Shobai, in all one hundred and thirty-nine.

29 The temple servants: the sons of Ziha,[u] the sons of Hasupha, the sons of Tabbaoth, the sons of Keros, the sons of Siaha,[v] the sons of Padon, the sons of Lebanah, the sons of Hagabah, [30] the sons of Akkub, the sons of Uthai, the sons of Ketab, the sons of Hagab, the sons of Shamlai,[w] the sons of Hana, the sons of Cathua, the sons of Gahar,[x] [31] the sons of Reaiah,[y] the sons of Rezin,[z] the sons of Nekoda,[a] the sons of Chezib, the sons of Gazzan,[b] the sons of Uzza, the sons of Paseah,[c] the sons of Hasrah, the sons of Besai,[d] the sons of Asnah, the sons of the Meunites,[e] the sons of Nephisim, the sons of Bakbuk,[f] the sons of Hakupha, the sons of Asur, the sons of Pharakim, the sons of Bazluth, [32] the sons of Mehida, the sons of Cutha, the sons of Charea, the sons of Barkos, the sons of Sisera,[g] the sons of Temah, the sons of Neziah, the sons of Hatipha.

33 The sons of Solomon's servants: the sons of Hassophereth,[h] the sons of Peruda, the sons of Jaalah, the

---

[n] Gk *Arsiphurith*   [o] Gk *Bethlomon*   [p] Gk *Kirama*   [q] Gk *Macalon*   [r] Gk *Betolio*   [s] Gk *Niphis*
[t] Gk *Calamolalus*   [u] Gk *Esau*   [v] Gk *Sua*   [w] Gk *Subai*   [x] Gk *Geddur*   [y] Gk *Jairus*
[z] Gk *Daisan*   [a] Gk *Noeba*   [b] Gk *Gazera*   [c] Gk *Phinoe*   [d] Gk *Basthai*   [e] Gk *Maani*
[f] Gk *Acub* or *Acuph* or *Acum*   [g] Gk *Serar*   [h] Gk *Assaphioth*

sons of Lozon, the sons of Giddel,[i] the sons of Shephatiah, [34] the sons of Hattil,[j] the sons of Pochereth-hazzebaim, the sons of Sarothie, the sons of Masiah, the sons of Gas, the sons of Addus, the sons of Subas, the sons of Apherra, the sons of Barodis, the sons of Shaphat, the sons of Ami.[k] 35 All the temple servants and the sons of Solomon's servants were three hundred and seventy-two.

36 The following are those who came up from Telmelah[l] and Tel-harsha, under the leadership of Cherub, Addan, and Immer, [37] though they could not prove by their fathers' houses or lineage that they belonged to Israel: the sons of Delaiah the son of Tobiah, the sons of Nekoda, six hundred and fifty-two.

38 Of the priests the following had assumed the priesthood but were not found registered: the sons of Habaiah, the sons of Hakkoz, the sons of Jaddus who had married Agia, one of the daughters of Barzillai, and was called by his name. 39 And when the genealogy of these men was sought in the register and was not found, they were excluded from serving as priests. 40 And Nehemiah and Attharias[m] told them not to share in the holy things until a high priest should appear wearing Urim and Thummim.[n]

41 All those of Israel, twelve or more years of age, besides menservants and maidservants, were forty-two thousand three hundred and sixty; 42 their menservants and maidservants were seven thousand three hundred and thirty-seven; there were two hundred and forty-five musicians and singers. 43 There were four hundred and thirty-five camels, and seven thousand and thirty-six horses, two hundred and forty-five mules, and five thousand five hundred and twenty-five asses.

44 Some of the heads of families, when they came to the temple of God which is in Jerusalem, vowed that they would erect the house on its site, to the best of their ability, 45 and that they would give to the sacred treasury for the work a thousand minas of gold, five thousand minas of silver, and one hundred priests' garments.

46 The priests, the Levites, and some of the people[o] settled in Jerusalem and its vicinity; and the temple singers, the gatekeepers, and all Israel in their towns.

47 When the seventh month came, and the sons of Israel were each in his own home, they gathered as one man in the square before the first gate toward the east. 48 Then Jeshua the son of Jozadak, with his fellow priests, and Zerubbabel the son of Shealtiel, with his kinsmen, took their places and prepared the altar of the God of Israel, 49 to offer burnt offerings upon it, in accordance with the directions in the book of Moses the man of God. 50 And some joined them from the other peoples of the land. And they erected the altar in its place, for all the peoples of the land were hostile to them and were stronger than they; and they offered sacrifices at the proper times and burnt offerings to the Lord morning and evening. 51 They kept the feast of booths, as it is commanded in the law, and offered the proper sacrifices every day, 52 and thereafter the continual offerings and sacrifices on sabbaths and at new moons and at all the consecrated feasts. 53 And all who had made any vow to God began to offer sacrifices to God, from the new moon of the seventh month, though the temple of God was not yet built. 54 And they gave money to the masons and the carpenters, and food and drink 55 and carts[p] to the Sidonians and the Tyrians, to bring cedar logs from Lebanon and convey

---

[i] Gk Isdael [j] Gk Agia [k] Gk Allon [l] Gk Thermeleth [m] Or the governor
[n] Gk Manifestation and Truth [o] Or those who were of the people
[p] The Greek text is uncertain at this point.

them in rafts to the harbour of Joppa, according to the decree which they had in writing from Cyrus king of the Persians.

56 In the second year after their coming to the temple of God in Jerusalem, in the second month, Zerubbabel the son of Shealtiel and Jeshua the son of Jozadak made a beginning, together with their brethren and the Levitical priests and all who had come to Jerusalem from the captivity; 57 and they laid the foundation of the temple of God on the new moon of the second month in the second year after they came to Judea and Jerusalem. 58 And they appointed the Levites who were twenty or more years of age to have charge of the work of the Lord. And Jeshua arose, and his sons and brethren and Kadmiel his brother and the sons of Jeshua Emadabun and the sons of Joda son of Iliadun, with their sons and brethren, all the Levites, as one man pressing forward the work on the house of God.

So the builders built the temple of the Lord. 59 And the priests stood arrayed in their garments, with musical instruments and trumpets, and the Levites, the sons of Asaph, with cymbals, 60 praising the Lord and blessing him, according to the directions of David king of Israel; 61 and they sang hymns, giving thanks to the Lord, because his goodness and his glory are for ever upon all Israel. 62 And all the people sounded trumpets and shouted with a great shout, praising the Lord for the erection of the house of the Lord. 63 Some of the Levitical priests and heads of fathers' houses, old men who had seen the former house, came to the building of this one with outcries and loud weeping, 64 while many came with trumpets and a joyful noise, 65 so that the people could not hear the trumpets because of the weeping of the people.

For the multitude sounded the trumpets loudly, so that the sound was heard afar; 66 and when the enemies of the tribe of Judah and Benjamin heard it, they came to find out what the sound of the trumpets meant. 67 And they learned that those who had returned from captivity were building the temple for the Lord God of Israel. 68 So they approached Zerubbabel and Jeshua and the heads of the fathers' houses and said to them, "We will build with you. 69 For we obey your Lord just as you do, and we have been sacrificing to him ever since the days of Esarhaddon *q* king of the Assyrians, who brought us here." 70 But Zerubbabel and Jeshua and the heads of the fathers' houses in Israel said to them, "You have nothing to do with us in building the house for the Lord our God, 71 for we alone will build it for the Lord of Israel, as Cyrus the king of the Persians has commanded us." 72 But the peoples of the land pressed hard *r* upon those in Judea, cut off their supplies, and hindered their building; 73 and by plots and demagoguery and uprisings they prevented the completion of the building as long as King Cyrus lived. And they were kept from building for two years, until the reign of Darius.

6 Now in the second year of the reign of Darius, the prophets Haggai and Zechariah the son of Iddo prophesied to the Jews who were in Judea and Jerusalem; they prophesied to them in the name of the Lord God of Israel. 2 Then Zerubbabel the son of Shealtiel and Jeshua the son of Jozadak arose and began to build the house of the Lord which is in Jerusalem, with the help of the prophets of the Lord who were with them.

3 At the same time Sisinnes the governor of Syria and Phoenicia and Sathrabuzanes and their associates came to them and said, 4 "By whose order are you building this house and

q Gk Asbasareth r The Greek text is uncertain at this point

this roof and finishing all the other things? And who are the builders that are finishing these things?" [5] Yet the elders of the Jews were dealt with kindly, for the providence of the Lord was over the captives; [6] and they were not prevented from building until word could be sent to Darius concerning them and a report made.

7 A copy of the letter which Sisinnes the governor of Syria and Phoenicia, and Sathrabuzanes, and their associates the local rulers in Syria and Phoenicia, wrote and sent to Darius:

8 "To King Darius, greeting. Let it be fully known to our lord the king that, when we went to the country of Judea and entered the city of Jerusalem, we found the elders of the Jews, who had been in captivity, [9] building in the city of Jerusalem a great new house for the Lord, of hewn stone, with costly timber laid in the walls. [10] These operations are going on rapidly, and the work is prospering in their hands and being completed with all splendour and care. [11] Then we asked these elders, 'At whose command are you building this house and laying the foundations of this structure?' [12] And in order that we might inform you in writing who the leaders are, we questioned them and asked them for a list of the names of those who are at their head. [13] They answered us, 'We are the servants of the Lord who created the heaven and the earth. [14] And the house was built many years ago by a king of Israel who was great and strong, and it was finished. [15] But when our fathers sinned against the Lord of Israel who is in heaven, and provoked him, he gave them over into the hands of Nebuchadnezzar king of Babylon, king of the Chaldeans; [16] and they pulled down the house, and burned it, and carried the people away captive to Babylon. [17] But in the first year that Cyrus reigned over the country of Babylonia, King Cyrus wrote that this house should be rebuilt. [18] And the holy vessels of gold and of silver, which Nebuchadnezzar had taken out of the house in Jerusalem and stored in his own temple, these Cyrus the king took out again from the temple in Babylon, and they were delivered to Zerubbabel and Sheshbazzar [8] the governor [19] with the command that he should take all these vessels back and put them in the temple at Jerusalem, and that this temple of the Lord should be rebuilt on its site. [20] Then this Sheshbazzar,[8] after coming here, laid the foundations of the house of the Lord which is in Jerusalem, and although it has been in process of construction from that time until now, it has not yet reached completion.' [21] Now therefore, if it seems wise, O king, let search be made in the royal archives of our lord [t] the king that are in Babylon; [22] and if it is found that the building of the house of the Lord in Jerusalem was done with the consent of King Cyrus, and if it is approved by our lord the king, let him send us directions concerning these things."

23 Then King Darius commanded that search be made in the royal archives that were deposited in Babylon. And in Ecbatana, the fortress which is in the country of Media, a scroll [u] was found in which this was recorded: [24] "In the first year of the reign of Cyrus, King Cyrus ordered the building of the house of the Lord in Jerusalem, where they sacrifice with perpetual fire; [25] its height to be sixty cubits and its breadth sixty cubits, with three courses of hewn stone and one course of new native timber; the cost to be paid from the treasury of Cyrus the king; [26] and that the holy vessels of the house of the Lord, both of gold and of silver, which Nebuchadnezzar took out of the house in Jerusalem and carried away to Babylon, should be restored to the house in Jerusalem, to be placed where they had been."

[8] Gk *Sanabassarus*   [t] Other authorities read *of Cyrus*   [u] Other authorities read *passage*

27 So Darius *v* commanded Sisinnes the governor of Syria and Phoenicia, and Sathrabuzanes, and their associates, and those who were appointed as local rulers in Syria and Phoenicia, to keep away from the place, and to permit Zerubbabel, the servant of the Lord and governor of Judea, and the elders of the Jews to build this house of the Lord on its site. 28 "And I command that it be built completely, and that full effort be made to help the men who have returned from the captivity of Judea, until the house of the Lord is finished; 29 and that out of the tribute of Coelesyria and Phoenicia a portion be scrupulously given to these men, that is, to Zerubbabel the governor, for sacrifices to the Lord, for bulls and rams and lambs, 30 and likewise wheat and salt and wine and oil, regularly every year, without quibbling, for daily use as the priests in Jerusalem may indicate, 31 in order that libations may be made to the Most High God for the king and his children, and prayers be offered for their life."

32 And he commanded that if any should transgress or nullify any of the things herein written,*w* a beam should be taken out of his house and he should be hanged upon it, and his property should be forfeited to the king.

33 "Therefore may the Lord, whose name is there called upon, destroy every king and nation that shall stretch out their hands to hinder or damage that house of the Lord in Jerusalem.

34 "I, King Darius, have decreed that it be done with all diligence as here prescribed."

7 Then Sisinnes the governor of Coelesyria and Phoenicia, and Sathrabuzanes, and their associates, following the orders of King Darius, 2 supervised the holy work with very great care, assisting the elders of the Jews and the chief officers of the temple. 3 And the holy work prospered, while the prophets Haggai and Zechariah prophesied; 4 and they completed it by the command of the Lord God of Israel. So with the consent of Cyrus and Darius and Artaxerxes, kings of the Persians, 5 the holy house was finished by the twenty-third day of the month of Adar, in the sixth year of King Darius. 6 And the people of Israel, the priests, the Levites, and the rest of those from the captivity who joined them, did according to what was written in the book of Moses. 7 They offered at the dedication of the temple of the Lord one hundred bulls, two hundred rams, four hundred lambs, 8 and twelve he-goats for the sins of all Israel, according to the number of the twelve leaders of the tribes of Israel; 9 and the priests and the Levites stood arrayed in their garments, according to kindred, for the services of the Lord God of Israel in accordance with the book of Moses; and the gatekeepers were at each gate.

10 The people of Israel who came from the captivity kept the passover on the fourteenth day of the first month, after the priests and the Levites were purified together. 11 Not all of the returned captives were purified, but the Levites were all purified together,*x* 12 and they sacrificed the passover lamb for all the returned captives and for their brethren the priests and for themselves. 13 And the people of Israel who came from the captivity ate it, all those who had separated themselves from the abominations of the peoples of the land and sought the Lord. 14 And they kept the feast of unleavened bread seven days, rejoicing before the Lord, 15 because he had changed the will of the king of the Assyrians concerning them, to strengthen their hands for the service of the Lord God of Israel.

v Gk *he* *w* Other authorities read *stated above* or *added in writing*
x The Greek text of this verse is uncertain

8 After these things, when Artaxerxes the king of the Persians was reigning, Ezra came, the son of Seraiah, son of Azariah, son of Hilkiah, son of Shallum, ² son of Zadok, son of Ahitub, son of Amariah, son of Uzzi, son of Bukki, son of Abishua, son of Phineas, son of Eleazar, son of Aaron the chief priest. ³ This Ezra came up from Babylon as a scribe skilled in the law of Moses, which was given by the God of Israel; ⁴ and the king showed him honour, for he found favour before the king ᵛ in all his requests. ⁵ There came up with him to Jerusalem some of the people of Israel and some of the priests and Levites and temple singers and gatekeepers and temple servants, ⁶ in the seventh year of the reign of Artaxerxes, in the fifth month (this was the king's seventh year); for they left Babylon on the new moon of the first month and arrived in Jerusalem on the new moon of the fifth month, by the prosperous journey which the Lord gave them.ᶻ ⁷ For Ezra possessed great knowledge, so that he omitted nothing from the law of the Lord or the commandments, but taught all Israel all the ordinances and judgments.

8 The following is a copy of the written commission from Artaxerxes the king which was delivered to Ezra the priest and reader of the law of the Lord:

9 "King Artaxerxes to Ezra the priest and reader of the law of the Lord, greeting. ¹⁰ In accordance with my gracious decision, I have given orders that those of the Jewish nation and of the priests and Levites and others in our realm, who freely choose to do so, may go with you to Jerusalem. ¹¹ Let as many as are so disposed, therefore, depart with you as I and the seven friends who are my counsellors have decided, ¹² in order to look into matters in Judea and Jerusalem, in accordance with what is in the law of the Lord, ¹³ and to carry to Jerusalem the gifts for the Lord of Israel which I and my friends have vowed, and to collect for the Lord in Jerusalem all the gold and silver that may be found in the country of Babylonia, ¹⁴ together with what is given by the nation for the temple of their Lord which is in Jerusalem, both gold and silver for bulls and rams and lambs and what goes with them, ¹⁵ so as to offer sacrifices upon the altar of their Lord which is in Jerusalem. ¹⁶ And whatever you and your brethren are minded to do with the gold and silver, perform it in accordance with the will of your God; ¹⁷ and deliver the holy vessels of the Lord which are given you for the use of the temple of your God which is in Jerusalem. ¹⁸ And whatever else occurs to you as necessary for the temple of your God, you may provide out of the royal treasury.

19 "And I, Artaxerxes the king, have commanded the treasurers of Syria and Phoenicia that whatever Ezra the priest and reader of the law of the Most High God sends for, they shall take care to give him, ²⁰ up to a hundred talents of silver, and likewise up to a hundred cors of wheat, a hundred baths of wine, and salt in abundance. ²¹ Let all things prescribed in the law of God be scrupulously fulfilled for the Most High God, so that wrath may not come upon the kingdom of the king and his sons. ²² You are also informed that no tribute or any other tax is to be laid on any of the priests or Levites or temple singers or gatekeepers or temple servants or persons employed in this temple, and that no one has authority to impose any tax upon them.

23 "And you, Ezra, according to the wisdom of God, appoint judges and justices to judge all those who know the law of your God, throughout all Syria and Phoenicia; and those who do not know it you shall teach. ²⁴ And all who transgress the law of your God or the law of the kingdom

ᵛ Gk *him*   ᶻ Other authorities add *for him* or *upon him*

13

shall be strictly punished, whether by death or some other punishment, either fine or imprisonment."

25 Blessed be the Lord alone, who put this into the heart of the king, to glorify his house which is in Jerusalem, 26 and who honoured me in the sight of the king and his counsellors and all his friends and nobles. 27 I was encouraged by the help of the Lord my God, and I gathered men from Israel to go up with me.

28 These are the principal men, according to their fathers' houses and their groups, who went up with me from Babylon, in the reign of Artaxerxes the king: 29 Of the sons of Phineas, Gershom. Of the sons of Ithamar, Gamael. Of the sons of David, Hattush the son of Shecaniah. 30 Of the sons of Parosh, Zechariah, and with him a hundred and fifty men enrolled. 31 Of the sons of Pahathmoab, Eliehoenai the son of Zerahiah, and with him two hundred men. 32 Of the sons of Zattu, Shecaniah the son of Jahaziel, and with him three hundred men. Of the sons of Adin, Obed the son of Jonathan, and with him two hundred and fifty men. 33 Of the sons of Elam, Jeshaiah the son of Gotholiah, and with him seventy men. 34 Of the sons of Shephatiah, Zeraiah the son of Michael, and with him seventy men. 35 Of the sons of Joab, Obadiah the son of Jehiel, and with him two hundred and twelve men. 36 Of the sons of Bani, Shelomith the son of Josiphiah, and with him a hundred and sixty men. 37 Of the sons of Bebai, Zechariah the son of Bebai, and with him twenty-eight men. 38 Of the sons of Azgad, Johanan the son of Hakkatan, and with him a hundred and ten men. 39 Of the sons of Adonikam, the last ones, their names being Eliphelet, Jeuel, and Shemaiah, and with them seventy men. 40 Of the sons of Bigvai, Uthai the son of Istalcurus, and with him seventy men.

41 I assembled them at the river called Theras, and we encamped there three days, and I inspected them. 42 When I found there none of the sons of the priests or of the Levites, 43 I sent word to Eliezar, Iduel, Maasmas, 44 Elnathan, Shemaiah, Jarib, Nathan, Elnathan, Zechariah, and Meshullam, who were leaders and men of understanding; 45 and I told them to go to Iddo, who was the leading man at the place of the treasury, 46 and ordered them to tell Iddo and his brethren and the treasurers at that place to send us men to serve as priests in the house of our Lord. 47 And by the mighty hand of our Lord they brought us competent men of the sons of Mahli the son of Levi, son of Israel, namely Sherebiah *a* with his sons and kinsmen, eighteen; 48 also Hashabiah and Annunus and Jeshaiah his brother, of the sons of Hananiah, and their sons, twenty men; 49 and of the temple servants, whom David and the leaders had given for the service of the Levites, two hundred and twenty temple servants; the list of all their names was reported.

50 There I proclaimed a fast for the young men before our Lord, to seek from him a prosperous journey for ourselves and for our children and the cattle that were with us. 51 For I was ashamed to ask the king for foot soldiers and horsemen and an escort to keep us safe from our adversaries; 52 for we had said to the king, "The power of our Lord will be with those who seek him, and will support them in every way." 53 And again we prayed to our Lord about these things, and we found him very merciful.

54 Then I set apart twelve of the leaders of the priests, Sherebiah and Hashabiah, and ten of their kinsmen with them; 55 and I weighed out to them the silver and the gold and the holy vessels of the house of our Lord, which the king himself and his coun-

a Gk Asebebias

14

sellors and the nobles and all Israel had given. ⁵⁶ I weighed and gave to them six hundred and fifty talents of silver, and silver vessels worth a hundred talents, and a hundred talents of gold, ⁵⁷ and twenty golden bowls, and twelve bronze vessels of fine bronze that glittered like gold. ⁵⁸ And I said to them, "You are holy to the Lord, and the vessels are holy, and the silver and the gold are vowed to the Lord, the Lord of our fathers. ⁵⁹ Be watchful and on guard until you deliver them to the leaders of the priests and the Levites, and to the heads of the fathers' houses of Israel, in Jerusalem, in the chambers of the house of our Lord." ⁶⁰ So the priests and the Levites who took the silver and the gold and the vessels which had been in Jerusalem carried them to the temple of the Lord.

61 We departed from the river Theras on the twelfth day of the first month; and we arrived in Jerusalem by the mighty hand of our Lord which was upon us; he delivered us from every enemy on the way, and so we came to Jerusalem. ⁶² When we had been there three days, the silver and the gold were weighed and delivered in the house of our Lord to Meremoth the priest, son of Uriah; ⁶³ and with him was Eleazar the son of Phinehas, and with them were Jozabad the son of Jeshua and Moeth the son of Binnui,ᵇ the Levites. ⁶⁴ The whole was counted and weighed, and the weight of everything was recorded at that very time. ⁶⁵ And those who had come back from captivity offered sacrifices to the Lord, the God of Israel, twelve bulls for all Israel, ninety-six rams, ⁶⁶ seventy-two lambs, and as a thank offering twelve he-goats—all as a sacrifice to the Lord. ⁶⁷ And they delivered the king's orders to the royal stewards and to the governors of Coelesyria and Phoenicia; and these officialsᶜ honoured the people and the temple of the Lord.

68 After these things had been done, the principal men came to me and said, ⁶⁹ "The people of Israel and the leaders and the priests and the Levites have not put away from themselves the alien peoples of the land and their pollutions, the Canaanites, the Hittites, the Perizzites, the Jebusites, the Moabites, the Egyptians, and the Edomites. ⁷⁰ For they and their sons have married the daughters of these people,ᵈ and the holy race has been mixed with the alien peoples of the land; and from the beginning of this matter the leaders and the nobles have been sharing in this iniquity."

71 As soon as I heard these things, I rent my garments and my holy mantle, and pulled out hair from my head and beard, and sat down in anxiety and grief. ⁷² And all who were ever moved at ᵉ the word of the Lord of Israel gathered round me, as I mourned over this iniquity, and I sat grief-stricken until the evening sacrifice. ⁷³ Then I rose from my fast, with my garments and my holy mantle rent, and kneeling down and stretching forth my hands to the Lord ⁷⁴ I said,

"O Lord, I am ashamed and confounded before thy face. ⁷⁵ For our sins have risen higher than our heads, and our mistakes have mounted up to heaven ⁷⁶ from the times of our fathers, and we are in great sin to this day. ⁷⁷ And because of our sins and the sins of our fathers we with our brethren and our kings and our priests were given over to the kings of the earth, to the sword and captivity and plundering, in shame until this day. ⁷⁸ And now in some measure mercy has come to us from thee, O Lord, to leave to us a root and a name in thy holy place, ⁷⁹ and to uncover a light for us in the house of the Lord our God, and to give us food in the time of our servitude. ⁸⁰ Even in our bondage we were not forsaken by our Lord, but he brought us into favour with the kings of the

ᵇ Gk *Sabannus*   ᶜ Gk *they*   ᵈ Gk *their daughters*   ᵉ Or *zealous for*

Persians, so that they have given us food ⁸¹ and glorified the temple of our Lord, and raised Zion from desolation, to give us a stronghold in Judea and Jerusalem.

82 "And now, O Lord, what shall we say, when we have these things? For we have transgressed thy commandments, which thou didst give by thy servants the prophets, saying, ⁸³ 'The land which you are entering to take possession of it is a land polluted with the pollution of the aliens of the land, and they have filled it with their uncleanness. ⁸⁴ Therefore do not give your daughters in marriage to their sons, and do not take their daughters for your sons; ⁸⁵ and do not seek ever to have peace with them, in order that you may be strong and eat the good things of the land and leave it for an inheritance to your children for ever.' ⁸⁶ And all that has happened to us has come about because of our evil deeds and our great sins. For thou, O Lord, didst lift the burden of our sins ⁸⁷ and give us such a root as this; but we turned back again to transgress thy law by mixing with the uncleanness of the peoples of the land. ⁸⁸ Wast thou not angry enough with us to destroy us without leaving a root or seed or name? ⁸⁹ O Lord of Israel, thou art true; for we are left as a root this day. ⁹⁰ Behold, we are now before thee in our iniquities; for we can no longer stand in thy presence because of these things."

91 While Ezra was praying and making his confession, weeping and lying upon the ground before the temple, there gathered about him a very great throng from Jerusalem, men and women and youths; for there was great weeping among the multitude. ⁹² Then Shecaniah the son of Jehiel, one of the men of Israel, called out, and said to Ezra, "We have sinned against the Lord, and have married foreign women from the peoples of the land; but even now there is hope for Israel. ⁹³ Let us take an oath to the Lord about this, that we will put away all our foreign wives, with their children, ⁹⁴ as seems good to you and to all who obey the law of the Lord. ⁹⁵ Arise*f* and take action, for it is your task, and we are with you to take strong measures." ⁹⁶ Then Ezra arose and had the leaders of the priests and Levites of all Israel take oath that they would do this. And they took the oath.

9 Then Ezra rose and went from the court of the temple to the chamber of Jehohanan the son of Eliashib, ² and spent the night there; and he did not eat bread or drink water, for he was mourning over the great iniquities of the multitude. ³ And a proclamation was made throughout Judea and Jerusalem to all who had returned from the captivity that they should assemble at Jerusalem, ⁴ and that if any did not meet there within two or three days, in accordance with the decision of the ruling elders, their cattle should be seized for sacrifice and the men themselves *g* expelled from the multitude of those who had returned from the captivity.

5 Then the men of the tribe of Judah and Benjamin assembled at Jerusalem within three days; this was the ninth month, on the twentieth day of the month. ⁶ And all the multitude sat in the open square before the temple, shivering because of the bad weather that prevailed. ⁷ Then Ezra rose and said to them, "You have broken the law and married foreign women, and so have increased the sin of Israel. ⁸ Now then make confession and give glory to the Lord the God of our fathers, ⁹ and do his will; separate yourselves from the peoples of the land and from your foreign wives." ¹⁰ Then all the multitude shouted and said with a loud voice, "We will do as you have said. ¹¹ But

---

f Other authorities read *as you decide. And all who obeyed the law of the Lord rose and said to Ezra, "Arise"*   *g* Gk *he himself*

the multitude is great and it is winter,
and we are not able to stand in the
open air. This is not a work we can do
in one day or two, for we have sinned
too much in these things. 12 So let the
leaders of the multitude stay, and let
all those in our settlements who have
foreign wives come at the time appointed, 13 with the elders and judges
of each place, until we are freed from
the wrath of the Lord over this matter." 14 Jonathan the son of Asahel
and Jahzeiah the son of Tikvah[h]
undertook the matter on these terms,
and Meshullam and Levi and Shabbethai served with them as judges.
15 And those who had returned from
the captivity acted in accordance with
all this.

16 Ezra the priest chose for himself the leading men of their fathers'
houses, all of them by name; and on
the new moon of the tenth month
they began their sessions to investigate the matter. 17 And the cases of
the men who had foreign wives were
brought to an end by the new moon
of the first month.

18 Of the priests those who were
brought in and found to have foreign
wives were: 19 of the sons of Jeshua
the son of Jozadak and his brethren,
Maaseiah, Eliezar, Jarib, and Jodan.
20 They pledged themselves to put
away their wives, and to give rams in
expiation of their error. 21 Of the sons
of Immer: Hanani and Zebadiah
and Maaseiah and Shemaiah and
Jehiel and Azariah. 22 Of the sons
of Pashhur: Elioenai, Maaseiah, Ish-
mael, and Nathanael, and Gedaliah,
and Elasah.[i]

23 And of the Levites: Jozabad
and Shimei and Kelaiah, who was
Kelita, and Pethahiah and Judah
and Jonah. 24 Of the temple singers:
Eliashib and Zaccur.[j] 25 Of the gatekeepers: Shallum and Telem.[k]

26 Of Israel: of the sons of Parosh:
Ramiah, Izziah, Malchijah, Mija-
min, and Eleazar, and Asibias, and
Benaiah. 27 Of the sons of Elam:
Mattaniah and Zechariah, Jehiel[l]
and Abdi, and Jeremoth and Elijah.
28 Of the sons of Zattu:[m] Elioenai,[n] Eliashib, Othoniah, Jeremoth,
and Zabad and Zerdaiah. 29 Of the
sons of Bebai: Jehohanan and Hananiah and Zabbai and Emathis.
30 Of the sons of Bani:[o] Meshullam,[p] Malluch,[q] Adaiah, Jashub, and
Sheal and Jeremoth. 31 Of the sons
of Addi: Naathus and Moossias, Lac-
cunus and Naidus, and Bescaspasmys
and Sesthel, and Belnuus and Manas-
seas. 32 Of the sons of Annan: Elionas
and Asaias and Melchias and Sabbaias
and Simon Chosamaeus. 33 Of the
sons of Hashum: Mattenai and Mat-
tattah and Zabad and Eliphelet and
Manasseh and Shimei. 34 Of the
sons of Bani: Jeremai, Maadai,[r]
Amram,[s] Joel, Mamdai and Bedeiah
and Vaniah, Carabasion and Eliashib and Machnadebai,[t] Eliasis,
Binnui, Elialis, Shimei, Shelemiah,
Nethaniah. Of the sons of Ezora:
Shashai, Azarel, Azael, Shemaiah,[u]
Amariah,[v] Joseph. 35 Of the sons of
Nebo:[w] Mattithiah,[x] Zabad, Iddo,
Joel, Benaiah. 36 All these had married foreign women, and they put
them away with their children.

37 The priests and the Levites and
the men of Israel settled in Jerusalem
and in the country. On the new moon
of the seventh month, when the sons
of Israel were in their settlements,
38 the whole multitude gathered with
one accord into the open square before the east gate of the temple; 39 and
they told Ezra the chief priest and
reader to bring the law of Moses
which had been given by the Lord
God of Israel. 40 So Ezra the chief
priest brought the law, for all the
multitude, men and women, and all
the priests to hear the law, on the
new moon of the seventh month.
41 And he read aloud in the open

[h] Gk *Thocanus* [i] Gk *Salthas* or *Saloas* [j] Gk *Bacchurus* [k] Gk *Tolbanes* [l] Gk *Jezrielus*
[m] Gk *Zamoth* [n] Gk *Eliadas* [o] Gk *Mani* [p] Gk *Olamus* [q] Gk *Mamuchus* [r] Gk *Momdius*
[s] Gk *Maerus* [t] Gk *Mamnitanemus* [u] Gk *Samatus* [v] Gk *Zambris* [w] Gk *Nooma* [x] Gk *Mazitias*

square before the gate of the temple from early morning until midday, in the presence of both men and women; and all the multitude gave attention to the law. [42] Ezra the priest and reader of the law stood on the wooden platform which had been prepared; [43] and beside him stood Mattathiah, Shema, Anaiah,[y] Azariah, Uriah, Hezekiah, and Baalsamus on his right hand, [44] and on his left Pedaiah, Mishael, Malchijah, Lothasubus, Nabariah, and Zechariah. [45] Then Ezra took up the book of the law in the sight of the multitude, for he had the place of honour in the presence of all. [46] And when he opened the law, they all stood erect. And Ezra blessed the Lord God Most High, the God of hosts, the Almighty; [47] and all the multitude answered, "Amen." And they lifted up their hands, and fell to the ground and worshipped the Lord. [48] Jeshua and Anniuth and Sherebiah, Jamin,[z] Akkub, Shabbethai, Hodiah, Massei-

ah[a] and Kelita, Azariah and Jozabad, Hanan, Pelaiah, the Levites, taught the law of the Lord,[b] at the same time explaining what was read.

[49] Then Attharates[c] said to Ezra the chief priest and reader, and to the Levites who were teaching the multitude, and to all, [50] "This day is holy to the Lord"—now they were all weeping as they heard the law— [51] "so go your way, eat the fat and drink the sweet, and send portions to those who have none; [52] for the day is holy to the Lord; and do not be sorrowful, for the Lord will exalt you." [53] And the Levites commanded all the people, saying, "This day is holy; do not be sorrowful." [54] Then they all went their way, to eat and drink and enjoy themselves, and to give portions to those who had none, and to make great rejoicing; [55] because they were inspired by the words which they had been taught. And they came together.[d]

[y] Gk Ananias [z] Gk Jadinus [a] Gk Maiannas [b] Other authorities add and read the law of the Lord to the multitude
[c] Or the governor [d] The Greek text ends abruptly: compare Nehemiah 8.13

THE SECOND BOOK OF

ESDRAS

1 The second book of the prophet Ezra the son of Seraiah, son of Azariah, son of Hilkiah, son of Shallum, son of Zadok, son of Ahitub, ²son of Ahijah, son of Phinehas, son of Eli, son of Amariah, son of Azariah, son of Meraioth, son of Arna, son of Uzzi, son of Borith, son of Abishua, son of Phinehas, son of Eleazar, ³son of Aaron, of the tribe of Levi, who was a captive in the country of the Medes in the reign of Artaxerxes, king of the Persians.

4 The word of the Lord came to me, saying, ⁵"Go and declare to my people their evil deeds, and to their children the iniquities which they have committed against me, so that they may tell their children's children ⁶that the sins of their parents have increased in them, for they have forgotten me and have offered sacrifices to strange gods. ⁷Was it not I who brought them out of the land of Egypt, out of the house of bondage? But they have angered me and despised my counsels. ⁸Pull out the hair of your head and hurl all evils upon them, for they have not obeyed my law—they are a rebellious people. ⁹How long shall I endure them, on whom I have bestowed such great benefits? ¹⁰For their sake I have overthrown many kings; I struck down Pharaoh with his servants, and all his army. ¹¹I have destroyed all nations before them, and scattered in the east the people of two provinces, Tyre and Sidon; I have slain all their enemies.

12 "But speak to them and say, Thus says the Lord: ¹³Surely it was I who brought you through the sea, and made safe highways for you where there was no road; I gave you Moses as leader and Aaron as priest; ¹⁴I provided light for you from a pillar of fire, and did great wonders among you. Yet you have forgotten me, says the Lord.

15 "Thus says the Lord Almighty: The quails were a sign to you; I gave you camps for your protection, and in them you complained. ¹⁶You have not exulted in my name at the destruction of your enemies, but to this day you still complain. ¹⁷Where are the benefits which I bestowed on you? When you were hungry and thirsty in the wilderness, did you not cry out to me, ¹⁸saying, 'Why hast thou led us into this wilderness to kill us? It would have been better for us to serve the Egyptians than to die in this wilderness.' ¹⁹I pitied your groanings and gave you manna for food; you ate the bread of angels. ²⁰When you were thirsty, did I not cleave the rock so that waters flowed in abundance? Because of the heat I covered you with the leaves of trees. ²¹I divided fertile lands among you; I drove out the Canaanites, the Perizzites, and the Philistines before you. What more can I do for you? says the Lord. ²²Thus says the Lord Almighty: When you were in the wilderness, at the bitter stream, thirsty and blaspheming my name, ²³I did not send fire upon you for your blasphemies, but threw a tree into the water and made the stream sweet.

24 "What shall I do to you, O Jacob? You would not obey me, O Judah. I will turn to other nations and will give them my name, that they may keep my statutes. ²⁵Because you have forsaken me, I also will forsake you. When you beg mercy of me, I will show you no mercy. ²⁶When you call upon me, I will not listen to you; for you have defiled your hands with blood, and your feet are swift to commit murder. ²⁷It is not as though you had

forsaken me; you have forsaken your-selves, says the Lord.

28 "Thus says the Lord Almighty: Have I not entreated you as a father entreats his sons or a mother her daughters or a nurse her children, 29 that you should be my people and I should be your God, and that you should be my sons and I should be your father? 30 I gathered you as a hen gathers her brood under her wings. But now, what shall I do to you? I will cast you out from my presence. 31 When you offer obla-tions to me, I will turn my face from you; for I have rejected your feast days, and new moons, and circumci-sions of the flesh. 32 I sent to you my servants the prophets, but you have taken and slain them and torn their bodies in pieces; their blood I will re-quire of you, says the Lord.

33 "Thus says the Lord Almighty: Your house is desolate; I will drive you out as the wind drives straw; 34 and your sons will have no chil-dren, because with you they have neglected my commandment and have done what is evil in my sight. 35 I will give your houses to a people that will come, who without having heard me will believe. Those to whom I have shown no signs will do what I have commanded. 36 They have seen no prophets, yet will recall their former state.*a* 37 I call to wit-ness the gratitude of the people that is to come, whose children rejoice with gladness; though they do not see me with bodily eyes, yet with the spirit they will believe the things I have said.

38 "And now, father, look with pride and see the people coming from the east; 39 to them I will give as leaders Abraham, Isaac, and Jacob and Hosea and Amos and Micah and Joel and Obadiah and Jonah 40 and Nahum and Habakkuk, Zephaniah, Haggai, Zechariah and Malachi, who is also called the messenger of the Lord.

2 "Thus says the Lord: I brought this people out of bond-age, and I gave them commandments through my servants the prophets; but they would not listen to them, and made my counsels void. 2 The mother who bore them says to them, 'Go, my children, because I am a widow and forsaken. 3 I brought you up with gladness; but with mourning and sorrow I have lost you, because you have sinned before the Lord God and have done what is evil in my sight. 4 But now what can I do for you? For I am a widow and forsaken. Go, my children, and ask for mercy from the Lord.' 5 I call upon you, father, as a witness in addition to the mother of the children, because they would not keep my covenant, 6 that you may bring confusion upon them and bring their mother to ruin, so that they may have no offspring. 7 Let them be scattered among the nations, let their names be blotted out from the earth, because they have despised my covenant.

8 "Woe to you, Assyria, who con-ceal the unrighteous in your midst! O wicked nation, remember what I did to Sodom and Gomor-rah, 9 whose land lies in lumps of pitch and heaps of ashes. So will I do to those who have not listened to me, says the Lord Al-mighty."

10 Thus says the Lord to Ezra: "Tell my people that I will give them the kingdom of Jerusalem, which I was going to give to Israel. 11 More-over, I will take back to myself their glory, and will give to these others the everlasting habitations, which I had prepared for Israel.*b* 12 The tree of life shall give them fragrant per-fume, and they shall neither toil nor become weary. 13 Ask and you will receive; pray that your days may be few, that they may be shortened. The kingdom is already prepared for you; watch! 14 Call, O call heaven and earth to witness, for I left out evil

---

a Other authorities read *their iniquities*   *b* Lat *those*

and created good, because I live, says the Lord.

15 "Mother, embrace your sons; bring them up with gladness, as does the dove; establish their feet, because I have chosen you, says the Lord. 16 And I will raise up the dead from their places, and will bring them out from their tombs, because I recognize my name in them. 17 Do not fear, mother of the sons, for I have chosen you, says the Lord. 18 I will send you help, my servants Isaiah and Jeremiah. According to their counsel I have consecrated and prepared for you twelve trees loaded with various fruits, 19 and the same number of springs flowing with milk and honey, and seven mighty mountains on which roses and lilies grow; by these I will fill your children with joy. 20 Guard the rights of the widow, secure justice for the fatherless, give to the needy, defend the orphan, clothe the naked, 21 care for the injured and the weak, do not ridicule a lame man, protect the maimed, and let the blind man have a vision of my splendour. 22 Protect the old and the young within your walls; 23 when you find any who are dead, commit them to the grave and mark it,*c* and I will give you the first place in my resurrection. 24 Pause and be quiet, my people, because your rest will come. 25 Good nurse, nourish your sons, and strengthen their feet. 26 Not one of the servants whom I have given you will perish, for I will require them from among your number. 27 Do not be anxious, for when the day of tribulation and anguish comes, others shall weep and be sorrowful, but you shall rejoice and have abundance. 28 The nations shall envy you but they shall not be able to do anything against you, says the Lord. 29 My hands will cover you, that your sons may not see Gehenna. 30 Rejoice, O mother, with your sons, because I will deliver you, says the Lord. 31 Remember your sons that sleep, because I will bring them out of the hiding places of the earth, and will show mercy to them; for I am merciful, says the Lord Almighty. 32 Embrace your children until I come, and proclaim mercy to them; because my springs run over, and my grace will not fail."

33 I, Ezra, received a command from the Lord on Mount Horeb to go to Israel. When I came to them they rejected me and refused the Lord's commandment. 34 Therefore I say to you, O nations that hear and understand, "Await your shepherd; he will give you everlasting rest, because he who will come at the end of the age is close at hand. 35 Be ready for the rewards of the kingdom, because the eternal light will shine upon you for evermore. 36 Flee from the shadow of this age, receive the joy of your glory; I publicly call on my Saviour to witness.*d* 37 Receive what the Lord has entrusted to you and be joyful, giving thanks to him who has called you to heavenly kingdoms. 38 Rise and stand, and see at the feast of the Lord the number of those who have been sealed. 39 Those who have departed from the shadow of this age have received glorious garments from the Lord. 40 Take again your full number, O Zion, and conclude the list of your people who are clothed in white, who have fulfilled the law of the Lord. 41 The number of your children, whom you desired, is full; beseech the Lord's power that your people, who have been called from the beginning, may be made holy."

42 I, Ezra, saw on Mount Zion a great multitude, which I could not number, and they all were praising the Lord with songs. 43 In their midst was a young man of great stature, taller than any of the others, and on the head of each of them he placed a crown, but he was more exalted

---

c Or seal it; or mark them and commit them to the grave
d Other authorities read I testify that my Saviour has been commissioned by the Lord

than they. And I was held spell-bound. ⁴⁴ Then I asked an angel, "Who are these, my lord?" ⁴⁵ He answered and said to me, "These are they who have put off mortal clothing and have put on the immortal, and they have confessed the name of God; now they are being crowned, and receive palms." ⁴⁶ Then I said to the angel, "Who is that young man who places crowns on them and puts palms in their hands?" ⁴⁷ He answered and said to me, "He is the Son of God, whom they confessed in the world." So I began to praise those who had stood valiantly for the name of the Lord. ⁴⁸ Then the angel said to me, "Go, tell my people how great and many are the wonders of the Lord God which you have seen."

3 In the thirtieth year after the destruction of our city, I Salathiel, who am also called Ezra, was in Babylon. I was troubled as I lay on my bed, and my thoughts welled up in my heart, ² because I saw the desolation of Zion and the wealth of those who lived in Babylon. ³ My spirit was greatly agitated, and I began to speak anxious words to the Most High, and said, ⁴ "O sovereign Lord, didst thou not speak at the beginning when thou didst form the earth—and that without help—and didst command the dust *ᵉ* ⁵ and it gave *ᶠ* thee Adam, a lifeless body? Yet he was the workmanship of thy hands, and thou didst breathe into him the breath of life, and he was made alive in thy presence. ⁶ And thou didst lead him into the garden which thy right hand had planted before the earth appeared. ⁷ And thou didst lay upon him one commandment of thine; but he transgressed it, and immediately thou didst appoint death for him and for his descendants. From him there sprang nations and tribes, peoples and clans, without number. ⁸ And every nation walked after its own will and did ungodly

things before thee and scorned thee, and thou didst not hinder them. ⁹ But again, in its time thou didst bring the flood upon the inhabitants of the world and destroy them. ¹⁰ And the same fate befell them: as death came upon Adam, so the flood upon them. ¹¹ But thou didst leave one of them, Noah with his household, and all the righteous who have descended from him.

12 "When those who dwelt on earth began to multiply, they produced children and peoples and many nations, and again they began to be more ungodly than were their ancestors. ¹³ And when they were committing iniquity before thee, thou didst choose for thyself one of them, whose name was Abraham; ¹⁴ and thou didst love him, and to him only didst thou reveal the end of the times, secretly by night. ¹⁵ Thou didst make with him an everlasting covenant, and promise him that thou wouldst never forsake his descendants; and thou gavest to him Isaac, and to Isaac thou gavest Jacob and Esau. ¹⁶ And thou didst set apart Jacob for thyself, but Esau thou didst reject; and Jacob became a great multitude. ¹⁷ And when thou didst lead his descendants out of Egypt, thou didst bring them to Mount Sinai. ¹⁸ Thou didst bend down the heavens and shake *ᵍ* the earth, and move the world, and make the depths to tremble, and trouble the times. ¹⁹ And thy glory passed through the four gates of fire and earthquake and wind and ice, to give the law to the descendants of Jacob, and thy commandment to the posterity of Israel.

20 "Yet thou didst not take away from them their evil heart, so that thy law might bring forth fruit in them. ²¹ For the first Adam, burdened with an evil heart, transgressed and was overcome, as were also all who were descended from him. ²² Thus the disease became per-

ᵉ Syr Ethiop   *ᶠ* Syr   *ᵍ* Syr Ethiop Arab 1 Georg: Lat *didst set fast*

manent; the law was in the people's heart along with the evil root, but what was good departed, and the evil remained. 23 So the times passed and the years were completed, and thou didst raise up for thyself a servant, named David. 24 And thou didst command him to build a city for thy name, and in it to offer thee oblations from what is thine. 25 This was done for many years; but the inhabitants of the city transgressed, 26 in everything doing as Adam and all his descendants had done, for they also had the evil heart. 27 So thou didst deliver the city into the hands of thy enemies.

28 "Then I said in my heart, Are the deeds of those who inhabit Babylon any better? Is that why she has gained dominion over Zion? 29 For when I came here I saw ungodly deeds without number, and my soul has seen many sinners during these thirty years.*h* And my heart failed me, 30 for I have seen how thou dost endure those who sin, and hast spared those who act wickedly, and hast destroyed thy people, and hast preserved thy enemies, 31 and hast not shown to any one how thy way may be comprehended.*i* Are the deeds of Babylon better than those of Zion? 32 Or has another nation known thee besides Israel? Or what tribes have so believed thy covenants as these tribes of Jacob? 33 Yet their reward has not appeared and their labour has borne no fruit. For I have travelled widely among the nations and have seen that they abound in wealth, though they are unmindful of thy commandments. 34 Now therefore weigh in a balance our iniquities and those of the inhabitants of the world; and so it will be found which way the turn of the scale will incline. 35 When have the inhabitants of the earth not sinned in thy sight? Or

what nation has kept thy commandments so well? 36 Thou mayest indeed find individual men who have kept thy commandments, but nations thou wilt not find."

4 Then the angel that had been sent to me, whose name was Uriel, answered 2 and said to me, "Your understanding has utterly failed regarding this world, and do you think you can comprehend the way of the Most High?" 3 Then I said, "Yes, my lord." And he replied to me, "I have been sent to show you three ways, and to put before you three problems. 4 If you can solve one of them for me, I also will show you the way you desire to see, and will teach you why the heart is evil."

5 I said, "Speak on, my lord." And he said to me, "Go, weigh for me the weight of fire, or measure for me a measure *j* of wind, or call back for me the day that is past."

6 I answered and said, "Who of those that have been born can do this, that you ask me concerning these things?"

7 And he said to me, "If I had asked you, 'How many dwellings are in the heart of the sea, or how many streams are at the source of the deep, or how many streams are above the firmament, or which are the exits of hell, or which are the entrances *k* of paradise?' 8 perhaps you would have said to me, 'I never went down into the deep, nor as yet into hell, neither did I ever ascend into heaven.' 9 But now I have asked you only about fire and wind and the day, things through which you have passed and without which you cannot exist,*l* and you have given me no answer about them!" 10 And he said to me, "You cannot understand the things with which you have grown up; 11 how then can your mind comprehend the way of the Most High? And how can

---

h Ethiop Arab 1 Arm: Lat Syr *in this thirtieth year*   *i* Syr: Lat *how this way should be forsaken*
j Syr Ethiop Arab 1 and 2 Georg: Latin *a blast*
k Syr Compare Ethiop Arab 2 Arm: Latin omits *of hell, or which are the entrances*
l Other Latin manuscripts read *from which you cannot be separated*

one who is already worn out [m] by the corrupt world understand incorruption?" [n] When I heard this, I fell on my face [o] 12 and said to him, "It would be better for us not to be here than to come here and live in ungodliness, and to suffer and not understand why."

13 He answered me and said, "I went into a forest of trees of the plain, and they made a plan 14 and said, 'Come, let us go and make war against the sea, that it may recede before us, and that we may make for ourselves more forests.' 15 And in like manner the waves of the sea also made a plan and said, 'Come, let us go up and subdue the forest of the plain so that there also we may gain more territory for ourselves.' 16 But the plan of the forest was in vain, for the fire came and consumed it; 17 likewise also the plan of the waves of the sea, for the sand stood firm and stopped them. 18 If now you were a judge between them, which would you undertake to justify, and which to condemn?"

19 I answered and said, "Each has made a foolish plan, for the land is assigned to the forest, and to the sea is assigned a place to carry its waves."

20 He answered me and said, "You have judged rightly, but why have you not judged so in your own case? 21 For as the land is assigned to the forest and the sea to its waves, so also those who dwell upon earth can understand only what is on the earth, and he who is above the heavens can understand what is above the height of the heavens."

22 Then I answered and said, "I beseech you, my lord, why [p] have I been endowed with the power of understanding? 23 For I did not wish to inquire about the ways above, but about those things which we daily experience: why Israel has been given over to the Gentiles as a reproach; why the people whom you loved has been given over to godless tribes, and the law of our fathers has been made of no effect and the written covenants no longer exist; 24 and why we pass from the world like locusts, and our life is like a mist, [q] and we are not worthy to obtain mercy. 25 But what will he do for his name, by which we are called? It is about these things that I have asked."

26 He answered me and said, "If you are alive, you will see, and if you live long, [r] you will often marvel, because the age is hastening swiftly to its end. 27 For it will not be able to bring the things that have been promised to the righteous in their appointed times, because this age is full of sadness and infirmities. 28 For the evil about which [s] you ask me has been sown, but the harvest of it has not yet come. 29 If therefore that which has been sown is not reaped, and if the place where the evil has been sown does not pass away, the field where the good has been sown will not come. 30 For a grain of evil seed was sown in Adam's heart from the beginning, and how much ungodliness it has produced until now, and will produce until the time of threshing comes! 31 Consider now for yourself how much fruit of ungodliness a grain of evil seed has produced. 32 When heads of grain without number are sown, how great a threshing floor they will fill!"

33 Then I answered and said, "How long [t] and when will these things be? Why are our years few and evil?" 34 He answered me and said, "You do not hasten faster than the Most High, for your haste is for yourself, [u] but the Highest hastens on behalf of many. 35 Did not the souls of the righteous in their chambers ask about these matters, saying, 'How

---

[m] The text here is uncertain [n] Syr Ethiop *the way of the incorruptible?*
[o] Syr Ethiop Arab 1; Latin is uncertain [p] Syr Ethiop Arm: Latin is corrupt
[q] Syr Ethiop Arab 1 and 2 Georg: Latin *a trembling* [r] Syr: Latin *live*
[s] Syr Ethiop: Latin is uncertain [t] Syr Ethiop: Latin is uncertain
[u] Syr Ethiop Arab 1 and 2 Arm: the Latin is corrupt

long are we to remain here? *v* And when will come the harvest of our reward?' [36] And Jeremiel the archangel answered them and said, 'When the number of those like yourselves is completed; *w* for he has weighed the age in the balance, [37] and measured the times by measure, and numbered the times by number; and he will not move or arouse them until that measure is fulfilled.' "

38 Then I answered and said, "O sovereign Lord, but all of us also are full of ungodliness. [39] And it is perhaps on account of us that the time of threshing is delayed for the righteous—on account of the sins of those who dwell on earth."

40 He answered me and said, "Go and ask a woman who is with child if, when her nine months have been completed, her womb can keep the child within her any longer."

41 And I said, "No, lord, it cannot."

And he said to me, "In Hades the chambers of the souls are like the womb. [42] For just as a woman who is in travail makes haste to escape the pangs of birth, so also do these places hasten to give back those things that were committed to them from the beginning. [43] Then the things that you desire to see will be disclosed to you."

44 I answered and said, "If I have found favour in your sight, and if it is possible, and if I am worthy, [45] show me this also: whether more time is to come than has passed, or whether for us the greater part has gone by. [46] For I know what has gone by, but I do not know what is to come."

47 And he said to me, "Stand at my right side, and I will show you the interpretation of a parable."

48 So I stood and looked, and behold, a flaming furnace passed by before me, and when the flame had gone by I looked, and behold, the smoke remained. [49] And after this a cloud full of water passed before me and poured down a heavy and violent rain, and when the rainstorm had passed, drops remained in the cloud.

50 And he said to me, "Consider it for yourself; for as the rain is more than the drops, and the fire is greater than the smoke, so the quantity that passed was far greater; but drops and smoke remained."

51 Then I prayed and said, "Do you think that I shall live until those days? Or who will be alive in those days?"

52 He answered me and said, "Concerning the signs about which you ask me, I can tell you in part; but I was not sent to tell you concerning your life, for I do not know.

5 "Now concerning the signs: behold, the days are coming when those who dwell on earth shall be seized with great terror,*x* and the way of truth shall be hidden, and the land shall be barren of faith. [2] And unrighteousness shall be increased beyond what you yourself see, and beyond what you heard of formerly. [3] And the land which you now see ruling shall be waste and untrodden,*y* and men shall see it desolate. [4] But if the Most High grants that you live, you shall see it thrown into confusion after the third period;*z*

and the sun shall suddenly shine
    forth at night,
and the moon during the day.

5 Blood shall drip from wood,
    and the stone shall utter its
    voice;
the peoples shall be troubled,
    and the stars shall fall.*a*

6 And one shall reign whom those who dwell on earth do not expect, and the birds shall fly away together;

---

v Syr Ethiop Arab 2 Georg: Lat *How long do I hope thus?*
w Syr Ethiop Arab 2: Lat *number of seeds is completed for you*
x Syr: Ethiop *confusion*: Latin is uncertain   *y* Syr: Latin is corrupt
z Literally *after the third*; Ethiop *after three months*; Arm *after the third vision*; Georg *after the third day*   *a* Ethiop Compare Syr and Arab: Latin is uncertain

7 and the sea of Sodom shall cast up fish; and one whom the many do not know shall make his voice heard by night, and all shall hear his voice.[b] **8** There shall be chaos also in many places, and fire shall often break out, and the wild beasts shall roam beyond their haunts, and menstruous women shall bring forth monsters. **9** And salt waters shall be found in the sweet, and all friends shall conquer one another; then shall reason hide itself, and wisdom shall withdraw into its chamber, **10** and it shall be sought by many but shall not be found, and unrighteousness and unrestraint shall increase on earth. **11** And one country shall ask its neighbour, 'Has righteousness, or any one who does right, passed through you?' And it will answer, 'No.' **12** And at that time men shall hope but not obtain; they shall labour but their ways shall not prosper. **13** These are the signs which I am permitted to tell you, and if you pray again, and weep as you do now, and fast for seven days, you shall hear yet greater things than these."

14 Then I awoke, and my body shuddered violently, and my soul was so troubled that it fainted. **15** But the angel who had come and talked with me held me and strengthened me and set me on my feet.

16 Now on the second night Phaltiel, a chief of the people, came to me and said, "Where have you been? And why is your face sad? **17** Or do you not know that Israel has been entrusted to you in the land of their exile? **18** Rise therefore and eat some bread, so that you may not forsake us, like a shepherd who leaves his flock in the power of cruel wolves."

19 Then I said to him, "Depart from me and do not come near me for seven days, and then you may come to me."

He heard what I said and left me.

20 So I fasted seven days, mourning and weeping, as Uriel the angel had commanded me.

21 And after seven days the thoughts of my heart were very grievous to me again. **22** Then my soul recovered the spirit of understanding, and I began once more to speak words in the presence of the Most High. **23** And I said, "O sovereign Lord, from every forest of the earth and from all its trees thou hast chosen one vine, **24** and from all the lands of the world thou hast chosen for thyself one region,[c] and from all the flowers of the world thou hast chosen for thyself one lily, **25** and from all the depths of the sea thou hast filled for thyself one river, and from all the cities that have been built thou hast consecrated Zion for thyself, **26** and from all the birds that have been created thou hast named for thyself one dove, and from all the flocks that have been made thou hast provided for thyself one sheep, **27** and from all the multitude of peoples thou hast gotten for thyself one people; and to this people, whom thou hast loved, thou hast given the law which is approved by all. **28** And now, O Lord, why hast thou given over the one to the many, and dishonoured[d] the one root beyond the others, and scattered thine only one among the many? **29** And those who opposed thy promises have trodden down those who believed thy covenants. **30** If thou dost really hate thy people, they should be punished at thy own hands."

31 When I had spoken these words, the angel who had come to me on a previous night was sent to me, **32** and he said to me, "Listen to me, and I will instruct you; pay attention to me, and I will tell you more."

33 And I said, "Speak, my lord." And he said to me, "Are you greatly

---

[b] Cn: Lat *fish; and it shall make its voice heard by night, which the many have not known, but all shall hear its voice.* [c] Ethiop: Latin *pit* [d] Syr Ethiop Arab: Lat *prepared*

disturbed in mind over Israel? *e* Or do you love him more than his Maker does?"

34 And I said, "No, my lord, but because of my grief I have spoken; for every hour I suffer agonies of heart, while I strive to understand the way of the Most High and to search out part of his judgment."

35 And he said to me, "You cannot." And I said, "Why not, my lord? Why then was I born? Or why did not my mother's womb become my grave, that I might not see the travail of Jacob and the exhaustion of the people of Israel?"

36 He said to me, "Count up for me those who have not yet come, and gather for me the scattered raindrops, and make the withered flowers bloom again for me; 37 open for me the closed chambers, and bring forth for me the winds shut up in them, or show me the picture of a voice; and then I will explain to you the travail that you ask to understand." *f*

38 And I said, "O sovereign Lord, who is able to know these things except he whose dwelling is not with men? 39 As for me, I am without wisdom, and how can I speak concerning the things which thou hast asked me?"

40 He said to me, "Just as you cannot do one of the things that were mentioned, so you cannot discover my judgment, or the goal of the love that I have promised my people."

41 And I said, "Yet behold, O Lord, thou dost have charge of those who are alive at the end, but what will those do who were before us, or we, or those who come after us?"

42 He said to me, "I shall liken my judgment to a circle; *g* just as for those who are last there is no slowness, so for those who are first there is no haste."

43 Then I answered and said, "Couldst thou not have created at one time those who have been and those who are and those who will be, that thou mightest show thy judgment the sooner?"

44 He replied to me and said, "The creation cannot make more haste than the Creator, neither can the world hold at one time those who have been created in it."

45 And I said, "How hast thou said to thy servant that thou *h* wilt certainly give life at one time to thy creation? If therefore all creatures will live at one time *i* and the creation will sustain them, it might even now be able to support all of them present at one time."

46 He said to me, "Ask a woman's womb, and say to it, 'If you bear ten *j* children, why one after another?' Request it therefore to produce ten at one time."

47 I said, "Of course it cannot, but only each in its own time."

48 He said to me, "Even so have I given the womb of the earth to those who from time to time are sown in it. 49 For as an infant does not bring forth, and a woman who has become old does not bring forth any longer, so have I organized the world which I created."

50 Then I inquired and said, "Since thou hast now given me the opportunity, let me speak before thee. Is our mother, of whom thou hast told me, still young? Or is she now approaching old age?"

51 He replied to me, "Ask a woman who bears children, and she will tell you. 52 Say to her, 'Why are those whom you have borne recently not like those whom you bore before, but smaller in stature?' 53 And she herself will answer you, 'Those born in the strength of youth are different from those born during the time of old age, when the womb is failing.' 54 Therefore you also should consider that you and your con-

---

e Or *you are greatly distracted in mind over Israel.*   *f* Lat *see*   *g* Or *crown*
h Syr Ethiop Arab 1: Latin text is uncertain   *i* Latin omits *If . . . one time*
j Syr Ethiop Arab 2 Arm: Latin text is corrupt

temporaries are smaller in stature than those who were before you, 55 and those who come after you will be smaller than you, as born of a creation which already is aging and passing the strength of youth."

56 And I said, "O Lord, I beseech thee, if I have found favour in thy sight, show thy servant through whom thou dost visit thy creation."

6 And he said to me, "At the beginning of the circle of the earth,ᵏ before the portals of the world were in place, and before the assembled winds blew, 2 and before the rumblings of thunder sounded, and before the flashes of lightning shone, and before the foundations of paradise were laid, 3 and before the beautiful flowers were seen, and before the powers of movement ˡ were established, and before the innumerable hosts of angels were gathered together, 4 and before the heights of the air were lifted up, and before the measures of the firmaments were named, and before the footstool of Zion was established, 5 and before the present years were reckoned, and before the imaginations of those who now sin were estranged, and before those who stored up treasures of faith were sealed—6 then I planned these things, and they were made through me and not through another, just as the end shall come through me and not through another."

7 And I answered and said, "What will be the dividing of the times? Or when will be the end of the first age and the beginning of the age that follows?"

8 He said to me, "From Abraham to Isaac,ᵐ because from him were born Jacob and Esau, for Jacob's hand held Esau's heel from the beginning. 9 For Esau is the end of this age, and Jacob is the beginning of the age that follows. 10 For the be-

ginning of a man is his hand, and the end of a man is his heel; ⁿ between the heel and the hand seek for nothing else, Ezra!"

11 I answered and said, "O sovereign Lord, if I have found favour in thy sight, 12 show thy servant the end of thy signs which thou didst show me in part on a previous night."

13 He answered and said to me, "Rise to your feet and you will hear a full, resounding voice. 14 And if the place where you are standing is greatly shaken 15 while the voice is speaking, do not be terrified; because the word concerns the end, and the foundations of the earth will understand 16 that the speech concerns them. They will tremble and be shaken, for they know that their end must be changed."

17 When I heard this, I rose to my feet and listened, and behold, a voice was speaking, and its sound was like the sound of many waters. 18 And it said, "Behold, the days are coming, and it shall be that when I draw near to visit the inhabitants of the earth, 19 and when I require from the doers of iniquity the penalty of their iniquity, and when the humiliation of Zion is complete, 20 and when the seal is placed upon the age which is about to pass away, then I will show these signs: the books shall be opened before the firmament, and all shall see it together. 21 Infants a year old shall speak with their voices, and women with child shall give birth to premature children at three or four months, and these shall live and dance. 22 Sown places shall suddenly appear unsown, and full storehouses shall suddenly be found to be empty; 23 and the trumpet shall sound aloud, and when all hear it, they shall suddenly be terrified. 24 At that time friends shall make war on friends like enemies, and the earth and those

---

ᵏ The text is uncertain: Compare Syr *The beginning by the hand of man, but the end by my own hands. For as before the land of the world existed there, and before:* Ethiop: *At first by the Son of Man, and afterwards I myself. For before the earth and the lands were created, and before*
ˡ Or *earthquake*   ᵐ Other authorities read *Abraham*   ⁿ Syr: Latin is defective here

who inhabit it shall be terrified, and the springs of the fountains shall stand still, so that for three hours they shall not flow.

25 "And it shall be that whoever remains after all that I have foretold to you shall himself be saved and shall see my salvation and the end of my world. 26 And they shall see the men who were taken up, who from their birth have not tasted death; and the heart of the earth's *o* inhabitants shall be changed and converted to a different spirit. 27 For evil shall be blotted out, and deceit shall be quenched; 28 faithfulness shall flourish, and corruption shall be overcome, and the truth, which has been so long without fruit, shall be revealed."

29 While he spoke to me, behold, little by little the place where I was standing began to rock to and fro.*p* 30 And he said to me, "I have come to show you these things this night.*q* 31 If therefore you will pray again and fast again for seven days, I will again declare to you greater things than these,*r* 32 because your voice has surely been heard before the Most High; for the Mighty One has seen your uprightness and has also observed the purity which you have maintained from your youth. 33 Therefore he sent me to show you all these things, and to say to you: 'Believe and do not be afraid! 34 Do not be quick to think vain thoughts concerning the former times, lest you be hasty concerning the last times.' "

35 Now after this I wept again and fasted seven days as before, in order to complete the three weeks as I had been told. 36 And on the eighth night my heart was troubled within me again, and I began to speak in the presence of the Most High. 37 For

my spirit was greatly aroused, and my soul was in distress.

38 I said, "O Lord, thou didst speak at the beginning of creation, and didst say on the first day, 'Let heaven and earth be made,' and thy word accomplished the work. 39 And then the Spirit was hovering, and darkness and silence embraced everything; the sound of man's voice was not yet there.*s* 40 Then thou didst command that a ray of light be brought forth from thy treasuries, so that thy works might then appear.

41 "Again, on the second day, thou didst create the spirit of the firmament, and didst command him to divide and separate the waters, that one part might move upward and the other part remain beneath.

42 "On the third day thou didst command the waters to be gathered together in the seventh part of the earth; six parts thou didst dry up and keep so that some of them might be planted and cultivated and be of service before thee. 43 For thy word went forth, and at once the work was done. 44 For immediately fruit came forth in endless abundance and of varied appeal to the taste; and flowers of inimitable colour; and odours of inexpressible fragrance. These were made on the third day.

45 "On the fourth day thou didst command the brightness of the sun, the light of the moon, and the arrangement of the stars to come into being; 46 and thou didst command them to serve man, who was about to be formed.

47 "On the fifth day thou didst command the seventh part, where the water had been gathered together, to bring forth living creatures, birds, and fishes; and so it was done. 48 The dumb and lifeless water produced living creatures, as it was commanded,*t* that therefore the nations

---

o Syr Compare Ethiop Arab 1 Arm: Latin omits *earth's*
p Syr Ethiop Compare Arab Arm: Latin is corrupt
q Syr Compare Ethiop: Latin is corrupt   *r* Syr Ethiop Arab I Arm: Latin adds *by day*
s Syr Ethiop: Lat *was not yet from thee*   *t* The text of this verse is uncertain

might declare thy wondrous works.

49 "Then thou didst keep in existence two living creatures; ⁿ the name of one thou didst call Behemoth and the name of the other Leviathan. ⁵⁰ And thou didst separate one from the other, for the seventh part where the water had been gathered together could not hold them both. ⁵¹ And thou didst give Behemoth one of the parts which had been dried up on the third day, to live in it, where there are a thousand mountains; ⁵² but to Leviathan thou didst give the seventh part, the watery part; and thou hast kept them to be eaten by whom thou wilt, and when thou wilt.

53 "On the sixth day thou didst command the earth to bring forth before thee cattle, beasts, and creeping things; ⁵⁴ and over these thou didst place Adam, as ruler over all the works which thou hadst made; and from him we have all come, the people whom thou hast chosen.

55 "All this I have spoken before thee, O Lord, because thou hast said that it was for us that thou didst create this world.ᵛ ⁵⁶ As for the other nations which have descended from Adam, thou hast said that they are nothing, and that they are like spittle, and thou hast compared their abundance to a drop from a bucket. ⁵⁷ And now, O Lord, behold, these nations, which are reputed as nothing, domineer over us and devour us. ⁵⁸ But we thy people, whom thou hast called thy first-born, only begotten, zealous for thee,ʷ and most dear, have been given into their hands. ⁵⁹ If the world has indeed been created for us, why do we not possess our world as an inheritance? How long will this be so?"

7 When I had finished speaking these words, the angel who had been sent to me on the former nights was sent to me again, ² and he said to me, "Rise, Ezra, and listen to the words that I have come to speak to you."

3 I said, "Speak, my lord." And he said to me, "There is a sea set in a wide expanse so that it is broad ˣ and vast, ⁴ but it has an entrance set in a narrow place, so that it is like a river. ⁵ If any one, then, wishes to reach the sea, to look at it or to navigate it, how can he come to the broad part unless he passes through the narrow part? ⁶ Another example: There is a city built and set on a plain, and it is full of all good things; ⁷ but the entrance to it is narrow and set in a precipitous place, so that there is fire on the right hand and deep water on the left; ⁸ and there is only one path lying between them, that is, between the fire and the water, so that only one man can walk upon that path. ⁹ If now that city is given to a man for an inheritance, how will the heir receive his inheritance unless he passes through the danger set before him?"

10 I said, "He cannot, lord." And he said to me, "So also is Israel's portion. ¹¹ For I made the world for their sake, and when Adam transgressed my statutes, what had been made was judged. ¹² And so the entrances of this world were made narrow and sorrowful and toilsome; they are few and evil, full of dangers and involved in great hardships. ¹³ But the entrances of the greater world are broad and safe, and really yield the fruit of immortality. ¹⁴ Therefore unless the living pass through the difficult and vain experiences, they can never receive those things that have been reserved for them. ¹⁵ But now why are you disturbed, seeing that you are to perish? And why are you moved, seeing that you are mortal? ¹⁶ And why have you not considered in your mind what is to come, rather than what is now present?"

17 Then I answered and said, "O

ⁿ Syr Ethiop: Lat *two souls*
ᵛ Syr Ethiop Arab 2: Lat *the first-born world* Compare Arab 1 *first world*
ʷ The meaning of the Latin text is obscure   ˣ Syr Compare Ethiop Arab 1: Lat *deep*

sovereign Lord, behold, thou hast ordained in thy law that the righteous shall inherit these things, but that the ungodly shall perish. 18 The righteous therefore can endure difficult circumstances while hoping for easier ones; but those who have done wickedly have suffered the difficult circumstances and will not see the easier ones."

19 And he said to me, "You are not a better judge than God, or wiser than the Most High! 20 Let many perish who are now living, rather than that the law of God which is set before them be disregarded! 21 For God strictly commanded those who came into the world, when they came, what they should do to live, and what they should observe to avoid punishment. 22 Nevertheless they were not obedient, and spoke against him;

they devised for themselves vain thoughts,
23 and proposed to themselves wicked frauds;
they even declared that the Most High does not exist,
and they ignored his ways!
24 They scorned his law,
and denied his covenants;
they have been unfaithful to his statutes,
and have not performed his works.

25 "Therefore, Ezra, empty things are for the empty, and full things are for the full. 26 For behold, the time will come, when the signs which I have foretold to you will come to pass, that the city which now is not seen shall appear,*v* and the land which now is hidden shall be disclosed. 27 And every one who has been delivered from the evils that I have foretold shall see my wonders. 28 For my son the Messiah *z* shall be revealed with those who are with him, and those who remain shall rejoice four

hundred years. 29 And after these years my son the Messiah shall die, and all who draw human breath. 30 And the world shall be turned back to primeval silence for seven days, as it was at the first beginnings; so that no one shall be left. 31 And after seven days the world, which is not yet awake, shall be roused, and that which is corruptible shall perish. 32 And the earth shall give up those who are asleep in it, and the dust those who dwell silently in it; and the chambers shall give up the souls which have been committed to them. 33 And the Most High shall be revealed upon the seat of judgment, and compassion shall pass away, and patience shall be withdrawn; *a* 34 but only judgment shall remain, truth shall stand, and faithfulness shall grow strong. 35 And recompense shall follow, and the reward shall be manifested; righteous deeds shall awake, and unrighteous deeds shall not sleep.*b* [36] Then the pit *c* of torment shall appear, and opposite it shall be the place of rest; and the furnace of hell *d* shall be disclosed, and opposite it the paradise of delight. [37] Then the Most High will say to the nations that have been raised from the dead, 'Look now, and understand whom you have denied, whom you have not served, whose commandments you have despised! [38] Look on this side and on that; here are delight and rest, and there are fire and torments!' Thus he will *e* speak to them on the day of judgment—[39] a day that has no sun or moon or stars, [40] or cloud or thunder or lightning or wind or water or air, or darkness or evening or morning, [41] or summer or spring or heat or winter *f* or frost or cold or hail or rain or dew, [42] or noon or night, or dawn or shining or brightness or light, but only the splendour of the glory of the Most High, by which

---

v Arm: Lat Syr *that the bride shall appear, even the city appearing*
z Syr Arab 1: Ethiop *my Messiah*; Arab 2 *the Messiah*; Arm *the Messiah of God*; Lat *my son Jesus*   *a* Lat *gather together*
b The passage from verse [36] to verse [105], formerly missing, has been restored to the text
c Syr Ethiop: Lat *place*   *d* Lat *gehenna*   *e* Syr Ethiop Arab 1: Lat *thou shalt*   *f* Or *storm*

all shall see what has been determined for them. [43] For it will last for about a week of years. [44] This is my judgment and its prescribed order; and to you alone have I shown these things."

[45] I answered and said, "O sovereign Lord, I said then and I say now: [g] Blessed are those who are alive and keep thy commandments! [46] But what of those for whom I prayed? For who among the living is there that has not sinned, or who among men that has not transgressed thy covenant? [47] And now I see that the world to come will bring delight to few, but torments to many. [48] For an evil heart has grown up in us, which has alienated us from God, [h] and has brought us into corruption and the ways of death, and has shown us the paths of perdition and removed us far from life—and that not just a few of us but almost all who have been created!"

[49] He answered me and said, "Listen to me, Ezra, [i] and I will instruct you, and will admonish you yet again. [50] For this reason the Most High has made not one world but two. [51] For whereas you have said that the righteous are not many but few, while the ungodly abound, hear the explanation for this.

[52] "If you have just a few precious stones, will you add to them lead and clay?" [j]

[53] I said, "Lord, how could that be?"

[54] And he said to me, "Not only that, but ask the earth and she will tell you; defer to her, and she will declare it to you. [55] Say to her, 'You produce gold and silver and brass, and also iron and lead and clay; [56] but silver is more abundant than gold, and brass than silver, and iron than brass, and lead than iron, and clay than lead.' [57] Judge therefore which

things are precious and desirable, those that are abundant or those that are rare?"

[58] I said, "O sovereign Lord, what is plentiful is of less worth, for what is more rare is more precious."

[59] He answered me and said, "Weigh within yourself [k] what you have thought, for he who has what is hard to get rejoices more than he who has what is plentiful. [60] So also will be the judgment [l] which I have promised; for I will rejoice over the few who shall be saved, because it is they who have made my glory to prevail now, and through them my name has now been honoured. [61] And I will not grieve over the multitude of those who perish; for it is they who are now like a mist, and are similar to a flame and smoke—they are set on fire and burn hotly, and are extinguished."

[62] I replied and said, "O earth, what have you brought forth, if the mind is made out of the dust like the other created things! [63] For it would have been better if the dust itself had not been born, so that the mind might not have been made from it. [64] But now the mind grows with us, and therefore we are tormented, because we perish and know it. [65] Let the human race lament, but let the beasts of the field be glad; let all who have been born lament, but let the four-footed beasts and the flocks rejoice! [66] For it is much better with them than with us; for they do not look for a judgment, nor do they know of any torment or salvation promised to them after death. [67] For what does it profit us that we shall be preserved alive but cruelly tormented? [68] For all who have been born are involved in iniquities, and are full of sins and burdened with transgressions. [69] And if we were not to come into judgment after

---

[g] Syr: Lat *And I answered, "I said then, O Lord, and I say now:*
[h] Cn: Lat Syr Ethiop *from these*   [i] Syr Arab 1 Georg: Lat Ethiop omit *Ezra*
[j] Arab 1: Lat Syr Ethiop *are corrupt*   [k] Syr Ethiop Arab 1: Latin is corrupt here
[l] Syr and Arab 1: Lat *creation*

death, perhaps it would have been better for us."

[70] He answered me and said, "When the Most High made the world and Adam and all who have come from him, he first prepared the judgment and the things that pertain to the judgment. [71] And now understand from your own words, for you have said that the mind grows with us. [72] For this reason, therefore, those who dwell on earth shall be tormented, because though they had understanding they committed iniquity, and though they received the commandments they did not keep them, and though they obtained the law they dealt unfaithfully with what they received. [73] What, then, will they have to say in the judgment, or how will they answer in the last times? [74] For how long the time is that the Most High has been patient with those who inhabit the world, and not for their sake, but because of the times which he has foreordained!"

[75] I answered and said, "If I have found favour in thy sight, O Lord, show this also to thy servant: whether after death, as soon as every one of us yields up his soul, we shall be kept in rest until those times come when thou wilt renew the creation, or whether we shall be tormented at once?"

[76] He answered me and said, "I will show you that also, but do not be associated with those who have shown scorn, nor number yourself among those who are tormented. [77] For you have a treasure of works laid up with the Most High; but it will not be shown to you until the last times. [78] Now, concerning death, the teaching is: When the decisive decree has gone forth from the Most High that a man shall die, as the spirit leaves the body to return again to him who gave it, first of all it adores the glory of the Most High. [79] And if it is one of those who

have shown scorn and have not kept the way of the Most High, and who have despised his law, and who have hated those who fear God—[80] such spirits shall not enter into habitations, but shall immediately wander about in torments, ever grieving and sad, in seven ways. [81] The first way, because they have scorned the law of the Most High. [82] The second way, because they cannot now make a good repentance that they may live. [83] The third way, they shall see the reward laid up for those who have trusted the covenants of the Most High. [84] The fourth way, they shall consider the torment laid up for themselves in the last days. [85] The fifth way, they shall see how the habitations of the others are guarded by angels in profound quiet. [86] The sixth way, they shall see how some of them will pass over *m* into torments. [87] The seventh way, which is worse *n* than all the ways that have been mentioned, because they shall utterly waste away in confusion and be consumed with shame,*o* and shall wither with fear at seeing the glory of the Most High before whom they sinned while they were alive, and before whom they are to be judged in the last times.

[88] "Now this is the order of those who have kept the ways of the Most High, when they shall be separated from their mortal body.*p* [89] During the time that they lived in it,*q* they laboriously served the Most High, and withstood danger every hour, that they might keep the law of the Lawgiver perfectly. [90] Therefore this is the teaching concerning them: [91] First of all, they shall see with great joy the glory of him who receives them, for they shall have rest in seven orders. [92] The first order, because they have striven with great effort to overcome the evil thought which was formed with them, that it might not lead them astray from life

---

m Cn: the text of this verse is corrupt   *n* Lat *greater*   *o* Syr Ethiop: Latin is corrupt
p Literally *the corruptible vessel*   *q* Syr Ethiop: Latin is corrupt

into death. [93] The second order, because they see the perplexity in which the souls of the ungodly wander, and the punishment that awaits them. [94] The third order, they see the witness which he who formed them bears concerning them, that while they were alive they kept the law which was given them in trust. [95] The fourth order, they understand the rest which they now enjoy, being gathered into their chambers and guarded by angels in profound quiet, and the glory which awaits them in the last days. [96] The fifth order, they rejoice that they have now escaped what is corruptible, and shall inherit what is to come; and besides they see the straits and toil *r* from which they have been delivered, and the spacious liberty which they are to receive and enjoy in immortality. [97] The sixth order, when it is shown to them how their face is to shine like the sun, and how they are to be made like the light of the stars, being incorruptible from then on. [98] The seventh order, which is greater than all that have been mentioned, because they shall rejoice with boldness, and shall be confident without confusion, and shall be glad without fear, for they hasten to behold the face of him whom they served in life and from whom they are to receive their reward when glorified. [99] This is the order of the souls of the righteous, as henceforth is announced; *s* and the aforesaid are the ways of torment which those who would not give heed shall suffer hereafter."

[100] I answered and said, "Will time therefore be given to the souls, after they have been separated from the bodies, to see what you have described to me?"

[101] He said to me, "They shall have freedom for seven days, so that during these seven days they may see the things of which you have been told, and afterwards they shall be gathered in their habitations."

[102] I answered and said, "If I have found favour in thy sight, show further to me, thy servant, whether on the day of judgment the righteous will be able to intercede for the ungodly or to entreat the Most High for them, [103] fathers for sons or sons for parents, brothers for brothers, relatives for their kinsmen, or friends *t* for those who are most dear."

[104] He answered me and said, "Since you have found favour in my sight, I will show you this also. The day of judgment is decisive *u* and displays to all the seal of truth. Just as now a father does not send his son, or a son his father, or a master his servant, or a friend his dearest friend, to be ill *v* or sleep or eat or be healed in his stead, [105] so no one shall ever pray for another on that day, neither shall any one lay a burden on another; *w* for then every one shall bear his own righteousness or unrighteousness."

36 [106] I answered and said, "How then do we find that first Abraham prayed for the people of Sodom, and Moses for our fathers who sinned in the desert, 37 [107] and Joshua after him for Israel in the days of Achan, 38 [108] and Samuel in the days of Saul,*x* and David for the plague, and Solomon for those in the sanctuary, 39 [109] and Elijah for those who received the rain, and for the one who was dead, that he might live, 40 [110] and Hezekiah for the people in the days of Sennacherib, and many others prayed for many? 41 [111] If therefore the righteous have prayed for the ungodly now, when corruption has increased and

---

r Syr Ethiop: Lat *fulness*   *s* Syr: Latin is corrupt here
t Syr Ethiop Arab 1: Lat *kinsmen for their nearest, friends* (literally *the confident*) *for their dearest*   *u* Lat *bold*   *v* Syr Ethiop Arm: Lat *understand*
w Syr: Latin omits *on that . . . another*   *x* Syr Ethiop Arab 1: Latin omits *in the days of Saul*

unrighteousness has multiplied, why will it not be so then as well?"

42 [112] He answered me and said, "This present world is not the end; the full glory does not *ᵛ* abide in it; *ᶻ* Therefore those who were strong prayed for the weak. 43 [113] But the day of judgment will be the end of this age and the beginning *ᵃ* of the immortal age to come, in which corruption has passed away, 44 [114] sinful indulgence has come to an end, unbelief has been cut off, and righteousness has increased and truth has appeared. 45 [115] Therefore no one will then be able to have mercy on him who has been condemned in the judgment, or to harm *ᵇ* him who is victorious."

46 [116] I answered and said, "This is my first and last word, that it would have been better if the earth had not produced Adam, or else, when it had produced him, had restrained him from sinning. 47 [117] For what good is it to all that they live in sorrow now and expect punishment after death? 48 [118] O Adam, what have you done? For though it was you who sinned, the fall was not yours alone, but ours also who are your descendants. 49 [119] For what good is it to us, if an eternal age has been promised to us, but we have done deeds that bring death? 50 [120] And what good is it that an everlasting hope has been promised us, but we have miserably failed? 51 [121] Or that safe and healthful habitations have been reserved for us, but we have lived wickedly? 52 [122] Or that the glory of the Most High will defend those who have led a pure life, but we have walked in the most wicked ways? 53 [123] Or that a paradise shall be revealed, whose fruit remains unspoiled and in which are abundance and healing, but we shall not enter it, 54 [124] because we have lived in unseemly places? 55 [125] Or that the

faces of those who practised self-control shall shine more than the stars, but our faces shall be blacker than darkness? 56 [126] For while we lived and committed iniquity we did not consider what we should suffer after death."

57 [127] He answered and said, "This is the meaning of the contest which every man who is born on earth shall wage, 58 [128] that if he is defeated he shall suffer what you have said, but if he is victorious he shall receive what I have said. *ᶜ* 59 [129] For this is the way of which Moses, while he was alive, spoke to the people, saying, 'Choose for yourself life, that you may live!' 60 [130] But they did not believe him, or the prophets after him, or even myself who have spoken to them. 61 [131] Therefore there shall not be *ᵈ* grief at their destruction, so much as joy over those to whom salvation is assured."

62 [132] I answered and said, "I know, O Lord, that the Most High is now called merciful, because he has mercy on those who have not yet come into the world; 63 [133] and gracious, because he is gracious to those who turn in repentance to his law; 64 [134] and patient, because he shows patience toward those who have sinned, since they are his own works; 65 [135] and bountiful, because he would rather give than take away; *ᵉ* 66 [136] and abundant in compassion, because he makes his compassions abound more and more to those now living and to those who are gone and to those yet to come, 67 [137] for if he did not make them abound, the world with those who inhabit it would not have life; 68 [138] and he is called giver, because if he did not give out of his goodness so that those who have committed iniquities might be relieved of them, not one ten-thousandth of mankind could have life; 69 [139] and judge, because

if he did not pardon those who were created by his word and blot out the multitude of their sins,*f* 70 [140] there would probably be left only very few of the innumerable multitude."

8 He answered me and said, "The Most High made this world for the sake of many, but the world to come for the sake of few. 2 But I will tell you a parable, Ezra. Just as, when you ask the earth, it will tell you that it provides very much clay from which earthenware is made, but only a little dust from which gold comes; so is the course of the present world. 3 Many have been created, but few shall be saved."

4 I answered and said, "Then drink your fill of understanding, O my soul, and drink wisdom, O my heart!*g* 5 For not of your own will did you come into the world,*h* and against your will you depart, for you have been given only a short time to live. 6 O Lord who art over us, grant to thy servant that we may pray before thee, and give us seed for our heart and cultivation of our understanding so that fruit may be produced, by which every mortal who bears the likeness*i* of a human being may be able to live. 7 For thou alone dost exist, and we are a work of thy hands, as thou hast declared. 8 And because thou dost give life to the body which is now fashioned in the womb, and dost furnish it with members, what thou hast created is preserved in fire and water, and for nine months the womb*j* which thou hast formed endures thy creation which has been created in it. 9 But that which keeps and that which is kept shall both be kept by thy keeping.*k* And when the womb gives up again what has been created in it, 10 thou hast commanded that from the members themselves (that is, from the

breasts) milk should be supplied which is the fruit of the breasts, 11 so that what has been fashioned may be nourished for a time; and afterwards thou wilt guide him in thy mercy. 12 Thou hast brought him up in thy righteousness, and instructed him in thy law, and reproved him in thy wisdom. 13 Thou wilt take away his life, for he is thy creation; and thou wilt make him live, for he is thy work. 14 If then thou wilt suddenly and quickly*l* destroy him who with so great labour was fashioned by thy command, to what purpose was he made? 15 And now I will speak out: About all mankind thou knowest best; but I will speak about thy people, for whom I am grieved, 16 and about thy inheritance, for whom I lament, and about Israel, for whom I am sad, and about the seed of Jacob, for whom I am troubled. 17 Therefore I will pray before thee for myself and for them, for I see the failings of us who dwell in the land, 18 and *m* I have heard of the swiftness of the judgment that is to come. 19 Therefore hear my voice, and understand my words, and I will speak before thee."

The beginning of the words of Ezra's prayer, before he was taken up. He said: 20 "O Lord who inhabitest eternity,*n* whose eyes are exalted *o* and whose upper chambers are in the air, 21 whose throne is beyond measure and whose glory is beyond comprehension, before whom the hosts of angels stand trembling 22 and at whose command they are changed to wind and fire,*p* whose word is sure and whose utterances are certain, whose ordinance is strong and whose command is terrible, 23 whose look dries up the depths and whose indignation makes the mountains melt away, and whose truth is established for ever *q*—24 hear, O Lord, the prayer

---

f Lat *contempts*   *g* Syr: Lat *let it feed on what it understands*   *h* Syr: Latin is corrupt here
i Syr: Lat *place*   *j* Literally *what thou hast formed*   *k* Syr: Latin is corrupt here
l Syr: Lat *shalt with a light command*   *m* Literally *but*   *n* Or *abidest for ever*
o Another Latin text reads *whose are the highest heavens*
p Syr: Lat *they whose service takes the form of wind and fire*
q Arab 2: other authorities read *bears witness*

of thy servant, and give ear to the petition of thy creature; attend to my words. ²⁵ For as long as I live I will speak, and as long as I have understanding I will answer. ²⁶ O look not upon the sins of thy people, but at those who have served thee in truth. ²⁷ Regard not the endeavours of those who act wickedly, but the endeavours of those who have kept thy covenants amid afflictions. ²⁸ Think not on those who have lived wickedly in thy sight; but remember those who have willingly acknowledged that thou art to be feared. ²⁹ Let it not be thy will to destroy those who have had the ways of cattle; but regard those who have gloriously taught thy law.ʳ ³⁰ Be not angry with those who are deemed worse than beasts; but love those who have always put their trust in thy glory. ³¹ For we and our fathers have passed our lives in ways that bring death;ˢ but thou, because of us sinners, art called merciful. ³² For if thou hast desired to have pity on us, who have no works of righteousness, then thou wilt be called merciful. ³³ For the righteous, who have many works laid up with thee, shall receive their reward in consequence of their own deeds. ³⁴ But what is man, that thou art angry with him; or what is a corruptible race, that thou art so bitter against it? ³⁵ For in truth there is no one among those who have been born who has not acted wickedly, and among those who have existed ᵗ there is no one who has not transgressed. ³⁶ For in this, O Lord, thy righteousness and goodness will be declared, when thou art merciful to those who have no store of good works."

37 He answered me and said, "Some things you have spoken rightly, and it will come to pass according to your words. ³⁸ For indeed I will not concern myself about the fashioning of those who have sinned, or about their death, their judgment, or their destruction; ³⁹ but I will rejoice over the creation of the righteous, over their pilgrimage also, and their salvation, and their receiving their reward. ⁴⁰ As I have spoken, therefore, so it shall be.

41 "For just as the farmer sows many seeds upon the ground and plants a multitude of seedlings, and yet not all that have been sown will come up ᵘ in due season, and not all that were planted will take root; so also those who have been sown in the world will not all be saved."

42 I answered and said, "If I have found favour before thee, let me speak.ᵛ ⁴³ For if the farmer's seed does not come up, because it has not received thy rain in due season, or if it has been ruined by too much rain, it perishes.ʷ ⁴⁴ But man, who has been formed by thy hands and is called thy own image because he is made like thee, and for whose sake thou hast formed all things—hast thou also made him like the farmer's seed? ⁴⁵ No, O Lord ˣ who art over us! But spare thy people and have mercy on thy inheritance, for thou hast mercy on thy own creation."

46 He answered me and said, "Things that are present are for those who live now, and things that are future are for those who will live hereafter. ⁴⁷ For you come far short of being able to love my creation more than I love it. But you have often compared yourself ʸ to the unrighteous. Never do so! ⁴⁸ But even in this respect you will be praiseworthy before the Most High, ⁴⁹ because you have humbled yourself, as is becoming for you, and have not deemed yourself to be among the righteous in order to receive ᶻ the greatest glory. ⁵⁰ For many miseries will affect those

---

ʳ Syr *have received the brightness of thy law*   ˢ Syr Ethiop: the Latin text is uncertain
ᵗ Syr: the Latin text is uncertain   ᵘ Syr Ethiop *will live;* Latin *will be saved*
ᵛ Or *If I have found favour, let me speak before thee*
ʷ Cn: Compare Syr Arab 1 Arm Georg 2: the Latin is corrupt
ˣ Ethiop Arab 1 and 2 Compare Syr: Latin om᾽ s *O Lord*   ʸ Syr Ethiop: Lat *brought yourself near*
ᶻ Or *righteous; so that you will receive*

who inhabit the world in the last times, because they have walked in great pride. [51] But think of your own case, and inquire concerning the glory of those who are like yourself, [52] because it is for you that paradise is opened, the tree of life is planted, the age to come is prepared, plenty is provided, a city is built, rest is appointed,[a] goodness is established and wisdom perfected beforehand. [53] The root of evil is sealed up from you, illness is banished from you, and death [b] is hidden; hell has fled and corruption has been forgotten; [c] [54] sorrows have passed away, and in the end the treasure of immortality is made manifest. [55] Therefore do not ask any more questions about the multitude of those who perish. [56] For they also received freedom, but they despised the Most High, and were contemptuous of his law, and forsook his ways. [57] Moreover they have even trampled upon his righteous ones, [58] and said in their hearts that there is no God—though knowing full well that they must die. [59] For just as the things which I have predicted await [d] you, so the thirst and torment which are prepared await them. For the Most High did not intend that men should be destroyed; [60] but they themselves who were created have defiled the name of him who made them, and have been ungrateful to him who prepared life for them. [61] Therefore my judgment is now drawing near; [62] I have not shown this to all men, but only to you and a few like you."

Then I answered and said, [63] "Behold, O Lord, thou hast now shown me a multitude of the signs which thou wilt do in the last times, but thou hast not shown me when thou wilt do them."

9 He answered me and said, "Measure carefully in your mind, and when you see that a certain part

of the predicted signs are past, [2] then you will know that it is the very time when the Most High is about to visit the world which he has made. [3] So when there shall appear in the world earthquakes, tumult of peoples, intrigues of nations, wavering of leaders, confusion of princes, [4] then you will know that it was of these that the Most High spoke from the days that were of old, from the beginning. [5] For just as with everything that has occurred in the world, the beginning is evident,[e] and the end manifest; [6] so also are the times of the Most High: the beginnings are manifest in wonders and mighty works, and the end in requital [f] and in signs. [7] And it shall be that every one who will be saved and will be able to escape on account of his works, or on account of the faith by which he has believed, [8] will survive the dangers that have been predicted, and will see my salvation in my land and within my borders, which I have sanctified for myself from the beginning. [9] Then those who have now abused my ways shall be amazed, and those who have rejected them with contempt shall dwell in torments. [10] For as many as did not acknowledge me in their lifetime, although they received my benefits, [11] and as many as scorned my law while they still had freedom, and did not understand but despised it [g] while an opportunity of repentance was still open to them, [12] these must in torment acknowledge it [h] after death. [13] Therefore, do not continue to be curious as to how the ungodly will be punished; but inquire how the righteous will be saved, those to whom the age belongs and for whose sake the age was made." [i]

[14] I answered and said, [15] "I said before, and I say now, and will say it again: there are more who perish than those who will be saved, [16] as

---

[a] Syr: Lat *allowed*   [b] Syr Ethiop Arm: Latin omits *death*
[c] Syr: Lat *Hades and corruption have fled into oblivion*, or *corruption has fled into Hades to be forgotten*   [d] Syr: Lat *will receive*   [e] Syr: Ethiop *in the word*: Latin is corrupt
[f] Syr: Lat Ethiop *in effects*   [g] Or *me*   [h] Or *me*
[i] Syr: Lat *saved, and whose is the age and for whose sake the age was made and when*

a wave is greater than a drop of water."

17 He answered me and said, "As is the field, so is the seed; and as are the flowers, so are the colours; and as is the work, so is the product; and as is the farmer, so is the threshing floor. 18 For there was a time in this age when I was preparing for those who now exist, before the world was made for them to dwell in, and no one opposed me then, for no one existed; 19 but now those who have been created in this world which is supplied both with an unfailing table and an inexhaustible pasture,ʲ have become corrupt in their ways. 20 So I considered my world, and behold, it was lost, and my earth, and behold, it was in peril because of the devices of those whoᵏ had come into it. 21 And I saw and spared some ˡ with great difficulty, and saved for myself one grape out of a cluster, and one plant out of a great forest.ᵐ 22 So let the multitude perish which has been born in vain, but let my grape and my plant be saved, because with much labour I have perfected them. 23 But if you will let seven days more pass—do not fast during them, however; 24 but go into a field of flowers where no house has been built, and eat only of the flowers of the field, and taste no meat and drink no wine, but eat only flowers, 25 and pray to the Most High continually—then I will come and talk with you."

26 So I went, as he directed me, into the field which is called Ardat;ⁿ and there I sat among the flowers and ate of the plants of the field, and the nourishment they afforded satisfied me. 27 And after seven days, as I lay on the grass, my heart was troubled again as it was before. 28 And my mouth was opened, and I began to speak before the Most High, and said, 29 "O Lord, thou didst show thyself among us, to our fathers in the wilder-

ness when they came out from Egypt and when they came into the untrodden and unfruitful wilderness; 30 and thou didst say, 'Hear me, O Israel, and give heed to my words, O descendants of Jacob. 31 For behold, I sow my law in you, and it shall bring forth fruit in you, and you shall be glorified through it for ever.' 32 But though our fathers received the law, they did not keep it, and did not observe the statutes; yet the fruit of the law did not perish—for it could not, because it was thine. 33 Yet those who received it perished, because they did not keep what had been sown in them. 34 And behold, it is the rule that, when the ground has received seed, or the sea a ship, or any dish food or drink, and when it happens that what was sown or what was launched or what was put in is destroyed, 35 they are destroyed, but the things that held them remain; yet with us it has not been so. 36 For we who have received the law and sinned will perish, as well as our heart which received it; 37 the law, however, does not perish but remains in its glory."

38 When I said these things in my heart, I lifted up my eyesᵒ and saw a woman on my right, and behold, she was mourning and weeping with a loud voice, and was deeply grieved at heart, and her clothes were rent, and there were ashes on her head. 39 Then I dismissed the thoughts with which I had been engaged, and turned to her 40 and said to her, "Why are you weeping, and why are you grieved at heart?"

41 And she said to me, "Let me alone, my lord, that I may weep for myself and continue to mourn, for I am greatly embittered in spirit and deeply afflicted."

42 And I said to her "What has happened to you? Tell me."

43 And she said to me, "Your servant was barren and had no child,

---

ʲ Cn: Lat *law*   ᵏ Cn: Lat *devices which*   ˡ Lat *them*   ᵐ Syr Ethiop Arab 1: Lat *tribe*
ⁿ Syr Ethiop *Arpad*: Arm *Ardab*   ᵒ Syr Arab Arm: Lat *I looked about me with my eyes*

though I lived with my husband thirty years. 44 And every hour and every day during those thirty years I besought the Most High, night and day. 45 And after thirty years God heard your handmaid, and looked upon my low estate, and considered my distress, and gave me a son. And I rejoiced greatly over him, I and my husband and all my neighbours;*p* and we gave great glory to the Mighty One. 46 And I brought him up with much care. 47 So when he grew up and I came to take a wife for him, I set a day for the marriage feast.

10 "But it happened that when my son entered his wedding chamber, he fell down and died. 2 Then we all put out the lamps, and all my neighbours*q* attempted to console me; and I remained quiet until evening of the second day. 3 But when they all had stopped consoling me, that I might be quiet, I got up in the night and fled, and came to this field, as you see. 4 And now I intend not to return to the city, but to stay here, and I will neither eat nor drink, but without ceasing mourn and fast until I die."

5 Then I broke off the reflections with which I was still engaged, and answered her in anger and said, 6 "You most foolish of women, do you not see our mourning, and what has happened to us? 7 For Zion, the mother of us all, is in deep grief and great affliction. 8 It is most appropriate to mourn now, because we are all mourning, and to be sorrowful, because we are all sorrowing; you are sorrowing for one son, but we, the whole world, for our mother.*r* 9 Now ask the earth, and she will tell you that it is she who ought to mourn over so many who have come into being upon her. 10 And from the beginning all have been born of her, and others will come; and behold, almost all go to perdition, and a multi-

tude of them are destined for destruction. 11 Who then ought to mourn the more, she*s* who lost so great a multitude, or you who are grieving for one? 12 But if you say to me, 'My lamentation is not like the earth's, for I have lost the fruit of my womb, which I brought forth in pain and bore in sorrow; 13 but it is with the earth according to the way of the earth—the multitude that is now in it goes as it came'; 14 then I say to you, 'As you brought forth in sorrow, so the earth also has from the beginning given her fruit, that is, man, to him who made her.' 15 Now, therefore, keep your sorrow to yourself, and bear bravely the troubles that have come upon you. 16 For if you acknowledge the decree of God to be just, you will receive your son back in due time, and will be praised among women. 17 Therefore go into the city to your husband."

18 She said to me, "I will not do so; I will not go into the city, but I will die here."

19 So I spoke again to her, and said, 20 "Do not say that, but let yourself be persuaded because of the troubles of Zion, and be consoled because of the sorrow of Jerusalem. 21 For you see that our sanctuary has been laid waste, our altar thrown down, our temple destroyed; 22 our harp has been laid low, our song has been silenced, and our rejoicing has been ended; the light of our lampstand has been put out, the ark of our covenant has been plundered, our holy things have been polluted, and the name by which we are called has been profaned; our free men *t* have suffered abuse, our priests have been burned to death, our Levites have gone into captivity, our virgins have been defiled, and our wives have been ravished; our righteous men have been carried off, our little ones have been cast out, our young men have been enslaved and

our strong men made powerless. [23] And, what is more than all, the seal of Zion—for she has now lost the seal of her glory, and has been given over into the hands of those that hate us. [24] Therefore shake off your great sadness and lay aside your many sorrows, so that the Mighty One may be merciful to you again, and the Most High may give you rest, a relief from your troubles."

[25] While I was talking to her, behold, her face suddenly shone exceedingly, and her countenance flashed like lightning, so that I was too frightened to approach her, and my heart was terrified. While [u] I was wondering what this meant, [26] behold, she suddenly uttered a loud and fearful cry, so that the earth shook at the sound. [27] And I looked, and behold, the woman was no longer visible to me, but there was an established city, [v] and a place of huge foundations showed itself. Then I was afraid, and cried with a loud voice and said, [28] "Where is the angel Uriel, who came to me at first? For it was he who brought me into this overpowering bewilderment; my end has become corruption, and my prayer a reproach."

[29] As I was speaking these words, behold, the angel who had come to me at first came to me, and he looked upon me; [30] and behold, I lay there like a corpse and I was deprived of my understanding. Then he grasped my right hand and strengthened me and set me on my feet, and said to me, [31] "What is the matter with you? And why are you troubled? And why are your understanding and the thoughts of your mind troubled?"

[32] I said, "Because you have forsaken me! I did as you directed, and went out into the field, and behold, I saw, and still see, what I am unable to explain."

[33] He said to me, "Stand up like a man, and I will instruct you."

[34] I said, "Speak, my lord; only do not forsake me, lest I die before my time. [w] [35] For I have seen what I did not know, and I have heard what I do not understand. [36] Or is my mind deceived, and my soul dreaming? [37] Now therefore I entreat you to give your servant an explanation of this bewildering vision."

[38] He answered me and said, "Listen to me and I will inform you, and tell you about the things which you fear, for the Most High has revealed many secrets to you. [39] For he has seen your righteous conduct, that you have sorrowed continually for your people, and mourned greatly over Zion. [40] This therefore is the meaning of the vision. [41] The woman who appeared to you a little while ago, whom you saw mourning and began to console—[42] but you do not now see the form of a woman, but an established city [x] has appeared to you—[43] and as for her telling you about the misfortune of her son, this is the interpretation: [44] This woman whom you saw, whom you now behold as an established city, is Zion. [y] [45] And as for her telling you that she was barren for thirty years, it is because there were three thousand [y] years in the world before any offering was offered in it. [z] [46] And after three thousand [y] years Solomon built the city, and offered offerings; then it was that the barren woman bore a son. [47] And as for her telling you that she brought him up with much care, that was the period of residence in Jerusalem. [48] And as for her saying to you, 'When my son entered his wedding chamber he died,' and that misfortune had overtaken her, [a] that was the destruction which befell Jerusalem. [49] And behold, you saw her likeness, how she mourned for her son, and you began to console her for

[u] Syr Ethiop Arab 1: Latin omits *I was too . . . terrified. While*
[v] Syr Ethiop Arab: Lat *a city was being built*
[w] Syr Ethiop Arab: Lat *die to no purpose*   [x] Syr Ethiop Arab: Lat *a city to be built*
[y] Syr Ethiop Arab Arm: Latin is corrupt   [z] Cn: Lat Syr Arab Arm *her*   [a] Or *him*

what had happened.[b] 50 For now the Most High, seeing that you are sincerely grieved and profoundly distressed for her, has shown you the brilliance of her glory, and the loveliness of her beauty. 51 Therefore I told you to remain in the field where no house had been built, 52 for I knew that the Most High would reveal these things to you. 53 Therefore I told you to go into the field where there was no foundation of any building, 54 for no work of man's building could endure in a place where the city of the Most High was to be revealed.

55 "Therefore do not be afraid, and do not let your heart be terrified; but go in and see the splendour and vastness of the building, as far as it is possible for your eyes to see it, 56 and afterward you will hear as much as your ears can hear. 57 For you are more blessed than many, and you have been called before the Most High, as but few have been. 58 But tomorrow night you shall remain here, 59 and the Most High will show you in those dream visions what the Most High will do to those who dwell on earth in the last days."

So I slept that night and the following one, as he had commanded me.

11 On the second night I had a dream, and behold, there came up from the sea an eagle that had twelve feathered wings and three heads. 2 And I looked, and behold, he spread his wings over[c] all the earth, and all the winds of heaven blew upon him, and the clouds were gathered about him.[d] 3 And I looked, and out of his wings there grew opposing wings; but they became little, puny wings. 4 But his heads were at rest; the middle head was larger than the other heads, but it also was at rest with them. 5 And I looked, and behold, the eagle flew with his wings,

to reign over the earth and over those who dwell in it. 6 And I saw how all things under heaven were subjected to him, and no one spoke against him, not even one creature that was on the earth. 7 And I looked, and behold, the eagle rose upon his talons, and uttered a cry to his wings, saying, 8 "Do not all watch at the same time; let each sleep in his own place, and watch in his turn; 9 but let the heads be reserved for the last."

10 And I looked, and behold, the voice did not come from his heads, but from the midst of his body. 11 And I counted his opposing wings, and behold, there were eight of them. 12 And I looked, and behold, on the right side one wing arose, and it reigned over all the earth. 13 And while it was reigning it came to its end and disappeared, so that its place was not seen. Then the next wing arose and reigned, and it continued to reign a long time. 14 And while it was reigning its end came also, so that it disappeared like the first. 15 And behold, a voice sounded, saying to it, 16 "Hear me, you who have ruled the earth all this time; I announce this to you before you disappear. 17 After you no one shall rule as long as you, or even half as long."

18 Then the third wing raised itself up, and held the rule like the former ones, and it also disappeared. 19 And so it went with all the wings; they wielded power one after another and then were never seen again. 20 And I looked, and behold, in due course the wings that followed[e] also rose up on the right[f] side, in order to rule. There were some of them that ruled, yet disappeared suddenly; 21 and others of them rose up, but did not hold the rule.

22 And after this I looked and behold, the twelve wings and the two little wings disappeared; 23 and noth-

---

[b] Most Latin manuscripts and Arab 1 add *these were the things to be opened to you*
[c] Arab 2 Arm: Lat Syr *in*
[d] Syr: Compare Ethiop Arab 1 and 2: Latin omits *the clouds* and *about him*
[e] Syr Arab 2 *the little wings*   [f] Some Ethiopic manuscripts read *left*

ing remained on the eagle's body except the three heads that were at rest and six little wings. 24 And I looked, and behold, two little wings separated from the six and remained under the head that was on the right side; but four remained in their place. 25 And I looked, and behold, these little wings *g* planned to set themselves up and hold the rule. 26 And I looked, and behold, one was set up, but suddenly disappeared; 27 a second also, and this disappeared more quickly than the first. 28 And I looked, and behold, the two that remained were planning between themselves to reign together; 29 and while they were planning, behold, one of the heads that were at rest (the one which was in the middle) awoke; for it was greater than the other two heads. 30 And I saw how it allied the two heads with itself, 31 and behold, the head turned with those that were with it, and it devoured the two little wings *h* which were planning to reign. 32 Moreover this head gained control of the whole earth, and with much oppression dominated its inhabitants; and it had greater power over the world than all the wings that had gone before.

33 And after this I looked, and behold, the middle head also suddenly disappeared, just as the wings had done. 34 But the two heads remained, which also ruled over the earth and its inhabitants. 35 And I looked, and behold, the head on the right side devoured the one on the left.

36 Then I heard a voice saying to me, "Look before you and consider what you see." 37 And I looked, and behold, a creature like a lion was aroused out of the forest, roaring; and I heard how he uttered a man's voice to the eagle, and spoke, saying, 38 "Listen and I will speak to you. The Most High says to you, 39 'Are you not the one that remains of the four beasts which I had made to reign in my world, so that the end of my times might come through them? 40 You, the fourth that has come, have conquered all the beasts that have gone before; and you have held sway over the world with much terror, and over all the earth with grievous oppression; and for so long you have dwelt on the earth with deceit.*i* 41 And you have judged the earth, but not with truth; 42 for you have afflicted the meek and injured the peaceable; you have hated those who tell the truth, and have loved liars; you have destroyed the dwellings of those who brought forth fruit, and have laid low the walls of those who did you no harm. 43 And so your insolence has come up before the Most High, and your pride to the Mighty One. 44 And the Most High has looked upon his times, and behold, they are ended, and his ages are completed! 45 Therefore you will surely disappear, you eagle, and your terrifying wings, and your most evil little wings, and your malicious heads, and your most evil talons, and your whole worthless body, 46 so that the whole earth, freed from your violence, may be refreshed and relieved, and may hope for the judgment and mercy of him who made it.'"

12 While the lion was saying these words to the eagle, I looked, 2 and behold, the remaining head disappeared. And the two wings that had gone over to it arose *j* and set themselves up to reign, and their reign was brief and full of tumult. 3 And I looked, and behold, they also disappeared, and the whole body of the eagle was burned, and the earth was exceedingly terrified.

Then I awoke in great perplexity of mind and great fear, and I said to my spirit, 4 "Behold, you have brought this upon me, because you search out the ways of the Most

---

g Syr: Lat *underwings*   *h* Syr: Lat *underwings*
i Syr Arab 1 Arab 2 Arm: Lat Ethiop *The fourth came, however, and conquered . . . and held sway . . . and for so long dwelt*   *j* Ethiop: Latin omits *arose*

High. 5 Behold, I am still weary in
mind and very weak in my spirit, and
not even a little strength is left in
me, because of the great fear with
which I have been terrified this
night. 6 Therefore I will now beseech the Most High that he may
strengthen me to the end."

7 And I said, "O sovereign Lord,
if I have found favour in thy sight,
and if I have been accounted righteous before thee beyond many
others, and if my prayer has indeed
come up before thy face, 8 strengthen
me and show me, thy servant, the
interpretation and meaning of this
terrifying vision, that thou mayest
fully comfort my soul. 9 For thou
hast judged me worthy to be shown
the end of the times and the last
events of the times."

10 He said to me, "This is the interpretation of this vision which you
have seen: 11 The eagle which you
saw coming up from the sea is the
fourth kingdom which appeared in a
vision to your brother Daniel. 12 But
it was not explained to him as I now
explain or have explained it to you.
13 Behold, the days are coming when
a kingdom shall arise on earth, and
it shall be more terrifying than all the
kingdoms that have been before it.
14 And twelve kings shall reign in it,
one after another. 15 But the second
that is to reign shall hold sway for a
longer time than any other of the
twelve. 16 This is the interpretation
of the twelve wings which you saw.
17 As for your hearing a voice that
spoke, coming not from the eagle's[k]
heads but from the midst of his body,
this is the interpretation: 18 In the
midst of[l] the time of that kingdom
great struggles shall arise, and it shall
be in danger of falling; nevertheless
it shall not fall then, but shall regain
its former power.[m] 19 As for your seeing eight little wings[n] clinging to
his wings, this is the interpretation:
20 Eight kings shall arise in it, whose
times shall be short and their years
swift; 21 and two of them shall perish
when the middle of its time draws
near; and four shall be kept for the
time when its end approaches; but
two shall be kept until the end. 22 As
for your seeing three heads at rest,
this is the interpretation: 23 In its
last days the Most High will raise up
three kings,[o] and they[p] shall renew
many things in it, and shall rule the
earth 24 and its inhabitants more op-
pressively than all who were before
them; therefore they are called the
heads of the eagle. 25 For it is they
who shall sum up his wickedness and
perform his last actions. 26 As for
your seeing that the large head disappeared, one of the kings[q] shall die
in his bed, but in agonies. 27 But as
for the two who remained, the sword
shall devour them. 28 For the sword
of one shall devour him who was
with him; but he also shall fall by the
sword in the last days. 29 As for your
seeing two little wings[r] passing over
to[s] the head which was on the right
side, 30 this is the interpretation: It
is these whom the Most High has
kept for the eagle's[t] end; this was
the reign which was brief and full of
tumult, as you have seen.

31 "And as for the lion whom you
saw rousing up out of the forest and
roaring and speaking to the eagle and
reproving him for his unrighteousness, and as for all his words that you
have heard, 32 this is the Messiah[u]
whom the Most High has kept until
the end of days, who will arise from
the posterity of David, and will come
and speak to them;[v] he will de-
nounce them for their ungodliness
and for their wickedness, and will
cast up before them their contemptuous dealings. 33 For first he will set
them living before his judgment seat,

[k] Lat *his* [l] Syr Arm: Lat *After* [m] Ethiop Arab 1 Arm: Lat Syr *beginning* [n] Syr: Lat *underwings*
[o] Syr Ethiop Arab Arm: Lat *kingdoms* [p] Syr Ethiop Arm: Lat *he* [q] Lat *them*
[r] Arab 1: Lat *underwings* [s] Syr Ethiop: Latin omits *to* [t] Lat *his* [u] Literally *anointed one*
[v] Syr: Latin omits *of days . . . and speak*

and when he has reproved them, then he will destroy them. ³⁴ But he will deliver in mercy the remnant of my people, those who have been saved throughout my borders, and he will make them joyful until the end comes, the day of judgment, of which I spoke to you at the beginning. ³⁵ This is the dream that you saw, and this is its interpretation. ³⁶ And you alone were worthy to learn this secret of the Most High. ³⁷ Therefore write all these things that you have seen in a book, and put it in a hidden place; ³⁸ and you shall teach them to the wise among your people, whose hearts you know are able to comprehend and keep these secrets. ³⁹ But wait here seven days more, so that you may be shown whatever it pleases the Most High to show you." Then he left me.

40 When all the people heard that the seven days were past and I had not returned to the city, they all gathered together, from the least to the greatest, and came to me and spoke to me, saying, ⁴¹ "How have we offended you, and what harm have we done you, that you have forsaken us and sit in this place? ⁴² For of all the prophets you alone are left to us, like a cluster of grapes from the vintage, and like a lamp in a dark place, and like a haven for a ship saved from a storm. ⁴³ Are not the evils which have befallen us sufficient? ⁴⁴ Therefore if you forsake us, how much better it would have been for us if we also had been consumed in the burning of Zion! ⁴⁵ For we are no better than those who died there." And they wept with a loud voice.

Then I answered them and said, ⁴⁶ "Take courage, O Israel; and do not be sorrowful, O house of Jacob; ⁴⁷ for the Most High has you in remembrance, and the Mighty One has not forgotten you in your struggle. ⁴⁸ As for me, I have neither forsaken you nor withdrawn from you;

but I have come to this place to pray on account of the desolation of Zion, and to seek mercy on account of the humiliation of our *ʷ* sanctuary. ⁴⁹ Now go, every one of you to his house, and after these days I will come to you." ⁵⁰ So the people went into the city, as I told them to do. ⁵¹ But I sat in the field seven days, as the angel *ˣ* had commanded me; and I ate only of the flowers of the field, and my food was of plants during those days.

13   After seven days I dreamed a dream in the night; ² and behold, a wind arose from the sea and stirred up all its waves. ³ And I looked, and behold, this wind made something like the figure of a man come up out of the heart of the sea. And I looked, and behold, *ʸ* that man flew *ᶻ* with the clouds of heaven; and wherever he turned his face to look, everything under his gaze trembled, ⁴ and whenever his voice issued from his mouth, all who heard his voice melted as wax melts *ᵃ* when it feels the fire.

5 After this I looked, and behold, an innumerable multitude of men were gathered together from the four winds of heaven to make war against the man who came up out of the sea. ⁶ And I looked, and behold, he carved out for himself a great mountain, and flew up upon it. ⁷ And I tried to see the region or place from which the mountain was carved, but I could not.

8 After this I looked, and behold, all who had gathered together against him, to wage war with him, were much afraid, yet dared to fight. ⁹ And behold, when he saw the onrush of the approaching multitude, he neither lifted his hand nor held a spear or any weapon of war; ¹⁰ but I saw only how he sent forth from his mouth as it were a stream of fire, and from his lips a flaming breath, and from his tongue he shot forth a storm

---

ʷ Syr Ethiop: Lat *your*   *ˣ* Literally *he*   *ʸ* Syr: Latin omits *this wind . . . and behold*
ᶻ Syr Ethiop Arab Arm: Lat *grew strong*   *ᵃ* Syr: Lat *burned as the earth rests*

of sparks.[b] 11 All these were mingled together, the stream of fire and the flaming breath and the great storm, and fell on the onrushing multitude which was prepared to fight, and burned them all up, so that suddenly nothing was seen of the innumerable multitude but only the dust of ashes and the smell of smoke. When I saw it, I was amazed.

12 After this I saw the same man come down from the mountain and call to him another multitude which was peaceable. 13 Then many people[c] came to him, some of whom were joyful and some sorrowful; some of them were bound, and some were bringing others as offerings. Then in great fear I awoke; and I besought the Most High, and said, 14 "From the beginning thou hast shown thy servant these wonders, and hast deemed me worthy to have my prayer heard by thee; 15 now show me also the interpretation of this dream. 16 For as I consider it in my mind, alas for those who will be left in those days! And still more, alas for those who are not left! 17 For those who are not left will be sad, 18 because they understand what is reserved for the last days, but cannot attain it. 19 But alas for those also who are left, and for that very reason! For they shall see great dangers and much distress, as these dreams show. 20 Yet it is better[d] to come into these things,[e] though incurring peril, than to pass from the world like a cloud, and not to see what shall happen in the last days."

He answered me and said, 21 "I will tell you the interpretation of the vision, and I will also explain to you the things which you have mentioned. 22 As for what you said about those who are left, this is the interpretation: 23 He who brings the peril at that time will himself protect those who fall into peril, who have works and have faith in the Almighty. 24 Understand therefore that those who are left are more blessed than those who have died. 25 This is the interpretation of the vision: As for your seeing a man come up from the heart of the sea, 26 this is he whom the Most High has been keeping for many ages, who will himself deliver his creation; and he will direct those who are left. 27 And as for your seeing wind and fire and a storm coming out of his mouth, 28 and as for his not holding a spear or weapon of war, yet destroying the onrushing multitude which came to conquer him, this is the interpretation: 29 Behold, the days are coming when the Most High will deliver those who are on the earth. 30 And bewilderment of mind shall come over those who dwell on the earth. 31 And they shall plan to make war against one another, city against city, place against place, people against people, and kingdom against kingdom. 32 And when these things come to pass and the signs occur which I showed you before, then my Son will be revealed, whom you saw as a man coming up from the sea.[f] 33 And when all the nations hear his voice, every man shall leave his own land and the warfare that they have against one another; 34 and an innumerable multitude shall be gathered together, as you saw, desiring to come and conquer him. 35 But he will stand on the top of Mount Zion. 36 And Zion will come and be made manifest to all people, prepared and built, as you saw the mountain carved out without hands. 37 And he, my Son, will reprove the assembled nations for their ungodliness (this was symbolized by the storm), 38 and will reproach them to their face with their evil thoughts and the torments with which they are to be tortured (which were symbolized by the

---

[b] The text is uncertain   [c] Lat Syr Arab 2 literally *the faces of many people*
[d] Ethiop, compare Arab 2: Lat *easier*   [e] Syr: Lat *this*
[f] Syr and most Latin manuscripts omit *from the sea*

flames), and will destroy them without effort by the law *g* (which was symbolized by the fire). 39 And as for your seeing him gather to himself another multitude that was peaceable, 40 these are the ten tribes which were led away from their own land into captivity in the days of King Hoshea, whom Shalmaneser the king of the Assyrians led captive; he took them across the river, and they were taken into another land. 41 But they formed this plan for themselves, that they would leave the multitude of the nations and go to a more distant region, where mankind had never lived, 42 that there at least they might keep their statutes which they had not kept in their own land. 43 And they went in by the narrow passages of the Euphrates river. 44 For at that time the Most High performed signs for them, and stopped the channels of the river until they had passed over. 45 Through that region there was a long way to go, a journey of a year and a half; and that country is called Arzareth.*h*

46 "Then they dwelt there until the last times; and now, when they are about to come again, 47 the Most High will stop *i* the channels of the river again, so that they may be able to pass over. Therefore you saw the multitude gathered together in peace. 48 But those who are left of your people, who are found within my holy borders, shall be saved.*j* 49 Therefore when he destroys the multitude of the nations that are gathered together, he will defend the people who remain. 50 And then he will show them very many wonders."

51 I said, "O sovereign Lord, explain this to me: Why did I see the man coming up from the heart of the sea?"

52 He said to me, "Just as no one can explore or know what is in the depths of the sea, so no one on earth can see my Son or those who are with him, except in the time of his day.*k* 53 This is the interpretation of the dream which you saw. And you alone have been enlightened about this, 54 because you have forsaken your own ways and have applied yourself to mine, and have searched out my law; 55 for you have devoted your life to wisdom, and called understanding your mother. 56 Therefore I have shown you this, for there is a reward laid up with the Most High. And after three more days I will tell you other things, and explain weighty and wondrous matters to you."

57 Then I arose and walked in the field, giving great glory and praise to the Most High because of his wonders, which he did from time to time, 58 and because he governs the times and whatever things come to pass in their seasons. And I stayed there three days.

14 On the third day, while I was sitting under an oak, behold, a voice came out of a bush opposite me and said, "Ezra, Ezra." 2 And I said, "Here I am, Lord," and I rose to my feet. 3 Then he said to me, "I revealed myself in a bush and spoke to Moses, when my people were in bondage in Egypt; 4 and I sent him and led *l* my people out of Egypt; and I led him up on Mount Sinai, where I kept him with me many days; 5 and I told him many wondrous things, and showed him the secrets of the times and declared to him *m* the end of the times. Then I commanded him, saying, 6 'These words you shall publish openly, and these you shall keep secret.' 7 And now I say to you: 8 Lay up in your heart the signs that I have shown you, the dreams that you have seen, and the interpretations that you have

---

g Syr: Lat *and the law*   *h* That is *Another Land*   *i* Syr: Lat *stops*
j Syr: Latin omits *shall be saved*
k Syr: Ethiop *except when his time and his day have come.* Latin omits *his*
l Other authorities read *he led*   *m* Syr Ethiop Arab Arm: Latin omits *declared to him*

heard; [9] for you shall be taken up from among men, and henceforth you shall live with my Son and with those who are like you, until the times are ended. [10] For the age has lost its youth, and the times begin to grow old. [11] For the age is divided into twelve parts, and nine [n] of its parts have already passed, [12] as well as half of the tenth part; so two of its parts remain, besides half of the tenth part.[o] [13] Now therefore, set your house in order, and reprove your people; comfort the lowly among them, and instruct those that are wise.[p] And now renounce the life that is corruptible, [14] and put away from you mortal thoughts; cast away from you the burdens of man, and divest yourself now of your weak nature, [15] and lay to one side the thoughts that are most grievous to you, and hasten to escape from these times. [16] For evils worse than those which you have now seen happen shall be done hereafter. [17] For the weaker the world becomes through old age, the more shall evils be multiplied among [q] its inhabitants. [18] For truth shall go farther away, and falsehood shall come near. For the eagle [r] which you saw in the vision is already hastening to come."

19 Then I answered and said, "Let me speak in thy presence, Lord.[s] [20] For behold, I will go, as thou hast commanded me, and I will reprove the people who are now living; but who will warn those who will be born hereafter? For the world lies in darkness, and its inhabitants are without light. [21] For thy law has been burned, and so no one knows the things which have been done or will be done by thee. [22] If then I have found favour before thee, send the Holy Spirit into me, and I will write everything that has happened in the world from the beginning, the things which were written in thy law, that men may be able to find the path, and that those who wish to live in the last days may live."

23 He answered me and said, "Go and gather the people, and tell them not to seek you for forty days. [24] But prepare for yourself many writing tablets, and take with you Sarea, Dabria, Selemia, Ethanus, and Asiel—these five, because they are trained to write rapidly; [25] and you shall come here, and I will light in your heart the lamp of understanding, which shall not be put out until what you are about to write is finished. [26] And when you have finished, some things you shall make public, and some you shall deliver in secret to the wise; tomorrow at this hour you shall begin to write."

27 Then I went as he commanded me, and I gathered all the people together, and said, [28] "Hear these words, O Israel. [29] At first our fathers dwelt as aliens in Egypt, and they were delivered from there, [30] and received the law of life, which they did not keep, which you also have transgressed after them. [31] Then land was given to you for a possession in the land of Zion; but you and your fathers committed iniquity and did not keep the ways which the Most High commanded you. [32] And because he is a righteous judge, in due time he took from you what he had given. [33] And now you are here, and your brethren are farther in the interior.[t] [34] If you, then, will rule over your minds and discipline your hearts, you shall be kept alive, and after death you shall obtain mercy. [35] For after death the judgment will come, when we shall live again; and then the names of the righteous will become manifest, and the deeds of the ungodly will be disclosed. [36] But let no one come to me now, and let no one seek me for forty days."

---

[n] Cn: Lat Ethiop *ten*
[o] Syr omits verses 11, 12: Ethiop *For the world is divided into ten parts, and has come to the tenth, and half of the tenth remains. Now* . . . [p] Lat omits *and . . . wise* [q] Literally *upon*
[r] Syr Ethiop Arab Arm: Latin is corrupt [s] Most Latin manuscripts omit *Let me speak*
[t] Syr Ethiop Arm: Lat *are among you*

37 So I took the five men, as he commanded me, and we proceeded to the field, and remained there. 38 And on the next day, behold, a voice called me, saying, "Ezra, open your mouth and drink what I give you to drink." 39 Then I opened my mouth, and behold, a full cup was offered to me; it was full of something like water, but its colour was like fire. 40 And I took it and drank; and when I had drunk it, my heart poured forth understanding, and wisdom increased in my breast, for my spirit retained its memory; 41 and my mouth was opened, and was no longer closed. 42 And the Most High gave understanding to the five men, and by turns they wrote what was dictated, in characters which they did not know.*u* They sat forty days, and wrote during the daytime, and ate their bread at night. 43 As for me, I spoke in the daytime and was not silent at night. 44 So during the forty days ninety-four *v* books were written. 45 And when the forty days were ended, the Most High spoke to me, saying, "Make public the twenty-four *w* books that you wrote first and let the worthy and the unworthy read them; 46 but keep the seventy that were written last, in order to give them to the wise among your people. 47 For in them is the spring of understanding, the fountain of wisdom, and the river of knowledge." 48 And I did so.*x*

15 *y* The Lord says, "Behold, speak in the ears of my people the words of the prophecy which I will put in your mouth, 2 and cause them to be written on paper; for they are trustworthy and true. 3 Do not fear the plots against you, and do not

be troubled by the unbelief of those who oppose you. 4 For every unbeliever shall die in his unbelief."

5 "Behold," says the Lord, "I bring evils upon the world, the sword and famine and death and destruction. 6 For iniquity has spread throughout every land, and their harmful deeds have reached their limit. 7 Therefore," says the Lord, 8 "I will be silent no longer concerning their ungodly deeds which they impiously commit, neither will I tolerate their wicked practices. Behold, innocent and righteous blood cries out to me, and the souls of the righteous cry out continually. 9 I will surely avenge them," says the Lord, "and will receive to myself all the innocent blood from among them. 10 Behold, my people is led like a flock to the slaughter; I will not allow them to live any longer in the land of Egypt, 11 but I will bring them out with a mighty hand and with an uplifted arm, and will smite Egypt with plagues, as before, and will destroy all its land."

12 Let Egypt mourn, and its foundations, for the plague of chastisement and punishment that the Lord will bring upon it. 13 Let the farmers that till the ground mourn, because their seed shall fail and their trees shall be ruined by blight and hail and by a terrible tempest. 14 Alas for the world and for those who live in it! 15 For the sword and misery draw near them, and nation shall rise up to fight against nation, with swords in their hands. 16 For there shall be unrest among men; growing strong against one another, they shall in their might have no respect for their king or the chief of their leaders. 17 For a man will desire to go into a

---

u Syr Compare Ethiop Arab 2 Arm: Latin is corrupt   *v* Syr Ethiop Arab 1 Arm: Latin is corrupt
w Syr Arab 1: Latin omits *twenty-four*
x Syr adds *in the seventh year of the sixth week, five thousand years and three months and twelve days after creation.*
At that time Ezra was caught up, and taken to the place of those who are like him, after he had written all these things. And he was called the Scribe of the knowledge of the Most High for ever and ever. Ethiop Arab 1 Arm have a similar ending.
y Chapters 15 and 16 (except 15:57–59 which has been found in Greek) are extant only in Latin

city, and shall not be able. ¹⁸ For because of their pride the cities shall be in confusion, the houses shall be destroyed, and people shall be afraid. ¹⁹ A man shall have no pity upon his neighbours, but shall make an assault upon their houses with the sword, and plunder their goods, because of hunger for bread and because of great tribulation.

20 "Behold," says God, "I call together all the kings of the earth to fear me, from the rising sun and from the south, from the east and from Lebanon; to turn and repay what they have given them. ²¹ Just as they have done to my elect until this day, so I will do, and will repay into their bosom." Thus says the Lord God: ²² "My right hand will not spare the sinners, and my sword will not cease from those who shed innocent blood on the earth." ²³ And a fire will go forth from his wrath, and will consume the foundations of the earth, and the sinners, like straw that is kindled. ²⁴ "Woe to those who sin and do not observe my commandments," says the Lord; ²⁵ "I will not spare them. Depart, you faithless children! Do not pollute my sanctuary." ²⁶ For the Lord knows all who transgress against him; therefore he will hand them over to death and slaughter. ²⁷ For now calamities have come upon the whole earth, and you shall remain in them; for God will not deliver you, because you have sinned against him.

28 Behold, a terrifying sight, appearing from the east! ²⁹ The nations of the dragons of Arabia shall come out with many chariots, and from the day that they set out, their hissing shall spread over the earth, so that all who hear them fear and tremble. ³⁰ Also the Carmonians, raging in wrath, shall go forth like wild boars of the forest, and with great power they shall come, and engage them in battle, and shall devastate a portion of the land of the Assyrians with

their teeth. ³¹ And then the dragons, remembering their origin, shall become still stronger; and if they combine in great power and turn to pursue them, ³² then these shall be disorganized and silenced by their power, and shall turn and flee. ³³ And from the land of the Assyrians an enemy in ambush shall beset them and destroy one of them, and fear and trembling shall come upon their army, and indecision upon their kings.

34 Behold, clouds from the east, and from the north to the south; and their appearance is very threatening, full of wrath and storm. ³⁵ They shall dash against one another and shall pour out a heavy tempest upon the earth, and their own tempest; and there shall be blood from the sword as high as a horse's belly ³⁶ and a man's thigh and a camel's hock. ³⁷ And there shall be fear and great trembling upon the earth; and those who see that wrath shall be horror-stricken, and they shall be seized with trembling. ³⁸ And, after that, heavy storm clouds shall be stirred up from the south, and from the north, and another part from the west. ³⁹ And the winds from the east shall prevail over the cloud that was ᵃ raised in wrath, and shall dispel it; and the tempest that was to cause destruction by the east wind shall be driven violently toward the south and west. ⁴⁰ And great and mighty clouds, full of wrath and tempest, shall rise, to destroy all the earth and its inhabitants, and shall pour out upon every high and lofty place ᵃ a terrible tempest, ⁴¹ fire and hail and flying swords and floods of water, that all the fields and all the streams may be filled with the abundance of those waters. ⁴² And they shall destroy cities and walls, mountains and hills, trees of the forests, and grass of the meadows, and their grain. ⁴³ And they shall go on steadily to Babylon, and shall destroy her. ⁴⁴ They shall come to her and

ᵃ Literally *that he*　　ᵃ Or *eminent person*

50

surround her; they shall pour out the tempest and all its wrath upon her; then the dust and smoke shall go up to heaven, and all who are about her shall wail over her. 45 And those who survive shall serve those who have destroyed her.

46 And you, Asia, who share in the glamour of Babylon and the glory of her person—47 woe to you, miserable wretch! For you have made yourself like her; you have decked out your daughters in harlotry to please and glory in your lovers, who have always lusted after you. 48 You have imitated that hateful harlot in all her deeds and devices; therefore God says, 49 "I will send evils upon you, widowhood, poverty, famine, sword, and pestilence, to lay waste your houses and bring you to destruction and death. 50 And the glory of your power shall wither like a flower, when the heat rises that is sent upon you. 51 You shall be weakened like a wretched woman who is beaten and wounded, so that you cannot receive your mighty lovers. 52 Would I have dealt with you so violently," says the Lord, 53 "if you had not always killed my chosen people, exulting and clapping your hands and talking about their death when you were drunk? 54 Trick out the beauty of your face! 55 The reward of a harlot is in your bosom, therefore you shall receive your recompense. 56 As you will do to my chosen people," says the Lord, "so God will do to you, and will hand you over to adversities. 57 Your children shall die of hunger, and you shall fall by the sword, and your cities shall be wiped out, and all your people who are in the open country shall fall by the sword. 58 And those who are in the mountains and highlands *b* shall perish of hunger, and they shall eat their own flesh in hunger for bread and drink their own blood in thirst for water. 59 Unhappy above all others, you shall come and suffer fresh afflictions. 60 And as they

pass they shall wreck the hateful *c* city, and shall destroy a part of your land and abolish a portion of your glory, as they return from devastated Babylon. 61 And you shall be broken down by them like stubble, and they shall be like fire to you. 62 And they shall devour you and your cities, your land and your mountains; they shall burn with fire all your forests and your fruitful trees. 63 They shall carry your children away captive, and shall plunder your wealth, and abolish the glory of your countenance."

16 Woe to you, Babylon and Asia! Woe to you, Egypt and Syria! 2 Gird yourselves with sackcloth and haircloth, and wail for your children, and lament for them; for your destruction is at hand. 3 The sword has been sent upon you, and who is there to turn it back? 4 A fire has been sent upon you, and who is there to quench it? 5 Calamities have been sent upon you, and who is there to drive them away? 6 Can one drive off a hungry lion in the forest, or quench a fire in the stubble, when once it has begun to burn? 7 Can one turn back an arrow shot by a strong archer? 8 The Lord God sends calamities, and who will drive them away? 9 Fire will go forth from his wrath, and who is there to quench it? 10 He will flash lightning, and who will not be afraid? He will thunder, and who will not be terrified? 11 The Lord will threaten, and who will not be utterly shattered at his presence? 12 The earth and its foundations quake, the sea is churned up from the depths, and its waves and the fish also shall be troubled at the presence of the Lord and before the glory of his power. 13 For his right hand that bends the bow is strong, and his arrows that he shoots are sharp and will not miss when they begin to be shot to the ends of the world. 14 Behold, calamities are sent forth and shall not return until they come over the earth. 15 The fire is kindled, and shall

b Gk: Latin omits *and highlands*   *c* Another reading is *idle* or *unprofitable*

not be put out until it consumes the foundations of the earth. 16 Just as an arrow shot by a mighty archer does not return, so the calamities that are sent upon the earth shall not return. 17 Alas for me! Alas for me! Who will deliver me in those days?

18 The beginning of sorrows, when there shall be much lamentation; the beginning of famine, when many shall perish; the beginning of wars, when the powers shall be terrified; the beginning of calamities, when all shall tremble. What shall they do in these circumstances, when the calamities come? 19 Behold, famine and plague, tribulation and anguish are sent as scourges for the correction of men. 20 Yet for all this they will not turn from their iniquities, nor be always mindful of the scourges. 21 Behold, provisions will be so cheap upon earth that men will imagine that peace is assured for them, and then the calamities shall spring up on the earth—the sword, famine, and great confusion. 22 For many of those who live on the earth shall perish by famine; and those who survive the famine shall die by the sword. 23 And the dead shall be cast out like dung, and there shall be no one to console them; for the earth shall be left desolate, and its cities shall be demolished. 24 No one shall be left to cultivate the earth or to sow it. 25 The trees shall bear fruit, and who will gather it? 26 The grapes shall ripen, and who will tread them? For in all places there shall be great solitude; 27 one man will long to see another, or even to hear his voice. 28 For out of a city, ten shall be left; and out of the field, two who have hidden themselves in thick groves and clefts in the rocks. 29 As in an olive orchard three or four olives may be left on every tree, 30 or as when a vineyard is gathered some clusters may be left by those who search carefully through the vineyard, 31 so in those days three or four shall be left by those who search

their houses with the sword. 32 And the earth shall be left desolate, and its fields shall be for briers, and its roads and all its paths shall bring forth thorns, because no sheep will go along them. 33 Virgins shall mourn because they have no bridegrooms; women shall mourn because they have no husbands; their daughters shall mourn, because they have no helpers. 34 Their bridegrooms shall be killed in war, and their husbands shall perish of famine.

35 Listen now to these things, and understand them, O servants of the Lord. 36 Behold the word of the Lord, receive it; do not disbelieve what the Lord says.*d* 37 Behold, the calamities draw near, and are not delayed. 38 Just as a woman with child, in the ninth month, when the time of her delivery draws near, has great pains about her womb for two or three hours beforehand, and when the child comes forth from the womb, there will not be a moment's delay, 39 so the calamities will not delay in coming forth upon the earth, and the world will groan, and pains will seize it on every side.

40 "Hear my words, O my people; prepare for battle, and in the midst of the calamities be like strangers on the earth. 41 Let him that sells be like one who will flee; let him that buys be like one who will lose; 42 let him that does business be like one who will not make a profit; and let him that builds a house be like one who will not live in it; 43 let him that sows be like one who will not reap; so also him that prunes the vines, like one who will not gather the grapes; 44 them that marry, like those who will have no children; and them that do not marry, like those who are widowed. 45 Because those who labour, labour in vain; 46 for strangers shall gather their fruits, and plunder their goods, and overthrow their houses, and take their children captive; for in captivity and famine they will beget

d Cn: Lat *do not believe the gods of whom the Lord speaks*

their children. ⁴⁷ Those who conduct business, do it only to be plundered; the more they adorn their cities, their houses and possessions, and their persons, ⁴⁸ the more angry I will be with them for their sins," says the Lord. ⁴⁹ Just as a respectable and virtuous woman abhors a harlot, ⁵⁰ so righteousness shall abhor iniquity, when she decks herself out, and shall accuse her to her face, when he comes who will defend him who searches out every sin on earth.

51 Therefore do not be like her or her works. ⁵² For behold, just a little while, and iniquity will be removed from the earth, and righteousness will reign over us. ⁵³ Let no sinner say that he has not sinned; for God*ᵉ* will burn coals of fire on the head of him who says, "I have not sinned before God and his glory." ⁵⁴ Behold, the Lord knows all the works of men, their imaginations and their thoughts and their hearts. ⁵⁵ He said, "Let the earth be made," and it was made; "Let the heaven be made," and it was made. ⁵⁶ At his word the stars were fixed, and he knows the number of the stars. ⁵⁷ It is he who searches the deep and its treasures, who has measured the sea and its contents; ⁵⁸ who has enclosed the sea in the midst of the waters, and by his word has suspended the earth over the water; ⁵⁹ who has spread out the heaven like an arch, and founded it upon the waters; ⁶⁰ who has put springs of water in the desert, and pools on the tops of the mountains, to send rivers from the heights to water the earth; ⁶¹ who formed man, and put a heart in the midst of his body, and gave him breath and life and understanding ⁶² and the spirit of Almighty God; who made all things and searches out hidden things in hidden places. ⁶³ Surely he knows your imaginations and what you think in your hearts! Woe to

those who sin and want to hide their sins! ⁶⁴ Because the Lord will strictly examine all their works, and will make a public spectacle of all of you. ⁶⁵ And when your sins come out before men, you shall be put to shame; and your own iniquities shall stand as your accusers in that day. ⁶⁶ What will you do? Or how will you hide your sins before God and his angels? ⁶⁷ Behold, God is the judge, fear him! Cease from your sins, and forget your iniquities, never to commit them again; so God will lead you forth and deliver you from all tribulation.

68 For behold, the burning wrath of a great multitude is kindled over you, and they shall carry off some of you and shall feed you what was sacrificed to idols. ⁶⁹ And those who consent to eat shall be held in*ᶠ* derision and contempt, and be trodden under foot. ⁷⁰ For in many places*ᵍ* and in neighbouring cities there shall be a great insurrection against those who fear the Lord. ⁷¹ They shall be like mad men, sparing no one, but plundering and destroying those who continue to fear the Lord. ⁷² For they shall destroy and plunder their goods, and drive them out of their houses. ⁷³ Then the tested quality of my elect shall be manifest, as gold that is tested by fire.

74 "Hear, my elect," says the Lord. "Behold, the days of tribulation are at hand, and I will deliver you from them. ⁷⁵ Do not fear or doubt, for God is your guide. ⁷⁶ You who keep my commandments and precepts," says the Lord God, "do not let your sins pull you down, or your iniquities prevail over you." ⁷⁷ Woe to those who are choked by their sins and overwhelmed by their iniquities, as a field is choked with underbrush and its path*ʰ* overwhelmed with thorns, so that no one can pass through! ⁷⁸ It is shut off and given up to be consumed by fire.

ᵉ Literally *he*   *ᶠ* Literally *consent to them shall be for these in*   *ᵍ* The Latin is uncertain
ʰ Another reading is *seed*

1 The book of the acts [a] of Tobit the son of Tobiel, son of Ananiel, son of Aduel, son of Gabael, of the descendants of Asiel and the tribe of Naphtali, [2] who in the days of Shalmaneser, [b] king of the Assyrians, was taken into captivity from Thisbe, which is to the south of Kedesh Naphtali in Galilee above Asher.

3 I, Tobit, walked in the ways of truth and righteousness all the days of my life, and I performed many acts of charity to my brethren and countrymen who went with me into the land of the Assyrians, to Nineveh. [4] Now when I was in my own country, in the land of Israel, while I was still a young man, the whole tribe of Naphtali my forefather deserted the house of Jerusalem. This was the place which had been chosen from among all the tribes of Israel, where all the tribes should sacrifice and where the temple of the dwelling of the Most High was consecrated and established for all generations for ever.

5 All the tribes that joined in apostasy used to sacrifice to the calf [c] Baal, and so did the house of Naphtali my forefather. [6] But I alone went often to Jerusalem for the feasts, as it is ordained for all Israel by an everlasting decree. Taking the first fruits and the tithes of my produce and the first shearings, I would give these to the priests, the sons of Aaron, at the altar. [7] Of all my produce I would give a tenth to the sons of Levi who ministered at Jerusalem; a second tenth I would sell, and I would go and spend the proceeds each year at Jerusalem; [8] the third tenth I would give to those to whom it was my duty, as Deborah my father's mother had commanded me, for I was left an orphan by my father. [9] When I became a man I married Anna, a member of our family, and by her I became the father of Tobias.

10 Now when I was carried away captive to Nineveh, all my brethren and my relatives ate the food of the Gentiles; [11] but I kept myself from eating it, [12] because I remembered God with all my heart. [13] Then the Most High gave me favour and good appearance in the sight of Shalmaneser, [b] and I was his buyer of provisions. [14] So I used to go into Media, and once at Rages in Media I left ten talents of silver in trust with Gabael, the brother of Gabrias. [15] But when Shalmaneser [b] died, Sennacherib his son reigned in his place; and under him the highways were unsafe, so that I could no longer go into Media.

16 In the days of Shalmaneser [b] I performed many acts of charity to my brethren. [17] I would give my bread to the hungry and my clothing to the naked; and if I saw any one of my people dead and thrown out behind the wall of Nineveh, I would bury him. [18] And if Sennacherib the king put to death any who came fleeing from Judea, I buried them secretly. For in his anger he put many to death. When the bodies were sought by the king, they were not found. [19] Then one of the men of Nineveh went and informed the king about me, that I was burying them; so I hid myself. When I learned that I was being searched for, to be put to death, I left home in fear. [20] Then all my property was confiscated and nothing was left to me except my wife Anna and my son Tobias.

21 But not fifty [d] days passed before two of Sennacherib's [e] sons killed him, and they fled to the mountains of Ararat. Then Esarhaddon, [f] his son, reigned in his place; and he appointed Ahikar, the son of my brother Anael, over all the accounts of his kingdom and over the entire

---

[a] Gk words   [b] Gk Enemessarus   [c] Other authorities read *heifer*
[d] Other authorities read *fifty-five*   [e] Gk *his*   [f] Gk *Sacherdonus*

administration. ²² Ahikar interceded for me, and I returned to Nineveh. Now Ahikar was cupbearer, keeper of the signet, and in charge of administration of the accounts, for Esarhaddon *ᶠ* had appointed him second to himself.*ᵍ* He was my nephew.

2 When I arrived home and my wife Anna and my son Tobias were restored to me, at the feast of Pentecost, which is the sacred festival of the seven weeks, a good dinner was prepared for me and I sat down to eat. ² Upon seeing the abundance of food I said to my son, "Go and bring whatever poor man of our brethren you may find who is mindful of the Lord, and I will wait for you." ³ But he came back and said, "Father, one of our people has been strangled and thrown into the market place." ⁴ So before I tasted anything I sprang up and removed the body *ʰ* to a place of shelter until sunset. ⁵ And when I returned I washed myself and ate my food in sorrow. ⁶ Then I remembered the prophecy of Amos, how he said,

> "Your feasts shall be turned into mourning,
> and all your festivities into lamentation."

And I wept.

⁷ When the sun had set I went and dug a grave and buried the body.*ʰ* ⁸ And my neighbours laughed at me and said, "He is no longer afraid that he will be put to death for doing this; he once ran away, and here he is burying the dead again!" ⁹ On the same night I returned from burying him, and because I was defiled I slept by the wall of the courtyard, and my face was uncovered. ¹⁰ I did not know that there were sparrows on the wall and their fresh droppings fell into my open eyes and white films formed on my eyes. I went to physicians, but they did not help me. Ahikar, however, took care of me until he *ⁱ* went to Elymais.

¹¹ Then my wife Anna earned money at women's work. ¹² She used to send the product to the owners. Once when they paid her wages, they also gave her a kid; ¹³ and when she returned to me it began to bleat. So I said to her, "Where did you get the kid? It is not stolen, is it? Return it to the owners; for it is not right to eat what is stolen." ¹⁴ And she said, "It was given to me as a gift in addition to my wages." But I did not believe her, and told her to return it to the owners; and I blushed for her. Then she replied to me, "Where are your charities and your righteous deeds? You seem to know everything!"

3 Then in my grief I wept, and I prayed in anguish, saying, ² "Righteous art thou, O Lord; all thy deeds and all thy ways are mercy and truth, and thou dost render true and righteous judgment for ever. ³ Remember me and look favourably upon me; do not punish me for my sins and for my unwitting offences and those which my fathers committed before thee. ⁴ For they disobeyed thy commandments, and thou gavest us over to plunder, captivity, and death; thou madest us a byword of reproach in all the nations among which we have been dispersed. ⁵ And now thy many judgments are true in exacting penalty from me for my sins and those of my fathers, because we did not keep thy commandments. For we did not walk in truth before thee. ⁶ And now deal with me according to thy pleasure; command my spirit to be taken up, that I may depart and become dust. For it is better for me to die than to live, because I have heard false reproaches, and great is the sorrow within me. Command that I now be released from my distress to go to the eternal abode; do not turn thy face away from me."

⁷ On the same day, at Ecbatana in Media, it also happened that Sarah, the daughter of Raguel, was re-

---

ᶠ Gk *Sacherdonus*　*ᵍ* Or *a second time*　*ʰ* Gk *him*　*ⁱ* Other authorities read *I*

proached by her father's maids, 8 because she had been given to seven husbands, and the evil demon Asmodeus had slain each of them before he had been with her as his wife. So the maids *j* said to her, "Do you not know that you strangle your husbands? You already have had seven and have had no benefit *k* from any of them. 9 Why do you beat us? If they are dead, go with them! May we never see a son or daughter of yours!"

10 When she heard these things she was deeply grieved, even to the thought of hanging herself. But she said, "I am the only child of my father; if I do this, it will be a disgrace to him, and I shall bring his old age down in sorrow to the grave." *l* 11 So she prayed by her window and said, "Blessed art thou, O Lord my God, and blessed is thy holy and honoured name for ever. May all thy works praise thee for ever. 12 And now, O Lord, I have turned my eyes and my face toward thee. 13 Command that I be released from the earth and that I hear reproach no more. 14 Thou knowest, O Lord, that I am innocent of any sin with man, 15 and that I did not stain my name or the name of my father in the land of my captivity. I am my father's only child, and he has no child to be his heir, no near kinsman or kinsman's *m* son for whom I should keep myself as wife. Already seven husbands of mine are dead. Why should I live? But if it be not pleasing to thee to take my life, command that respect be shown to me and pity be taken upon me, and that I hear reproach no more."

16 The prayer of both was heard in the presence of the glory of the great God. 17 And Raphael *n* was sent to heal the two of them: to scale away the white films from Tobit's eyes; to give Sarah the daughter of Raguel in marriage to Tobias the son of Tobit, and to bind Asmodeus

the evil demon, because Tobias was entitled to possess her. At that very moment Tobit returned and entered his house and Sarah the daughter of Raguel came down from her upper room.

4 On that day Tobit remembered the money which he had left in trust with Gabael at Rages in Media, and he said to himself: 2 "I have asked for death. Why do I not call my son Tobias so that I may explain to him about the money *o* before I die?" 3 So he called him and said, "My son, when I die, bury me, and do not neglect your mother. Honour her all the days of your life; do what is pleasing to her, and do not grieve her. 4 Remember, my son, that she faced many dangers for you while you were yet unborn. When she dies, bury her beside me in the same grave.

5 "Remember the Lord our God all your days, my son, and refuse to sin or to transgress his commandments. Live uprightly all the days of your life, and do not walk in the ways of wrongdoing. 6 For if you do what is true, your ways will prosper through your deeds. 7 Give alms from your possessions to all who live uprightly, and do not let your eye begrudge the gift when you make it. Do not turn your face away from any poor man, and the face of God will not be turned away from you. 8 If you have many possessions, make your gift from them in proportion; if few, do not be afraid to give according to the little you have. 9 So you will be laying up a good treasure for yourself against the day of necessity. 10 For charity delivers from death and keeps you from entering the darkness; 11 and for all who practise it charity is an excellent offering in the presence of the Most High.

12 "Beware, my son, of all immorality. First of all take a wife from

---

j Gk *they*   *k* Other authorities read *have not borne the name of*   *l* Gk *to Hades*   *m* Gk *his*
n Other authorities read *the great Raphael. And he*   *o* Other authorities omit *about the money*

among the descendants of your fathers and do not marry a foreign woman, who is not of your father's tribe; for we are the sons of the prophets. Remember, my son, that Noah, Abraham, Isaac, and Jacob, our fathers of old, all took wives from among their brethren. They were blessed in their children, and their posterity will inherit the land. 13 So now, my son, love your brethren, and in your heart do not disdain your brethren and the sons and daughters of your people by refusing to take a wife for yourself from among them. For in pride there is ruin and great confusion; and in shiftlessness there is loss and great want, because shiftlessness is the mother of famine. 14 Do not hold over till the next day the wages of any man who works for you, but pay him at once; and if you serve God you will receive payment.

"Watch yourself, my son, in everything you do, and be disciplined in all your conduct. 15 And what you hate, do not do to any one. Do not drink wine to excess or let drunkenness go with you on your way. 16 Give of your bread to the hungry, and of your clothing to the naked. Give all your surplus to charity, and do not let your eye begrudge the gift when you make it. 17 Place your bread on the grave of the righteous, but give none to sinners. 18 Seek advice from every wise man, and do not despise any useful counsel. 19 Bless the Lord God on every occasion; ask him that your ways may be made straight and that all your paths and plans may prosper. For none of the nations has understanding; but the Lord himself gives all good things, and according to his will he humbles whomever he wishes.

"So, my son, remember my commands, and do not let them be blotted out of your mind. 20 And now let me explain to you about the ten talents of silver which I left in trust with Gabael the son of Gabrias at Rages in Media. 21 Do not be afraid, my son, because we have become poor. You have great wealth if you fear God and refrain from every sin and do what is pleasing in his sight."

5 Then Tobias answered him, "Father, I will do everything that you have commanded me; 2 but how can I obtain the money when I do not know the man?" 3 Then Tobit gave him the receipt, and said to him, "Find a man to go with you and I will pay him wages as long as I live; and go and get the money." 4 So he went to look for a man; and he found Raphael, who was an angel, 5 but Tobias *p* did not know it. Tobias *p* said to him, "Can you go with me to Rages in Media? Are you acquainted with that region?" 6 The angel replied, "I will go with you; I am familiar with the way, and I have stayed with our brother Gabael." 7 Then Tobias said to him, "Wait for me, and I shall tell my father." 8 And he said to him, "Go, and do not delay." So he went in and said to his father, "I have found some one to go with me." He said, "Call him to me, so that I may learn to what tribe he belongs, and whether he is a reliable man to go with you."

9 So Tobias *p* invited him in; he entered and they greeted each other. 10 Then Tobit said to him, "My brother, to what tribe and family do you belong? Tell me." 11 But he answered, "Are you looking for a tribe and a family or for a man whom you will pay to go with your son?" And Tobit said to him, "I should like to know, my brother, your people and your name." 12 He replied, "I am Azarias the son of the great Ananias, one of your relatives." 13 Then Tobit said to him, "You are welcome, my brother. Do not be angry with me because I tried to learn your tribe and family. You are a relative of mine, of a good and noble lineage. For I used to know Ananias and Jathan, the sons of the great Shemai-

p Gk *he*

ah, when we went together to Jerusalem to worship and offered the first-born of our flocks and the tithes of our produce. They did not go astray in the error of our brethren. My brother, you come of good stock. 14 But tell me, what wages am I to pay you—a drachma a day, and expenses for yourself as for my son? 15 And besides, I will add to your wages if you both return safe and sound." So they agreed to these terms.

16 Then he said to Tobias, "Get ready for the journey, and good success to you both." So his son made the preparations for the journey. And his father said to him, "Go with this man; God who dwells in heaven will prosper your way, and may his angel attend you." So they both went out and departed, and the young man's dog was with them.

17 But Anna,*q* his mother, began to weep, and said to Tobit, "Why have you sent our child away? Is he not the staff of our hands as he goes in and out before us? 18 Do not add money to money, but consider it rubbish as compared to our child. 19 For the life that is given to us by the Lord is enough for us." 20 And Tobit said to her, "Do not worry, my sister; he will return safe and sound, and your eyes will see him. 21 For a good angel will go with him; his journey will be successful, and he will come back safe and sound." So she stopped weeping.

6 Now as they proceeded on their way they came at evening to the Tigris river and camped there. 2 Then the young man went down to wash himself. A fish leaped up from the river and would have swallowed the young man; 3 and the angel said to him, "Catch the fish." So the young man seized the fish and threw it up on the land. 4 Then the angel said to him, "Cut open the fish and take the heart and liver and gall and

put them away safely." 5 So the young man did as the angel told him; and they roasted and ate the fish.

And they both continued on their way until they came near to Ecbatana. 6 Then the young man said to the angel, "Brother Azarias, of what use is the liver and heart and gall of the fish?" He replied, "As for the heart and the liver, if a demon or evil spirit gives trouble to any one, you make a smoke from these before the man or woman, and that person will never be troubled again. 8 And as for the gall, anoint with it a man who has white films in his eyes, and he will be cured."

9 When they approached Ecbatana,*r* 10 the angel said to the young man, "Brother, today we shall stay with Raguel. He is your relative, and he has an only daughter named Sarah. I will suggest that she be given to you in marriage, 11 because you are entitled to her and to her inheritance, for you are her only eligible kinsman. 12 The girl is also beautiful and sensible. Now listen to my plan. I will speak to her father, and as soon as we return from Rages we will celebrate the marriage. For I know that Raguel, according to the law of Moses, cannot give her to another man without incurring the penalty of death, because you rather than any other man are entitled to the inheritance."

13 Then the young man said to the angel, "Brother Azarias, I have heard that the girl has been given to seven husbands and that each died in the bridal chamber. 14 Now I am the only son my father has, and I am afraid that if I go in I will die as those before me did, for a demon is in love with her, and he harms no one except those who approach her. So now I fear that I may die and bring the lives of my father and mother to the grave in sorrow on my account. And they have no other son to bury them."

q Other authorities omit Anna   r Other authorities read Rages

15 But the angel said to him, "Do you remember the words with which your father commanded you to take a wife from among your own people? Now listen to me, brother, for she will become your wife; and do not worry about the demon, for this very night she will be given to you in marriage. 16 When you enter the bridal chamber, you shall take live ashes of incense and lay upon them some of the heart and liver of the fish so as to make a smoke. 17 Then the demon will smell it and flee away, and will never again return. And when you approach her, rise up, both of you, and cry out to the merciful God, and he will save you and have mercy on you. Do not be afraid, for she was destined for you from eternity. You will save her, and she will go with you, and I suppose that you will have children by her." When Tobias heard these things, he fell in love with her and yearned deeply for her.

7 When they reached Ecbatana and arrived at the house of Raguel, Sarah met them and greeted them. They returned her greeting, and she brought them into the house. 2 Then Raguel said to his wife Edna, "How much the young man resembles my cousin Tobit!" 3 And Raguel asked them, "Where are you from, brethren?" They answered him, "We belong to the sons of Naphtali, who are captives in Nineveh." 4 So he said to them, "Do you know our brother Tobit?" And they said, "Yes, we do." And he asked them, "Is he in good health?" 5 They replied, "He is alive and in good health." And Tobias said, "He is my father." 6 Then Raguel sprang up and kissed him and wept. 7 And he blessed him and exclaimed, "Son of that good and noble man!" When he heard that Tobit had lost his sight, he was stricken with grief and wept. 8 And his wife Edna and his daughter

Sarah wept. They received them very warmly; and they killed a ram from the flock and set large servings of food before them.

Then Tobias said to Raphael, "Brother Azarias, speak of those things which you talked about on the journey, and let the matter be settled." 9 So he communicated the proposal to Raguel. And Raguel said to Tobias, "Eat, drink, and be merry; 10 for it is your right to take my child. But let me explain the true situation to you. 11 I have given my daughter to seven husbands, and when each came to her he died in the night. But for the present be merry." And Tobias said, "I will eat nothing here until you make a binding agreement with me." 12 So Raguel said, "Take her right now, in accordance with the law. You are her relative, and she is yours. The merciful God will guide you both for the best." 13 Then he called his daughter Sarah, and taking her by the hand he gave her to Tobias to be his wife, saying, "Here she is; take her according to the law of Moses, and take her with you to your father." And he blessed them. 14 Next he called his wife Edna, and took a scroll and wrote out the contract; and they set their seals to it. 15 Then they began to eat.

16 And Raguel called his wife Edna and said to her, "Sister, make up the other room, and take her into it." 17 So she did as he said, and took her there; and the girl[s] began to weep. But the mother[s] comforted her daughter in her tears, and said to her, 18 "Be brave, my child; the Lord of heaven and earth grant you joy[t] in place of this sorrow of yours. Be brave, my daughter."

8 When they had finished eating, they escorted Tobias in to her. 2 As he went he remembered the words of Raphael, and he took the live ashes of incense and put the heart and liver of the fish upon them and made a smoke. 3 And when the

s Gk *she*   *t* Other authorities read *favour*

demon smelled the odour he fled to the remotest parts of Egypt, and the angel bound him. 4 When the door was shut and the two were alone, Tobias got up from the bed and said, "Sister, get up, and let us pray that the Lord may have mercy upon us." 5 And Tobias began to pray,

"Blessed art thou, O God of our fathers,
and blessed be thy holy and glorious name for ever.
Let the heavens and all of thy creatures bless thee.
6 Thou madest Adam and gavest him Eve his wife
as a helper and support.
From them the race of mankind has sprung.
Thou didst say, 'It is not good that the man should be alone;
let us make a helper for him like himself.'

7 And now, O Lord, I am not taking this sister of mine because of lust, but with sincerity. Grant that I may find mercy and may grow old together with her." 8 And she said with him, "Amen." 9 Then they both went to sleep for the night.

But Raguel arose and went and dug a grave, 10 with the thought, "Perhaps he too will die." 11 Then Raguel went into his house 12 and said to his wife Edna, "Send one of the maids to see whether he is alive; and if he is not, let us bury him without any one knowing about it." 13 So the maid opened the door and went in, and found them both asleep. 14 And she came out and told them that he was alive. 15 Then Raguel blessed God and said,

"Blessed art thou, O God, with every pure and holy blessing.
Let thy saints and all thy creatures bless thee;
let all thy angels and thy chosen people bless thee for ever.
16 Blessed art thou, because thou hast made me glad.

It has not happened to me as I expected;
but thou hast treated us according to thy great mercy.
17 Blessed art thou, because thou hast had compassion on two only children.
Show them mercy, O Lord;
and bring their lives to fulfilment in health and happiness and mercy."

18 Then he ordered his servants to fill in the grave.

19 After this he gave a wedding feast for them which lasted fourteen days. 20 And before the days of the feast were over, Raguel declared by oath to Tobias *u* that he should not leave until the fourteen days of the wedding feast were ended, 21 that then he should take half of Raguel's *v* property and return in safety to his father, and that the rest would be his "when my wife and I die."

9 Then Tobias called Raphael and said to him, 2 "Brother Azarias, take a servant and two camels with you and go to Gabael at Rages in Media and get the money for me; and bring him to the wedding feast. 3 For Raguel has sworn that I should not leave; 4 but my father is counting the days, and if I delay long he will be greatly distressed." 5 So Raphael made the journey and stayed over night with Gabael. He gave him the receipt, and Gabael *w* brought out the money bags with their seals intact and gave them to him. 6 In the morning they both got up early and came to the wedding feast. And Gabael blessed Tobias and his wife.*x*

10 Now his father Tobit was counting each day, and when the days for the journey had expired and they did not arrive, 2 he said, "Is it possible that he has been detained? *y* Or is it possible that Gabael has died and there is no one to give him the money?" 3 And he was greatly distressed. 4 And his wife said

u Gk *him*　*v* Gk *his*　*w* Gk *he*　*x* Cn: Gk *And Tobias blessed his wife*
y One Gk Ms Lat: Gk *they are put to shame* or *they are disappointed*

60

to him, "The lad has perished; his long delay proves it." Then she began to mourn for him, and said, 5 "Am I not distressed, my child, that I let you go, you who are the light of my eyes?" 6 But Tobit said to her, "Be still and stop worrying; he is well." 7 And she answered him, "Be still and stop deceiving me; my child has perished." And she went out every day to the road by which they had left; she ate nothing in the daytime, and throughout the nights she never stopped mourning for her son Tobias, until the fourteen days of the wedding feast had expired which Raguel had sworn that he should spend there.

At that time Tobias said to Raguel, "Send me back, for my father and mother have given up hope of ever seeing me again." 8 But his father-in-law said to him, "Stay with me, and I will send messengers to your father, and they will inform him how things are with you." 9 Tobias replied, "No, send me back to my father." 10 So Raguel arose and gave him his wife Sarah and half of his property in slaves, cattle, and money. 11 And when he had blessed them he sent them away, saying, "The God of heaven will prosper you, my children, before I die." 12 He said also to his daughter, "Honour your father-in-law and your mother-in-law; they are now your parents. Let me hear a good report of you." And he kissed her. And Edna said to Tobias, "The Lord of heaven bring you back safely, dear brother, and grant me to see your children by my daughter Sarah, that I may rejoice before the Lord. See, I am entrusting my daughter to you; do nothing to grieve her."

11 After this Tobias went on his way, praising God because he had made his journey a success. And he blessed Raguel and his wife Edna.

So he continued on his way until they came near to Nineveh. 2 Then

Raphael said to Tobias, "Are you not aware, brother, of how you left your father? 3 Let us run ahead of your wife and prepare the house. 4 And take the gall of the fish with you." So they went their way, and the dog went along behind them.

5 Now Anna sat looking intently down the road for her son. 6 And she caught sight of him coming, and said to his father, "Behold, your son is coming, and so is the man who went with him!"

7 Raphael said, "I know, Tobias, that your father will open his eyes. 8 You therefore must anoint his eyes with the gall; and when they smart he will rub them, and will cause the white films to fall away, and he will see you."

9 Then Anna ran to meet them, and embraced her son, and said to him, "I have seen you, my child; now I am ready to die." And they both wept. 10 Tobit started toward the door, and stumbled. But his son ran to him 11 and took hold of his father, and he sprinkled the gall upon his father's eyes, saying, "Be of good cheer, father." 12 And when his eyes began to smart he rubbed them, 13 and the white films scaled off from the corners of his eyes. 14 Then he saw his son and embraced him, and he wept and said, "Blessed art thou, O God, and blessed is thy name for ever, and blessed are all thy holy angels. 15 For thou hast afflicted me, but thou hast had mercy upon me; here I see my son Tobias!" And his son went in rejoicing, and he reported to his father the great things that had happened to him in Media.

16 Then Tobit went out to meet his daughter-in-law at the gate of Nineveh, rejoicing and praising God. Those who saw him as he went were amazed because he could see. 17 And Tobit gave thanks before them that God had been merciful to him. When Tobit came near to Sarah his daughter-in-law, he blessed her, saying, "Welcome, daughter! Blessed is God

who has brought you to us, and blessed are your father and your mother." So there was rejoicing among all his brethren in Nineveh. [18] Ahikar and his nephew Nadab[z] came, [19] and Tobias' marriage was celebrated for seven days with great festivity.

12 Tobit then called his son Tobias and said to him, "My son, see to the wages of the man who went with you; and he must also be given more." [2] He replied, "Father, it would do me no harm to give him half of what I have brought back. [3] For he has led me back to you safely, he cured my wife, he obtained the money for me, and he also healed you." [4] The old man said, "He deserves it." [5] So he called the angel and said to him, "Take half of all that you two have brought back."

[6] Then the angel[a] called the two of them privately and said to them: "Praise God and give thanks to him; exalt him and give thanks to him in the presence of all the living for what he has done for you. It is good to praise God and to exalt his name, worthily declaring the works of God. Do not be slow to give him thanks. [7] It is good to guard the secret of a king, but gloriously to reveal the works of God. Do good, and evil will not overtake you. [8] Prayer is good when accompanied by fasting, almsgiving, and righteousness. A little with righteousness is better than much with wrongdoing. It is better to give alms than to treasure up gold. [9] For almsgiving delivers from death, and it will purge away every sin. Those who perform deeds of charity and of righteousness will have fulness of life; [10] but those who commit sin are the enemies of their own lives. [11] "I will not conceal anything from you. I have said, 'It is good to guard the secret of a king, but gloriously to reveal the works of God.'

[12] And so, when you and your daughter-in-law Sarah prayed, I brought a reminder of your prayer before the Holy One; and when you buried the dead, I was likewise present with you. [13] When you did not hesitate to rise and leave your dinner in order to go and lay out the dead, your good deed was not hidden from me, but I was with you. [14] So now God sent me to heal you and your daughter-in-law Sarah. [15] I am Raphael, one of the seven holy angels who present the prayers of the saints and enter into the presence of the glory of the Holy One."

[16] They were both alarmed; and they fell upon their faces, for they were afraid. [17] But he said to them, "Do not be afraid; you will be safe. But praise God for ever. [18] For I did not come as a favour on my part, but by the will of our God. Therefore praise him for ever. [19] All these days I merely appeared to you and did not eat or drink, but you were seeing a vision. [20] And now give thanks to God, for I am ascending to him who sent me. Write in a book everything that has happened." [21] Then they stood up; but they saw him no more. [22] So they confessed the great and wonderful works of God, and acknowledged that the angel of the Lord had appeared to them.

13 Then Tobit wrote a prayer of rejoicing, and said:
"Blessed is God who lives for ever,
   and blessed is his kingdom.
[2] For he afflicts, and he shows mercy;
   he leads down to Hades, and
     brings up again,
   and there is no one who can
     escape his hand.
[3] Acknowledge him before the nations, O sons of Israel;
   for he has scattered us among
     them.
[4] Make his greatness known there,
   and exalt him in the presence
     of all the living;

---

[z] Other authorities read *Nasbas*   [a] Gk *he*

because he is our Lord and God,
  he is our Father for ever.
5 He will afflict us for our iniquities;
  and again he will show mercy,
  and will gather us from all the na-
    tions
  among whom you*b* have been
    scattered.
6 If you turn to him with all your
    heart and with all your soul,
  to do what is true before him,
  then he will turn to you
  and will not hide his face from
    you.
But see what he will do with you;
  give thanks to him with your
    full voice.
Praise the Lord of righteousness,
  and exalt the King of the ages.
I give him thanks in the land of
    my captivity,
  and I show his power and maj-
    esty to a nation of sinners.
Turn back, you sinners, and do
    right before him;
  who knows if he will accept you
    and have mercy on you?
7 I exalt my God;
  my soul exalts the King of
    heaven,
  and will rejoice in his majesty.
8 Let all men speak,
  and give him thanks in Jeru-
    salem.
9 O Jerusalem, the holy city,
  he will afflict you for the deeds
    of your sons,
  but again he will show mercy to
    the sons of the righteous.
10 Give thanks worthily to the Lord,
  and praise the King of the ages,
  that his tent may be raised for
    you again with joy.
May he cheer those within you
    who are captives,
  and love those within you who
    are distressed,
  to all generations for ever.
11 Many nations will come from afar
    to the name of the Lord God,
  bearing gifts in their hands, gifts
    for the King of heaven.

Generations of generations will
    give you joyful praise.
12 Cursed are all who hate you;
  blessed for ever will be all who
    love you.
13 Rejoice and be glad for the sons of
    the righteous;
  for they will be gathered to-
    gether,
  and will praise the Lord of the
    righteous.
14 How blessed are those who love
    you!
  They will rejoice in your peace.
Blessed are those who grieved over
    all your afflictions;
  for they will rejoice for you upon
    seeing all your glory,
  and they will be made glad for
    ever.
15 Let my soul praise God the great
    King.
16 For Jerusalem will be built with
    sapphires and emeralds,
  her*c* walls with precious stones,
  and her towers and battlements
    with pure gold.
17 The streets of Jerusalem will be
    paved*d* with beryl and ruby
    and stones of Ophir;
18 all her lanes will cry 'Hallelujah!'
    and will give praise,
  saying, 'Blessed is God, who has
    exalted you for ever.' "

14 Here Tobit ended his words
of praise. 2 He was fifty-eight
years old when he lost his sight, and
after eight years he regained it. He
gave alms, and he continued to fear
the Lord God and to praise him.
3 When he had grown very old he
called his son and grandsons, and
said to him, "My son, take your sons;
behold, I have grown old and am
about to depart this life. 4 Go to
Media, my son, for I fully believe
what Jonah the prophet said about
Nineveh, that it will be overthrown.
But in Media there will be peace for
a time. Our brethren will be scattered
over the earth from the good land,

b Other authorities read *we*   *c* Gk *your*   *d* Or *inlaid*

and Jerusalem will be desolate. The house of God in it will be burned down and will be in ruins for a time. [5] But God will again have mercy on them, and bring them back into their land; and they will rebuild the house of God,[e] though it will not be like the former one until the times of the age are completed. After this they will return from the places of their captivity, and will rebuild Jerusalem in splendour. And the house of God will be rebuilt there with a glorious building for all generations for ever, just as the prophets said of it. [6] Then all the Gentiles will turn to fear the Lord God in truth, and will bury their idols. [7] All the Gentiles will praise the Lord, and his people will give thanks to God, and the Lord will exalt his people. And all who love the Lord God in truth and righteousness will rejoice, showing mercy to our brethren.

[8] "So now, my son, leave Nineveh, because what the prophet Jonah said will surely happen. [9] But keep the law and the commandments, and be merciful and just, so that it may be well with you. [10] Bury me properly, and your mother with me. And do not live in Nineveh any longer. See,

my son, what Nadab[f] did to Ahikar who had reared him, how he brought him from light into darkness, and with what he repaid him. But Ahikar was saved, and the other received repayment as he himself went down into the darkness. Ahikar[g] gave alms and escaped the deathtrap which Nadab[h] had set for him; but Nadab[f] fell into the trap and perished. [11] So now, my children, consider what almsgiving accomplishes and how righteousness delivers." As he said this he died in his bed. He was a hundred and fifty-eight years old; and Tobias[h] gave him a magnificent funeral. [12] And when Anna died he buried her with his father.

Then Tobias returned with his wife and his sons to Ecbatana, to Raguel his father-in-law. [13] He grew old with honour, and he gave his father-in-law and mother-in-law magnificent funerals. He inherited their property and that of his father Tobit. [14] He died in Ecbatana of Media at the age of a hundred and twenty-seven years. [15] But before he died he heard of the destruction of Nineveh, which Nebuchadnezzar and Ahasuerus had captured. Before his death he rejoiced over Nineveh.

[e] Gk *house*   [f] Other authorities read *Aman*   [g] Other authorities read *Manasses*   [h] Gk *he*

1 In the twelfth year of the reign of Nebuchadnezzar, who ruled over the Assyrians in the great city of Nineveh, in the days of Arphaxad, who ruled over the Medes in Ecbatana—² he is the king who built walls about Ecbatana with hewn stones three cubits thick and six cubits long; he made the walls seventy cubits high and fifty cubits wide; ³ at the gates he built towers a hundred cubits high and sixty cubits wide at the foundations; ⁴ and he made its gates, which were seventy cubits high and forty cubits wide, so that his armies could march out in force and his infantry form their ranks—⁵ it was in those days that King Nebuchadnezzar made war against King Arphaxad in the great plain which is on the borders of Ragae. ⁶ He was joined by all the people of the hill country and all those who lived along the Euphrates and the Tigris and the Hydaspes and in the plain where Arioch ruled the Elymaeans. Many nations joined the forces of the Chaldeans.

⁷ Then Nebuchadnezzar king of the Assyrians sent to all who lived in Persia and to all who lived in the west, those who lived in Cilicia and Damascus and Lebanon and Antilebanon and all who lived along the seacoast, ⁸ and those among the nations of Carmel and Gilead, and Upper Galilee and the great Plain of Esdraelon, ⁹ and all who were in Samaria and its surrounding towns, and beyond the Jordan as far as Jerusalem and Bethany and Chelous and Kadesh and the river of Egypt, and Tahpanhes and Raamses and the whole land of Goshen, ¹⁰ even beyond Tanis and Memphis, and all who lived in Egypt as far as the borders of Ethiopia. ¹¹ But all who lived in the whole region disregarded the orders of Nebuchadnezzar king of the Assyrians, and refused to join him in the war; for they were not afraid of him, but looked upon him as only one man,ᵃ and they sent back his messengers empty-handed and shamefaced.

¹² Then Nebuchadnezzar was very angry with this whole region, and swore by his throne and kingdom that he would surely take revenge on the whole territory of Cilicia and Damascus and Syria and kill them by the sword, and also all the inhabitants of the land of Moab, and the people of Ammon, and all Judea, and every one in Egypt, as far as the coasts of the two seas. ¹³ In the seventeenth year he led his forces against King Arphaxad, and defeated him in battle, and overthrew the whole army of Arphaxad, and all his cavalry and all his chariots. ¹⁴ Thus he took possession of his cities, and came to Ecbatana, captured its towers, plundered its markets, and turned its beauty into shame. ¹⁵ He captured Arphaxad in the mountains of Ragae and struck him down with hunting spears; and he utterly destroyed him, to this day. ¹⁶ Then he returned with them to Nineveh, he and all his combined forces, a vast body of troops; and there he and his forces rested and feasted for one hundred and twenty days.

2 In the eighteenth year, on the twenty-second day of the first month, there was talk in the palace of Nebuchadnezzar king of the Assyrians about carrying out his revenge on the whole region, just as he had said. ² He called together all his officers and all his nobles and set forth to them his secret plan and recounted fully, with his own lips, all the wickedness of the region;ᵇ ³ and it was decided that every one who had not obeyed his command should be destroyed. ⁴ When he had finished setting forth his plan, Nebuchadnezzar king of the Assyrians

---

ᵃ Or *a man*   ᵇ The meaning of the Greek of the last clause of this verse is uncertain.

called Holofernes, the chief general of his army, second only to himself, and said to him,

5 "Thus says the Great King, the lord of the whole earth: When you leave my presence, take with you men confident in their strength, to the number of one hundred and twenty thousand foot soldiers and twelve thousand cavalry. 6 Go and attack the whole west country, because they disobeyed my orders. 7 Tell them to prepare earth and water, for I am coming against them in my anger, and will cover the whole face of the earth with the feet of my armies, and will hand them over to be plundered by my troops,[c] 8 till their wounded shall fill their valleys, and every brook and river shall be filled with their dead, and overflow; 9 and I will lead them away captive to the ends of the whole earth. 10 You shall go and seize all their territory for me in advance. They will yield themselves to you, and you shall hold them for me till the day of their punishment. 11 But if they refuse, your eye shall not spare and you shall hand them over to slaughter and plunder throughout your whole region. 12 For as I live, and by the power of my kingdom, what I have spoken my hand will execute. 13 And you—take care not to transgress any of your sovereign's commands, but be sure to carry them out just as I have ordered you; and do not delay about it."

14 So Holofernes left the presence of his master, and called together all the commanders, generals, and officers of the Assyrian army, 15 and mustered the picked troops by divisions as his lord had ordered him to do, one hundred and twenty thousand of them, together with twelve thousand archers on horseback, 16 and he organized them as a great army is marshalled for a campaign. 17 He collected a vast number of camels and asses and mules for trans-

port, and innumerable sheep and oxen and goats for provision; 18 also plenty of food for every man, and a huge amount of gold and silver from the royal palace. 19 So he set out with his whole army, to go ahead of King Nebuchadnezzar and to cover the whole face of the earth to the west with their chariots and horsemen and picked troops of infantry. 20 Along with them went a mixed crowd like a swarm of locusts, like the dust of the earth—a multitude that could not be counted.

21 They marched for three days from Nineveh to the plain of Bectileth, and camped opposite Bectileth near the mountain which is to the north of Upper Cilicia. 22 From there Holofernes[d] took his whole army, his infantry, cavalry, and chariots, and went up into the hill country 23 and ravaged Put and Lud, and plundered all the people of Rassis and the Ishmaelites who lived along the desert, south of the country of the Chelleans. 24 Then he followed[e] the Euphrates and passed through Mesopotamia and destroyed all the hilltop cities along the brook Abron, as far as the sea. 25 He also seized the territory of Cilicia, and killed every one who resisted him, and came to the southern borders of Japheth, fronting toward Arabia. 26 He surrounded all the Midianites, and burned their tents and plundered their sheepfolds. 27 Then he went down into the plain of Damascus during the wheat harvest, and burned all their fields and destroyed their flocks and herds and sacked their cities and ravaged their lands and put to death all their young men with the edge of the sword.

28 So fear and terror of him fell upon all the people who lived along the seacoast, at Sidon and Tyre, and those who lived in Sur and Ocina and all who lived in Jamnia. Those who lived in Azotus and Ascalon feared him exceedingly.

[c] Gk *them*   [d] Gk *he*   [e] Or *crossed*

3 So they sent messengers to sue for peace, and said, "Behold, we the servants of Nebuchadnezzar, the Great King, lie prostrate before you. Do with us whatever you will. ³ Behold, our buildings, and all our land, and all our wheat fields, and our flocks and herds, and all our sheepfolds with their tents, lie before you; do with them whatever you please. ⁴ Our cities also and their inhabitants are your slaves; come and deal with them in any way that seems good to you."

5 The men came to Holofernes and told him all this. ⁶ Then he went down to the seacoast with his army and stationed garrisons in the hilltop cities and took picked men from them as his allies. ⁷ And these people and all in the country round about welcomed him with garlands and dances and tambourines. ⁸ And he demolished all their shrines *f* and cut down their sacred groves; for it had been given to him to destroy all the gods of the land, so that all nations should worship Nebuchadnezzar only, and all their tongues and tribes should call upon him as god.

9 Then he came to the edge of Esdraelon, near Dothan, fronting the great ridge of Judea; ¹⁰ here he camped between Geba and Scythopolis, and remained for a whole month in order to assemble all the supplies for his army.

4 By this time the people of Israel living in Judea heard of everything that Holofernes, the general of Nebuchadnezzar the king of the Assyrians, had done to the nations, and how he had plundered and destroyed all their temples; ² they were therefore very greatly terrified at his approach, and were alarmed both for Jerusalem and for the temple of the Lord their God. ³ For they had only recently returned from the captivity, and all the people of Judea were newly gathered together, and the sacred vessels and the

altar and the temple had been consecrated after their profanation. ⁴ So they sent to every district of Samaria, and to Kona and Beth-horon and Belmain and Jericho and to Choba and Aesora and the valley of Salem, ⁵ and immediately seized all the high hilltops and fortified the villages on them and stored up food in preparation for war—since their fields had recently been harvested. ⁶ And Joakim, the high priest, who was in Jerusalem at that time, wrote to the people of Bethulia and Betomesthaim, which faces Esdraelon opposite the plain near Dothan, ⁷ ordering them to seize the passes up into the hills, since by them Judea could be invaded, and it was easy to stop any who tried to enter, for the approach was narrow, only wide enough for two men at the most.

8 So the Israelites did as Joakim the high priest and the senate of the whole people of Israel, in session at Jerusalem, had given order. ⁹ And every man of Israel cried out to God with great fervour, and they humbled themselves with much fasting. ¹⁰ They and their wives and their children and their cattle and every resident alien and hired labourer and purchased slave—they all girded themselves with sackcloth. ¹¹ And all the men and women of Israel, and their children, living at Jerusalem, prostrated themselves before the temple and put ashes on their heads and spread out their sackcloth before the Lord. ¹² They even surrounded the altar with sackcloth and cried out in unison, praying earnestly to the God of Israel not to give up their infants as prey and their wives as booty, and the cities they had inherited to be destroyed, and the sanctuary to be profaned and desecrated to the malicious joy of the Gentiles. ¹³ So the Lord heard their prayers and looked upon their affliction; for the people fasted many days throughout Judea and in Jerusalem

f Syr: Gk *borders.*

3a

before the sanctuary of the Lord Almighty. ¹⁴ And Joakim the high priest and all the priests who stood before the Lord and ministered to the Lord, with their loins girded with sackcloth, offered the continual burnt offerings and the vows and freewill offerings of the people. ¹⁵ With ashes upon their turbans, they cried out to the Lord with all their might to look with favour upon the whole house of Israel.

5 When Holofernes, the general of the Assyrian army, heard that the people of Israel had prepared for war and had closed the passes in the hills and had fortified all the high hilltops and set up barricades in the plains, ² he was very angry. So he called together all the princes of Moab and the commanders of Ammon and all the governors of the coastland, ³ and said to them, "Tell me, you Canaanites, what people is this that lives in the hill country? What cities do they inhabit? How large is their army, and in what does their power or strength consist? Who rules over them as king, leading their army? ⁴ And why have they alone, of all who live in the west, refused to come out and meet me?"

5 Then Achior, the leader of all the Ammonites, said to him, "Let my lord now hear a word from the mouth of your servant, and I will tell you the truth about this people that dwells in the nearby mountain district. No falsehood shall come from your servant's mouth. ⁶ This people is descended from the Chaldeans. ⁷ At one time they lived in Mesopotamia, because they would not follow the gods of their fathers who were in Chaldea. ⁸ For they had left the ways of their ancestors, and they worshipped the God of heaven, the God they had come to know; hence they drove them out from the presence of their gods; and they fled to Mesopotamia, and lived there for a long time. ⁹ Then their God commanded them to leave the place where they were living and go to the land of Canaan. There they settled, and prospered, with much gold and silver and very many cattle. ¹⁰ When a famine spread over Canaan they went down to Egypt and lived there as long as they had food; and there they became a great multitude—so great that they could not be counted. ¹¹ So the king of Egypt became hostile to them; he took advantage of them and set them to making bricks, and humbled them and made slaves of them. ¹² Then they cried out to their God, and he afflicted the whole land of Egypt with incurable plagues; and so the Egyptians drove them out of their sight. ¹³ Then God dried up the Red Sea before them, ¹⁴ and he led them by the way of Sinai and Kadesh-barnea, and drove out all the people of the wilderness. ¹⁵ So they lived in the land of the Amorites, and by their might destroyed all the inhabitants of Heshbon; and crossing over the Jordan they took possession of all the hill country. ¹⁶ And they drove out before them the Canaanites and the Perizzites and the Jebusites and the Shechemites and all the Gergesites, and lived there a long time. ¹⁷ As long as they did not sin against their God they prospered, for the God who hates iniquity is with them. ¹⁸ But when they departed from the way which he had appointed for them, they were utterly defeated in many battles and were led away captive to a foreign country; the temple of their God was razed to the ground, and their cities were captured by their enemies. ¹⁹ But now they have returned to their God, and have come back from the places to which they were scattered, and have occupied Jerusalem, where their sanctuary is, and have settled in the hill country, because it was uninhabited. ²⁰ Now therefore, my master and lord, if there is any unwitting error in this people and they sin against their God and we find out their offence, then we will go up and defeat them.

21 But if there is no transgression in their nation, then let my lord pass them by; for their Lord will defend them, and their God will protect them, and we shall be put to shame before the whole world."

22 When Achior had finished saying this, all the men standing around the tent began to complain; Holofernes' officers and all the men from the seacoast and from Moab insisted that he must be put to death. 23 "For," they said, "we will not be afraid of the Israelites; they are a people with no strength or power for making war. 24 Therefore let us go up, Lord Holofernes, and they will be devoured by your vast army."

6 When the disturbance made by the men outside the council died down, Holofernes, the commander of the Assyrian army, said to Achior and all the Moabites in the presence of all the foreign contingents:

2 "And who are you, Achior, and you hirelings of Ephraim, to prophesy among us as you have done today and tell us not to make war against the people of Israel because their God will defend them? Who is God except Nebuchadnezzar? 3 He will send his forces and will destroy them from the face of the earth, and their God will not deliver them—we the king's *f* servants will destroy them as one man. They cannot resist the might of our cavalry. 4 We will burn them up, *g* and their mountains will be drunk with their blood, and their fields will be full of their dead. They *h* cannot withstand us, but will utterly perish. So says King Nebuchadnezzar, the lord of the whole earth. For he has spoken; none of his words shall be in vain.

5 "But you, Achior, you Ammonite hireling, who have said these words on the day of your iniquity, you shall not see my face again from this day until I take revenge on this race that

came out of Egypt. 6 Then the sword of my army and the spear *i* of my servants shall pierce your sides, and you shall fall among their wounded, when I return. 7 Now my slaves are going to take you back into the hill country and put you in one of the cities beside the passes, 8 and you will not die until you perish along with them. 9 If you really hope in your heart that they will not be taken, do not look downcast! I have spoken and none of my words shall fail."

10 Then Holofernes ordered his slaves, who waited on him in his tent, to seize Achior and take him to Bethulia and hand him over to the men of Israel. 11 So the slaves took him and led him out of the camp into the plain, and from the plain they went up into the hill country and came to the springs below Bethulia. 12 When the men of the city saw them, *j* they caught up their weapons and ran out of the city to the top of the hill, and all the slingers kept them from coming up by casting stones at them. 13 However, they got under the shelter of the hill and they bound Achior and left him lying at the foot of the hill, and returned to their master.

14 Then the men of Israel came down from their city and found him; and they untied him and brought him into Bethulia and placed him before the magistrates of their city, 15 who in those days were Uzziah the son of Micah, of the tribe of Simeon, and Chabris the son of Gothoniel, and Charmis the son of Melchiel. 16 They called together all the elders of the city, and all their young men and their women ran to the assembly; and they set Achior in the midst of all their people, and Uzziah asked him what had happened. 17 He answered and told them what had taken place at the council of Holofernes, and all that he had said in the presence of the Assyrian lead-

---

f Gk *his*   *g* Other authorities add *with it*   *h* Gk *the track of their feet*   *i* Lat Syr: Gk *people*
j Other authorities add *on the top of the hill*

69

ers, and all that Holofernes had said so boastfully against the house of Israel. 18 Then the people fell down and worshipped God, and cried out to him, and said,

19 "O Lord God of heaven, behold their arrogance, and have pity on the humiliation of our people, and look this day upon the faces of those who are consecrated to thee."

20 Then they consoled Achior, and praised him greatly. 21 And Uzziah took him from the assembly to his own house and gave a banquet for the elders; and all that night they called on the God of Israel for help.

7 The next day Holofernes ordered his whole army, and all the allies who had joined him, to break camp and move against Bethulia, and to seize the passes up into the hill country and make war on the Israelites. 2 So all their warriors moved their camp that day; their force of men of war was one hundred and seventy thousand infantry and twelve thousand cavalry, together with the baggage and the foot soldiers handling it, a very great multitude. 3 They encamped in the valley near Bethulia, beside the spring, and they spread out in breadth over Dothan as far as Balbaim and in length from Bethulia to Cyamon, which faces Esdraelon.

4 When the Israelites saw their vast numbers they were greatly terrified, and every one said to his neighbour, "These men will now lick up the face of the whole land; neither the high mountains nor the valleys nor the hills will bear their weight." 5 Then each man took up his weapons, and when they had kindled fires on their towers they remained on guard all that night.

6 On the second day Holofernes led out all his cavalry in full view of the Israelites in Bethulia, 7 and examined the approaches to the city, and visited the springs that supplied their water, and seized them and set guards of soldiers over them, and then returned to his army.

8 Then all the chieftains of the people of Esau and all the leaders of the Moabites and the commanders of the coastland came to him and said, 9 "Let our lord hear a word, lest his army be defeated. 10 For these people, the Israelites, do not rely on their spears but on the height of the mountains where they live, for it is not easy to reach the tops of their mountains. 11 Therefore, my lord, do not fight against them in battle array, and not a man of your army will fall. 12 Remain in your camp, and keep all the men in your forces with you; only let your servants take possession of the spring of water that flows from the foot of the mountain —13 for this is where all the people of Bethulia get their water. So thirst will destroy them, and they will give up their city. We and our people will go up to the tops of the nearby mountains and camp there to keep watch that not a man gets out of the city. 14 They and their wives and children will waste away with famine, and before the sword reaches them they will be strewn about in the streets where they live. 15 So you will pay them back with evil, because they rebelled and did not receive you peaceably."

16 These words pleased Holofernes and all his servants, and he gave orders to do as they had said. 17 So the army of the Ammonites moved forward, together with five thousand Assyrians, and they encamped in the valley and seized the water supply and the springs of the Israelites. 18 And the sons of Esau and the sons of Ammon went up and encamped in the hill country opposite Dothan; and they sent some of their men toward the south and the east, toward Acraba, which is near Chusi beside the brook Mochmur. The rest of the Assyrian army encamped in the plain, and covered the whole face of the land, and their tents and supply trains spread out in great number, and they formed a vast multitude.

19 The people of Israel cried out

to the Lord their God, for their courage failed, because all their enemies had surrounded them and there was no way of escape from them. ²⁰ The whole Assyrian army, their infantry, chariots, and cavalry, surrounded them for thirty-four days, until all the vessels of water belonging to every inhabitant of Bethulia were empty; ²¹ their cisterns were going dry, and they did not have enough water to drink their fill for a single day, because it was measured out to them to drink. ²² Their children lost heart, and the women and young men fainted from thirst and fell down in the streets of the city and in the passages through the gates; there was no strength left in them any longer.

23 Then all the people, the young men, the women, and the children, gathered about Uzziah and the rulers of the city and cried out with a loud voice, and said before all the elders, ²⁴ "God be judge between you and us! For you have done us a great injury in not making peace with the Assyrians. ²⁵ For now we have no one to help us; God has sold us into their hands, to strew us on the ground before them with thirst and utter destruction. ²⁶ Now call them in and surrender the whole city to the army of Holofernes and to all his forces, to be plundered. ²⁷ For it would be better for us to be captured by them; *k* for we will be slaves, but our lives will be spared, and we shall not witness the death of our babes before our eyes, or see our wives and children draw their last breath. ²⁸ We call to witness against you heaven and earth and our God, the Lord of our fathers, who punishes us according to our sins and the sins of our fathers. Let him not do this day the things which we have described!"

29 Then great and general lamentation arose throughout the assembly, and they cried out to the Lord God with a loud voice. ³⁰ And Uzziah said

to them, "Have courage, my brothers! Let us hold out for five more days; by that time the Lord our God will restore to us his mercy, for he will not forsake us utterly. ³¹ But if these days pass by, and no help comes for us, I will do what you say."

32 Then he dismissed the people to their various posts, and they went up on the walls and towers of their city. The women and children he sent home. And they were greatly depressed in the city.

8 At that time Judith heard about these things: she was the daughter of Merari the son of Ox, son of Joseph, son of Oziel, son of Elkiah, son of Ananias, son of Gideon, son of Raphaim, son of Ahitub, son of Elijah, son of Hilkiah, son of Eliab, son of Nathanael, son of Salamiel, son of Sarasadai, son of Israel. ² Her husband Manasseh, who belonged to her tribe and family, had died during the barley harvest. ³ For as he stood overseeing the men who were binding sheaves in the field, he was overcome by the burning heat, and took to his bed and died in Bethulia his city. So they buried him with his fathers in the field between Dothan and Balamon. ⁴ Judith had lived at home as a widow for three years and four months. ⁵ She set up a tent for herself on the roof of her house, and girded sackcloth about her loins and wore the garments of her widowhood. ⁶ She fasted all the days of her widowhood, except the day before the sabbath and the sabbath itself, the day before the new moon and the day of the new moon, and the feasts and days of rejoicing of the house of Israel. ⁷ She was beautiful in appearance, and had a very lovely face; and her husband Manasseh had left her gold and silver, and men and women slaves, and cattle, and fields; and she maintained this estate. ⁸ No one spoke ill of her, for she feared God with great devotion.

9 When Judith heard the wicked

k Other authorities add *than to die of thirst*

71

words spoken by the people against the ruler, because they were faint for lack of water, and when she heard all that Uzziah said to them, and how he promised them under oath to surrender the city to the Assyrians after five days, [10] she sent her maid, who was in charge of all she possessed, to summon [l] Chabris and Charmis, the elders of her city. [11] They came to her, and she said to them,

"Listen to me, rulers of the people of Bethulia! What you have said to the people today is not right; you have even sworn and pronounced this oath between God and you, promising to surrender the city to our enemies unless the Lord turns and helps us within so many days. [12] Who are you, that have put God to the test this day, and are setting yourselves up in the place of [m] God among the sons of men? [13] You are putting the Lord Almighty to the test—but you will never know anything! [14] You cannot plumb the depths of the human heart, nor find out what a man is thinking; how do you expect to search out God, who made all these things, and find out his mind or comprehend his thought? No, my brethren, do not provoke the Lord our God to anger. [15] For if he does not choose to help us within these five days, he has power to protect us within any time he pleases, or even to destroy us in the presence of our enemies. [16] Do not try to bind the purposes of the Lord our God; for God is not like man, to be threatened, nor like a human being, to be won over by pleading. [17] Therefore, while we wait for his deliverance, let us call upon him to help us, and he will hear our voice, if it pleases him.

[18] "For never in our generation, nor in these present days, has there been any tribe or family or people or city of ours which worshipped gods made with hands, as was done in days gone by—[19] and that was why our fathers were handed over to the sword, and to be plundered, and so they suffered a great catastrophe before our enemies. [20] But we know no other god but him, and therefore we hope that he will not disdain us or any of our nation. [21] For if we are captured all Judea will be captured and our sanctuary will be plundered; and he will exact of us [n] the penalty for its desecration. [22] And the slaughter of our brethren and the captivity of the land and the desolation of our inheritance—all this he will bring upon our heads among the Gentiles, wherever we serve as slaves; and we shall be an offence and a reproach in the eyes of those who acquire us. [23] For our slavery will not bring us into favour, but the Lord our God will turn it to dishonour.

[24] "Now therefore, brethren, let us set an example to our brethren, for their lives depend upon us, and the sanctuary and the temple and the altar rest upon us. [25] In spite of everything let us give thanks to the Lord our God, who is putting us to the test as he did our forefathers. [26] Remember what he did with Abraham, and how he tested Isaac, and what happened to Jacob in Mesopotamia in Syria, while he was keeping the sheep of Laban, his mother's brother. [27] For he has not tried us with fire, as he did them, to search their hearts, nor has he taken revenge upon us; but the Lord scourges those who draw near to him, in order to admonish them."

[28] Then Uzziah said to her, "All that you have said has been spoken out of a true heart, and there is no one who can deny your words. [29] Today is not the first time your wisdom has been shown, but from the beginning of your life all the people have recognized your understanding, for your heart's disposition is right. [30] But the people were very thirsty, and they compelled us to do for them what we have promised, and made us take an oath which we cannot

---

[l] Some authorities add *Uzziah and* (See verses 28 and 35)　　[m] Or *above*　　[n] Gk *our blood*

break. ³¹ So pray for us, since you are a devout woman, and the Lord will send us rain to fill our cisterns and we will no longer be faint."

32 Judith said to them, "Listen to me. I am about to do a thing which will go down through all generations of our descendants. ³³ Stand at the city gate tonight, and I will go out with my maid; and within the days after which you have promised to surrender the city to our enemies, the Lord will deliver Israel by my hand. ³⁴ Only, do not try to find out what I plan; for I will not tell you until I have finished what I am about to do."

35 Uzziah and the rulers said to her, "Go in peace, and may the Lord God go before you, to take revenge upon our enemies." ³⁶ So they returned from the tent and went to their posts.

9 Then Judith fell upon her face, and put ashes on her head, and uncovered the sackcloth she was wearing; and at the very time when that evening's incense was being offered in the house of God in Jerusalem, Judith cried out to the Lord with a loud voice, and said,

2 "O Lord God of my father Simeon, to whom thou gavest a sword to take revenge on the strangers who had loosed the girdle ° of a virgin to defile her, and uncovered her thigh to put her to shame, and polluted her womb to disgrace her; for thou hast said, 'It shall not be done'—yet they did it. ³ So thou gavest up their rulers to be slain, and their bed, which was ashamed of the deceit they had practised, to be stained with blood, and thou didst strike down slaves along with princes, and princes on their thrones; ⁴ and thou gavest their wives for a prey and their daughters to captivity, and all their booty to be divided among thy beloved sons, who were zealous for thee, and abhorred the pollution of their blood, and called on thee for

° Cn: Gk *womb*

help—O God, my God, hear me also, a widow.

5 "For thou hast done these things and those that went before and those that followed; thou hast designed the things that are now, and those that are to come. Yea, the things thou didst intend came to pass, ⁶ and the things thou didst will presented themselves and said, 'Lo, we are here'; for all thy ways are prepared in advance, and thy judgment is with foreknowledge.

7 "Behold now, the Assyrians are increased in their might; they are exalted, with their horses and riders; they glory in the strength of their foot soldiers; they trust in shield and spear, in bow and sling, and know not that thou art the Lord who crushest wars; the Lord is thy name. ⁸ Break their strength by thy might, and bring down their power in thy anger; for they intend to defile thy sanctuary, and to pollute the tabernacle where thy glorious name rests, and to cast down the horn of thy altar with the sword. ⁹ Behold their pride, and send thy wrath upon their heads; give to me, a widow, the strength to do what I plan. ¹⁰ By the deceit of my lips strike down the slave with the prince and the prince with his servant; crush their arrogance by the hand of a woman.

11 "For thy power depends not upon numbers, nor thy might upon men of strength; for thou art God of the lowly, helper of the oppressed, upholder of the weak, protector of the forlorn, saviour of those without hope. ¹² Hear, O hear me, God of my father, God of the inheritance of Israel, Lord of heaven and earth, Creator of the waters, King of all thy creation, hear my prayer! ¹³ Make my deceitful words to be their wound and stripe, for they have planned cruel things against thy covenant, and against thy consecrated house, and against the top of Zion, and against the house possessed by thy

children. ¹⁴ And cause thy whole nation and every tribe to know and understand that thou art God, the God of all power and might, and that there is no other who protects the people of Israel but thou alone!"

10 When Judith ᵖ had ceased crying out to the God of Israel, and had ended all these words, ² she rose from where she lay prostrate and called her maid and went down into the house where she lived on sabbaths and on her feast days; ³ and she removed the sackcloth which she had been wearing, and took off her widow's garments, and bathed her body with water, and anointed herself with precious ointment, and combed her hair and put on a tiara, and arrayed herself in her gayest apparel, which she used to wear while her husband Manasseh was living. ⁴ And she put sandals on her feet, and put on her anklets and bracelets and rings, and her earrings and all her ornaments, and made herself very beautiful, to entice the eyes of all men who might see her. ⁵ And she gave her maid a bottle of wine and a flask of oil, and filled a bag with parched grain and a cake of dried fruit and fine bread; and she wrapped up all her vessels and gave them to her to carry.

6 Then they went out to the city gate of Bethulia, and found Uzziah standing there with the elders of the city, Chabris and Charmis. ⁷ When they saw her, and noted how her face was altered and her clothing changed, they greatly admired her beauty, and said to her, ⁸ "May the God of our fathers grant you favour and fulfil your plans, that the people of Israel may glory and Jerusalem may be exalted." And she worshipped God.

9 Then she said to them, "Order the gate of the city to be opened for me, and I will go out and accomplish the things about which you spoke with me." So they ordered the young men to open the gate for her, as she

had said. ¹⁰ When they had done this, Judith went out, she and her maid with her; and the men of the city watched her until she had gone down the mountain and passed through the valley and they could no longer see her.

11 The women ᵠ went straight on through the valley; and an Assyrian patrol met her ¹² and took her into custody, and asked her, "To what people do you belong, and where are you coming from, and where are you going?" She replied, "I am a daughter of the Hebrews, but I am fleeing from them, for they are about to be handed over to you to be devoured. ¹³ I am on my way to the presence of Holofernes the commander of your army, to give him a true report; and I will show him a way by which he can go and capture all the hill country without losing one of his men, captured or slain."

14 When the men heard her words, and observed her face—she was in their eyes marvellously beautiful—they said to her, ¹⁵ "You have saved your life by hurrying down to the presence of our lord. Go at once to his tent; some of us will escort you and hand you over to him. ¹⁶ And when you stand before him, do not be afraid in your heart, but tell him just what you have said, and he will treat you well."

17 They chose from their number a hundred men to accompany her and her maid, and they brought them to the tent of Holofernes. ¹⁸ There was great excitement in the whole camp, for her arrival was reported from tent to tent, and they came and stood around her as she waited outside the tent of Holofernes while they told him about her. ¹⁹ And they marvelled at her beauty, and admired the Israelites, judging them by her, and every one said to his neighbour, "Who can despise these people, who have women like this among them? Surely not a man of them had better be left

ᵖ Gk *she* ᵠ Gk *They*

alive, for if we let them go they will be able to ensnare the whole world!"

20 Then Holofernes' companions and all his servants came out and led her into the tent. 21 Holofernes was resting on his bed, under a canopy which was woven with purple and gold and emeralds and precious stones. 22 When they told him of her he came forward to the front of the tent, with silver lamps carried before him. 23 And when Judith came into the presence of Holofernes *r* and his servants, they all marvelled at the beauty of her face; and she prostrated herself and made obeisance to him, and his slaves raised her up.

11 Then Holofernes said to her, "Take courage, woman, and do not be afraid in your heart, for I have never hurt any one who chose to serve Nebuchadnezzar, the king of all the earth. 2 And even now, if your people who live in the hill country had not slighted me, I would never have lifted my spear against them; but they have brought all this on themselves. 3 And now tell me why you have fled from them and have come over to us —since you have come to safety. 4 Have courage; you will live, tonight and from now on. No one will hurt you, but all will treat you well, as they do the servants of my lord King Nebuchadnezzar."

5 Judith replied to him, "Accept the words of your servant, and let your maidservant speak in your presence, and I will tell nothing false to my lord this night. 6 And if you follow out the words of your maidservant, God will accomplish something through you, and my lord will not fail to achieve his purposes. 7 Nebuchadnezzar the king of the whole earth lives, and as his power endures, who has sent you to direct every living soul, not only do men serve him because of you, but also the beasts of the field and the cattle and the birds of the air will live by your power under Nebuchadnezzar and all his

house. 8 For we have heard of your wisdom and skill, and it is reported throughout the whole world that you are the one good man in the whole kingdom, thoroughly informed and marvellous in military strategy.

9 "Now as for the things Achior said in your council, we have heard his words, for the men of Bethulia spared him and he told them all he had said to you. 10 Therefore, my lord and master, do not disregard what he said, but keep it in your mind, for it is true: our nation cannot be punished, nor can the sword prevail against them, unless they sin against their God.

11 "And now, in order that my lord may not be defeated and his purpose frustrated, death will fall upon them, for a sin has overtaken them by which they are about to provoke their God to anger when they do what is wrong. 12 Since their food supply is exhausted and their water has almost given out, they have planned to kill their cattle and have determined to use all that God by his laws has forbidden them to eat. 13 They have decided to consume the first fruits of the grain and the tithes of the wine and oil, which they had consecrated and set aside for the priests who minister in the presence of our God at Jerusalem— although it is not lawful for any of the people so much as to touch these things with their hands. 14 They have sent men to Jerusalem, because even the people living there have been doing this, to bring back to them permission from the senate. 15 When the word reaches them and they proceed to do this, on that very day they will be handed over to you to be destroyed.

16 "Therefore, when I, your servant, learned all this, I fled from them; and God has sent me to accomplish with you things that will astonish the whole world, as many as shall hear about them. 17 For your servant is religious, and serves the God of

r Gk *him*

heaven day and night; therefore, my lord, I will remain with you, and every night your servant will go out into the valley, and I will pray to God and he will tell me when they have committed their sins. 18 And I will come and tell you, and then you shall go out with your whole army, and not one of them will withstand you. 19 Then I will lead you through the middle of Judea, till you come to Jerusalem; and I will set your throne [s] in the midst of it; and you will lead them like sheep that have no shepherd, and not a dog will so much as open its mouth to growl at you. For this has been told me, by my foreknowledge; it was announced to me, and I was sent to tell you."

20 Her words pleased Holofernes and all his servants, and they marvelled at her wisdom and said, 21 "There is not such a woman from one end of the earth to the other, either for beauty of face or wisdom of speech!" 22 And Holofernes said to her, "God has done well to send you before the people, to lend strength to our hands and to bring destruction upon those who have slighted my lord. 23 You are not only beautiful in appearance, but wise in speech; and if you do as you have said, your God shall be my God, and you shall live in the house of King Nebuchadnezzar and be renowned throughout the whole world."

12 Then he commanded them to bring her in where his silver dishes were kept, and ordered them to set a table for her with some of his own food and to serve her with his own wine. 2 But Judith said, "I cannot eat it, lest it be an offence; but I will be provided from the things I have brought with me." 3 Holofernes said to her, "If your supply runs out, where can we get more like it for you? For none of your people is here with us." 4 Judith replied, "As your soul lives, my lord, your servant will not use up the things I have

with me before the Lord carries out by my hand what he has determined to do."

5 Then the servants of Holofernes brought her into the tent, and she slept until midnight. Along toward the morning watch she arose 6 and sent to Holofernes and said, "Let my lord now command that your servant be permitted to go out and pray." 7 So Holofernes commanded his guards not to hinder her. And she remained in the camp for three days, and went out each night to the valley of Bethulia, and bathed at the spring in the camp.[t] 8 When she came up from the spring she prayed the Lord God of Israel to direct her way for the raising up of her people. 9 So she returned clean and stayed in the tent until she ate her food toward evening.

10 On the fourth day Holofernes held a banquet for his slaves only, and did not invite any of his officers. 11 And he said to Bagoas, the eunuch who had charge of all his personal affairs, "Go now and persuade the Hebrew woman who is in your care to join us and eat and drink with us. 12 For it will be a disgrace if we let such a woman go without enjoying her company, for if we do not embrace her she will laugh at us." 13 So Bagoas went out from the presence of Holofernes, and approached her and said, "This beautiful maidservant will please come to my lord and be honoured in his presence, and drink wine and be merry with us, and become today like one of the daughters of the Assyrians who serve in the house of Nebuchadnezzar." 14 And Judith said, "Who am I, to refuse my lord? Surely whatever pleases him I will do at once, and it will be a joy to me until the day of my death!" 15 So she got up and arrayed herself in all her woman's finery, and her maid went and spread on the ground for her before Holofernes the soft fleeces which she had received from

[s] Or *chariot*   [t] Other authorities omit *in the camp*

Bagoas for her daily use, so that she might recline on them when she ate.

16 Then Judith came in and lay down, and Holofernes' heart was ravished with her and he was moved with great desire to possess her; for he had been waiting for an opportunity to deceive her, ever since the day he first saw her. 17 So Holofernes said to her, "Drink now, and be merry with us!" 18 Judith said, "I will drink now, my lord, because my life means more to me today than in all the days since I was born." 19 Then she took and ate and drank before him what her maid had prepared. 20 And Holofernes was greatly pleased with her, and drank a great quantity of wine, much more than he had ever drunk in any one day since he was born.

13 When evening came, his slaves quickly withdrew, and Bagoas closed the tent from outside and shut out the attendants from his master's presence; and they went to bed, for they all were weary because the banquet had lasted long. 2 So Judith was left alone in the tent, with Holofernes stretched out on his bed, for he was overcome with wine.

3 Now Judith had told her maid to stand outside the bedchamber and to wait for her to come out, as she did every day; for she said she would be going out for her prayers. And she had said the same thing to Bagoas. 4 So every one went out, and no one, either small or great, was left in the bedchamber. Then Judith, standing beside his bed, said in her heart, "O Lord God of all might, look in this hour upon the work of my hands for the exaltation of Jerusalem. 5 For now is the time to help thy inheritance, and to carry out my undertaking for the destruction of the enemies who have risen up against us."

6 She went up to the post at the end of the bed, above Holofernes' head, and took down his sword that hung there. 7 She came close to his bed and took hold of the hair of his head, and said, "Give me strength this day, O Lord God of Israel!" 8 And she struck his neck twice with all her might, and severed his head from his body. 9 Then she tumbled his body off the bed and pulled down the canopy from the posts; after a moment she went out, and gave Holofernes' head to her maid, 10 who placed it in her food bag.

Then the two of them went out together, as they were accustomed to go for prayer; and they passed through the camp and circled around the valley and went up the mountain to Bethulia and came to its gates. 11 Judith called out from afar to the watchmen at the gates, "Open, open the gate! God, our God, is still with us, to show his power in Israel, and his strength against our enemies, even as he has done this day!"

12 When the men of her city heard her voice, they hurried down to the city gate and called together the elders of the city. 13 They all ran together, both small and great, for it was unbelievable that she had returned; they opened the gate and admitted them, and they kindled a fire for light, and gathered around them. 14 Then she said to them with a loud voice, "Praise God, O praise him! Praise God, who has not withdrawn his mercy from the house of Israel, but has destroyed our enemies by my hand this very night!"

15 Then she took the head out of the bag and showed it to them, and said, "See, here is the head of Holofernes, the commander of the Assyrian army, and here is the canopy beneath which he lay in his drunken stupor. The Lord has struck him down by the hand of a woman. 16 As the Lord lives, who has protected me in the way I went, it was my face that tricked him to his destruction, and yet he committed no act of sin with me, to defile and shame me."

17 All the people were greatly astonished, and bowed down and wor-

shipped God, and said with one accord, "Blessed art thou, our God, who hast brought into contempt this day the enemies of thy people."

18 And Uzziah said to her, "O daughter, you are blessed by the Most High God above all women on earth; and blessed be the Lord God, who created the heavens and the earth, who has guided you to strike the head of the leader of our enemies. 19 Your hope will never depart from the hearts of men, as they remember the power of God. 20 May God grant this to be a perpetual honour to you, and may he visit you with blessings, because you did not spare your own life when our nation was brought low, but have avenged our ruin, walking in the straight path before our God." And all the people said, "So be it, so be it!"

14 Then Judith said to them, "Listen to me, my brethren, and take this head and hang it upon the parapet of your wall. 2 And as soon as morning comes and the sun rises, let every valiant man take his weapons and go out of the city, and set a captain over them, as if you were going down to the plain against the Assyrian outpost; only do not go down. 3 Then they will seize their arms and go into the camp and rouse the officers of the Assyrian army; and they will rush into the tent of Holofernes, and will not find him. Then fear will come over them, and they will flee before you, 4 and you and all who live within the borders of Israel shall pursue them and cut them down as they flee. 5 But before you do all this, bring Achior the Ammonite to me, and let him see and recognize the man who despised the house of Israel and sent him to us as if to his death."

6 So they summoned Achior from the house of Uzziah. And when he came and saw the head of Holofernes in the hand of one of the men at the gathering of the people, he fell down

on his face and his spirit failed him. 7 And when they raised him up he fell at Judith's feet, and knelt before her, and said, "Blessed are you in every tent of Judah! In every nation those who hear your name will be alarmed. 8 Now tell me what you have done during these days."

Then Judith described to him in the presence of the people all that she had done, from the day she left until the moment of her speaking to them. 9 And when she had finished, the people raised a great shout and made a joyful noise in their city. 10 And when Achior saw all that the God of Israel had done, he believed firmly in God, and was circumcised, and joined the house of Israel, remaining so to this day.

11 As soon as it was dawn they hung the head of Holofernes on the wall, and every man took his weapons, and they went out in companies to the passes in the mountains. 12 And when the Assyrians saw them they sent word to their commanders, and they went to the generals and the captains and to all their officers. 13 So they came to Holofernes' tent and said to the steward in charge of all his personal affairs, "Wake up our lord, for the slaves have been so bold as to come down against us to give battle, in order to be destroyed completely."

14 So Bagoas went in and knocked at the door of the tent, for he supposed that he was sleeping with Judith. 15 But when no one answered, he opened it and went into the bedchamber and found him thrown down on the platform dead, with his head cut off and missing. 16 And he cried out with a loud voice and wept and groaned and shouted, and rent his garments. 17 Then he went to the tent where Judith had stayed, and when he did not find her he rushed out to the people and shouted, 18 "The slaves have tricked us! One Hebrew woman has brought disgrace upon the house of King Nebuchad-

nezzar! For look, here is Holofernes
lying on the ground, and his head is
not on him!"

19 When the leaders of the Assyrian army heard this, they rent their
tunics and were greatly dismayed,
and their loud cries and shouts arose
in the midst of the camp.

15 When the men in the tents
heard it, they were amazed at
what had happened. ² Fear and trembling came over them, so that they
did not wait for one another, but
with one impulse all rushed out and
fled by every path across the plain
and through the hill country. ³ Those
who had camped in the hills around
Bethulia also took to flight. Then
the men of Israel, every one that was
a soldier, rushed out upon them.
⁴ And Uzziah sent men to Betomas-
thaim and Bebai and Choba and
Kola, and to all the frontiers of Israel, to tell what had taken place and
to urge all to rush out upon their
enemies to destroy them. ⁵ And
when the Israelites heard it, with one
accord they fell upon the enemy,ᵘ
and cut them down as far as Choba.
Those in Jerusalem and all the hill
country also came, for they were told
what had happened in the camp of
the enemy; and those in Gilead and
in Galilee outflanked them with great
slaughter, even beyond Damascus
and its borders. ⁶ The rest of the people of Bethulia fell upon the Assyrian camp and plundered it, and were
greatly enriched. ⁷ And the Israelites,
when they returned from the slaughter, took possession of what remained,
and the villages and towns in the hill
country and in the plain got a great
amount of booty, for there was a
vast quantity of it.

8 Then Joakim the high priest, and
the senate of the people of Israel
who lived at Jerusalem, came to witness the good things which the Lord
had done for Israel, and to see Judith
and to greet her. ⁹ And when they
met her they all blessed her with one

accord and said to her, "You are the
exaltation of Jerusalem, you are the
great glory of Israel, you are the great
pride of our nation! ¹⁰ You have done
all this singlehanded; you have done
great good to Israel, and God is well
pleased with it. May the Almighty
Lord bless you for ever!" And all the
people said, "So be it!"

11 So all the people plundered the
camp for thirty days. They gave
Judith the tent of Holofernes and
all his silver dishes and his beds and
his bowls and all his furniture; and
she took them and loaded her mule
and hitched up her carts and piled
the things on them.

12 Then all the women of Israel
gathered to see her, and blessed her,
and some of them performed a dance
for her; and she took branches in
her hands and gave them to the
women who were with her; ¹³ and
they crowned themselves with olive
wreaths, she and those who were
with her; and she went before all the
people in the dance, leading all the
women, while all the men of Israel
followed, bearing their arms and
wearing garlands and with songs on
their lips.

16 Then Judith began this
thanksgiving before all Israel,
and all the people loudly sang this
song of praise. ² And Judith said,

Begin a song to my God with
    tambourines,
  sing to my Lord with cymbals.
Raise to him a new psalm;ᵛ
  exalt him, and call upon his
    name.
³ For God is the Lord who crushes
    wars;
  for he has delivered me out of
    the hands of my pursuers,
  and brought me into his camp,
    in the midst of the people.

⁴ The Assyrian came down from the
    mountains of the north;
  he came with myriads of his
    warriors;

ᵘ Gk *them*   ᵛ Other authorities read *a psalm and praise*

their multitude blocked up the
    valleys,
  their cavalry covered the hills.
5 He boasted that he would burn up
    my territory,
    and kill my young men with the
      sword,
and dash my infants to the ground
  and seize my children as prey,
  and take my virgins as booty.

6 But the Lord Almighty has foiled
    them
  by the hand of a woman.
7 For their mighty one did not fall
    by the hands of the young
    men,
  nor did the sons of the Titans
    smite him,
  nor did tall giants set upon him;
but Judith the daughter of Merari
    undid him
  with the beauty of her counte-
    nance.

8 For she took off her widow's
    mourning
  to exalt the oppressed in Israel.
She anointed her face with oint-
    ment
  and fastened her hair with a
    tiara
  and put on a linen gown to de-
    ceive him.
9 Her sandal ravished his eyes,
  her beauty captivated his mind,
  and the sword severed his neck.
10 The Persians trembled at her bold-
    ness,
  the Medes were daunted at her
    daring.

11 Then my oppressed people shouted
    for joy;
  my weak people shouted *w* and
    the enemy *x* trembled;
  they lifted up their voices, and
    the enemy *x* were turned back.
12 The sons of maidservants have
    pierced them through;
  they were wounded like the chil-
    dren of fugitives,

they perished before the army
  of my Lord.

13 I will sing to my God a new song:
  O Lord, thou art great and glorious,
    wonderful in strength, invin-
    cible.
14 Let all thy creatures serve thee,
  for thou didst speak, and they
    were made.
Thou didst send forth thy Spirit, *y*
  and it formed them;
  there is none that can resist thy
    voice.
15 For the mountains shall be shaken
    to their foundations with the
    waters;
  at thy presence the rocks shall
    melt like wax,
but to those who fear thee
  thou wilt continue to show
    mercy.
16 For every sacrifice as a fragrant
    offering is a small thing,
  and all fat for burnt offerings to
    thee is a very little thing,
but he who fears the Lord shall be
  great for ever.

17 Woe to the nations that rise up
    against my people!
  The Lord Almighty will take
    vengeance on them in the day
    of judgment;
  fire and worms he will give to their
    flesh;
  they shall weep in pain for ever.

18 When they arrived at Jerusalem
they worshipped God. As soon as the
people were purified, they offered
their burnt offerings, their freewill
offerings, and their gifts. 19 Judith
also dedicated to God all the vessels
of Holofernes, which the people had
given her; and the canopy which she
took for herself from his bedchamber
she gave as a votive offering to the
Lord. 20 So the people continued
feasting in Jerusalem before the
sanctuary for three months, and
Judith remained with them.

w Other authorities read *feared*   *x* Gk *they*   *y* Or *breath*

21 After this every one returned home to his own inheritance, and Judith went to Bethulia, and remained on her estate, and was honoured in her time throughout the whole country. 22 Many desired to marry her, but she remained a widow all the days of her life after Manasseh her husband died and was gathered to his people. 23 She became more and more famous, and grew old in her husband's house, until she was one hundred and five years old.

She set her maid free. She died in Bethulia, and they buried her in the cave of her husband Manasseh, 24 and the house of Israel mourned for her seven days. Before she died she distributed her property to all those who were next of kin to her husband Manasseh, and to her own nearest kindred. 25 And no one ever again spread terror among the people of Israel in the days of Judith, or for a long time after her death.

THE ADDITIONS TO THE
BOOK OF ESTHER

*Translated in the order of the Greek version of Esther but with the
chapter and verse numbers of the King James Version*

11 ² In the second year of the
reign of Artaxerxes the Great,
on the first day of Nisan, Mordecai
the son of Jair, son of Shimei, son
of Kish, of the tribe of Benjamin,
had a dream. ³ He was a Jew, dwelling
in the city of Susa, a great man, serving in the court of the king. ⁴ He was
one of the captives whom Nebuchadnezzar king of Babylon had brought
from Jerusalem with Jeconiah king
of Judea. And this was his dream:

5 Behold, noise *a* and confusion,
thunders and earthquake, tumult
upon the earth! ⁶ And behold, two
great dragons came forward, both
ready to fight, and they roared terribly. ⁷ And at their roaring every nation prepared for war, to fight against
the nation of the righteous. ⁸ And
behold, a day of darkness and gloom,
tribulation and distress, affliction and
great tumult upon the earth! ⁹ And
the whole righteous nation was troubled; they feared the evils that
threatened them, and were ready to
perish. ¹⁰ Then they cried to God;
and from their cry, as though from
a tiny spring, there came a great
river, with abundant water; ¹¹ light
came, and the sun rose, and the lowly
were exalted and consumed those
held in honour.

12 Mordecai saw in this dream
what God had determined to do, and
after he awoke he had it on his mind
and sought all day to understand it
in every detail.

12 Now Mordecai took his rest
in the courtyard with Gabatha
and Tharra, the two eunuchs of the
king who kept watch in the courtyard. ² He overheard their conversation and inquired into their purposes,
and learned that they were preparing

a Or *voices*

to lay hands upon Artaxerxes the
king; and he informed the king concerning them. ³ Then the king examined the two eunuchs, and when
they confessed they were led to execution. ⁴ The king made a permanent
record of these things, and Mordecai
wrote an account of them. ⁵ And the
king ordered Mordecai to serve in
the court and rewarded him for these
things. ⁶ But Haman, the son of
Hammedatha, a Bougaean, was in
great honour with the king, and he
sought to injure Mordecai and his
people because of the two eunuchs of
the king.

*Esther 1.1–3.13 follows
here in the Greek*

13 This is a copy of the letter:
"The Great King, Artaxerxes,
to the rulers of the hundred and
twenty-seven provinces from India to
Ethiopia and to the governors under
them, writes thus:

2 "Having become ruler of many
nations and master of the whole
world, not elated with presumption
of authority but always acting rea-
sonably and with kindness, I have
determined to settle the lives of my
subjects in lasting tranquillity and, in
order to make my kingdom peaceable
and open to travel throughout all
its extent, to re-establish the peace
which all men desire.

3 "When I asked my counsellors
how this might be accomplished,
Haman, who excels among us in
sound judgment, and is distinguished
for his unchanging good will and
steadfast fidelity, and has attained
the second place in the kingdom,
⁴ pointed out to us that among all

the nations in the world there is scattered a certain hostile people, who have laws contrary to those of every nation and continually disregard the ordinances of the kings, so that the unifying of the kingdom which we honourably intend cannot be brought about. 5 We understand that this people, and it alone, stands constantly in opposition to all men, perversely following a strange manner of life and laws, and is ill-disposed to our government, doing all the harm they can so that our kingdom may not attain stability.

6 "Therefore we have decreed that those indicated to you in the letters of Haman, who is in charge of affairs and is our second father, shall all, with their wives and children, be utterly destroyed by the sword of their enemies, without pity or mercy, on the fourteenth day of the twelfth month, Adar, of this present year, 7 so that those who have long been and are now hostile may in one day go down in violence to Hades, and leave our government completely secure and untroubled hereafter."

Esther 3.14–4.17 follows here in the Greek

8 Then Mordecai *b* prayed to the Lord, calling to remembrance all the works of the Lord. He said:

9 "O Lord, Lord, King who rulest over all things, for the universe is in thy power and there is no one who can oppose thee if it is thy will to save Israel. 10 For thou hast made heaven and earth and every wonderful thing under heaven, 11 and thou art Lord of all, and there is no one who can resist thee, who art the Lord. 12 Thou knowest all things; thou knowest, O Lord, that it was not in insolence or pride or for any love of glory that I did this, and refused to bow down to this proud Haman. 13 For I would have been

willing to kiss the soles of his feet, to save Israel! 14 But I did this, that I might not set the glory of man above the glory of God, and I will not bow down to any one but to thee, who art my Lord; and I will not do these things in pride. 15 And now, O Lord God and King, God of Abraham, spare thy people; for the eyes of our foes are upon us *c* to annihilate us, and they desire to destroy the inheritance that has been thine from the beginning. 16 Do not neglect thy portion, which thou didst redeem for thyself out of the land of Egypt. 17 Hear my prayer, and have mercy upon thy inheritance; turn our mourning into feasting, that we may live and sing praise to thy name, O Lord; do not destroy the mouth of those who praise thee."

18 And all Israel cried out mightily, for their death was before their eyes.

14 And Esther the queen, seized with deathly anxiety, fled to the Lord; 2 she took off her splendid apparel and put on the garments of distress and mourning, and instead of costly perfumes she covered her head with ashes and dung, and she utterly humbled her body, and every part that she loved to adorn she covered with her tangled hair. 3 And she prayed to the Lord God of Israel, and said:

"O my Lord, thou only art our King; help me, who am alone and have no helper but thee, 4 for my danger is in my hand. 5 Ever since I was born I have heard in the tribe of my family that thou, O Lord, didst take Israel out of all the nations, and our fathers from among all their ancestors, for an everlasting inheritance, and that thou didst do for them all that thou didst promise. 6 And now we have sinned before thee, and thou hast given us into the hands of our enemies, 7 because we glorified their gods. Thou art righteous, O Lord! 8 And now they are

b Gk *he*   *c* Gk *for they are looking upon us*

not satisfied that we are in bitter slavery, but they have covenanted with their idols [9]to abolish what thy mouth has ordained and to destroy thy inheritance, to stop the mouths of those who praise thee and to quench thy altar and the glory of thy house, [10] to open the mouths of the nations for the praise of vain idols, and to magnify for ever a mortal king. [11] O Lord, do not surrender thy sceptre to what has no being; and do not let them mock at our downfall; but turn their plan against themselves, and make an example of the man who began this against us. [12] Remember, O Lord; make thyself known in this time of our affliction, and give me courage, O King of the gods and Master of all dominion! [13] Put eloquent speech in my mouth before the lion, and turn his heart to hate the man who is fighting against us, so that there may be an end of him and those who agree with him. [14] But save us by thy hand, and help me, who am alone and have no helper but thee, O Lord. [15] Thou hast knowledge of all things; and thou knowest that I hate the splendour of the wicked and abhor the bed of the uncircumcised and of any alien. [16] Thou knowest my necessity—that I abhor the sign of my proud position, which is upon my head on the days when I appear in public. I abhor it like a menstruous rag, and I do not wear it on the days when I am at leisure. [17] And thy servant has not eaten at Haman's table, and I have not honoured the king's feast or drunk the wine of the libations. [18] Thy servant has had no joy since the day that I was brought here until now, except in thee, O Lord God of Abraham. [19] O God, whose might is over all, hear the voice of the despairing, and save us from the hands of evil-doers. And save me from my fear!"

15 On the third day, when she ended her prayer, she took off the garments in which she had worshipped, and arrayed herself in splendid attire. [2] Then, majestically adorned, after invoking the aid of the all-seeing God and Saviour, she took her two maids with her, [3] leaning daintily on one, [4] while the other followed carrying her train. [5] She was radiant with perfect beauty, and she looked happy, as if beloved, but her heart was frozen with fear. [6] When she had gone through all the doors, she stood before the king. He was seated on his royal throne, clothed in the full array of his majesty, all covered with gold and precious stones. And he was most terrifying.

7 Lifting his face, flushed with splendour, he looked at her in fierce anger. And the queen faltered, and turned pale and faint, and collapsed upon the head of the maid who went before her. [8] Then God changed the spirit of the king to gentleness, and in alarm he sprang from his throne and took her in his arms until she came to herself. And he comforted her with soothing words, and said to her, [9] "What is it, Esther? I am your brother. Take courage; [10] you shall not die, for our law applies only to the people.[d] Come near."

11 Then he raised the golden sceptre and touched it to her neck; [12] and he embraced her, and said, "Speak to me." [13] And she said to him, "I saw you, my lord, like an angel of God, and my heart was shaken with fear at your glory. [14] For you are wonderful, my lord, and your countenance is full of grace." [15] But as she was speaking, she fell fainting. [16] And the king was agitated, and all his servants sought to comfort her.

*Esther 5.3–8.12 follows
here in the Greek*

16 The following is a copy of this letter:
"The Great King, Artaxerxes, to the rulers of the provinces from India

[d] The meaning of the Greek text of this clause is obscure

to Ethiopia, one hundred and twenty-seven satrapies, and to those who are loyal to our government, greeting.

2 "The more often they are honoured by the too great kindness of their benefactors, the more proud do many men become. 3 They not only seek to injure our subjects, but in their inability to stand prosperity they even undertake to scheme against their own benefactors. 4 They not only take away thankfulness from among men, but, carried away by the boasts of those who know nothing of goodness, they suppose that they will escape the evil-hating justice of God, who always sees everything. 5 And often many of those who are set in places of authority have been made in part responsible for the shedding of innocent blood, and have been involved in irremediable calamities, by the persuasion of friends who have been entrusted with the administration of public affairs, 6 when these men by the false trickery of their evil natures beguile the sincere good will of their sovereigns.

7 "What has been wickedly accomplished through the pestilent behaviour of those who exercise authority unworthily, can be seen not so much from the more ancient records which we hand on as from investigation of matters close at hand. 8 For the future we will take care to render our kingdom quiet and peaceable for all men, 9 by changing our methods and always judging what comes before our eyes with more equitable consideration. 10 For Haman, the son of Hammedatha, a Macedonian (really an alien to the Persian blood, and quite devoid of our kindliness), having become our guest, 11 so far enjoyed the good will that we have for every nation that he was called our father and was continually bowed down to by all as the person second to the royal throne. 12 But, unable to restrain his arrogance, he undertook to deprive us of our kingdom and our life, 13 and with intricate craft and deceit asked for the destruction of Mordecai, our saviour and perpetual benefactor, and of Esther, the blameless partner of our kingdom, together with their whole nation. 14 He thought that in this way he would find us undefended and would transfer the kingdom of the Persians to the Macedonians.

15 "But we find that the Jews, who were consigned to annihilation by this thrice accursed man, are not evildoers but are governed by most righteous laws 16 and are sons of the Most High, the most mighty living God, who has directed the kingdom both for us and for our fathers in the most excellent order.

17 "You will therefore do well not to put in execution the letters sent by Haman the son of Hammedatha, 18 because the man himself who did these things has been hanged at the gate of Susa, with all his household. For God, who rules over all things, has speedily inflicted on him the punishment he deserved.

19 "Therefore post a copy of this letter publicly in every place, and permit the Jews to live under their own laws. 20 And give them reinforcements, so that on the thirteenth day of the twelfth month, Adar, on that very day they may defend themselves against those who attack them at the time of their affliction. 21 For God, who rules over all things, has made this day to be a joy to his chosen people instead of a day of destruction for them.

22 "Therefore you shall observe this with all good cheer as a notable day among your commemorative festivals, 23 so that both now and hereafter it may mean salvation for us and the loyal Persians, but that for those who plot against us it may be a reminder of destruction.

24 "Every city and country, without exception, which does not act accordingly, shall be destroyed in wrath with spear and fire. It shall be made not only impassable for men,

but also most hateful for all time to beasts and birds."

This is followed in the Greek by 8.13–10.3, where the Hebrew Esther ends. The Greek version adds the following:

10 ⁴ And Mordecai said, "These things have come from God. ⁵ For I remember the dream that I had concerning these matters, and none of them has failed to be fulfilled. ⁶ The tiny spring which became a river, and there was light and the sun and abundant water—the river is Esther, whom the king married and made queen. ⁷ The two dragons are Haman and myself. ⁸ The nations are those that gathered to destroy the name of the Jews. ⁹ And my nation, this is Israel, who cried out to God and were saved. The Lord has saved his people; the Lord has delivered us from all these evils; God has done great

^e Or *priest, and Levitas*   ^f Cn: Gk *brought in*

signs and wonders, which have not occurred among the nations. ¹⁰ For this purpose he made two lots, one for the people of God and one for all the nations. ¹¹ And these two lots came to the hour and moment and day of decision before God and among all the nations. ¹² And God remembered his people and vindicated his inheritance. ¹³ So they will observe these days in the month of Adar, on the fourteenth and fifteenth of that month, with an assembly and joy and gladness before God, from generation to generation for ever among his people Israel."

11 ¹ In the fourth year of the reign of Ptolemy and Cleopatra, Dositheus, who said that he was a priest and a Levite,^e and Ptolemy his son brought to Egypt^f the preceding Letter of Purim, which they said was genuine and had been translated by Lysimachus the son of Ptolemy, one of the residents of Jerusalem.

THE WISDOM OF SOLOMON

1 Love righteousness, you rulers
of the earth,
think of the Lord with uprightness,
and seek him with sincerity of
heart;
2 because he is found by those who
do not put him to the test,
and manifests himself to those who
do not distrust him.
3 For perverse thoughts separate
men from God,
and when his power is tested, it
convicts the foolish;
4 because wisdom will not enter a
deceitful soul,
nor dwell in a body enslaved to sin.
5 For a holy and disciplined spirit
will flee from deceit,
and will rise and depart from foolish thoughts,
and will be ashamed at the approach of unrighteousness.

6 For wisdom is a kindly spirit
and will not free a blasphemer
from the guilt of his words;
because God is witness of his in-
most feelings,
and a true observer of his heart,
and a hearer of his tongue.
7 Because the Spirit of the Lord has
filled the world,
and that which holds all things together knows what is said;
8 therefore no one who utters unrighteous things will escape
notice,
and justice, when it punishes, will
not pass him by.
9 For inquiry will be made into the
counsels of an ungodly man,
and a report of his words will come
to the Lord,
to convict him of his lawless deeds;
10 because a jealous ear hears all
things,
and the sound of murmurings does
not go unheard.
11 Beware then of useless murmuring,
and keep your tongue from slander;

because no secret word is without
result,[a]
and a lying mouth destroys the soul.

12 Do not invite death by the error
of your life,
nor bring on destruction by the
works of your hands;
13 because God did not make death,
and he does not delight in the
death of the living.
14 For he created all things that they
might exist,
and the generative forces[b] of the
world are wholesome,
and there is no destructive poison
in them;
and the dominion[c] of Hades is
not on earth.
15 For righteousness is immortal.

16 But ungodly men by their words
and deeds summoned death;[d]
considering him a friend, they
pined away,
and they made a covenant with
him,
because they are fit to belong to
his party.

2 For they reasoned unsoundly,
saying to themselves,
"Short and sorrowful is our life,
and there is no remedy when a
man comes to his end,
and no one has been known to return from Hades.
2 Because we were born by mere
chance,
and hereafter we shall be as though
we had never been;
because the breath in our nostrils
is smoke,
and reason is a spark kindled by
the beating of our hearts.
3 When it is extinguished, the body
will turn to ashes,
and the spirit will dissolve like
empty air.
4 Our name will be forgotten in
time,

a Or will go unpunished   b Or the creatures   c Or palace   d Gk him

87

and no one will remember our
works;
our life will pass away like the
traces of a cloud,
and be scattered like mist
that is chased by the rays of the
sun
and overcome by its heat.
⁵ For our allotted time is the passing
of a shadow,
and there is no return from our
death,
because it is sealed up and no one
turns back.

⁶ "Come, therefore, let us enjoy the
good things that exist,
and make use of the creation to
the full as in youth.
⁷ Let us take our fill of costly wine
and perfumes,
and let no flower of spring pass
by us.
⁸ Let us crown ourselves with rose-
buds before they wither.
⁹ Let none of us fail to share in our
revelry,
everywhere let us leave signs of
enjoyment,
because this is our portion, and
this our lot.
¹⁰ Let us oppress the righteous poor
man;
let us not spare the widow
nor regard the grey hairs of the
aged.
¹¹ But let our might be our law of
right,
for what is weak proves itself to
be useless.

¹² "Let us lie in wait for the righteous
man,
because he is inconvenient to us
and opposes our actions;
he reproaches us for sins against
the law,
and accuses us of sins against our
training.
¹³ He professes to have knowledge of
God,

and calls himself a child *e* of the
Lord.
¹⁴ He became to us a reproof of our
thoughts;
¹⁵ the very sight of him is a burden
to us,
because his manner of life is un-
like that of others,
and his ways are strange.
¹⁶ We are considered by him as something base,
and he avoids our ways as unclean;
he calls the last end of the righteous happy,
and boasts that God is his father.
¹⁷ Let us see if his words are true,
and let us test what will happen at
the end of his life;
¹⁸ for if the righteous man is God's
son, he will help him,
and will deliver him from the hand
of his adversaries.
¹⁹ Let us test him with insult and
torture,
that we may find out how gentle
he is,
and make trial of his forbearance.
²⁰ Let us condemn him to a shameful death,
for, according to what he says, he
will be protected."

²¹ Thus they reasoned, but they were
led astray,
for their wickedness blinded them,
²² and they did not know the secret
purposes of God,
nor hope for the wages of holiness,
nor discern the prize for blameless
souls;
²³ for God created man for incorruption,
and made him in the image of his
own eternity,*f*
²⁴ but through the devil's envy death
entered the world,
and those who belong to his party
experience it.

3   But the souls of the righteous
are in the hand of God,

---

e Or *servant* *f* Other ancient authorities read *nature*

and no torment will ever touch
them.

2 In the eyes of the foolish they
seemed to have died,
and their departure was thought to
be an affliction,

3 and their going from us to be their
destruction;
but they are at peace.

4 For though in the sight of men
they were punished,
their hope is full of immortality.

5 Having been disciplined a little,
they will receive great good,
because God tested them and
found them worthy of himself;

6 like gold in the furnace he tried
them,
and like a sacrificial burnt offering
he accepted them.

7 In the time of their visitation they
will shine forth,
and will run like sparks through
the stubble.

8 They will govern nations and rule
over peoples,
and the Lord will reign over them
for ever.

9 Those who trust in him will understand truth,
and the faithful will abide with
him in love,
because grace and mercy are upon
his elect,
and he watches over his holy ones.*g*

10 But the ungodly will be punished
as their reasoning deserves,
who disregarded the righteous
man *h* and rebelled against the
Lord;

11 for whoever despises wisdom and
instruction is miserable.
Their hope is vain, their labours
are unprofitable,
and their works are useless.

12 Their wives are foolish, and their
children evil;

13 their offspring are accursed.
For blessed is the barren woman
who is undefiled,

who has not entered into a sinful
union;
she will have fruit when God examines souls.

14 Blessed also is the eunuch whose
hands have done no lawless
deed,
and who has not devised wicked
things against the Lord;
for special favour will be shown
him for his faithfulness,
and a place of great delight in the
temple of the Lord.

15 For the fruit of good labours is renowned,
and the root of understanding does
not fail.

16 But children of adulterers will not
come to maturity,
and the offspring of an unlawful
union will perish.

17 Even if they live long they will be
held of no account,
and finally their old age will be
without honour.

18 If they die young, they will have
no hope
and no consolation in the day of
decision.

19 For the end of an unrighteous
generation is grievous.

4 Better than this is childlessness
with virtue,
for in the memory of virtue *i* is
immortality,
because it is known both by God
and by men.

2 When it is present, men imitate *j*
it,
and they long for it when it has
gone;
and throughout all time it marches
crowned in triumph,
victor in the contest for prizes that
are undefiled.

3 But the prolific brood of the ungodly will be of no use,
and none of their illegitimate seedlings will strike a deep root
or take a firm hold.

g The text of this line is uncertain, and it is omitted here by some ancient authorities. Compare 4.15
h Or *what is right* *i* Gk *it* *j* Other ancient authorities read *honour*

⁴ For even if they put forth boughs
for a while,
standing insecurely they will be
shaken by the wind,
and by the violence of the winds
they will be uprooted

⁵ The branches will be broken off
before they come to maturity,
and their fruit will be useless,
not ripe enough to eat, and good
for nothing.

⁶ For children born of unlawful
unions
are witnesses of evil against their
parents when God examines
them.*ᵏ*

⁷ But the righteous man, though he
die early, will be at rest.

⁸ For old age is not honoured for
length of time,
nor measured by number of years;

⁹ but understanding is grey hair for
men,
and a blameless life is ripe old age.

¹⁰ There was one who pleased God
and was loved by him,
and while living among sinners he
was taken up.

¹¹ He was caught up lest evil change
his understanding
or guile deceive his soul.

¹² For the fascination of wickedness
obscures what is good,
and roving desire perverts the innocent mind.

¹³ Being perfected in a short time, he
fulfilled long years;

¹⁴ for his soul was pleasing to the
Lord,
therefore he took him quickly from
the midst of wickedness.

¹⁵ Yet the peoples saw and did not
understand,
nor take such a thing to heart,
that God's grace and mercy are
with his elect,
and he watches over his holy ones.

¹⁶ The righteous man who has died

will condemn the ungodly who
are living,
and youth that is quickly perfected *ˡ* will condemn the pro-
longed old age of the unrighteous man.

¹⁷ For they will see the end of the
wise man,
and will not understand what the
Lord purposed for him,
and for what he kept him safe.

¹⁸ They will see, and will have contempt for him,
but the Lord will laugh them to
scorn.
After this they will become dishonoured corpses,
and an outrage among the dead
for ever;

¹⁹ because he will dash them speechless to the ground,
and shake them from the foundations;
they will be left utterly dry and
barren,
and they will suffer anguish,
and the memory of them will
perish.

²⁰ They will come with dread when
their sins are reckoned up,
and their lawless deeds will convict them to their face.

5 Then the righteous man will
stand with great confidence
in the presence of those who have
afflicted him,
and those who make light of his
labours.

² When they see him, they will be
shaken with dreadful fear,
and they will be amazed at his unexpected salvation.

³ They will speak to one another in
repentance,
and in anguish of spirit they will
groan, and say,

⁴ "This is the man whom we once
held in derision
and made a byword of reproach—
we fools!

ᵏ Gk *at their examination*   *ˡ* Or *ended*

We thought that his life was madness
and that his end was without honour.
5 Why has he been numbered
among the sons of God?
And why is his lot among the
saints?
6 So it was we who strayed from the
way of truth,
and the light of righteousness did
not shine on us,
and the sun did not rise upon us.
7 We took our fill of the paths of
lawlessness and destruction,
and we journeyed through trackless deserts,
but the way of the Lord we have
not known.
8 What has our arrogance profited
us?
And what good has our boasted
wealth brought us?
9 "All those things have vanished
like a shadow,
and like a rumour that passes by;
10 like a ship that sails through the
billowy water,
and when it has passed no trace
can be found,
nor track of its keel in the waves;
11 or as, when a bird flies through the
air,
no evidence of its passage is found;
the light air, lashed by the beat of
its pinions
and pierced by the force of its
rushing flight,
is traversed by the movement of
its wings,
and afterward no sign of its coming
is found there;
12 or as, when an arrow is shot at a
target,
the air, thus divided, comes together at once,
so that no one knows its pathway.
13 So we also, as soon as we were born,
ceased to be,
and we had no sign of virtue to
show,

but were consumed in our wickedness."
14 Because the hope of the ungodly
man is like chaff *m* carried by
the wind,
and like a light hoarfrost *n* driven
away by a storm;
it is dispersed like smoke before
the wind,
and it passes like the remembrance
of a guest who stays but a day.

15 But the righteous live for ever,
and their reward is with the Lord;
the Most High takes care of them.
16 Therefore they will receive a glorious crown
and a beautiful diadem from the
hand of the Lord,
because with his right hand he will
cover them,
and with his arm he will shield
them.
17 The Lord *o* will take his zeal as his
whole armour,
and will arm all creation to repel *p*
his enemies;
18 he will put on righteousness as a
breastplate,
and wear impartial justice as a helmet;
19 he will take holiness as an invincible shield,
20 and sharpen stern wrath for a
sword,
and creation will join with him to
fight against the madmen.
21 Shafts of lightning will fly with
true aim,
and will leap to the target as from a
well-drawn bow of clouds,
22 and hailstones full of wrath will be
hurled as from a catapult;
the water of the sea will rage
against them,
and rivers will relentlessly overwhelm them;
23 a mighty wind will rise against
them,
and like a tempest it will winnow
them away.

Lawlessness will lay waste the
whole earth,
and evil-doing will overturn the
thrones of rulers.

6 Listen therefore, O kings, and
understand;
learn, O judges of the ends of the
earth.
2 Give ear, you that rule over multitudes,
and boast of many nations.
3 For your dominion was given you
from the Lord,
and your sovereignty from the Most
High,
who will search out your works and
inquire into your plans.
4 Because as servants of his kingdom
you did not rule rightly,
nor keep the law,
nor walk according to the purpose
of God,
5 he will come upon you terribly and
swiftly,
because severe judgment falls on
those in high places.
6 For the lowliest man may be par-
doned in mercy,
but mighty men will be mightily
tested.
7 For the Lord of all will not stand
in awe of any one,
nor show deference to greatness;
because he himself made both
small and great,
and he takes thought for all
alike.
8 But a strict inquiry is in store for
the mighty.
9 To you then, O monarchs, my
words are directed,
that you may learn wisdom and not
transgress.
10 For they will be made holy who
observe holy things in holiness,
and those who have been taught
them will find a defence.
11 Therefore set your desire on my
words;
long for them, and you will be instructed.

q Gk Her beginning

12 Wisdom is radiant and unfading,
and she is easily discerned by those
who love her,
and is found by those who seek
her.
13 She hastens to make herself known
to those who desire her.
14 He who rises early to seek her will
have no difficulty,
for he will find her sitting at his
gates.
15 To fix one's thought on her is perfect understanding,
and he who is vigilant on her account will soon be free from
care,
16 because she goes about seeking
those worthy of her,
and she graciously appears to them
in their paths,
and meets them in every thought.

17 The beginning of wisdom *q* is the
most sincere desire for instruction,
and concern for instruction is love
of her,
18 and love of her is the keeping of her
laws,
and giving heed to her laws is as-
surance of immortality,
19 and immortality brings one near to
God;
20 so the desire for wisdom leads to a
kingdom.

21 Therefore if you delight in thrones
and sceptres, O monarchs over
the peoples,
honour wisdom, that you may reign
for ever.
22 I will tell you what wisdom is and
how she came to be,
and I will hide no secrets from
you,
but I will trace her course from
the beginning of creation,
and make the knowledge of her
clear,
and I will not pass by the truth;
23 neither will I travel in the company of sickly envy,

for envy[r] does not associate with
wisdom.

24 A multitude of wise men is the salvation of the world,
and a sensible king is the stability
of his people.

25 Therefore be instructed by my
words, and you will profit.

7 I also am mortal, like all men,
a descendant of the first-formed
child of earth;
and in the womb of a mother I was
moulded into flesh,

2 within the period of ten months,
compacted with blood,
from the seed of a man and the
pleasure of marriage.

3 And when I was born, I began to
breathe the common air,
and fell upon the kindred earth,
and my first sound was a cry, like
that of all.

4 I was nursed with care in swad-
dling cloths.

5 For no king has had a different beginning of existence;

6 there is for all mankind one entrance into life, and a common
departure.

7 Therefore I prayed, and understanding was given me;
I called upon God, and the spirit
of wisdom came to me.

8 I preferred her to sceptres and
thrones,
and I accounted wealth as nothing
in comparison with her.

9 Neither did I liken to her any
priceless gem,
because all gold is but a little sand
in her sight,
and silver will be accounted as clay
before her.

10 I loved her more than health and
beauty,
and I chose to have her rather than
light,
because her radiance never ceases.

11 All good things came to me along
with her,

and in her hands uncounted
wealth.

12 I rejoiced in them all, because wisdom leads them;
but I did not know that she was
their mother.

13 I learned without guile and I impart without grudging;
I do not hide her wealth,

14 for it is an unfailing treasure for
men;
those who get it obtain friendship
with God,
commended for the gifts that come
from instruction.

15 May God grant that I speak with
judgment
and have thoughts worthy of what
I have received,
for he is the guide even of wisdom
and the corrector of the wise.

16 For both we and our words are in
his hand,
as are all understanding and skill
in crafts.

17 For it is he who gave me unerring
knowledge of what exists,
to know the structure of the world
and the activity of the elements;

18 the beginning and end and middle of times,
the alternations of the solstices and
the changes of the seasons,

19 the cycles of the year and the con-
stellations of the stars,

20 the natures of animals and the
tempers of wild beasts,
the powers of spirits[s] and the rea-
sonings of men,
the varieties of plants and the virtues of roots;

21 I learned both what is secret and
what is manifest,

22 for wisdom, the fashioner of all
things, taught me.

For in her there is a spirit that is
intelligent, holy,
unique, manifold, subtle,
mobile, clear, unpolluted,

[r] Gk *this*　[s] Or *winds*

distinct, invulnerable, loving the good, keen,

irresistible, 23 beneficent, humane, steadfast, sure, free from anxiety, all-powerful, overseeing all, and penetrating through all spirits that are intelligent and pure and most subtle.

24 For wisdom is more mobile than any motion;

because of her pureness she pervades and penetrates all things.

25 For she is a breath of the power of God,

and a pure emanation of the glory of the Almighty;

therefore nothing defiled gains entrance into her.

26 For she is a reflection of eternal light,

a spotless mirror of the working of God,

and an image of his goodness.

27 Though she is but one, she can do all things,

and while remaining in herself, she renews all things;

in every generation she passes into holy souls

and makes them friends of God, and prophets;

28 for God loves nothing so much as the man who lives with wisdom.

29 For she is more beautiful than the sun,

and excels every constellation of the stars.

Compared with the light she is found to be superior,

30 for it is succeeded by the night,

but against wisdom evil does not prevail.

8 She reaches mightily from one end of the earth to the other, and she orders all things well.

2 I loved her and sought her from my youth,

and I desired to take her for my bride,

and I became enamoured of her beauty.

3 She glorifies her noble birth by living with God,

and the Lord of all loves her.

4 For she is an initiate in the knowledge of God,

and an associate in his works.

5 If riches are a desirable possession in life,

what is richer than wisdom who effects all things?

6 And if understanding is effective, who more than she is fashioner of what exists?

7 And if any one loves righteousness, her labours are virtues;

for she teaches self-control and prudence,

justice and courage;

nothing in life is more profitable for men than these.

8 And if any one longs for wide experience,

she knows the things of old, and infers the things to come;

she understands turns of speech and the solutions of riddles;

she has foreknowledge of signs and wonders

and of the outcome of seasons and times.

9 Therefore I determined to take her to live with me,

knowing that she would give me good counsel

and encouragement in cares and grief.

10 Because of her I shall have glory among the multitudes

and honour in the presence of the elders, though I am young.

11 I shall be found keen in judgment, and in the sight of rulers I shall be admired.

12 When I am silent they will wait for me,

and when I speak they will give heed;

and when I speak at greater length they will put their hands on their mouths.

13 Because of her I shall have immortality,

and leave an everlasting remembrance to those who come after me.

14 I shall govern peoples,
and nations will be subject to me;
15 dread monarchs will be afraid of
me when they hear of me;
among the people I shall show
myself capable, and courageous
in war.
16 When I enter my house, I shall
find rest with her,
for companionship with her has
no bitterness,
and life with her has no pain, but
gladness and joy.
17 When I considered these things
inwardly,
and thought upon them in my
mind,
that in kinship with wisdom there
is immortality,
18 and in friendship with her, pure
delight,
and in the labours of her hands,
unfailing wealth,
and in the experience of her company, understanding,
and renown in sharing her words,
I went about seeking how to get
her for myself.
19 As a child I was by nature well-
endowed,
and a good soul fell to my lot;
20 or rather, being good, I entered an
undefiled body.
21 But I perceived that I would not
possess wisdom unless God gave
her to me—
and it was a mark of insight to
know whose gift she was—
so I appealed to the Lord and besought him,
and with my whole heart I said:

9 "O God of my fathers and Lord
of mercy,
who hast made all things by thy
word,
2 and by thy wisdom hast formed
man,
to have dominion over the creatures thou hast made,
3 and rule the world in holiness and
righteousness,

and pronounce judgment in uprightness of soul,
4 give me the wisdom that sits by
thy throne,
and do not reject me from among
thy servants.
5 For I am thy slave and the son of
thy maidservant,
a man who is weak and short-lived,
with little understanding of judgment and laws;
6 for even if one is perfect among
the sons of men,
yet without the wisdom that comes
from thee he will be regarded as
nothing.
7 Thou hast chosen me to be king of
thy people
and to be judge over thy sons and
daughters.
8 Thou hast given command to build
a temple on thy holy mountain,
and an altar in the city of thy
habitation,
a copy of the holy tent which thou
didst prepare from the beginning.
9 With thee is wisdom, who knows
thy works
and was present when thou didst
make the world,
and who understands what is
pleasing in thy sight
and what is right according to thy
commandments.
10 Send her forth from the holy
heavens,
and from the throne of thy glory
send her,
that she may be with me and toil,
and that I may learn what is pleasing to thee.
11 For she knows and understands all
things,
and she will guide me wisely in my
actions
and guard me with her glory.
12 Then my works will be acceptable,
and I shall judge thy people justly,
and shall be worthy of the throne *t*
of my father.

t Gk *thrones*

¹³ For what man can learn the counsel of God?

Or who can discern what the Lord wills?

¹⁴ For the reasoning of mortals is worthless,

and our designs are likely to fail,

¹⁵ for a perishable body weighs down the soul,

and this earthy tent burdens the thoughtful [u] mind.

¹⁶ We can hardly guess at what is on earth,

and what is at hand we find with labour;

but who has traced out what is in the heavens?

¹⁷ Who has learned thy counsel, unless thou hast given wisdom

and sent thy holy Spirit from on high?

¹⁸ And thus the paths of those on earth were set right,

and men were taught what pleases thee,

and were saved by wisdom."

10 Wisdom [v] protected the first-formed father of the world,

when he alone had been created;

she delivered him from his transgression,

² and gave him strength to rule all things.

³ But when an unrighteous man departed from her in his anger,

he perished because in rage he slew his brother.

⁴ When the earth was flooded because of him, wisdom again saved it,

steering the righteous man by a paltry piece of wood.

⁵ Wisdom [w] also, when the nations in wicked agreement had been confounded,

recognized the righteous man and preserved him blameless before God,

and kept him strong in the face of his compassion for his child.

⁶ Wisdom [w] rescued a righteous man when the ungodly were perishing;

he escaped the fire that descended on the Five Cities.[x]

⁷ Evidence of their wickedness still remains:

a continually smoking wasteland,

plants bearing fruit that does not ripen,

and a pillar of salt standing as a monument to an unbelieving soul.

⁸ For because they passed wisdom by,

they not only were hindered from recognizing the good,

but also left for mankind a reminder of their folly,

so that their failures could never go unnoticed.

⁹ Wisdom rescued from troubles those who served her.

¹⁰ When a righteous man fled from his brother's wrath,

she guided him on straight paths;

she showed him the kingdom of God,

and gave him knowledge of angels; [y]

she prospered him in his labours,

and increased the fruit of his toil.

¹¹ When his oppressors were covetous,

she stood by him and made him rich.

¹² She protected him from his enemies,

and kept him safe from those who lay in wait for him;

in his arduous contest she gave him the victory,

so that he might learn that godliness is more powerful than anything.

¹³ When a righteous man was sold, wisdom [z] did not desert him,

but delivered him from sin.

She descended with him into the dungeon,

---

[u] Or *anxious*   [v] Gk *She*   [w] Gk *She*   [x] Or *Pentapolis*   [y] Or *of holy things*   [z] Gk *she*

14 and when he was in prison she did
not leave him.
until she brought him the sceptre
of a kingdom
and authority over his masters.
Those who accused him she showed
to be false,
and she gave him everlasting honour.

15 A holy people and blameless race
wisdom *a* delivered from a nation
of oppressors.
16 She entered the soul of a servant
of the Lord,
and withstood dread kings with
wonders and signs.
17 She gave to holy men the reward
of their labours;
she guided them along a marvellous way,
and became a shelter to them by
day,
and a starry flame through the
night.
18 She brought them over the Red
Sea,
and led them through deep waters;
19 but she drowned their enemies,
and cast them up from the depth
of the sea.
20 Therefore the righteous plundered
the ungodly;
they sang hymns, O Lord, to thy
holy name,
and praised with one accord thy
defending hand,
21 because wisdom opened the mouth
of the dumb,
and made the tongues of babes
speak clearly.

11 Wisdom *a* prospered their
works by the hand of a holy
prophet.
2 They journeyed through an uninhabited wilderness,
and pitched their tents in untrodden places.
3 They withstood their enemies and
fought off their foes.
4 When they thirsted they called
upon thee,

and water was given them out of
flinty rock,
and slaking of thirst from hard stone.
5 For through the very things by
which their enemies were punished,
they themselves received benefit
in their need.
6 Instead of the fountain of an everflowing river,
stirred up and defiled with blood
7 in rebuke for the decree to slay
the infants,
thou gavest them abundant water
unexpectedly,
8 showing by their thirst at that time
how thou didst punish their enemies.
9 For when they were tried, though
they were being disciplined in
mercy,
they learned how the ungodly were
tormented when judged in
wrath.
10 For thou didst test them as a father
does in warning,
but thou didst examine the ungodly *b* as a stern king does in
condemnation.
11 Whether absent or present, they
were equally distressed,
12 for a twofold grief possessed them,
and a groaning at the memory of
what had occurred.
13 For when they heard that through
their own punishments
the righteous *c* had received benefit, they perceived it was the
Lord's doing.
14 For though they had mockingly
rejected him who long before
had been cast out and exposed,
at the end of the events they marvelled at him,
for their thirst was not like that of
the righteous.

15 In return for their foolish and
wicked thoughts,
which led them astray to worship
irrational serpents and worthless
animals,

a Gk *She*   *b* Gk *those*   *c* Gk *they*

thou didst send upon them a multitude of irrational creatures to punish them,

16 that they might learn that one is punished by the very things by which he sins.

17 For thy all-powerful hand,
which created the world out of formless matter,
did not lack the means to send upon them a multitude of bears, or bold lions,

18 or newly created unknown beasts full of rage,
or such as breathe out fiery breath,
or belch forth a thick pall of smoke,
or flash terrible sparks from their eyes;

19 not only could their damage exterminate men,[d]
but the mere sight of them could kill by fright.

20 Even apart from these, men[e] could fall at a single breath
when pursued by justice
and scattered by the breath of thy power.
But thou hast arranged all things by measure and number and weight.

21 For it is always in thy power to show great strength,
and who can withstand the might of thy arm?

22 Because the whole world before thee is like a speck that tips the scales,
and like a drop of morning dew that falls upon the ground.

23 But thou art merciful to all, for thou canst do all things,
and thou dost overlook men's sins, that they may repent.

24 For thou lovest all things that exist,
and hast loathing for none of the things which thou hast made,
for thou wouldst not have made anything if thou hadst hated it.

25 How would anything have endured if thou hadst not willed it?
Or how would anything not called forth by thee have been preserved?

26 Thou sparest all things, for they are thine, O Lord who lovest the living.

12 For thy immortal spirit is in all things.

2 Therefore thou dost correct little by little those who trespass,
and dost remind and warn them of the things wherein they sin,
that they may be freed from wickedness and put their trust in thee, O Lord.

3 Those who dwelt of old in thy holy land

4 thou didst hate for their detestable practices,
their works of sorcery and unholy rites,

5 their merciless slaughter[f] of children,
and their sacrificial feasting on human flesh and blood.
These initiates from the midst of a heathen cult,[g]

6 these parents who murder helpless lives,
thou didst will to destroy by the hands of our fathers,

7 that the land most precious of all to thee
might receive a worthy colony of the servants[h] of God.

8 But even these thou didst spare, since they were but men,
and didst send wasps[i] as forerunners of thy army,
to destroy them little by little,

9 though thou wast not unable to give the ungodly into the hands of the righteous in battle,
or to destroy them at one blow by dread wild beasts or thy stern word.

10 But judging them little by little thou gavest them a chance to repent,

---

[d] Gk *them*   [e] Gk *they*   [f] Cn: Gk *slaughterers*   [g] The Gk text of this line is uncertain
[h] Or *children*   [i] Or *hornets*

though thou wast not unaware
that their origin [j] was evil
and their wickedness inborn,
and that their way of thinking
would never change.
11 For they were an accursed race
from the beginning,
and it was not through fear of any
one that thou didst leave them
unpunished for their sins.

12 For who will say, "What hast thou
done?"
Or who will resist thy judgment?
Who will accuse thee for the destruction of nations which thou
didst make?
Or who will come before thee to
plead as an advocate for unrighteous men?
13 For neither is there any god besides
thee, whose care is for all men, [k]
to whom thou shouldst prove that
thou hast not judged unjustly;
14 nor can any king or monarch con-
front thee about those whom
thou hast punished.
15 Thou art righteous and rulest all
things righteously,
deeming it alien to thy power
to condemn him who does not deserve to be punished.
16 For thy strength is the source of
righteousness,
and thy sovereignty over all causes
thee to spare all.
17 For thou dost show thy strength
when men doubt the complete-
ness of thy power,
and dost rebuke any insolence
among those who know it. [l]
18 Thou who art sovereign in strength
dost judge with mildness,
and with great forebearance thou
dost govern us;
for thou hast power to act whenever thou dost choose.

19 Through such works thou hast
taught thy people

that the righteous man must be
kind,
and thou hast filled thy sons with
good hope,
because thou givest repentance for
sins.
20 For if thou didst punish with such
great care and indulgence [m]
the enemies of thy servants [n] and
those deserving of death,
granting them time and opportunity to give up their wickedness,
21 with what strictness thou hast
judged thy sons,
to whose fathers thou gavest oaths
and covenants full of good promises!
22 So while chastening us thou
scourgest our enemies ten thousand times more,
so that we may meditate upon thy
goodness when we judge,
and when we are judged we may
expect mercy.

23 Therefore those who in folly of
life lived unrighteously
thou didst torment through their
own abominations.
24 For they went far astray on the
paths of error,
accepting as gods those animals
which even their enemies [o] despised;
they were deceived like foolish
babes.
25 Therefore, as to thoughtless children,
thou didst send thy judgment to
mock them.
26 But those who have not heeded
the warning of light rebukes
will experience the deserved judgment of God.
27 For when in their suffering they
became incensed
at those creatures which they had
thought to be gods, being punished by means of them,
they saw and recognized as the true

j Or *nature*   k Or *all things*   l The Gk text of this line is uncertain
m Some ancient authorities omit *and indulgence*; others read *and entreaty*   n Or *children*
o Gk *they*

God him whom they had before
refused to know.
Therefore the utmost condemnation came upon them.

13

For all men who were ignor-
ant of God were foolish by
nature;
and they were unable from the
good things that are seen to
know him who exists,
nor did they recognize the craftsman while paying heed to his
works;
2 but they supposed that either fire
or wind or swift air,
or the circle of the stars, or turbu-
lent water,
or the luminaries of heaven were
the gods that rule the world.
3 If through delight in the beauty
of these things men [p] assumed
them to be gods,
let them know how much better
than these is their Lord,
for the author of beauty created
them.
4 And if men [p] were amazed at their
power and working,
let them perceive from them
how much more powerful is he
who formed them.
5 For from the greatness and beauty
of created things
comes a corresponding perception
of their Creator.
6 Yet these men are little to be
blamed,
for perhaps they go astray
while seeking God and desiring to
find him.
7 For as they live among his works
they keep searching,
and they trust in what they see,
because the things that are seen
are beautiful.
8 Yet again, not even they are to be
excused;
9 for if they had the power to know
so much
that they could investigate the
world,

how did they fail to find sooner
the Lord of these things?

10 But miserable, with their hopes
set on dead things, are the men
who give the name "gods" to the
works of men's hands,
gold and silver fashioned with skill,
and likenesses of animals,
or a useless stone, the work of an
ancient hand.
11 A skilled woodcutter may saw
down a tree easy to handle
and skilfully strip off all its bark,
and then with pleasing workmanship
make a useful vessel that serves
life's needs,
12 and burn the castoff pieces of his
work
to prepare his food, and eat his fill.
13 But a castoff piece from among
them, useful for nothing,
a stick crooked and full of knots,
he takes and carves with care in his
leisure,
and shapes it with skill gained in
idleness; [q]
he forms it like the image of a
man,
14 or makes it like some worthless
animal,
giving it a coat of red paint and
colouring its surface red
and covering every blemish in it
with paint;
15 then he makes for it a niche that
befits it,
and sets it in the wall, and fastens
it there with iron.
16 So he takes thought for it, that it
may not fall,
because he knows that it cannot
help itself,
for it is only an image and has
need of help.
17 When he prays about possessions
and his marriage and children,
he is not ashamed to address a lifeless thing.
18 For health he appeals to a thing
that is weak;

[p] Gk *they*   [q] Other authorities read *with intelligent skill*

for life he prays to a thing that is
dead;

for aid he entreats a thing that is
utterly inexperienced;

for a prosperous journey, a thing
that cannot take a step;

19 for money-making and work and
success with his hands

he asks strength of a thing whose
hands have no strength.

14 Again, one preparing to sail
and about to voyage over
raging waves

calls upon a piece of wood more
fragile than the ship which carries him.

2 For it was desire for gain that
planned that vessel,

and wisdom was the craftsman who
built it;

3 but it is thy providence, O Father,
that steers its course,

because thou hast given it a path
in the sea,

and a safe way through the waves,

4 showing that thou canst save from
every danger,

so that even if a man lacks skill, he
may put to sea.

5 It is thy will that the works of thy
wisdom should not be without
effect;

therefore men trust their lives even
to the smallest piece of wood,

and passing through the billows on
a raft they come safely to land.

6 For even in the beginning, when
arrogant giants were perishing,

the hope of the world took refuge
on a raft,

and guided by thy hand left to the
world the seed of a new generation.

7 For blessed is the wood by which
righteousness comes.

8 But the idol made with hands is
accursed, and so is he who made
it;

because he did the work, and the
perishable thing was named a god.

9 For equally hateful to God are the
ungodly man and his ungodliness,

10 for what was done will be punished
together with him who did it.

11 Therefore there will be a visitation
also upon the heathen idols,

because, though part of what God
created, they became an abomination,

and became traps for the souls of
men

and a snare to the feet of the foolish.

12 For the idea of making idols was
the beginning of fornication,

and the invention of them was the
corruption of life,

13 for neither have they existed from
the beginning

nor will they exist for ever.

14 For through the vanity of men
they entered the world,

and therefore their speedy end has
been planned.

15 For a father, consumed with grief
at an untimely bereavement,

made an image of his child, who
had been suddenly taken from
him:

and he now honoured as a god what
was once a dead human being,

and handed on to his dependents
secret rites and initiations.

16 Then the ungodly custom, grown
strong with time, was kept as a
law,

and at the command of monarchs
graven images were worshipped.

17 When men could not honour monarchs *r* in their presence, since
they lived at a distance,

they imagined their appearance
far away,

and made a visible image of the
king whom they honoured,

so that by their zeal they might
flatter the absent one as though
present.

18 Then the ambition of the craftsman impelled

r Gk *them*

101

even those who did not know the
king to intensify their worship.

19 For he, perhaps wishing to please
his ruler,
skilfully forced the likeness to take
more beautiful form,

20 and the multitude, attracted by the
charm of his work,
now regarded as an object of worship the one whom shortly before they had honoured as a man.

21 And this became a hidden trap for
mankind,
because men, in bondage to misfortune or to royal authority,
bestowed on objects of stone or
wood the name that ought not
to be shared.

22 Afterward it was not enough for
them to err about the knowledge of God,
but they live in great strife due to
ignorance,
and they call such great evils
peace.

23 For whether they kill children in
their initiations, or celebrate secret mysteries,
or hold frenzied revels with strange
customs,

24 they no longer keep either their
lives or their marriages pure,
but they either treacherously kill
one another, or grieve one another by adultery,

25 and all is a raging riot of blood and
murder, theft and deceit, corruption, faithlessness, tumult,
perjury,

26 confusion over what is good, forgetfulness of favours,
pollution of souls, sex perversion,
disorder in marriage, adultery, and
debauchery.

27 For the worship of idols not to be
named
is the beginning and cause and end
of every evil.

28 For their worshippers *s* either rave
in exultation, or prophesy lies,

or live unrighteously, or readily
commit perjury;

29 for because they trust in lifeless
idols
they swear wicked oaths and expect to suffer no harm.

30 But just penalties will overtake
them on two counts:
because they thought wickedly of
God in devoting themselves to
idols,
and because in deceit they swore
unrighteously through contempt
for holiness.

31 For it is not the power of the things
by which men swear,*t*
but the just penalty for those who
sin,
that always pursues the transgression of the unrighteous.

15 But thou, our God, art kind
and true,
patient, and ruling all things *u* in
mercy.

2 For even if we sin we are thine,
knowing thy power;
but we will not sin, because we
know that we are accounted
thine.

3 For to know thee is complete
righteousness,
and to know thy power is the root
of immortality.

4 For neither has the evil intent of
human art misled us,
nor the fruitless toil of painters,
a figure stained with varied colours,

5 whose appearance arouses yearn-
ing in fools,
so that they desire *v* the lifeless
form of a dead image.

6 Lovers of evil things and fit for
such objects of hope *w*
are those who either make or desire or worship them.

7 For when a potter kneads the soft
earth
and laboriously moulds each vessel
for our service,

---

s Gk *they*   *t* Or *of the oaths men swear*   *u* Or *ruling the universe*   *v* Gk *and he desires*
w Gk *such hopes*

he fashions out of the same clay
both the vessels that serve clean
uses
and those for contrary uses, making all in like manner;
but which shall be the use of each
of these
the worker in clay decides.

8 With misspent toil, he forms a
futile god from the same clay—
this man who was made of earth
a short time before
and after a little while goes to the
earth from which he was taken,
when he is required to return the
soul that was lent him.

9 But he is not concerned that he is
destined to die
or that his life is brief,
but he competes with workers in
gold and silver,
and imitates workers in copper;
and he counts it his glory that he
moulds counterfeit gods.

10 His heart is ashes, his hope is
cheaper than dirt,
and his life is of less worth than
clay,

11 because he failed to know the one
who formed him
and inspired him with an active
soul
and breathed into him a living
spirit.

12 But he *x* considered our existence
an idle game,
and life a festival held for profit,
for he says one must get money
however one can, even by base
means.

13 For this man, more than all others,
knows that he sins
when he makes from earthy matter
fragile vessels and graven images.

14 But most foolish, and more miserable than an infant,
are all the enemies who oppressed
thy people.

15 For they thought that all their
heathen idols were gods,

though these have neither the use
of their eyes to see with,
nor nostrils with which to draw
breath,
nor ears with which to hear,
nor fingers to feel with,
and their feet are of no use for
walking.

16 For a man made them,
and one whose spirit is borrowed
formed them;
for no man can form a god which
is like himself.

17 He is mortal, and what he makes
with lawless hands is dead,
for he is better than the objects he
worships,
since *v* he has life, but they never
have.

18 The enemies of thy people *z* worship even the most hateful animals,
which are worse than all others,
when judged by their lack of intelligence;

19 and even as animals they are not
so beautiful in appearance that
one would desire them,
but they have escaped both the
praise of God and his blessing.

16 Therefore those men were de-
servedly punished through
such creatures,
and were tormented by a multitude of animals.

2 Instead of this punishment thou
didst show kindness to thy
people,
and thou didst prepare quails to
eat,
a delicacy to satisfy the desire of
appetite;

3 in order that those men, when
they desired food,
might lose the least remnant of
appetite *a*
because of the odious creatures
sent to them,
while thy people,*b* after suffering
want a short time,

x Other authorities read *they*   *v* Other authorities read *of which*   *z* Gk *They*
a Gk *loathed the necessary appetite*   *b* Gk *they*

might partake of delicacies.

⁴ For it was necessary that upon
   those oppressors inexorable want
   should come,
 while to these it was merely shown
   how their enemies were being
   tormented.

⁵ For when the terrible rage of wild
   beasts came upon thy people *c*
 and they were being destroyed by
   the bites of writhing serpents,
 thy wrath did not continue to the
   end;
⁶ they were troubled for a little
   while as a warning,
 and received a token of deliverance
   to remind them of thy law's
   command.
⁷ For he who turned toward it was
   saved, not by what he saw,
 but by thee, the Saviour of all.
⁸ And by this also thou didst con-
   vince our enemies
 that it is thou who deliverest from
   every evil.
⁹ For they were killed by the bites
   of locusts and flies,
 and no healing was found for them,
 because they deserved to be punished by such things;
¹⁰ but thy sons were not conquered
   even by the teeth of venomous
   serpents,
 for thy mercy came to their help
   and healed them.
¹¹ To remind them of thy oracles
   they were bitten,
 and then were quickly delivered,
 lest they should fall into deep forgetfulness
 and become unresponsive *d* to thy
   kindness.
¹² For neither herb nor poultice cured
   them,
 but it was thy word, O Lord, which
   heals all men.
¹³ For thou hast power over life and
   death;
 thou dost lead men down to the
   gates of Hades and back again.

¹⁴ A man in his wickedness kills
   another,
 but he cannot bring back the departed spirit,
 nor set free the imprisoned soul.

¹⁵ To escape from thy hand is impossible;
¹⁶ for the ungodly, refusing to know
   thee,
 were scourged by the strength of
   thy arm,
 pursued by unusual rains and hail
   and relentless storms,
 and utterly consumed by fire.
¹⁷ For—most incredible of all—in
   the water, which quenches all
   things,
 the fire had still greater effect,
 for the universe defends the righteous.
¹⁸ At one time the flame was restrained,
 so that it might not consume the
   creatures sent against the ungodly,
 but that seeing this they might
   know
 that they were being pursued by
   the judgment of God;
¹⁹ and at another time even in the
   midst of water it burned more
   intensely than fire,
 to destroy the crops of the unrighteous land.
²⁰ Instead of these things thou didst
   give thy people the food of
   angels,
 and without their toil thou didst
   supply them from heaven with
   bread ready to eat,
 providing every pleasure and suited
   to every taste.
²¹ For thy sustenance manifested thy
   sweetness toward thy children;
 and the bread, ministering *e* to the
   desire of the one who took it,
 was changed to suit every one's
   liking.
²² Snow and ice withstood fire without melting,

c Gk *them*   *d* The meaning of the Greek is obscure   *e* Gk *and it, ministering*

so that they might know that the
crops of their enemies
were being destroyed by the fire
that blazed in the hail
and flashed in the showers of rain;
23 whereas the fire,*f* in order that the
righteous might be fed,
even forgot its native power.

24 For the creation, serving thee who
hast made it,
exerts itself to punish the unrighteous,
and in kindness relaxes on behalf
of those who trust in thee.
25 Therefore at that time also,
changed into all forms,
it served thy all-nourishing bounty,
according to the desire of those
who had need,*g*
26 so that thy sons, whom thou didst
love, O Lord, might learn
that it is not the production of
crops that feeds man,
but that thy word preserves those
who trust in thee.
27 For what was not destroyed by fire
was melted when simply warmed
by a fleeting ray of the sun,
28 to make it known that one must rise
before the sun to give thee thanks,
and must pray to thee at the dawning of the light;
29 for the hope of an ungrateful man
will melt like wintry frost,
and flow away like waste water.

17 Great are thy judgments and
hard to describe;
therefore uninstructed souls have
gone astray.
2 For when lawless men supposed
that they held the holy nation
in their power,
they themselves lay as captives of
darkness and prisoners of long
night,
shut in under their roofs, exiles
from eternal providence.

3 For thinking that in their secret
sins they were unobserved
behind a dark curtain of forgetfulness,
they were scattered, terribly *h*
alarmed,
and appalled by spectres.
4 For not even the inner chamber
that held them protected them
from fear,
but terrifying sounds rang out
around them,
and dismal phantoms with gloomy
faces appeared.
5 And no power of fire was able to
give light,
nor did the brilliant flames of the
stars
avail to illumine that hateful night.
6 Nothing was shining through to
them
except a dreadful, self-kindled fire,
and in terror they deemed the
things which they saw
to be worse than that unseen appearance.
7 The delusions of their magic art
lay humbled,
and their boasted wisdom was
scornfully rebuked.
8 For those who promised to drive
off the fears and disorders of a
sick soul
were sick themselves with ridicu-
lous fear.
9 For even if nothing disturbing
frightened them,
yet, scared by the passing of beasts
and the hissing of serpents,
10 they perished in trembling fear,
refusing to look even at the air,
though it nowhere could be
avoided.
11 For wickedness is a cowardly thing,
condemned by its own testi-
mony;*i*
distressed by conscience, it has always exaggerated *j* the difficulties.

---

f Gk *this*   *g* Or *who made supplication*
h Or, with other authorities, *unobserved, they were darkened behind a dark curtain of forgetfulness,
terribly*   *i* The Gk text of this line is uncertain and probably corrupt
j Other ancient authorities read *anticipated*

12 For fear is nothing but surrender
of the helps that come from
reason;
13 and the inner expectation of help,
being weak,
prefers ignorance of what causes
the torment.
14 But throughout the night, which
was really powerless,
and which beset them from the
recesses of powerless Hades,
they all slept the same sleep,
15 and now were driven by monstrous
spectres,
and now were paralyzed by their
souls' surrender,
for sudden and unexpected fear
overwhelmed them.
16 And whoever was there fell down,
and thus was kept shut up in a
prison not made of iron;
17 for whether he was a farmer or a
shepherd
or a workman who toiled in the
wilderness,
he was seized, and endured the
inescapable fate;
for with one chain of darkness they
all were bound.
18 Whether there came a whistling
wind,
or a melodious sound of birds in
wide-spreading branches,
or the rhythm of violently rushing
water,
19 or the harsh crash of rocks hurled
down,
or the unseen running of leaping
animals,
or the sound of the most savage
roaring beasts,
or an echo thrown back from a
hollow of the mountains,
it paralyzed them with terror.
20 For the whole world was illumined
with brilliant light,
and was engaged in unhindered
work,
21 while over those men alone heavy
night was spread,
an image of the darkness that was
destined to receive them;

but still heavier than darkness
were they to themselves.

18 But for thy holy ones there
was very great light.
Their enemies [k] heard their voices
but did not see their forms,
and counted them happy for not
having suffered,
2 and were thankful that thy
holy ones,[l] though previously
wronged, were doing them no
injury;
and they begged their pardon for
having been at variance with
them.[l]
3 Therefore thou didst provide a
flaming pillar of fire
as a guide for thy people's [m] unknown journey,
and a harmless sun for their glorious wandering.
4 For their enemies [n] deserved to be
deprived of light and imprisoned
in darkness,
those who had kept thy sons imprisoned,
through whom the imperishable
light of the law was to be given
to the world.

5 When they had resolved to kill the
babes of thy holy ones,
and one child had been exposed
and rescued,
thou didst in punishment take
away a multitude of their children;
and thou didst destroy them all
together by a mighty flood.
6 That night was made known beforehand to our fathers,
so that they might rejoice in sure
knowledge of the oaths in which
they trusted.
7 The deliverance of the righteous
and the destruction of their
enemies
were expected by thy people.
8 For by the same means by which
thou didst punish our enemies
thou didst call us to thyself and
glorify us.

k Gk *they*   l The meaning of the Greek of this line is uncertain   m Gk *their*   n Gk *those men*

9 For in secret the holy children of
good men offered sacrifices,
and with one accord agreed to the
divine law,
that the saints would share alike
the same things,
both blessings and dangers;
and already they were singing the
praises of the fathers.*o*

10 But the discordant cry of their
enemies echoed back,
and their piteous lament for their
children was spread abroad.

11 The slave was punished with the
same penalty as the master,
and the common man suffered the
same loss as the king;

12 and they all together, by the one
form of death,
had corpses too many to count.
For the living were not sufficient
even to bury them,
since in one instant their most
valued children had been destroyed.

13 For though they had disbelieved
everything because of their
magic arts,
yet, when their first-born were destroyed, they acknowledged thy
people to be God's son.

14 For while gentle silence enveloped
all things,
and night in its swift course was
now half gone,

15 thy all-powerful word leaped from
heaven, from the royal throne,
into the midst of the land that was
doomed,
a stern warrior 16 carrying the
sharp sword of thy authentic
command,
and stood and filled all things
with death,
and touched heaven while standing on the earth.

17 Then at once apparitions in dreadful dreams greatly troubled
them,
and unexpected fears assailed
them;

18 and one here and another there,
hurled down half dead,
made known why they were dying;

19 for the dreams which disturbed
them forewarned them of this,
so that they might not perish
without knowing why they suffered.

20 The experience of death touched
also the righteous,
and a plague came upon the multitude in the desert,
but the wrath did not long continue.

21 For a blameless man was quick to
act as their champion;
he brought forward the shield of
his ministry,
prayer and propitiation by incense;
he withstood the anger and put an
end to the disaster,
showing that he was thy servant.

22 He conquered the wrath *p* not by
strength of body,
and not by force of arms,
but by his word he subdued the
punisher,
appealing to the oaths and covenants given to our fathers.

23 For when the dead had already
fallen on one another in heaps,
he intervened and held back the
wrath,
and cut off its way to the living.

24 For upon his long robe the whole
world was depicted,
and the glories of the fathers were
engraved on the four rows of
stones,
and thy majesty on the diadem
upon his head.

25 To these the destroyer yielded,
these he *q* feared;
for merely to test the wrath was
enough.

19 But the ungodly were assailed
to the end by pitiless anger,
for God *r* knew in advance even
their future actions,

o Other authorities read *dangers, the fathers already leading the songs of praise*
p Cn. Gk *multitude*   *q* Other authorities read *they*   *r* Gk *he*

² that, though they themselves had
permitted ˢ thy people to depart
and hastily sent them forth,
they would change their minds
and pursue them.
³ For while they were still busy at
mourning,
and were lamenting at the graves
of their dead,
they reached another foolish decision,
and pursued as fugitives those
whom they had begged and compelled to depart.
⁴ For the fate they deserved drew
them on to this end,
and made them forget what had
happened,
in order that they might fill up the
punishment which their torments still lacked,
⁵ and that thy people might experience ᵗ an incredible journey,
but they themselves might meet a
strange death.

⁶ For the whole creation in its nature was fashioned anew,
complying with thy commands,
that thy children ᵘ might be kept
unharmed.
⁷ The cloud was seen overshadowing
the camp,
and dry land emerging where
water had stood before,
an unhindered way out of the Red
Sea,
and a grassy plain out of the raging
waves,
⁸ where those protected by thy hand
passed through as one nation,
after gazing on marvellous wonders.
⁹ For they ranged like horses,
and leaped like lambs,
praising thee, O Lord, who didst
deliver them.
¹⁰ For they still recalled the events
of their sojourn,
how instead of producing animals
the earth brought forth gnats,

and instead of fish the river spewed
out vast numbers of frogs.
¹¹ Afterward they saw also a new
kind ᵛ of birds,
when desire led them to ask for
luxurious food;
¹² for, to give them relief, quails
came up from the sea.

¹³ The punishments did not come
upon the sinners
without prior signs in the violence
of thunder,
for they justly suffered because of
their wicked acts;
for they practised a more bitter
hatred of strangers.
¹⁴ Others had refused to receive
strangers when they came to
them,
but these made slaves of guests
who were their benefactors.
¹⁵ And not only so, but punishment
of some sort will come upon the
former
for their hostile reception of the
aliens;
¹⁶ but the latter, after receiving them
with festal celebrations,
afflicted with terrible sufferings
those who had already shared the
same rights.
¹⁷ They were stricken also with loss
of sight—
just as were those at the door of
the righteous man—
when, surrounded by yawning
darkness,
each tried to find the way through
his own door.

¹⁸ For the elements changed ʷ places
with one another,
as on a harp the notes vary the
nature of the rhythm,
while each note remains the same.ˣ
This may be clearly inferred from
the sight of what took place.
¹⁹ For land animals were transformed
into water creatures,

ˢ Other authorities read *had changed their minds to permit*
ᵗ Other authorities read *accomplish*   ᵘ Or *servants*   ᵛ Or *production*
ʷ Gk *changing*   ˣ The meaning of this verse is uncertain

and creatures that swim moved
over to the land.

20 Fire even in water retained its nor-
mal power,
and water forgot its fire-quenching
nature.

21 Flames, on the contrary, failed to
consume
the flesh of perishable creatures
that walked among them,

nor did they melt *y* the crystalline,
easily melted kind of heavenly
food.

22 For in everything, O Lord, thou
hast exalted and glorified thy
people;
and thou hast not neglected to
help them at all times and in all
places.

y Cn: Gk *nor could be melted*

ECCLESIASTICUS, OR THE WISDOM
OF JESUS THE SON OF

SIRACH

The Prologue

Whereas many great teachings have been given to us through the law and the prophets and the others that followed them, on account of which we should praise Israel for instruction and wisdom; and since it is necessary not only that the readers themselves should acquire understanding but also that those who love learning should be able to help the outsiders by both speaking and writing, my grandfather Jesus, after devoting himself especially to the reading of the law and the prophets and the other books of our fathers, and after acquiring considerable proficiency in them, was himself also led to write something pertaining to instruction and wisdom, in order that, by becoming conversant with this also, those who love learning should make even greater progress in living according to the law.

You are urged therefore to read with good will and attention, and to be indulgent[a] in cases where, despite our diligent labour in translating, we may seem to have rendered some phrases imperfectly. For what was originally expressed in Hebrew does not have exactly the same sense when translated into another language. Not only this work, but even the law itself, the prophecies, and the rest of the books differ not a little as originally expressed.

When I came to Egypt in the thirty-eighth year of the reign of Euergetes and stayed for some time, I found opportunity for no little instruction.[b] It seemed highly necessary that I should myself devote some pains and labour to the translation of the following book, using in that period of time great watchfulness and skill in order to complete and publish the book for those living abroad who wished to gain learning, being prepared in character to live according to the law.

1 All wisdom comes from the
    Lord
    and is with him for ever.
2 The sand of the sea, the drops of
    rain,
    and the days of eternity--who
    can count them?
3 The height of heaven, the breadth
    of the earth,
    the abyss, and wisdom--who
    can search them out?
4 Wisdom was created before all
    things,
    and prudent understanding from
    eternity.[c]
6 The root of wisdom--to whom has
    it been revealed?
    Her clever devices--who knows
    them? [d]
8 There is One who is wise, greatly
    to be feared,
    sitting upon his throne.
9 The Lord himself created wis-
    dom;[e]
    he saw her and apportioned her,

---

[a] Or *Please read therefore with good will and attention, and be indulgent*
[b] Other authorities read *a copy affording no little instruction*
[c] Other authorities add as verse 5, *The source of wisdom is God's word in the highest heaven, and her ways are the eternal commandments.*
[d] Other authorities add as verse 7, *The knowledge of wisdom—to whom was it manifested? And her abundant experience—who has understood it?* [e] Gk *her*

he poured her out upon all his
works.

¹⁰ She dwells with all flesh according
to his gift,
and he supplied her to those
who love him.

¹¹ The fear of the Lord is glory and
exultation,
and gladness and a crown of rejoicing.
¹² The fear of the Lord delights the
heart,
and gives gladness and joy and
long life.
¹³ With him who fears the Lord it
will go well at the end;
on the day of his death he will
be blessed.

¹⁴ To fear the Lord is the beginning
of wisdom;
she is created with the faithful
in the womb.
¹⁵ She made *f* among men an eternal
foundation,
and among their descendants
she will be trusted.
¹⁶ To fear the Lord is wisdom's full
measure;
she satisfies *g* men with her
fruits;
¹⁷ she fills their whole house with
desirable goods,
and their storehouses with her
produce.
¹⁸ The fear of the Lord is the crown
of wisdom,
making peace and perfect health
to flourish.
¹⁹ He saw her and apportioned her;
he rained down knowledge and
discerning comprehension,
and he exalted the glory of those
who held her fast.
²⁰ To fear the Lord is the root of
wisdom,

and her branches are long life.*h*

²² Unrighteous anger cannot be justified,
for a man's anger tips the scale
to his ruin.
²³ A patient man will endure until
the right moment,
and then joy will burst forth for
him.
²⁴ He will hide his words until the
right moment,
and the lips of many will tell of
his good sense.
²⁵ In the treasuries of wisdom are
wise sayings,
but godliness is an abomination
to a sinner.
²⁶ If you desire wisdom, keep the
commandments,
and the Lord will supply it for
you.
²⁷ For the fear of the Lord is wisdom
and instruction,
and he delights in fidelity and
meekness.
²⁸ Do not disobey the fear of the
Lord;
do not approach him with a divided mind.
²⁹ Be not a hypocrite in men's sight,*i*
and keep watch over your lips.
³⁰ Do not exalt yourself lest you fall,
and thus bring dishonour upon
yourself.
The Lord will reveal your secrets
and cast you down in the midst
of the congregation,
because you did not come in the
fear of the Lord,
and your heart was full of deceit.

2 My son, if you come forward
to serve the Lord,
prepare yourself for temptation.*j*
² Set your heart right and be steadfast,

---

f Gk *made as nest*   *g* Gk *intoxicates*   *h* Other authorities add as verse 21, *The fear of the Lord
drives away sins; and where it abides, it will turn away all anger.*
i Syr: Gk *in the mouths of men*   *j* Or *trials*

111

and do not be hasty in time of
    calamity.
3 Cleave to him and do not depart,
    that you may be honoured at the
    end of your life.
4 Accept whatever is brought upon
    you,
    and in changes that humble you
    be patient.
5 For gold is tested in the fire,
    and acceptable men in the fur-
    nace of humiliation.
6 Trust in him, and he will help you;
    make your ways straight, and
    hope in him.

7 You who fear the Lord, wait for
    his mercy;
    and turn not aside, lest you fall.
8 You who fear the Lord, trust in
    him,
    and your reward will not fail;
9 you who fear the Lord, hope for
    good things,
    for everlasting joy and mercy.
10 Consider the ancient generations
    and see;
    who ever trusted in the Lord
    and was put to shame?
    Or who ever persevered in the fear
    of the Lord *k* and was for-
    saken?
    Or who ever called upon him
    and was overlooked?
11 For the Lord is compassionate and
    merciful;
    he forgives sins and saves in
    time of affliction.

12 Woe to timid hearts and to slack
    hands,
    and to the sinner who walks
    along two ways!
13 Woe to the faint heart, for it has
    no trust!
    Therefore it will not be sheltered.
14 Woe to you who have lost your
    endurance!
    What will you do when the
    Lord punishes you?

15 Those who fear the Lord will not
    disobey his words,
    and those who love him will
    keep his ways.
16 Those who fear the Lord will seek
    his approval,
    and those who love him will be
    filled with the law.
17 Those who fear the Lord will pre-
    pare their hearts,
    and will humble themselves be-
    fore him.
18 Let us fall *l* into the hands of the
    Lord,
    but not into the hands of men;
for as his majesty is,
    so also is his mercy.

3 Listen to me your father, O
    children;
    and act accordingly, that you
    may be kept in safety.
2 For the Lord honoured the father
    above the children,
    and he confirmed the right of
    the mother over her sons.
3 Whoever honours his father atones
    for sins,
4   and whoever glorifies his mother
    is like one who lays up treas-
    ure.
5 Whoever honours his father will be
    gladdened by his own chil-
    dren,
    and when he prays he will be
    heard.
6 Whoever glorifies his father will
    have long life,
    and whoever obeys the Lord
    will refresh his mother;
7   he will serve his parents as his
    masters.*m*
8 Honour your father by word and
    deed,
    that a blessing from him may
    come upon you.
9 For a father's blessing strengthens
    the houses of the children,
    but a mother's curse uproots
    their foundations.

k Gk *of him*   *l* Gk *We shall fall*
m In other authorities this line is preceded by *Whoever fears the Lord will honour his father*

10 Do not glorify yourself by dishonouring your father,
  for your father's dishonour is no glory to you.

11 For a man's glory comes from honouring his father,
  and it is a disgrace for children not to respect their mother.

12 O son, help your father in his old age,
  and do not grieve him as long as he lives;

13 even if he is lacking in understanding, show forbearance;
  in all your strength do not despise him.

14 For kindness to a father will not be forgotten,
  and against your sins it will be credited to you;

15 in the day of your affliction it will be remembered in your favour;
  as frost in fair weather, your sins will melt away.

16 Whoever forsakes his father is like a blasphemer,
  and whoever angers his mother is cursed by the Lord.

17 My son, perform your tasks in meekness;
  then you will be loved by those whom God accepts.

18 The greater you are, the more you must humble yourself;
  so you will find favour in the sight of the Lord.ⁿ

20 For great is the might of the Lord;
  he is glorified by the humble.

21 Seek not what is too difficult for you,
  nor investigate what is beyond your power.

22 Reflect upon what has been assigned to you,
  for you do not need what is hidden.

23 Do not meddle in what is beyond your tasks,

for matters too great for human understanding have been shown you.

24 For their hasty judgment has led many astray,
  and wrong opinion has caused their thoughts to slip.º

26 A stubborn mind will be afflicted at the end,
  and whoever loves danger will perish by it.

27 A stubborn mind will be burdened by troubles,
  and the sinner will heap sin upon sin.

28 The affliction of the proud has no healing,
  for a plant of wickedness has taken root in him.

29 The mind of the intelligent man will ponder a parable,
  and an attentive ear is the wise man's desire.

30 Water extinguishes a blazing fire:
  so almsgiving atones for sin.

31 Whoever requites favours gives thought to the future;
  at the moment of his falling he will find support.

4 My son, deprive not the poor of his living,
  and do not keep needy eyes waiting.

2 Do not grieve the one who is hungry,
  nor anger a man in want.

3 Do not add to the troubles of an angry mind,
  nor delay your gift to a beggar.

4 Do not reject an afflicted suppliant,
  nor turn your face away from the poor.

5 Do not avert your eye from the needy,
  nor give a man occasion to curse you;

ⁿ Other authorities add as verse 19, *Many are lofty and renowned, but to the meek he reveals his secrets.*
º Other authorities add as verse 25, *If you have no eyes you will be without light; if you lack knowledge do not profess to have it.*

6 for if in bitterness of soul he calls
down a curse upon you,
his Creator will hear his prayer.
7 Make yourself beloved in the congregation;
bow your head low to a great man.
8 Incline your ear to the poor,
and answer him peaceably and gently.
9 Deliver him who is wronged from the hand of the wrongdoer;
and do not be fainthearted in judging a case.
10 Be like a father to orphans,
and instead of a husband to their mother;
you will then be like a son of the Most High,
and he will love you more than does your mother.

11 Wisdom exalts her sons
and gives help to those who seek her.
12 Whoever loves her loves life,
and those who seek her early will be filled with joy.
13 Whoever holds her fast will obtain glory,
and the Lord will bless the place she[p] enters.
14 Those who serve her will minister to the Holy One;[q]
the Lord loves those who love her.
15 He who obeys her will judge the nations,
and whoever gives heed to her will dwell secure.
16 If he has faith in her he will obtain her;
and his descendants will remain in possession of her.
17 For at first she will walk with him on tortuous paths,
she will bring fear and cowardice upon him,
and will torment him by her discipline
until she trusts him,
and she will test him with her ordinances.
18 Then she will come straight back to him and gladden him,
and will reveal her secrets to him.
19 If he goes astray she will forsake him,
and hand him over to his ruin.

20 Observe the right time, and beware of evil;[r]
and do not bring shame on yourself.
21 For there is a shame which brings sin,
and there is a shame which is glory and favour.
22 Do not show partiality, to your own harm,
or deference, to your downfall.
23 Do not refrain from speaking at the crucial time,[s]
and do not hide your wisdom.[t]
24 For wisdom is known through speech,
and education through the words of the tongue.
25 Never speak against the truth,
but be mindful of your ignorance.
26 Do not be ashamed to confess your sins,
and do not try to stop the current of a river.
27 Do not subject yourself to a foolish fellow,
nor show partiality to a ruler.
28 Strive even to death for the truth
and the Lord God will fight for you.

29 Do not be reckless in your speech,
or sluggish and remiss in your deeds.
30 Do not be like a lion in your home,
nor be a faultfinder with your servants.
31 Let not your hand be extended to receive,

[p] Or *he* [q] Or *at the holy place* [r] Or *an evil man* [s] Cn: Gk *at a time of salvation*
[t] So some Gk Mss and Heb Syr Vg: other Gk Mss omit *and do not hide your wisdom*

but withdrawn when it is time
to repay.

5 Do not set your heart on your
wealth,
nor say, "I have enough."

2 Do not follow your inclination and
strength,
walking according to the desires
of your heart.

3 Do not say, "Who will have power
over me?"
for the Lord will surely punish
you.

4 Do not say, "I sinned, and what
happened to me?"
for the Lord is slow to anger.

5 Do not be so confident of atonement
that you add sin to sin.

6 Do not say, "His mercy is great,
he will forgive *u* the multitude of
my sins,"
for both mercy and wrath are with
him,
and his anger rests on sinners.

7 Do not delay to turn to the Lord,
nor postpone it from day to day;
for suddenly the wrath of the Lord
will go forth,
and at the time of punishment
you will perish.

8 Do not depend on dishonest
wealth,
for it will not benefit you in the
day of calamity.

9 Do not winnow with every wind,
nor follow every path:
the double-tongued sinner does
that.

10 Be steadfast in your understanding,
and let your speech be consist-
ent.

11 Be quick to hear,
and be deliberate in answering.

12 If you have understanding, answer
your neighbour;
but if not, put your hand on your
mouth.

13 Glory and dishonour come from
speaking,
and a man's tongue is his downfall.

14 Do not be called a slanderer,
and do not lie in ambush with
your tongue;
for shame comes to the thief,
and severe condemnation to the
double-tongued.

15 In great or small matters do not
act amiss,
and do not become an enemy
instead of a friend;

6 for a bad name incurs shame
and reproach:
so fares the double-tongued sinner.

2 Do not exalt yourself through your
soul's counsel,
lest your soul be torn in pieces
like a bull.*v*

3 You will devour your leaves and
destroy your fruit,
and will be left like a withered
tree.

4 An evil soul will destroy him who
has it,
and make him the laughingstock
of his enemies.

5 A pleasant voice multiplies friends,
and a gracious tongue multiplies
courtesies.

6 Let those that are at peace with
you be many,
but let your advisers be one in a
thousand.

7 When you gain a friend, gain him
through testing,
and do not trust him hastily.

8 For there is a friend who is such
at his own convenience,
but will not stand by you in
your day of trouble.

9 And there is a friend who changes
into an enemy,
and will disclose a quarrel to
your disgrace.

---

u Heb: Gk *he* (or *it*) *will atone for*   *v* The meaning of the Greek of this verse is obscure.

10 And there is a friend who is a table companion,
> but will not stand by you in your day of trouble.
11 In your prosperity he will make himself your equal,
> and be bold with your servants;
12 but if you are brought low he will turn against you,
> and will hide himself from your presence.
13 Keep yourself far from your enemies,
> and be on guard toward your friends.

14 A faithful friend is a sturdy shelter:
> he that has found one has found a treasure.
15 There is nothing so precious as a faithful friend,
> and no scales can measure his excellence.
16 A faithful friend is an elixir of life;
> and those who fear the Lord will find him.
17 Whoever fears the Lord directs his friendship aright,
> for as he is, so is his neighbour also.

18 My son, from your youth up choose instruction,
> and until you are old you will keep finding wisdom.
19 Come to her like one who ploughs and sows,
> and wait for her good harvest.
> For in her service you will toil a little while,
> and soon you will eat of her produce.
20 She seems very harsh to the uninstructed;
> a weakling will not remain with her.
21 She will weigh him down like a heavy testing stone,
> and he will not be slow to cast her off.

22 For wisdom is like her name,
> and is not manifest to many.
23 Listen, my son, and accept my judgment;
> do not reject my counsel.
24 Put your feet into her fetters,
> and your neck into her collar.
25 Put your shoulder under her and carry her,
> and do not fret under her bonds.
26 Come to her with all your soul,
> and keep her ways with all your might.
27 Search out and seek, and she will become known to you;
> and when you get hold of her, do not let her go.
28 For at last you will find the rest she gives,
> and she will be changed into joy for you.
29 Then her fetters will become for you a strong protection,
> and her collar a glorious robe.
30 Her yoke *w* is a golden ornament,
> and her bonds are a cord of blue.
31 You will wear her like a glorious robe,
> and put her on like a crown of gladness.

32 If you are willing, my son, you will be taught,
> and if you apply yourself you will become clever.
33 If you love to listen you will gain knowledge,
> and if you incline your ear you will become wise.
34 Stand in the assembly of the elders.
> Who is wise? Cleave to him.
35 Be ready to listen to every *x* narrative,
> and do not let wise proverbs escape you.
36 If you see an intelligent man, visit him early;
> let your foot wear out his doorstep.
37 Reflect on the statutes of the Lord,

w Heb: Gk *Upon her*   *x* Heb: Gk adds *divine*

and meditate at all times on his
commandments.
It is he who will give insight to [y]
your mind,
and your desire for wisdom will
be granted.

7 Do no evil, and evil will never
befall you.
2 Stay away from wrong, and it
will turn away from you.
3 My son, do not sow the furrows of
injustice,
and you will not reap a sevenfold
crop.

4 Do not seek from the Lord the
highest office,
nor the seat of honour from the
king.
5 Do not assert your righteousness
before the Lord,
nor display your wisdom before
the king.
6 Do not seek to become a judge,
lest you be unable to remove iniquity,
lest you be partial to a powerful
man,
and thus put a blot on your integrity.
7 Do not offend against the public,
and do not disgrace yourself
among the people.

8 Do not commit a sin twice;
even for one you will not go unpunished.
9 Do not say, "He will consider the
multitude of my gifts,
and when I make an offering to
the Most High God he will
accept it."
10 Do not be fainthearted in your
prayer,
nor neglect to give alms.

11 Do not ridicule a man who is bitter
in soul,

for there is One who abases and
exalts.
12 Do not devise [z] a lie against your
brother,
nor do the like to a friend.
13 Refuse to utter any lie,
for the habit of lying serves no
good.
14 Do not prattle in the assembly of
the elders,
nor repeat yourself in your
prayer.

15 Do not hate toilsome labour,
or farm work, which were created by the Most High.
16 Do not count yourself among the
crowd of sinners;
remember that wrath does not
delay.
17 Humble yourself greatly,
for the punishment of the ungodly is fire and worms. [a]

18 Do not exchange a friend for
money,
or a real brother for the gold of
Ophir.
19 Do not deprive yourself of a wise
and good wife,
for her charm is worth more than
gold.
20 Do not abuse a servant who per-
forms his work faithfully,
or a hired labourer who devotes
himself to you.
21 Let your soul love [b] an intelligent
servant;
do not withhold from him his
freedom.

22 Do you have cattle? Look after
them;
if they are profitable to you, keep
them.
23 Do you have children? Discipline
them,
and make them obedient [c] from
their youth.

[y] Heb: Gk *will confirm*   [z] Heb: Gk *plough*
[a] The Hebrew text reads *for the expectation of man is worms*
[b] The Hebrew text reads *Love like yourself*   [c] Gk *bend their necks*

24 Do you have daughters? Be concerned for their chastity,[d]
and do not show yourself too indulgent with them.

25 Give a daughter in marriage; you will have finished a great task.
But give her to a man of understanding.

26 If you have a wife who pleases you,[e] do not cast her out;
but do not trust yourself to one whom you detest.

27 With all your heart honour your father,
and do not forget the birth pangs of your mother.

28 Remember that through your parents[f] you were born;
and what can you give back to them that equals their gift to you?

29 With all your soul fear the Lord, and honour his priests.

30 With all your might love your Maker,
and do not forsake his ministers.

31 Fear the Lord and honour the priest, and give him his portion, as is commanded you:
the first fruits, the guilt offering, the gift of the shoulders,
the sacrifice of sanctification, and the first fruits of the holy things.

32 Stretch forth your hand to the poor,
so that your blessing may be complete.

33 Give graciously to all the living, and withhold not kindness from the dead.

34 Do not fail those who weep, but mourn with those who mourn.

35 Do not shrink from visiting a sick man,
because for such deeds you will be loved.

36 In all you do, remember the end of your life,
and then you will never sin.

8 Do not contend with a powerful man,
lest you fall into his hands.

2 Do not quarrel with a rich man,
lest his resources outweigh yours;
for gold has ruined many,
and has perverted the minds of kings.

3 Do not argue with a chatterer,
nor heap wood on his fire.

4 Do not jest with an ill-bred person,
lest your ancestors be disgraced.

5 Do not reproach a man who is turning away from sin;
remember that we all deserve punishment.

6 Do not disdain a man when he is old,
for some of us are growing old.

7 Do not rejoice over any one's death;
remember that we all must die.

8 Do not slight the discourse of the sages,
but busy yourself with their maxims;
because from them you will gain instruction
and learn how to serve great men.

9 Do not disregard the discourse of the aged,
for they themselves learned from their fathers;
because from them you will gain understanding
and learn how to give an answer in time of need.

10 Do not kindle the coals of a sinner,
lest you be burned in his flaming fire.

11 Do not get up and leave an insolent fellow,
lest he lie in ambush against your words.

---

d Gk *body*   *e* Heb Syr omit *who pleases you*   *f* Gk *them*

12 Do not lend to a man who is
   stronger than you;
   but if you do lend anything, be
      as one who has lost it.
13 Do not give surety beyond your
   means,
   but if you give surety, be con-
      cerned as one who must pay.

14 Do not go to law against a judge,
   for the decision will favour him
      because of his standing.
15 Do not travel on the road with a
      foolhardy fellow,
   lest he be burdensome to you;
   for he will act as he pleases,
   and through his folly you will
      perish with him.
16 Do not fight with a wrathful man,
   and do not cross the wilderness
      with him;
   because blood is as nothing in his
      sight,
   and where no help is at hand,
      he will strike you down.
17 Do not consult with a fool,
   for he will not be able to keep
      a secret.
18 In the presence of a stranger do
   nothing that is to be kept se-
      cret,
   for you do not know what he
      will divulge.*g*
19 Do not reveal your thoughts to
      every one,
   lest you drive away your good
      luck.*h*

9 Do not be jealous of the wife
   of your bosom,
   and do not teach her an evil les-
      son to your own hurt.
2 Do not give yourself to a woman
   so that she gains mastery over
      your strength.
3 Do not go to meet a loose woman,
   lest you fall into her snares.
4 Do not associate with a woman
      singer,
   lest you be caught in her in-
      trigues.

5 Do not look intently at a virgin,
   lest you stumble and incur pen-
      alties for her.
6 Do not give yourself to harlots
   lest you lose your inheritance.
7 Do not look around in the streets
      of a city,
   nor wander about in its deserted
      sections.
8 Turn away your eyes from a shapely
      woman,
   and do not look intently at
      beauty belonging to another;
   many have been misled by a wom-
      an's beauty,
   and by it passion is kindled like
      a fire.
9 Never dine with another man's wife,
   nor revel with her at wine;
   lest your heart turn aside to her,
   and in blood *i* you be plunged
      into destruction.

10 Forsake not an old friend,
   for a new one does not compare
      with him.
   A new friend is like new wine;
   when it has aged you will drink
      it with pleasure.

11 Do not envy the honours of a sin-
      ner,
   for you do not know what his
      end will be.
12 Do not delight in what pleases the
      ungodly;
   remember that they will not be
      held guiltless as long as they
      live.

13 Keep far from a man who has the
      power to kill,
   and you will not be worried by
      the fear of death.
   But if you approach him, make no
      misstep,
   lest he rob you of your life.
   Know that you are walking in the
      midst of snares,
   and that you are going about
      on the city battlements.

g Or *it will bring forth*   *h* Heb: Gk *let him not return a favour to you*   *i* Heb: Gk *by your spirit*

14 As much as you can, aim to know
   your neighbours,
   and consult with the wise.
15 Let your conversation be with men
   of understanding,
   and let all your discussion be
   about the law of the Most
   High.
16 Let righteous men be your dinner
   companions,
   and let your glorying be in the
   fear of the Lord.
17 A work will be praised for the skill
   of the craftsmen;
   so a people's leader is proved
   wise by his words.
18 A babbler is feared in his city,
   and the man who is reckless in
   speech will be hated.

10 A wise magistrate will edu-
   cate his people,
   and the rule of an understanding
   man will be well ordered.
2 Like the magistrate of the people,
   so are his officials;
   and like the ruler of the city, so
   are all its inhabitants.
3 An undisciplined king will ruin his
   people,
   but a city will grow through the
   understanding of its rulers.
4 The government of the earth is in
   the hands of the Lord,
   and over it he will raise up the
   right man for the time.
5 The success of a man is in the
   hands of the Lord,
   and he confers his honour upon
   the person of the scribe.*j*

6 Do not be angry with your neighbour for any injury,
   and do not attempt anything by
   acts of insolence.
7 Arrogance is hateful before the
   Lord and before men,
   and injustice is outrageous to
   both.
8 Sovereignty passes from nation to
   nation

on account of injustice and insolence and wealth.
9 How can he who is dust and ashes
   be proud?
   for even in life his bowels decay.*k*
10 A long illness baffles the physician;*l*
   the king of today will die tomorrow.
11 For when a man is dead,
   he will inherit creeping things,
   and wild beasts, and worms.
12 The beginning of man's pride is to
   depart from the Lord;
   his heart has forsaken his Maker.
13 For the beginning of pride is sin,
   and the man who clings to it
   pours out abominations.
   Therefore the Lord brought upon
   them extraordinary afflictions,
   and destroyed them utterly.
14 The Lord has cast down the thrones
   of rulers,
   and has seated the lowly in their
   place.
15 The Lord has plucked up the roots
   of the nations,*m*
   and has planted the humble in
   their place.
16 The Lord has overthrown the lands
   of the nations,
   and has destroyed them to the
   foundations of the earth.
17 He has removed some of them and
   destroyed them,
   and has extinguished the memory of them from the earth.
18 Pride was not created for men,
   nor fierce anger for those born of
   women.

19 What race is worthy of honour?
   The human race.
   What race is worthy of honour?
   Those who fear the Lord.
   What race is unworthy of honour?
   The human race.
   What race is unworthy of hon-
   our? Those who transgress the
   commandments.
20 Among brothers their leader is
   worthy of honour,

j Or *the official* *k* Heb: Gk is obscure *l* Heb Vg: Gk is uncertain
m Some authorities read *proud nations*

120

and those who fear the Lord are worthy of honour in his eyes.[n]

22 The rich, and the eminent, and the poor—
their glory is the fear of the Lord.

23 It is not right to despise an intelligent poor man,
nor is it proper to honour a sinful man.

24 The nobleman, and the judge, and the ruler will be honoured,
but none of them is greater than the man who fears the Lord.

25 Free men will be at the service of a wise servant,
and a man of understanding will not grumble.

26 Do not make a display of your wisdom when you do your work,
nor glorify yourself at a time when you are in want.

27 Better is a man who works and has an abundance of everything,
than one who goes about boasting, but lacks bread.

28 My son, glorify yourself with humility,
and ascribe to yourself honour according to your worth.

29 Who will justify the man that sins against himself?
And who will honour the man that dishonours his own life?

30 A poor man is honoured for his knowledge,
while a rich man is honoured for his wealth.

31 A man honoured in poverty, how much more in wealth!
And a man dishonoured in wealth, how much more in poverty!

11 The wisdom of a humble man will lift up his head,
and will seat him among the great.

2 Do not praise a man for his good looks,

nor loathe a man because of his appearance.

3 The bee is small among flying creatures,
but her product is the best of sweet things.

4 Do not boast about wearing fine clothes,
nor exalt yourself in the day that you are honoured;
for the works of the Lord are wonderful,
and his works are concealed from men.

5 Many kings have had to sit on the ground,
but one who was never thought of has worn a crown.

6 Many rulers have been greatly disgraced,
and illustrious men have been handed over to others.

7 Do not find fault before you investigate;
first consider, and then reprove.

8 Do not answer before you have heard,
nor interrupt a speaker in the midst of his words.

9 Do not argue about a matter which does not concern you,
nor sit with sinners when they judge a case.

10 My son, do not busy yourself with many matters;
if you multiply activities you will not go unpunished,
and if you pursue you will not overtake,
and by fleeing you will not escape.

11 There is a man who works, and toils, and presses on,
but is so much the more in want.

12 There is another who is slow and needs help,
who lacks strength and abounds in poverty;

---

[n] Other authorities add as verse 21, *The fear of the Lord is the beginning of acceptance; obduracy and pride are the beginning of rejection.*

but the eyes of the Lord look upon
him for his good;
he lifts him out of his low estate
¹³ and raises up his head,
so that many are amazed at him.

¹⁴ Good things and bad, life and
death,
poverty and wealth, come from
the Lord.^o
¹⁷ The gift of the Lord endures for
those who are godly,
and what he approves will have
lasting success.
¹⁸ There is a man who is rich through
his diligence and self-denial,
and this is the reward allotted to
him:
¹⁹ when he says, "I have found rest,
and now I shall enjoy^p my
goods!"
he does not know how much time
will pass
until he leaves them to others
and dies.
²⁰ Stand by your covenant^q and at-
tend to it,
and grow old in your work.

²¹ Do not wonder at the works of a
sinner,
but trust in the Lord and keep at
your toil;
for it is easy in the sight of the Lord
to enrich a poor man quickly
and suddenly.
²² The blessing of the Lord is^r the
reward of the godly,
and quickly God causes his blessing to flourish.
²³ Do not say, "What do I need,
and what prosperity could be
mine in the future?"
²⁴ Do not say, "I have enough,
and what calamity could hap-
pen to me in the future?"
²⁵ In the day of prosperity, adversity
is forgotten,

and in the day of adversity,
prosperity is not remembered.
²⁶ For it is easy in the sight of the
Lord
to reward a man on the day of
death according to his conduct.
²⁷ The misery of an hour makes one
forget luxury,
and at the close of a man's life
his deeds will be revealed.
²⁸ Call no one happy before his death;
a man will be known through
his children.

²⁹ Do not bring every man into your
home,
for many are the wiles of the
crafty.
³⁰ Like a decoy partridge in a cage,
so is the mind of a proud man,
and like a spy he observes your
weakness;^s
³¹ for he lies in wait, turning good
into evil,
and to worthy actions he will at-
tach blame.
³² From a spark of fire come many
burning coals,
and a sinner lies in wait to shed
blood.
³³ Beware of a scoundrel, for he de-
vises evil,
lest he give you a lasting blemish.
³⁴ Receive a stranger into your home
and he will upset you with
commotion,
and will estrange you from your
family.

12 If you do a kindness, know to
whom you do it,
and you will be thanked for your
good deeds.
² Do good to a godly man, and you
will be repaid—
if not by him, certainly by the
Most High.

---

^o Other authorities add as verses 15 and 16, ¹⁵ *Wisdom, understanding, and knowledge of the law
come from the Lord; affection and the ways of good works come from him.* ¹⁶ *Error and darkness
were created with sinners; evil will grow old with those who take pride in malice.*   ^p Gk *eat of*
^q Heb *task*   ^r Gk *is in*   ^s Heb: Gk *downfall*

3 No good will come to the man who
   persists in evil
   or to him who does not give
      alms.
4 Give to the godly man, but do not
   help the sinner.
5   Do good to the humble, but do
      not give to the ungodly;
   hold back his bread, and do not
      give it to him,
   lest by means of it he subdue
      you;
   for you will receive twice as much
      evil
   for all the good which you do to
      him.
6 For the Most High also hates sin-
      ners
   and will inflict punishment on
      the ungodly.[t]
7 Give to the good man, but do not
   help the sinner.

8 A friend will not be known[u] in
      prosperity,
   nor will an enemy be hidden in
      adversity.
9 A man's enemies are grieved when
      he prospers,
   and in his adversity even his
      friend will separate from him.
10 Never trust your enemy,
   for like the rusting of copper, so
      is his wickedness.
11 Even if he humbles himself and
      goes about cringing,
   watch yourself, and be on your
      guard against him;
   and you will be to him like one
      who has polished a mirror,
   and you will know that it was
      not hopelessly tarnished.
12 Do not put him next to you,
   lest he overthrow you and take
      your place;
   do not have him sit at your right,
   lest he try to take your seat of
      honour,
   and at last you will realize the
      truth of my words,
   and be stung by what I have said.

13 Who will pity a snake charmer bit-
      ten by a serpent,
   or any who go near wild beasts?
14 So no one will pity a man who as-
      sociates with a sinner
   and becomes involved in his sins.
15 He will stay with you for a time,
   but if you falter, he will not
      stand by you.

16 An enemy will speak sweetly with
      his lips,
   but in his mind he will plan to
      throw you into a pit;
   an enemy will weep with his eyes,
   but if he finds an opportunity
      his thirst for blood will be
      insatiable.
17 If calamity befalls you, you will
      find him there ahead of you;
   and while pretending to help
      you, he will trip you by the
      heel;
18 he will shake his head, and clap
      his hands,
   and whisper much, and change
      his expression.

13   Whoever touches pitch will
         be defiled,
   and whoever associates with a
      proud man will become like
      him.
2 Do not lift a weight beyond your
      strength,
   nor associate with a man might-
      ier and richer than you.
   How can the clay pot associate
      with the iron kettle?
   The pot will strike against it,
      and will itself be broken.
3 A rich man does wrong, and he
      even adds reproaches;
   a poor man suffers wrong, and
      he must add apologies.
4 A rich man[v] will exploit you if you
      can be of use to him,
   but if you are in need he will
      forsake you.
5 If you own something, he will live
      with you;

---

[t] Other authorities add *and he is keeping them for the mighty day of their punishment*
[u] Other authorities read *punished*   [v] Gk *He*

he will drain your resources and
he will not care.
⁶ When he needs you he will deceive you,
he will smile at you and give you
hope.
He will speak to you kindly and
say, "What do you need?"
⁷ He will shame you with his foods,
until he has drained you two or
three times;
and finally he will deride you.
Should he see you afterwards, he
will forsake you,
and shake his head at you.

⁸ Take care not to be led astray,
and not to be humiliated in your
feasting.ʷ
⁹ When a powerful man invites you,
be reserved;
and he will invite you the more
often.
¹⁰ Do not push forward, lest you be
repulsed;
and do not remain at a distance,
lest you be forgotten.
¹¹ Do not try to treat him as an equal,
nor trust his abundance of
words;
for he will test you through much
talk,
and while he smiles he will be
examining you.
¹² Cruel is he who does not keep
words to himself;
he will not hesitate to injure or
to imprison.
¹³ Keep words to yourself and be very
watchful,
for you are walking about with
your own downfall.ˣ

¹⁵ Every creature loves its like,
and every person his neighbour;
¹⁶ all living beings associate by species,
and a man clings to one like himself.

¹⁷ What fellowship has a wolf with a
lamb?
No more has a sinner with a
godly man.
¹⁸ What peace is there between a
hyena and a dog?
And what peace between a rich
man and a poor man?
¹⁹ Wild asses in the wilderness are
the prey of lions;
likewise the poor are pastures
for the rich.
²⁰ Humility is an abomination to a
proud man;
likewise a poor man is an abomination to a rich one.

²¹ When a rich man totters, he is
steadied by friends,
but when a humble man falls, he
is even pushed away by
friends.
²² If a rich man slips, his helpers are
many;
he speaks unseemly words, and
they justify him.
If a humble man slips, they even
reproach him;
he speaks sensibly, and receives
no attention.
²³ When the rich man speaks all are
silent,
and they extol to the clouds what
he says.
When the poor man speaks they
say, "Who is this fellow?"
And should he stumble, they
even push him down.

²⁴ Riches are good if they are free
from sin,
and poverty is evil in the opinion of the ungodly.
²⁵ A man's heart changes his countenance,
either for good or for evil.ʸ
²⁶ The mark of a happy heart is a
cheerful face,

ʷ Other authorities read _folly_
ˣ Other authorities add _When you hear these things in your sleep, wake up!_ ¹⁴ _During all your life
love the Lord, and call on him for your salvation._
ʸ Other authorities add _and a glad heart makes a cheerful countenance_

but to devise proverbs requires
　　painful thinking.

14 Blessed is the man who does
　　not blunder with his lips
　and need not suffer grief for sin.
² Blessed is he whose heart does not
　　condemn him,
　and who has not given up his
　　hope.

³ Riches are not seemly for a stingy
　　man;
　and of what use is property to
　　an envious man?
⁴ Whoever accumulates by depriv-
　　ing himself, accumulates for
　　others;
　and others will live in luxury on
　　his goods.
⁵ If a man is mean to himself, to
　　whom will he be generous?
　He will not enjoy his own riches.
⁶ No one is meaner than the man
　　who is grudging to himself,
　and this is the retribution for
　　his baseness;
⁷ even if he does good, he does it
　　unintentionally,
　and betrays his baseness in the
　　end.
⁸ Evil is the man with a grudging
　　eye;
　he averts his face and disregards
　　people.
⁹ A greedy man's eye is not satisfied
　　with a portion,
　and mean injustice withers the
　　soul.
¹⁰ A stingy man's eye begrudges
　　bread,
　and it is lacking at his table.

¹¹ My son, treat yourself well, ac-
　　cording to your means,
　and present worthy offerings to
　　the Lord.
¹² Remember that death will not de-
　　lay,
　and the decree ᶻ of Hades has
　　not been shown to you.
¹³ Do good to a friend before you die,

and reach out and give to him
　　as much as you can.
¹⁴ Do not deprive yourself of a happy
　　day;
　let not your share of desired
　　good pass by you.
¹⁵ Will you not leave the fruit of your
　　labours to another,
　and what you acquired by toil
　　to be divided by lot?
¹⁶ Give, and take, and beguile your-
　　self,
　because in Hades one cannot
　　look for luxury.
¹⁷ All living beings become old like a
　　garment,
　for the decree ᵃ from of old is,
　　"You must surely die!"
¹⁸ Like flourishing leaves on a spread-
　　ing tree
　which sheds some and puts
　　forth others,
　so are the generations of flesh and
　　blood:
　one dies and another is born.
¹⁹ Every product decays and ceases to
　　exist,
　and the man who made it will
　　pass away with it.

²⁰ Blessed is the man who meditates
　　on ᵇ wisdom
　and who reasons intelligently.
²¹ He who reflects in his mind on her
　　ways
　will also ponder her secrets.
²² Pursue wisdom ᶜ like a hunter,
　and lie in wait on her paths.
²³ He who peers through her windows
　will also listen at her doors;
²⁴ he who encamps near her house
　will also fasten his tent peg to
　　her walls;
²⁵ he will pitch his tent near her,
　and will lodge in an excellent
　　lodging place;
²⁶ he will place his children under
　　her shelter,
　and will camp under her boughs;
²⁷ he will be sheltered by her from
　　the heat,

ᶻ Gk *covenant*　ᵃ Gk *covenant*　ᵇ Other authorities read *dies in*　ᶜ Gk *her*

and will dwell in the midst of her
glory.

15 The man who fears the Lord
will do this,
and he who holds to the law will
obtain wisdom.[d]
2 She will come to meet him like a
mother,
and like the wife of his youth
she will welcome him.
3 She will feed him with the bread
of understanding,
and give him the water of wisdom to drink.
4 He will lean on her and will not
fall,
and he will rely on her and will
not be put to shame.
5 She will exalt him above his neighbours,
and will open his mouth in the
midst of the assembly.
6 He will find gladness and a crown
of rejoicing,
and will acquire an everlasting
name.
7 Foolish men will not obtain her,
and sinful men will not see her.
8 She is far from men of pride,
and liars will never think of her.

9 A hymn of praise is not fitting on
the lips of a sinner,
for it has not been sent from the
Lord.
10 For a hymn of praise should be uttered in wisdom,
and the Lord will prosper it.
11 Do not say, "Because of the Lord
I left the right way";
for he [e] will not do what he hates.
12 Do not say, "It was he who led me
astray";
for he has no need of a sinful
man.
13 The Lord hates all abominations,
and they are not loved by those
who fear him.
14 It was he who created man in the
beginning,

and he left him in the power of
his own inclination.
15 If you will, you can keep the commandments,
and to act faithfully is a matter
of your own choice.
16 He has placed before you fire and
water:
stretch out your hand for whichever you wish.
17 Before a man [f] are life and death,
and whichever he chooses will be
given to him.
18 For great is the wisdom of the
Lord;
he is mighty in power and sees
everything;
19 his eyes are on those who fear him,
and he knows every deed of man.
20 He has not commanded any one
to be ungodly,
and he has not given any one
permission to sin.

16 Do not desire a multitude
of useless children,
nor rejoice in ungodly sons.
2 If they multiply, do not rejoice in
them,
unless the fear of the Lord is in
them.
3 Do not trust in their survival,
and do not rely on their multitude;
for one is better than a thousand,[g]
and to die childless is better
than to have ungodly children.
4 For through one man of understanding a city will be filled
with people,
but through a tribe of lawless
men it will be made desolate.
5 Many such things my eye has seen,
and my ear has heard things
more striking than these.

6 In an assembly of sinners a fire will
be kindled,
and in a disobedient nation
wrath was kindled.
7 He was not propitiated for the ancient giants

d Gk *her*   e Heb: Gk *you*   f Gk *men*   g The text of this line is uncertain

126

who revolted in their might.

⁸ He did not spare the neighbours of
Lot,

whom he loathed on account of
their insolence.

⁹ He showed no pity for a nation
devoted to destruction,

for those destroyed in their sins;

¹⁰ nor for the six hundred thousand
men on foot,

who rebelliously assembled in
their stubbornness.

¹¹ Even if there is only one stiff-
necked person,

it will be a wonder if he remains
unpunished.

For mercy and wrath are with the
Lord; *ʰ*

he is mighty to forgive, and he
pours out wrath.

¹² As great as his mercy, so great is
also his reproof;

he judges a man according to
his deeds.

¹³ The sinner will not escape with his
plunder,

and the patience of the godly
will not be frustrated.

¹⁴ He will make room for every act
of mercy;

every one will receive in accordance with his deeds.*ⁱ*

¹⁷ Do not say, "I shall be hidden from
the Lord,

and who from on high will remember me?

Among so many people I shall not
be known,

for what is my soul in the bound-
less creation?

¹⁸ Behold, heaven and the highest
heaven,

the abyss and the earth, will
tremble at his visitation.

¹⁹ The mountains also and the foundations of the earth

shake with trembling when he
looks upon them.

²⁰ And no mind will reflect on this.
Who will ponder his ways?

²¹ Like a tempest which no man can
see,

so most of his works are concealed.

²² Who will announce his acts of justice?

Or who will await them? For
the covenant is far off."

²³ This is what one devoid of understanding thinks;

a senseless and misguided man
thinks foolishly.

²⁴ Listen to me, my son, and acquire
knowledge,

and pay close attention to my
words.

²⁵ I will impart instruction by weight,
and declare knowledge accu-
rately.

²⁶ The works of the Lord have existed
from the beginning by his
creation,*ʲ*

and when he made them, he determined their divisions.

²⁷ He arranged his works in an eternal
order,

and their dominion *ᵏ* for all *ˡ*
generations;

they neither hunger nor grow
weary,

and they do not cease from their
labours.

²⁸ They do not crowd one another
aside,

and they will never disobey his
word.

²⁹ After this the Lord looked upon
the earth,

and filled it with his good things;

³⁰ with all kinds of living beings he
covered its surface,

and to it they return.

17 The Lord created man out
of earth,

ʰ Gk *him*
ⁱ Other authorities add ¹⁵ *The Lord hardened Pharaoh so that he did not know him; in order that
his works might be known under heaven.* ¹⁶ *His mercy is manifest to the whole of creation, and
he divided his light and darkness with a plumb line.* *ʲ* Heb: Gk *judgment*
ᵏ Or *elements* *ˡ* Gk *their*

and turned him back to it again.

2 He gave to men[m] few days, a limited time,

but granted them authority over the things upon the earth.[n]

3 He endowed them with strength like his own,[o]

and made them in his own image.

4 He placed the fear of them[p] in all living beings,

and granted them dominion over beasts and birds.[q]

6 He made for them[r] tongue and eyes;

he gave them ears and a mind for thinking.

7 He filled them with knowledge and understanding,

and showed them good and evil.

8 He set his eye upon their hearts

to show them the majesty of his works.[s]

10 And they will praise his holy name,

to proclaim the grandeur of his works.

11 He bestowed knowledge upon them,

and allotted to them the law of life.

12 He established with them an eternal covenant,

and showed them his judgments.

13 Their eyes saw his glorious majesty,

and their ears heard the glory of his voice.

14 And he said to them, "Beware of all unrighteousness."[t]

And he gave commandment to each of them concerning his neighbour.

15 Their ways are always before him,

they will not be hid from his eyes.[u]

17 He appointed a ruler for every nation,

but Israel is the Lord's own portion.[v]

19 All their works are as the sun before him,

and his eyes are continually upon their ways.

20 Their iniquities are not hidden from him,

and all their sins are before the Lord.[w]

22 A man's almsgiving is like a signet with the Lord,[x]

and he will keep a person's kindness like the apple of his eye.

23 Afterward he will arise and requite them,

and he will bring their recompense on their heads.

24 Yet to those who repent he grants a return,

and he encourages those whose endurance is failing.

25 Turn to the Lord and forsake your sins;

pray in his presence and lessen your offences.

26 Return to the Most High and turn away from iniquity,[y]

and hate abominations intensely.

27 Who will sing praises to the Most High in Hades,

as do those who are alive and give thanks?

28 From the dead, as from one who

---

[m] Gk *them*   [n] Gk *it*   [o] Cn: Gk *proper to them*   [p] Syr: Gk *him*

[q] Other authorities add 5 *They obtained the use of the five operations of the Lord; as sixth he distributed to them the gift of mind, and as seventh reason, the interpreter of his operations.*

[r] Syr: Gk *Inclination and*

[s] Other authorities add 9 *and he gave them to boast of his marvels for ever*

[t] Or *every unrighteous man*

[u] Other authorities add 16 *Their ways from youth tend toward evil, and they are unable to make for themselves hearts of flesh in place of their stony hearts.* 17 *For in the division of the nations of the whole earth*

[v] Other authorities add 18 *whom, being his first-born, he brings up with discipline, and allotting to him the light of his love, he does not neglect him.*

[w] Other authorities add 21 *But the Lord, who is gracious and knows his creatures, has neither left nor abandoned them, but spared them*   [x] Gk *him*

[y] Other authorities add *for he will lead you out of darkness to the light of health*

does not exist, thanksgiving has ceased;
he who is alive and well sings the Lord's praises.

29 How great is the mercy of the Lord,
and his forgiveness for those who turn to him!

30 For all things cannot be in men,[z]
since a son of man is not immortal.

31 What is brighter than the sun? Yet its light fails.[a]
So flesh and blood devise evil.

32 He marshals the host of the height of heaven;
but all men are dust and ashes.

18 He who lives for ever created the whole universe;
2 the Lord alone will be declared righteous.[b]

1 To none has he given power to proclaim his works;
and who can search out his mighty deeds?

5 Who can measure his majestic power?
And who can fully recount his mercies?

6 It is not possible to diminish or increase them,
nor is it possible to trace the wonders of the Lord.

7 When a man has finished, he is just beginning,
and when he stops, he will be at a loss.

8 What is man, and of what use is he?
What is his good and what is his evil?

9 The number of a man's days is great if he reaches a hundred years.

9 Like a drop of water from the sea and a grain [c] of sand
so are a few years in the day of eternity.

11 Therefore the Lord is patient with them
and pours out his mercy upon them.

12 He sees and recognizes that their end will be evil;
therefore he grants them forgiveness in abundance.

13 The compassion of man is for his neighbour,
but the compassion of the Lord is for all living beings.
He rebukes and trains and teaches them,
and turns them back, as a shepherd his flock.

14 He has compassion on those who accept his discipline
and who are eager for his judgments.

15 My son, do not mix reproach with your good deeds,
nor cause grief by your words when you present a gift.

16 Does not the dew assuage the scorching heat?
So a word is better than a gift.

17 Indeed, does not a word surpass a good gift?
Both are to be found in a gracious man.

18 A fool is ungracious and abusive,
and the gift of a grudging man makes the eyes dim.

19 Before you speak, learn,
and before you fall ill, take care of your health.

20 Before judgment, examine yourself,
and in the hour of visitation you will find forgiveness.

21 Before falling ill, humble yourself,
and when you are on the point of sinning, turn back.

22 Let nothing hinder you from paying a vow promptly,
and do not wait until death to be released from it.

---

[z] The Greek text of this line is uncertain   [a] Or *suffers eclipse*
[b] Other authorities add *and there is no other beside him;* 3 *he steers the world with the span of his hand, and all things obey his will; for he is king of all things, by his power separating among them the holy things from the profane.*   [c] Gk *pebble*

23 Before making a vow,*d* prepare
   yourself;
   and do not be like a man who
   tempts the Lord.
24 Think of his wrath on the day of
   death,
   and of the moment of vengeance
   when he turns away his face.
25 In the time of plenty think of the
   time of hunger;
   in the days of wealth think of
   poverty and need.
26 From morning to evening conditions change,
   and all things move swiftly before the Lord.

27 A wise man is cautious in everything,
   and in days of sin he guards
   against wrongdoing.
28 Every intelligent man knows wisdom,
   and he praises the one who finds
   her.
29 Those who understand sayings become skilled themselves,
   and pour forth apt proverbs.

30 Do not follow your base desires,
   but restrain your appetites.
31 If you allow your soul to take
   pleasure in base desire,
   it will make you the laughingstock of your enemies.
32 Do not revel in great luxury,
   lest you become impoverished
   by its expense.
33 Do not become a beggar by feasting with borrowed money,
   when you have nothing in your
   purse.

19 A workman who is a drunk-
   ard will not become rich;
   he who despises small things
   will fail little by little.
2 Wine and women lead intelligent
   men astray,

and the man who consorts with
   harlots is very reckless.
3 Decay and worms will inherit him,
   and the reckless soul will be
   snatched away.

4 One who trusts others too quickly
   is lightminded,
   and one who sins does wrong to
   himself.
5 One who rejoices in wickedness *e*
   will be condemned,*f*
6   and for one who hates gossip
   evil is lessened.
7 Never repeat a conversation,
   and you will lose nothing at all.
8 With friend or foe do not report it,
   and unless it would be a sin for
   you, do not disclose it;
9 for some one has heard you and
   watched you,
   and when the time comes he
   will hate you.
10 Have you heard a word? Let it die
   with you.
   Be brave! It will not make you
   burst!
11 With such a word a fool will suffer
   pangs
   like a woman in labour with a
   child.
12 Like an arrow stuck in the flesh of
   the thigh,
   so is a word inside a fool.
13 Question a friend, perhaps he did
   not do it;
   but if he did anything, so that
   he may do it no more.
14 Question a neighbour, perhaps he
   did not say it;
   but if he said it, so that he may
   not say it again.
15 Question a friend, for often it is
   slander;
   so do not believe everything you
   hear.
16 A person may make a slip without
   intending it.

d Or *offering a prayer* *e* Other authorities read *heart*
f Other authorities add *but he who withstands pleasures crowns his life.* 6 *He who controls his
tongue will live without strife,*

Who has never sinned with his
tongue?

17 Question your neighbour before you
threaten him;

and let the law of the Most
High take its course.*g*

20 All wisdom is the fear of the Lord,
and in all wisdom there is the
fulfilment of the law.*h*

22 But the knowledge of wickedness
is not wisdom,

nor is there prudence where
sinners take counsel.

23 There is a cleverness which is
abominable,

but there is a fool who merely
lacks wisdom.

24 Better is the God-fearing man who
lacks intelligence,

than the highly prudent man
who transgresses the law.

25 There is a cleverness which is
scrupulous but unjust,

and there are people who dis-
tort kindness to gain a verdict.

26 There is a rascal bowed down in
mourning,*i*

but inwardly he is full of deceit.

27 He hides his face and pretends not
to hear;

but where no one notices, he
will forestall you.

28 And if by lack of strength he is
prevented from sinning,

he will do evil when he finds an
opportunity.

29 A man is known by his appearance,
and a sensible man is known by
his face, when you meet him.

30 A man's attire and open-mouthed
laughter,

and a man's manner of walking,
show what he is.

20 There is a reproof which is
not timely;

and there is a man who keeps
silent but is wise.

2 How much better it is to reprove
than to stay angry!

And the one who confesses his
fault will be kept from loss.*j*

4 Like a eunuch's desire to violate a
maiden

is a man who executes judgments by violence.

5 There is one who by keeping silent
is found wise,

while another is detested for being too talkative.

6 There is one who keeps silent because he has no answer,

while another keeps silent because he knows when to speak.

7 A wise man will be silent until the
right moment,

but a braggart and fool goes beyond the right moment.

8 Whoever uses too many words will
be loathed,

and whoever usurps the right to
speak will be hated.

9 There may be good fortune for a
man in adversity,

and a windfall may result in a
loss.

10 There is a gift that profits you
nothing,

and there is a gift that brings a
double return.

11 There are losses because of glory,
and there are men who have
raised their heads from humble circumstances.

12 There is a man who buys much for
a little,

but pays for it seven times over.

---

g Other authorities add *and do not be angry.* 18 *The fear of the Lord is the beginning of acceptance,
and wisdom obtains his love.* 19 *The knowledge of the Lord's commandments is life-giving discipline; and those who do what is pleasing to him enjoy the fruit of the tree of immortality.*
h Other authorities add, *and the knowledge of his omnipotence.* 21 *When a servant says to his
master, "I will not act as you wish," even if later he does it, he angers the one who supports him.*
i Gk *blackness*
j Other authorities add 3 *How good it is to show repentance when you are reproved, for so you
will escape deliberate sin!*

¹³ The wise man makes himself beloved through his words,
    but the courtesies of fools are
      wasted.
¹⁴ A fool's gift will profit you nothing,
    for he has many eyes instead of
      one.
¹⁵ He gives little and upbraids much,
    he opens his mouth like a herald;
  today he lends and tomorrow he
    asks it back;
  such a one is a hateful man.
¹⁶ A fool will say, "I have no friend,
    and there is no gratitude for my
      good deeds;
  those who eat my bread speak
    unkindly."
¹⁷ How many will ridicule him, and
    how often!

¹⁸ A slip on the pavement is better
    than a slip of the tongue;
  so the downfall of the wicked
    will occur speedily.
¹⁹ An ungracious man is like a story
    told at the wrong time,
  which is continually on the lips
    of the ignorant.
²⁰ A proverb from a fool's lips will
    be rejected,
  for he does not tell it at its
    proper time.

²¹ A man may be prevented from
    sinning by his poverty,
  so when he rests he feels no re-
    morse.
²² A man may lose his life through
    shame,
  or lose it because of his foolish
    look.
²³ A man may for shame make prom-
    ises to a friend,
  and needlessly make him an
    enemy.

²⁴ A lie is an ugly blot on a man;
    it is continually on the lips of
      the ignorant.
²⁵ A thief is preferable to a habitual
    liar,

but the lot of both is ruin.
²⁶ The disposition of a liar brings dis-
    grace,
  and his shame is ever with him.

²⁷ He who speaks wisely will advance
    himself,
  and a sensible man will please
    great men.
²⁸ Whoever cultivates the soil will
    heap up his harvest,
  and whoever pleases great men
    will atone for injustice.
²⁹ Presents and gifts blind the eyes of
    the wise;
  like a muzzle on the mouth they
    avert reproofs.
³⁰ Hidden wisdom and unseen treas-
    ure,
  what advantage is there in either
    of them?
³¹ Better is the man who hides his
    folly
  than the man who hides his wis-
    dom.ᵏ

21 Have you sinned, my son?
        Do so no more,
      but pray about your former sins.
² Flee from sin as from a snake;
    for if you approach sin, it will
      bite you.
  Its teeth are lion's teeth,
    and destroy the souls of men.
³ All lawlessness is like a two-edged
    sword;
  there is no healing for its wound.

⁴ Terror and violence will lay waste
    riches;
  thus the house of the proud will
    be laid waste.
⁵ The prayer of a poor man goes
    from his lips to the ears of
      God,ˡ
  and his judgment comes speed-
    ily.
⁶ Whoever hates reproof walks in
    the steps of the sinner,
  but he that fears the Lord will
    repent in his heart.

ᵏ Other authorities add ³² *Unwearied patience in seeking the Lord is better than a masterless chariot of one's own life.* ˡ Gk *his ears*

7 He who is mighty in speech is
  known from afar;
  but the sensible man, when he
  slips, is aware of it.

8 A man who builds his house with
  other people's money
  is like one who gathers stones
  for his burial mound.*m*
9 An assembly of the wicked is like
  tow gathered together,
  and their end is a flame of fire.
10 The way of sinners is smoothly
  paved with stones,
  but at its end is the pit of Hades.

11 Whoever keeps the law controls
  his thoughts,
  and wisdom is the fulfilment of
  the fear of the Lord.
12 He who is not clever cannot be
  taught,
  but there is a cleverness which
  increases bitterness.
13 The knowledge of a wise man will
  increase like a flood,
  and his counsel like a flowing
  spring.
14 The mind of a fool is like a broken
  jar;
  it will hold no knowledge.

15 When a man of understanding
  hears a wise saying,
  he will praise it and add to it;
  when a reveller hears it, he dislikes
  it
  and casts it behind his back.
16 A fool's narration is like a burden
  on a journey,
  but delight will be found in the
  speech of the intelligent.
17 The utterance of a sensible man
  will be sought in the assembly,
  and they will ponder his words
  in their minds.

18 Like a house that has vanished, so
  is wisdom to a fool;

and the knowledge of the ig-
  norant is unexamined talk.
19 To a senseless man education is
  fetters on his feet,
  and like manacles on his right
  hand.
20 A fool raises his voice when he
  laughs,
  but a clever man smiles quietly.
21 To a sensible man education is like
  a golden ornament,
  and like a bracelet on the right
  arm.

22 The foot of a fool rushes into a
  house,
  but a man of experience stands
  respectfully before it.
23 A boor peers into the house from
  the door,
  but a cultivated man remains
  outside.
24 It is ill-mannered for a man to
  listen at a door,
  and a discreet man is grieved by
  the disgrace.
25 The lips of strangers will speak of
  these things,*n*
  but the words of the prudent
  will be weighed in the balance.
26 The mind of fools is in their
  mouth,
  but the mouth of wise men is
  in *o* their mind.
27 When an ungodly man curses his
  adversary,*p*
  he curses his own soul.
28 A whisperer defiles his own soul
  and is hated in his neighbour-
  hood.

22 The indolent may be compared to a filthy stone,
  and every one hisses at his disgrace.
2 The indolent may be compared to
  the filth of dunghills;
  any one that picks it up will
  shake it off his hand.

m Other authorities read *for the winter*   *n* The Greek text of this line is uncertain
o Other authorities omit *in*   *p* Or *curses Satan*

[3] It is a disgrace to be the father of
an undisciplined son,
and the birth of a daughter is a
loss.
[4] A sensible daughter obtains her
husband,
but one who acts shamefully
brings grief to her father.
[5] An impudent daughter disgraces
father and husband,
and will be despised by both.
[6] Like music in mourning is a tale
told at the wrong time,
but chastising and discipline are
wisdom at all times.

[7] He who teaches a fool is like one
who glues potsherds together,
or who rouses a sleeper from
deep slumber.
[8] He who tells a story to a fool tells
it to a drowsy man;
and at the end he will say,
"What is it?"[q]
[11] Weep for the dead, for he lacks
the light;
and weep for the fool, for he
lacks intelligence;
weep less bitterly for the dead, for
he has attained rest;
but the life of the fool is worse
than death.
[12] Mourning for the dead lasts seven
days,
but for a fool or an ungodly man
it lasts all his life.

[13] Do not talk much with a foolish
man,
and do not visit an unintelligent
man;
guard yourself from him to escape
trouble,
and you will not be soiled when
he shakes himself off;
avoid him and you will find rest,
and you will never be wearied by
his madness.
[14] What is heavier than lead?
And what is its name except
"Fool"?
[15] Sand, salt, and a piece of iron
are easier to bear than a stupid
man.

[16] A wooden beam firmly bonded
into a building
will not be torn loose by an
earthquake;
so the mind firmly fixed on a reasonable counsel
will not be afraid in a crisis.
[17] A mind settled on an intelligent
thought
is like the stucco decoration on
the wall of a colonnade.[r]
[18] Fences set on a high place
will not stand firm against the
wind;
so a timid heart with a fool's purpose
will not stand firm against any
fear.

[19] A man who pricks an eye will
make tears fall,
and one who pricks the heart
makes it show feeling.
[20] One who throws a stone at birds
scares them away,
and one who reviles a friend will
break off the friendship.
[21] Even if you have drawn your sword
against a friend,
do not despair, for a renewal of
friendship is possible.
[22] If you have opened your mouth
against your friend,
do not worry, for reconciliation
is possible;
but as for reviling, arrogance, disclosure of secrets, or a treacherous blow—
in these cases any friend will flee.

[23] Gain the trust of your neighbour in
his poverty,
that you may rejoice with him
in his prosperity;

[q] Other authorities add [9] *Children who are brought up in a good life, conceal the lowly birth of their parents.* [10] *Children who are disdainfully and boorishly haughty stain the nobility of their kindred.* [r] Or *on a smooth wall*

stand by him in time of affliction,
   that you may share with him in
   his inheritance.[s]

24 The vapour and smoke of the furnace precede the fire;
   so insults precede bloodshed.

25 I will not be ashamed to protect
   a friend,
   and I will not hide from him;

26 but if some harm should happen
   to me because of him,
   whoever hears of it will beware
   of him.

27 O that a guard were set over my
   mouth,
   and a seal of prudence upon my
   lips,
   that it may keep me from falling,
   so that my tongue may not destroy me! [t]

23 O Lord, Father and Ruler
   of my life,
   do not abandon me to their
   counsel,
   and let me not fall because of
   them!

2 O that whips were set over my
   thoughts,
   and the discipline of wisdom
   over my mind! [u]
   That they may not spare me in my
   errors,
   and that it may not pass by my [v]
   sins;

3 in order that my mistakes may not
   be multiplied,
   and my sins may not abound;
   then I will not fall before my adversaries,
   and my enemy will not rejoice
   over me.

4 O Lord, Father and God of my life,
   do not give me haughty eyes,

5   and remove from me evil desire.

6 Let neither gluttony nor lust overcome me,
   and do not surrender me to a
   shameless soul.

7 Listen, my children, to instruction
   concerning speech;
   the one who observes it will
   never be caught.

8 The sinner is overtaken through
   his lips,
   the reviler and the arrogant are
   tripped by them.

9 Do not accustom your mouth to
   oaths,
   and do not habitually utter the
   name of the Holy One;

10 for as a servant who is continually
   examined under torture
   will not lack bruises,
   so also the man who always swears
   and utters the Name
   will not be cleansed from sin.

11 A man who swears many oaths will
   be filled with iniquity,
   and the scourge will not leave
   his house;
   if he offends, his sin remains on
   him,
   and if he disregards it, he sins
   doubly;
   if he has sworn needlessly, he will
   not be justified,
   for his house will be filled with
   calamities.

12 There is an utterance which is
   comparable to death; [w]
   may it never be found in the inheritance of Jacob!
   For all these errors will be far from
   the godly,
   and they will not wallow in sins.

13 Do not accustom your mouth to
   lewd vulgarity,
   for it involves sinful speech.

14 Remember your father and mother
   when [x] you sit among great men;
   lest you be forgetful in their presence,
   and be deemed a fool on account of your habits;
   then you will wish that you had
   never been born,

---

[s] Other authorities add *For one should not always despise restricted circumstances, nor admire a rich man who is stupid.*   [t] Or *Who will set a guard . . . destroy me?*
[u] Or *Who will set whips . . . my mind*   [v] Gk *their*
[w] Other authorities read *clothed about with death*   [x] Gk *for*

and you will curse the day of
your birth.

15 A man accustomed to use insulting
words
will never become disciplined
all his days.

16 Two sorts of men multiply sins,
and a third incurs wrath.
The soul heated like a burning fire
will not be quenched until it is
consumed;
a man who commits fornication
with his near of kin *y*
will never cease until the fire
burns him up.

17 To a fornicator all bread tastes
sweet;
he will never cease until he dies.

18 A man who breaks his marriage
vows
says to himself, "Who sees me?
Darkness surrounds me, and the
walls hide me,
and no one sees me. Why should
I fear?
The Most High will not take notice
of my sins."

19 His fear is confined to the eyes of
men,
and he does not realize that the
eyes of the Lord
are ten thousand times brighter
than the sun;
they look upon all the ways of
men,
and perceive even the hidden
places.

20 Before the universe was created, it
was known to him;
so it was also after it was finished.

21 This man will be punished in the
streets of the city,
and where he least suspects it,
he will be seized.

22 So it is with a woman who leaves
her husband
and provides an heir by a
stranger.

23 For first of all, she has disobeyed
the law of the Most High;
second, she has committed an
offence against her husband;
and third, she has committed
adultery through harlotry
and brought forth children by
another man.

24 She herself will be brought before
the assembly,
and punishment will fall on her
children.

25 Her children will not take root,
and her branches will not bear
fruit.

26 She will leave her memory for a
curse,
and her disgrace will not be
blotted out.

27 Those who survive her will recognize
that nothing is better than the
fear of the Lord,
and nothing sweeter than to heed
the commandments of the
Lord.*z*

24 Wisdom will praise herself,
and will glory in the
midst of her people.*a*

2 In the assembly of the Most High
she will open her mouth,
and in the presence of his host
she will glory:

3 "I came forth from the mouth of
the Most High,
and covered the earth like a mist.

4 I dwelt in high places,
and my throne was in a pillar of
cloud.

5 Alone I have made the circuit of
the vault of heaven
and have walked in the depths
of the abyss.

6 In the waves of the sea, in the
whole earth,
and in every people and nation
I have gotten a possession.

7 Among all these I sought a resting
place;

---

y Gk *in the body of his flesh*
z Other authorities add 28*It is a great honour to follow God, and to be received by him is long life.*
a Or *will glorify herself in the midst of the people*

I sought in whose territory I might lodge.

8 "Then the Creator of all things gave me a commandment,
and the one who created me assigned a place for my tent.
And he said, 'Make your dwelling in Jacob,
and in Israel receive your inheritance.'
9 From eternity, in the beginning, he created me,
and for eternity I shall not cease to exist.
10 In the holy tabernacle I ministered before him,
and so I was established in Zion.
11 In the beloved city likewise he gave me a resting place,
and in Jerusalem was my dominion.
12 So I took root in an honoured people,
in the portion of the Lord, who is their inheritance.

13 "I grew tall like a cedar in Lebanon,
and like a cypress on the heights of Hermon.
14 I grew tall like a palm tree in Engedi,[b]
and like rose plants in Jericho;
like a beautiful olive tree in the field,
and like a plane tree I grew tall.
15 Like cassia and camel's thorn I gave forth the aroma of spices,
and like choice myrrh I spread a pleasant odour,
like galbanum, onycha, and stacte,
and like the fragrance of frankincense in the tabernacle.
16 Like a terebinth I spread out my branches,
and my branches are glorious and graceful.
17 Like a vine I caused loveliness to bud,

and my blossoms became glorious and abundant fruit.[c]

19 "Come to me, you who desire me,
and eat your fill of my produce.
20 For the remembrance of me is sweeter than honey,
and my inheritance sweeter than the honeycomb.
21 Those who eat me will hunger for more,
and those who drink me will thirst for more.
22 Whoever obeys me will not be put to shame,
and those who work with my help will not sin."

23 All this is the book of the covenant of the Most High God,
the law which Moses commanded us
as an inheritance for the congregations of Jacob.[d]
25 It fills men with wisdom, like the Pishon,
and like the Tigris at the time of the first fruits.
26 It makes them full of understanding, like the Euphrates,
and like the Jordan at harvest time.
27 It makes instruction shine forth like light,
like the Gihon at the time of vintage.
28 Just as the first man did not know her perfectly,
the last one has not fathomed her;
29 for her thought is more abundant than the sea,
and her counsel deeper than the great abyss.

30 I went forth like a canal from a river
and like a water channel into a garden.

---

b Other authorities read *on the beaches*
c Other authorities add 18 *I am the mother of beautiful love, of fear, of knowledge, and of holy hope; being eternal, I therefore am given to all my children, to those who are named by him*
d Other authorities add 24 *"Do not cease to be strong in the Lord, cleave to him so that he may strengthen you; the Lord Almighty alone is God, and besides him there is no saviour."*

31 I said, "I will water my orchard
    and drench my garden plot";
and lo, my canal became a river,
    and my river became a sea.
32 I will again make instruction shine
    forth like the dawn,
    and I will make it shine afar;
33 I will again pour out teaching like
    prophecy,
    and leave it to all future gen-
    erations.
34 Observe that I have not laboured
    for myself alone,
    but for all who seek instruction.*e*

25 My soul takes pleasure in
    three things,
    and they are beautiful in the
    sight of the Lord and of men:*f*
agreement between brothers, friend-
    ship between neighbours,
    and a wife and husband who
    live in harmony.
2 My soul hates three kinds of men,
    and I am greatly offended at
    their life:
a beggar who is proud, a rich man
    who is a liar,
and an adulterous old man who
    lacks good sense.

3 You have gathered nothing in your
    youth;
    how then can you find anything
    in your old age?
4 What an attractive thing is judg-
    ment in grey-haired men,
    and for the aged to possess good
    counsel!
5 How attractive is wisdom in the
    aged,
    and understanding and counsel
    in honourable men!
6 Rich experience is the crown of the
    aged,
    and their boast is the fear of the
    Lord.

7 With nine thoughts I have glad-
    dened my heart,
    and a tenth I shall tell with my
    tongue:
a man rejoicing in his children;
    a man who lives to see the
    downfall of his foes;
8 happy is he who lives with an in-
    telligent wife,
    and he who has not made a slip
    with his tongue,
    and he who has not served a
    man inferior to himself;
9 happy is he who has gained good
    sense,
    and he who speaks to attentive
    listeners.
10 How great is he who has gained
    wisdom!
    But there is no one superior to
    him who fears the Lord.
11 The fear of the Lord surpasses
    everything;
    to whom shall be likened the
    one who holds it fast? *g*

13 Any wound, but not a wound of
    the heart!
    Any wickedness, but not the
    wickedness of a wife!
14 Any attack, but not an attack from
    those who hate!
    And any vengeance, but not the
    vengeance of enemies!
15 There is no venom *h* worse than a
    snake's venom,*h*
    and no wrath worse than an en-
    emy's wrath.

16 I would rather dwell with a lion
    and a dragon
    than dwell with an evil wife.
17 The wickedness of a wife changes
    her appearance,
    and darkens her face like that of
    a bear.
18 Her husband takes his meals among
    the neighbours,

---

e Gk *it*
f Syr Vg: Gk *In three things I was beautified and I stood in beauty before the Lord and men*
g Other authorities add 12 *The fear of the Lord is the beginning of love for him, and faith is the beginning of clinging to him*   *h* Cn: Gk *head*

and he cannot help sighing[i]
  bitterly.

19 Any iniquity is insignificant compared to a wife's iniquity;
  may a sinner's lot befall her!

20 A sandy ascent for the feet of the
  aged—
  such is a garrulous wife for a
  quiet husband.

21 Do not be ensnared by a woman's
  beauty,
  and do not desire a woman for
  her possessions.[j]

22 There is wrath and impudence and
  great disgrace
  when a wife supports her husband.

23 A dejected mind, a gloomy face,
  and a wounded heart are caused
  by an evil wife.
  Drooping hands and weak knees
  are caused by the wife who does
  not make her husband happy.

24 From a woman sin had its beginning,
  and because of her we all die.

25 Allow no outlet to water,
  and no boldness of speech in an
  evil wife.

26 If she does not go as you direct,
  separate her from yourself.

26 Happy is the husband of a
  good wife;
  the number of his days will be
  doubled.

2 A loyal wife rejoices her husband,
  and he will complete his years
  in peace.

3 A good wife is a great blessing;
  she will be granted among the
  blessings of the man who fears
  the Lord.

4 Whether rich or poor, his heart is
  glad,
  and at all times his face is cheerful.

5 Of three things my heart is afraid,
  and of a fourth I am frightened:[k]

The slander of a city, the gathering of a mob,
  and false accusation—all these
  are worse than death.

6 There is grief of heart and sorrow
  when a wife is envious of a
  rival,
  and a tongue-lashing makes it
  known to all.

7 An evil wife is an ox yoke which
  chafes;
  taking hold of her is like grasping
  a scorpion.

8 There is great anger when a wife
  is drunken;
  she will not hide her shame.

9 A wife's harlotry shows in her lustful eyes,
  and she is known by her eyelids.

10 Keep strict watch over a headstrong
  daughter,
  lest, when she finds liberty, she
  use it to her hurt.

11 Be on guard against her impudent
  eye,
  and do not wonder if she sins
  against you.

12 As a thirsty wayfarer opens his
  mouth
  and drinks from any water near
  him,
  so will she sit in front of every post
  and open her quiver to the arrow.

13 A wife's charm delights her husband,
  and her skill puts fat on his
  bones.

14 A silent wife is a gift of the Lord,
  and there is nothing so precious
  as a disciplined soul.

15 A modest wife adds charm to
  charm,
  and no balance can weigh the
  value of a chaste soul.

16 Like the sun rising in the heights
  of the Lord,
  so is the beauty of a good wife in
  her well-ordered home.

17 Like the shining lamp on the holy
  lampstand,

---

i Other authorities read *and listening he sighs*
j Heb Syr: Some Gk authorities read *for her beauty*   k The Greek of this line is uncertain

so is a beautiful face on a stately figure.

¹⁸ Like pillars of gold on a base of silver,
  so are beautiful feet with a steadfast heart.[l]

²⁸ At two things my heart is grieved,
  and because of a third anger comes over me:
a warrior in want through poverty,
  and intelligent men who are treated contemptuously;
a man who turns back from righteousness to sin—
  the Lord will prepare him for the sword!

²⁹ A merchant can hardly keep from wrongdoing,
  and a tradesman will not be declared innocent of sin.

27

Many have committed sin for a trifle,[m]
and whoever seeks to get rich will avert his eyes.
² As a stake is driven firmly into a fissure between stones,
  so sin is wedged in between selling and buying.
³ If a man is not steadfast and zealous in the fear of the Lord,
  his house will be quickly overthrown.

⁴ When a sieve is shaken, the refuse remains;
  so a man's filth remains in his thoughts.
⁵ The kiln tests the potter's vessels;
  so the test of a man is in his reasoning.
⁶ The fruit discloses the cultivation of a tree;
  so the expression of a thought discloses the cultivation of a man's mind.
⁷ Do not praise a man before you hear him reason,
  for this is the test of men.

⁸ If you pursue justice, you will attain it
  and wear it as a glorious robe.
⁹ Birds flock with their kind;
  so truth returns to those who practise it.
¹⁰ A lion lies in wait for prey;
  so does sin for the workers of iniquity.
¹¹ The talk of the godly man is always wise,
  but the fool changes like the moon.
¹² Among stupid people watch for a chance to leave,
  but among thoughtful people stay on.

---

[l] Other authorities add verses 19–27:
¹⁹ *My son, keep sound the bloom of your youth,*
  and do not give your strength to strangers.
²⁰ *Seek a fertile field within the whole plain,*
  and sow it with your own seed, trusting in your fine stock.
²¹ *So your offspring will survive*
  and, having confidence in their good descent, will grow great.
²² *A harlot is regarded as spittle,*
  and a married woman as a tower of death to her lovers,
²³ *A godless wife is given as a portion to a lawless man,*
  but a pious wife is given to the man who fears the Lord.
²⁴ *A shameless woman constantly acts disgracefully,*
  but a modest daughter will even be embarrassed before her husband.
²⁵ *A headstrong wife is regarded as a dog,*
  but one who has a sense of shame will fear the Lord.
²⁶ *A wife honouring her husband will seem wise to all,*
  but if she dishonours him in her pride she will be known to all as ungodly.
  Happy is the husband of a good wife;
  for the number of his years will be doubled.
²⁷ *A loud-voiced and garrulous wife is regarded as a war trumpet for putting the enemy to flight,*
  and every person like this lives in the anarchy of war.
[m] One ancient authority reads *gain*

13 The talk of fools is offensive,
and their laughter is wantonly
sinful.
14 The talk of men given to swearing
makes one's hair stand on end,
and their quarrels make a man
stop his ears.
15 The strife of the proud leads to
bloodshed,
and their abuse is grievous to
hear.

16 Whoever betrays secrets destroys
confidence,
and he will never find a con-
genial friend.
17 Love your friend and keep faith
with him;
but if you betray his secrets, do
not run after him.
18 For as a man destroys his enemy,
so you have destroyed the friendship of your neighbour.
19 And as you allow a bird to escape
from your hand,
so you have let your neighbour go,
and will not catch him again.
20 Do not go after him, for he is too
far off,
and has escaped like a gazelle
from a snare.
21 For a wound may be bandaged,
and there is reconciliation after
abuse,
but whoever has betrayed secrets is
without hope.

22 Whoever winks his eye plans evil
deeds,
and no one can keep him from
them.
23 In your presence his mouth is all
sweetness,
and he admires your words;
but later he will twist his speech
and with your own words he will
give offence.
24 I have hated many things, but none
to be compared to him;
even the Lord will hate him.

25 Whoever throws a stone straight
up throws it on his own head;
and a treacherous blow opens up
wounds.
26 He who digs a pit will fall into it,
and he who sets a snare will be
caught in it.
27 If a man does evil, it will roll back
upon him,
and he will not know where it
came from.
28 Mockery and abuse issue from the
proud man,*
but vengeance lies in wait for
him like a lion.
29 Those who rejoice in the fall of the
godly will be caught in a snare,
and pain will consume them before their death.

30 Anger and wrath, these also are
abominations,
and the sinful man will possess
them.

28 He that takes vengeance will
suffer vengeance from the
Lord,
and he will firmly establish *o* his
sins.
2 Forgive your neighbour the wrong
he has done,
and then your sins will be par-
doned when you pray.
3 Does a man harbour anger against
another,
and yet seek for healing from
the Lord?
4 Does he have no mercy toward a
man like himself,
and yet pray for his own sins?
5 If he himself, being flesh, main-
tains wrath,
who will make expiation for his
sins?
6 Remember the end of your life, and
cease from enmity,
remember destruction and
death, and be true to the commandments.
7 Remember the commandments,

---

* Other authorities read *proud men*   *o* Other authorities read *closely observe*

141

and do not be angry with your
neighbour;
remember the covenant of the
Most High, and overlook ignorance.

8 Refrain from strife, and you will
lessen sins;
for a man given to anger will
kindle strife,
9 and a sinful man will disturb
friends
and inject enmity among those
who are at peace.
10 In proportion to the fuel for the
fire, so will be the burning,
and in proportion to the obstin-
acy of strife will be the burning; *p*
in proportion to the strength of the
man will be his anger,
and in proportion to his wealth
he will heighten his wrath.
11 A hasty quarrel kindles fire,
and urgent strife sheds blood.
12 If you blow on a spark, it will glow;
if you spit on it, it will be put
out;
and both come out of your
mouth.

13 Curse the whisperer and deceiver,
for he has destroyed many who
were at peace.
14 Slander *q* has shaken many,
and scattered them from nation
to nation,
and destroyed strong cities,
and overturned the houses of
great men.
15 Slander *q* has driven away courageous women,
and deprived them of the fruit
of their toil.
16 Whoever pays heed to slander *r*
will not find rest,
nor will he settle down in peace.
17 The blow of a whip raises a welt,
but a blow of the tongue crushes
the bones.

18 Many have fallen by the edge of
the sword,
but not so many as have fallen
because of the tongue.
19 Happy is the man who is protected
from it,
who has not been exposed to its
anger,
who has not borne its yoke,
and has not been bound with its
fetters;
20 for its yoke is a yoke of iron,
and its fetters are fetters of
bronze;
21 its death is an evil death,
and Hades is preferable to it.
22 It will not be master over the godly,
and they will not be burned in its
flame.
23 Those who forsake the Lord will
fall into its power;
it will burn among them and will
not be put out.
It will be sent out against them like
a lion;
like a leopard it will mangle
them.
24 See that you fence in your property with thorns,
lock up your silver and gold,
25 make balances and scales for your
words,
and make a door and a bolt for
your mouth.
26 Beware lest you err with your
tongue, *s*
lest you fall before him who lies
in wait.

29 He that shows mercy will
lend to his neighbour,
and he that strengthens him with
his hand keeps the commandments.
2 Lend to your neighbour in the time
of his need;
and in turn, repay your neighbour promptly.
3 Confirm your word and keep faith
with him,

---

p Other authorities place this line at the end of the verse, or omit it
q Gk *a third tongue*   *r* Gk *it*   *s* Gk *with it*

and on every occasion you will
    find what you need.
4 Many persons regard a loan as a
    windfall,
    and cause trouble to those who
      help them.
5 A man will kiss another's hands
    until he gets a loan,
    and will lower his voice in speak-
      ing of his neighbour's money;
    but at the time for repayment he
      will delay,
    and will pay in words of uncon-
      cern,
    and will find fault with the time.
6 If the lender *t* exerts pressure, he
    will hardly get back half,
    and will regard that as a wind-
      fall.
    If he does not, the borrower *u* has
      robbed him of his money,
    and he has needlessly made him
      his enemy;
    he will repay him with curses and
      reproaches,
    and instead of glory will repay
      him with dishonour.
7 Because of such wickedness, there-
    fore,*v* many have refused to
    lend;
    they have been afraid of being
      defrauded needlessly.

8 Nevertheless, be patient with a
    man in humble circumstances,
    and do not make him wait for
      your alms.
9 Help a poor man for the command-
    ment's sake,
    and because of his need do not
      send him away empty.
10 Lose your silver for the sake of a
    brother or a friend,
    and do not let it rust under a
      stone and be lost.
11 Lay up your treasure according to
    the commandments of the
    Most High,
    and it will profit you more than
      gold.

12 Store up almsgiving in your treas-
    ury,
    and it will rescue you from all
      affliction;
13 more than a mighty shield and
    more than a heavy spear,
    it will fight on your behalf
      against your enemy.

14 A good man will be surety for his
    neighbour,
    but a man who has lost his
      sense of shame will fail him.
15 Do not forget all the kindness of
    your surety,
    for he has given his life for you.
16 A sinner will overthrow the pros-
    perity of his surety,
17   and one who does not feel grate-
      ful will abandon his rescuer.
18 Being surety has ruined many men
    who were prosperous,
    and has shaken them like a wave
      of the sea;
    it has driven men of power into
      exile,
    and they have wandered among
      foreign nations.
19 The sinner who has fallen into
    suretyship
    and pursues gain will fall into
      lawsuits.
20 Assist your neighbour according to
    your ability,
    but take heed to yourself lest
      you fall.

21 The essentials for life are water
    and bread
    and clothing and a house to
      cover one's nakedness.
22 Better is the life of a poor man
    under the shelter of his roof
    than sumptuous food in another
      man's house.
23 Be content with little or much.*w*
24 It is a miserable life to go from
    house to house,
    and where you are a stranger you
      may not open your mouth;

---

t Gk *he*   *u* Gk *he*   *v* Other authorities read *It is not because of wickedness that*
w Other authorities add: *and you will not hear reproach for your sojourning.*

25 you will play the host and provide
    drink without being thanked,
  and besides this you will hear
    bitter words:
26 "Come here, stranger, prepare the
    table,
  and if you have anything at
    hand, let me have it to eat."
27 "Give place, stranger, to an hon-
    oured person;
  my brother has come to stay
    with me; I need my house."
28 These things are hard to bear for
    a man who has feeling:
  scolding about lodging *x* and the
    reproach of the moneylender.

30 He who loves his son will
    whip him often,
  in order that he may rejoice at
    the way he turns out.
2 He who disciplines his son will
    profit by him,
  and will boast of him among
    acquaintances.
3 He who teaches his son will make
    his enemies envious,
  and will glory in him in the
    presence of friends.
4 The *y* father may die, and yet he
    is not dead,
  for he has left behind him one
    like himself;
5 while alive he saw and rejoiced,
  and when he died he was not
    grieved;
6 he has left behind him an avenger
    against his enemies,
  and one to repay the kindness
    of his friends.

7 He who spoils his son will bind up
    his wounds,
  and his feelings will be troubled
    at every cry.
8 A horse that is untamed turns out
    to be stubborn,
  and a son unrestrained turns out
    to be wilful.

9 Pamper a child, and he will
    frighten you;
  play with him, and he will give
    you grief.
10 Do not laugh with him, lest you
    have sorrow with him,
  and in the end you will gnash
    your teeth.
11 Give him no authority in his youth,
  and do not ignore his errors.
12 Bow down his neck in his youth,*z*
  and beat his sides while he is
    young,
  lest he become stubborn and dis-
    obey you,
  and you have sorrow of soul
    from him.*a*
13 Discipline your son and take pains
    with him,
  that you may not be offended by
    his shamelessness.

14 Better off is a poor man who is well
    and strong in constitution
  than a rich man who is severely
    afflicted in body.
15 Health and soundness are better
    than all gold,
  and a robust body than count-
    less riches.
16 There is no wealth better than
    health of body,
  and there is no gladness above
    joy of heart.
17 Death is better than a miserable
    life,
  and eternal rest *b* than chronic
    sickness.

18 Good things poured out upon a
    mouth that is closed
  are like offerings of food placed
    upon a grave.
19 Of what use to an idol is an offer-
    ing of fruit?
  For it can neither eat nor smell.
  So is he who is afflicted by the
    Lord;
20 he sees with his eyes and groans,

x Or *from the household,* or (Syr) *from the host*   *y* Greek *His*
z Other authorities omit this line and the preceding line   *a* Other authorities omit this line
b Some authorities omit *eternal rest*

like a eunuch who embraces a
maiden and groans.

21 Do not give yourself over to sorrow,
and do not afflict yourself de-
liberately.
22 Gladness of heart is the life of man,
and the rejoicing of a man is
length of days.
23 Delight your soul and comfort your
heart,
and remove sorrow far from you,
for sorrow has destroyed many,
and there is no profit in it.
24 Jealousy and anger shorten life,
and anxiety brings on old age
too soon.
25 A man of cheerful and good heart
will give heed to the food he
eats.

31 Wakefulness over wealth
wastes away one's flesh,
and anxiety about it removes
sleep.
2 Wakeful anxiety prevents slumber,
and a severe illness carries off
sleep.*c*
3 The rich man toils as his wealth
accumulates,
and when he rests he fills himself with his dainties.
4 The poor man toils as his liveli-
hood diminishes,
and when he rests he becomes
needy.

5 He who loves gold will not be
justified,
and he who pursues money will
be led astray *d* by it.
6 Many have come to ruin because
of gold,
and their destruction has met
them face to face.
7 It is a stumbling block to those
who are devoted to it,
and every fool will be taken
captive by it.

8 Blessed is the rich man who is
found blameless,
and who does not go after gold.
9 Who is he? And we will call him
blessed,
for he has done wonderful things
among his people.
10 Who has been tested by it and
been found perfect?
Let it be for him a ground for
boasting.
Who has had the power to transgress and did not transgress,
and to do evil and did not do it?
11 His prosperity will be established,
and the assembly will relate his
acts of charity.

12 Are you seated at the table of a
great man? *e*
Do not be greedy *f* at it,
and do not say, "There is certainly much upon it!"
13 Remember that a greedy *g* eye is
a bad thing.
What has been created more
greedy *g* than the eye?
Therefore it sheds tears from
every face.
14 Do not reach out your hand for
everything you see,
and do not crowd your neighbour *h* at the dish.
15 Judge your neighbour's feelings by
your own,
and in every matter be thoughtful.
16 Eat like a human being what is set
before you,
and do not chew greedily, lest
you be hated.
17 Be the first to stop eating, for the
sake of good manners,
and do not be insatiable, lest
you give offence.
18 If you are seated among many
persons,
do not reach out your hand before they do.

c Other authorities read *sleep carries off a severe illness*   *d* Heb Syr: Gk *will be filled*
e Heb Syr: Gk *at a great table*   *f* Gk *open your throat*   *g* Gk *evil*   *h* Gk *him*

19 How ample a little is for a well
    disciplined man!
  He does not breathe heavily
    upon his bed.
20 Healthy sleep depends on mod-
    erate eating;
  he rises early, and feels fit.[i]
  The distress of sleeplessness and
    of nausea
  and colic are with the glutton.
21 If you are overstuffed with food,
  get up in the middle of the
    meal, and you will have relief.
22 Listen to me, my son, and do not
    disregard me,
  and in the end you will appreci-
    ate my words.
  In all your work be industrious,
  and no sickness will overtake you.

23 Men will praise the one who is
    liberal with food,
  and their testimony to his excel-
    lence is trustworthy.
24 The city will complain of the one
    who is niggardly with food,
  and their testimony to his nig-
    gardliness is accurate.

25 Do not aim to be valiant over wine,
    for wine has destroyed many.
26 Fire and water prove[j] the temper
    of steel,
  so wine tests hearts in the strife
    of the proud.
27 Wine is like life to men,
  if you drink it in moderation.
  What is life to a man who is with-
    out wine?
  It has been created to make men
    glad.
28 Wine drunk in season and tem-
    perately
  is rejoicing of heart and glad-
    ness of soul.
29 Wine drunk to excess is bitterness
    of soul,
  with provocation and stumbling.
30 Drunkenness increases the anger
    of a fool to his injury,
  reducing his strength and adding
    wounds.

31 Do not reprove your neighbour at
    a banquet of wine,
  and do not despise him in his
    merrymaking;
  speak no word of reproach to him,
  and do not afflict him by mak-
    ing demands of him.

32 If they make you master of
    the feast, do not exalt
    yourself;
  be among them as one of them;
  take good care of them and then
    be seated;
2 when you have fulfilled your
    duties, take your place,
  that you may be merry on their
    account
  and receive a wreath for your
    excellent leadership.

3 Speak, you who are older, for it is
    fitting that you should,
  but with accurate knowledge,
  and do not interrupt the
    music.
4 Where there is entertainment, do
    not pour out talk;
  do not display your cleverness
    out of season.
5 A ruby seal in a setting of gold
  is a concert of music at a ban-
    quet of wine.
6 A seal of emerald in a rich setting
    of gold
  is the melody of music with
    good wine.

7 Speak, young man, if there is need
    of you,
  but no more than twice, and
    only if asked.
8 Speak concisely, say much in few
    words;
  be as one who knows and yet
    holds his tongue.
9 Among the great do not act as
    their equal;
  and when another is speaking,
    do not babble.

10 Lightning speeds before the thun-
    der,

---

i Gk *his soul is with him*   j Gk *The furnace by dipping proves*

and approval precedes a modest
  man.
11 Leave in good time and do not be
  the last;
  go home quickly and do not
  linger.
12 Amuse yourself there, and do what
  you have in mind,
  but do not sin through proud
    speech.
13 And for these things bless him who
    made you
  and satisfies you with his good
    gifts.

14 He who fears the Lord will accept
  his discipline,
  and those who rise early to seek
    him *k* will find favour.
15 He who seeks the law will be filled
    with it,
  but the hypocrite will stumble
    at it.
16 Those who fear the Lord will form
    true judgments,
  and like a light they will kindle
    righteous deeds.
17 A sinful man will shun reproof,
  and will find a decision accord-
    ing to his liking.

18 A man of judgment will not over-
    look an idea,
  and an insolent *l* and proud man
    will not cower in fear.*m*
19 Do nothing without deliberation;
  and when you have acted, do not
    regret it.
20 Do not go on a path full of
    hazards,
  and do not stumble over stony
    ground.
21 Do not be overconfident on a
    smooth *n* way,
22   and give good heed to your
    paths.*o*
23 Guard *p* yourself in every act,
  for this is the keeping of the
    commandments.

24 He who believes the law gives heed
    to the commandments,
  and he who trusts the Lord will
    not suffer loss.

33

No evil will befall the man
  who fears the Lord,
but in trial he will deliver him
    again and again.
2 A wise man will not hate the law,
  but he who is hypocritical about
    it is like a boat in a storm.
3 A man of understanding will trust
    in the law;
  for him the law is as dependable
    as an inquiry by means of
    Urim.

4 Prepare what to say, and thus you
    will be heard;
  bind together your instruction,
    and make your answer.
5 The heart of a fool is like a cart
    wheel,
  and his thoughts like a turning
    axle.
6 A stallion is like a mocking friend;
  he neighs under every one who
    sits on him.

7 Why is any day better than
    another,
  when all the daylight in the
    year is from the sun?
8 By the Lord's decision they were
    distinguished,
  and he appointed the different
    seasons and feasts;
9 some of them he exalted and hal-
    lowed,
  and some of them he made or-
    dinary days.
10 All men are from the ground,
  and Adam was created of the
    dust.
11 In the fulness of his knowledge
    the Lord distinguished them
  and appointed their different
    ways;

---

k Other authorities omit *to seek him*   *l* Heb: Gk *alien*
m The meaning of this line is uncertain. Other authorities add the phrases *and after acting, with
him, without deliberation*   *n* Or *an unexplored*   *o* Syr Vg: Gk *and beware of your children*
p Heb Syr: Gk *Trust*

12 some of them he blessed and exalted,

and some of them he made holy and brought near to himself;

but some of them he cursed and brought low,

and he turned them out of their place.

13 As clay in the hand of the potter—

for all his ways are as he pleases—

so men are in the hand of him who made them,

to give them as he decides.

14 Good is the opposite of evil, and life the opposite of death;

so the sinner is the opposite of the godly.

15 Look upon all the works of the Most High;

they likewise are in pairs, one the opposite of the other.

16 I was the last on watch;

I was like one who gleans after the grape-gatherers;

by the blessing of the Lord I excelled,

and like a grape-gatherer I filled my wine press.

17 Consider that I have not laboured for myself alone,

but for all who seek instruction.

18 Hear me, you who are great among the people,

and you leaders of the congregation, hearken.

19 To son or wife, to brother or friend,

do not give power over yourself, as long as you live;

and do not give your property to another,

lest you change your mind and must ask for it.

20 While you are still alive and have breath in you,

do not let any one take your place.

21 For it is better that your children should ask from you

than that you should look to the hand of your sons.

22 Excel in all that you do;

bring no stain upon your honour.

23 At the time when you end the days of your life,

in the hour of death, distribute your inheritance.

24 Fodder and a stick and burdens for an ass;

bread and discipline and work for a servant.

25 Set your slave to work, and you will find rest;

leave his hands idle, and he will seek liberty.

26 Yoke and thong will bow the neck,

and for a wicked servant there are racks and tortures.

27 Put him to work, that he may not be idle,

for idleness teaches much evil.

28 Set him to work, as is fitting for him,

and if he does not obey, make his fetters heavy.

29 Do not act immoderately toward anybody,

and do nothing without discretion.

30 If you have a servant, let him be as yourself,

because you have bought him with blood.

31 If you have a servant, treat him as a brother,

for as your own soul you will need him.

If you ill-treat him, and he leaves and runs away,

which way will you go to seek him?

34 A man of no understanding has vain and false hopes,

and dreams give wings to fools.

2 As one who catches at a shadow and pursues the wind,

so is he who gives heed to dreams.

3 The vision of dreams is this against that,

the likeness of a face confront-
ing a face.

4 From an unclean thing what will
be made clean?
And from something false what
will be true?

5 Divinations and omens and dreams
are folly,
and like a woman in travail the
mind has fancies.

6 Unless they are sent from the Most
High as a visitation,
do not give your mind to them.

7 For dreams have deceived many,
and those who put their hope in
them have failed.

8 Without such deceptions the law
will be fulfilled,
and wisdom is made perfect in
truthful lips.

9 An educated *q* man knows many
things,
and one with much experience
will speak with understanding.

10 He that is inexperienced knows
few things,
but he that has travelled acquires much cleverness.

11 I have seen many things in my
travels,
and I understand more than I
can express.

12 I have often been in danger of
death,
but have escaped because of
these experiences.

13 The spirit of those who fear the
Lord will live,
for their hope is in him who
saves them.

14 He who fears the Lord will not be
timid,
nor play the coward, for he is
his hope.

15 Blessed is the soul of the man who
fears the Lord!
To whom does he look? And
who is his support?

16 The eyes of the Lord are upon
those who love him,
a mighty protection and strong
support,
a shelter from the hot wind and a
shade from noonday sun,
a guard against stumbling and
a defence against falling.

17 He lifts up the soul and gives light
to the eyes;
he grants healing, life, and
blessing.

18 If one sacrifices from what has
been wrongfully obtained, the
offering is blemished; *r*
the gifts *s* of the lawless are not
acceptable.

19 The Most High is not pleased
with the offerings of the ungodly;
and he is not propitiated for sins
by a multitude of sacrifices.

20 Like one who kills a son before his
father's eyes
is the man who offers a sacrifice
from the property of the poor.

21 The bread of the needy is the life
of the poor;
whoever deprives them of it is
a man of blood.

22 To take away a neighbour's living
is to murder him;
to deprive an employee of his
wages is to shed blood.

23 When one builds and another
tears down,
what do they gain but toil?

24 When one prays and another
curses,
to whose voice will the Lord
listen?

25 If a man washes after touching a
dead body, and touches it
again,
what has he gained by his wash-
ing?

26 So if a man fasts for his sins,
and goes again and does the
same things,

q Other authorities read *A travelled*   r Other authorities read *is made in mockery*
s Other authorities read *mockeries*

who will listen to his prayer?
And what has he gained by
humbling himself?

35

He who keeps the law makes
many offerings;
he who heeds the command-
ments sacrifices a peace offering.

2 He who returns a kindness offers
fine flour,
and he who gives alms sacrifices
a thank offering.

3 To keep from wickedness is pleasing to the Lord,
and to forsake unrighteousness
is atonement.

4 Do not appear before the Lord
empty-handed,

5 for all these things are to be
done because of the com-
mandment.

6 The offering of a righteous man
anoints the altar,
and its pleasing odour rises before the Most High.

7 The sacrifice of a righteous man is
acceptable,
and the memory of it will not
be forgotten.

8 Glorify the Lord generously,
and do not stint the first fruits
of your hands.

9 With every gift show a cheerful
face,
and dedicate your tithe with
gladness.

10 Give to the Most High as he has
given,
and as generously as your hand
has found.

11 For the Lord is the one who repays,
and he will repay you sevenfold.

12 Do not offer him a bribe, for he
will not accept it;
and do not trust to an unrighteous sacrifice;
for the Lord is the judge,
and with him is no partiality.

13 He will not show partiality in the
case of a poor man;
and he will listen to the prayer
of one who is wronged.

14 He will not ignore the supplication
of the fatherless,
nor the widow when she pours
out her story.

15 Do not the tears of the widow run
down her cheek
as she cries out against him who
has caused them to fall?

16 He whose service is pleasing to the
Lord will be accepted,
and his prayer will reach to the
clouds.

17 The prayer of the humble pierces
the clouds,
and he will not be consoled until it reaches the Lord; [t]
he will not desist until the Most
High visits him,
and does justice for the righteous, and executes judgment.

18 And the Lord will not delay,
neither will he be patient with
them,
till he crushes the loins of the un-
merciful
and repays vengeance on the
nations;
till he takes away the multitude of
the insolent,
and breaks the sceptres of the
unrighteous;

19 till he repays man according to his
deeds,
and the works of men according
to their devices;
till he judges the case of his people
and makes them rejoice in his
mercy.

20 Mercy is as welcome when he
afflicts them
as clouds of rain in the time of
drought.

36

Have mercy upon us, O
Lord, the God of all, and
look upon us,

[t] Or *until the Lord draws near*

2 and cause the fear of thee to fall
  upon all the nations.
3 Lift up thy hand against foreign
  nations
  and let them see thy might.
4 As in us thou hast been sanctified
  before them,
  so in them be thou magnified
  before us;
5 and let them know thee, as we
  have known
  that there is no God but thee,
  O Lord.
6 Show signs anew, and work further
  wonders;
  make thy hand and thy right
  arm glorious.
7 Rouse thy anger and pour out thy
  wrath;
  destroy the adversary and wipe
  out the enemy.
8 Hasten the day, and remember the
  appointed time,[u]
  and let people recount thy
  mighty deeds.
9 Let him who survives be consumed
  in the fiery wrath,
  and may those who harm thy
  people meet destruction.
10 Crush the heads of the rulers of
  the enemy,
  who say, "There is no one but
  ourselves."
11 Gather all the tribes of Jacob,
  and give[v] them their inheritance, as at the beginning.
12 Have mercy, O Lord, upon the
  people called by thy name,
  upon Israel, whom thou hast
  likened to a[w] first-born son.
13 Have pity on the city of thy sanctuary,[x]
  Jerusalem, the place of thy rest.
14 Fill Zion with the celebration of
  thy wondrous deeds,
  and thy temple[y] with thy glory.
15 Bear witness to those whom thou
  didst create in the beginning,

and fulfil the prophecies spoken
  in thy name.
16 Reward those who wait for thee,
  and let thy prophets be found
  trustworthy.
17 Hearken, O Lord, to the prayer of
  thy servants,
  according to the blessing of
  Aaron for thy people,
  and all who are on the earth will
  know
  that thou art the Lord, the God
  of the ages.

18 The stomach will take any food,
  yet one food is better than
  another.
19 As the palate tastes the kinds of
  game,
  so an intelligent mind detects
  false words.
20 A perverse mind will cause grief,
  but a man of experience will pay
  him back.
21 A woman will accept any man,
  but one daughter is better than
  another.
22 A woman's beauty gladdens the
  countenance,
  and surpasses every human desire.
23 If kindness and humility mark her
  speech,
  her husband is not like other
  men.
24 He who acquires a wife gets his
  best possession,[z]
  a helper fit for him and a pillar
  of support.[a]
25 Where there is no fence, the property will be plundered;
  and where there is no wife, a
  man will wander about and
  sigh.
26 For who will trust a nimble robber
  that skips from city to city?
  So who will trust a man that has
  no home,

---

u Other authorities read *remember thy oath*   v Other authorities read *gave*
w Other authorities read *hast named thy*   x Or *on thy holy city*   y Heb Syr: Gk Vg *people*
z Heb: Gk *enters upon a possession*   a Heb: Gk *rest*

and lodges wherever night finds him?

37

Every friend will say, "I too am a friend";
but some friends are friends only in name.
2 Is it not a grief to the death
when a companion and friend turns to enmity?
3 O evil imagination, why were you formed
to cover the land with deceit?
4 Some companions rejoice in the happiness of a friend,
but in time of trouble are against him.
5 Some companions help a friend for their stomachs' sake,
and in the face of battle take up the shield.
6 Do not forget a friend in your heart,
and be not unmindful of him in your wealth.

7 Every counsellor praises counsel,
but some give counsel in their own interest.
8 Be wary of a counsellor,
and learn first what is his interest—
for he will take thought for himself—
lest he cast the lot against you
9 and tell you, "Your way is good,"
and then stand aloof to see what will happen to you.
10 Do not consult with one who looks at you suspiciously;
hide your counsel from those who are jealous of you.
11 Do not consult with a woman about her rival
or with a coward about war,
with a merchant about barter
or with a buyer about selling,
with a grudging man about gratitude
or with a merciless man about kindness,
with an idler about any work
or with a man hired for a year about completing his work,
with a lazy servant about a big task—
pay no attention to these in any matter of counsel.
12 But stay constantly with a godly man
whom you know to be a keeper of the commandments,
whose soul is in accord with your soul,
and who will sorrow with you if you fail.
13 And establish the counsel of your own heart,
for no one is more faithful to you than it is.
14 For a man's soul sometimes keeps him better informed
than seven watchmen sitting high on a watchtower.
15 And besides all this pray to the Most High
that he may direct your way in truth.

16 Reason is the beginning of every work,
and counsel precedes every undertaking.
17 As a clue to changes of heart
18 four turns of fortune appear,
good and evil, life and death;
and it is the tongue that continually rules them.
19 A man may be shrewd and the teacher of many,
and yet be unprofitable to himself.
20 A man skilled in words may be hated;
he will be destitute of all food,
21 for grace was not given him by the Lord,
since he is lacking in all wisdom.
22 A man may be wise to his own advantage,
and the fruits of his understanding may be trustworthy on his lips.
23 A wise man will instruct his own people,

and the fruits of his understanding will be trustworthy.
24 A wise man will have praise heaped
upon him,
and all who see him will call him
happy.
25 The life of a man is numbered by
days,
but the days of Israel are without number.
26 He who is wise among his people
will inherit confidence,*b*
and his name will live for ever.

27 My son, test your soul while you
live;
see what is bad for it and do not
give it that.
28 For not everything is good for
every one,
and not every person enjoys
everything.
29 Do not have an insatiable appetite
for any luxury,
and do not give yourself up to
food;
30 for overeating brings sickness,
and gluttony leads to nausea.
31 Many have died of gluttony,
but he who is careful to avoid
it prolongs his life.

38 Honour the physician with
the honour due him,*c* according to your need of
him,
for the Lord created him;
2 for healing comes from the Most
High,
and he will receive a gift from
the king.
3 The skill of the physician lifts up
his head,
and in the presence of great
men he is admired.
4 The Lord created medicines from
the earth,
and a sensible man will not despise them.

5 Was not water made sweet with a
tree
in order that his *d* power might
be known?
6 And he gave skill to men
that he *e* might be glorified in
his marvellous works.
7 By them he heals and takes away
pain;
8 the pharmacist makes of them
a compound.
His works will never be finished;
and from him health *f* is upon
the face of the earth.

9 My son, when you are sick do not
be negligent,
but pray to the Lord, and he
will heal you.
10 Give up your faults and direct your
hands aright,
and cleanse your heart from all
sin.
11 Offer a sweet-smelling sacrifice,
and a memorial portion of
fine flour,
and pour oil on your offering,
as much as you can afford.*g*
12 And give the physician his place,
for the Lord created him;
let him not leave you, for there
is need of him.
13 There is a time when success lies
in the hands of physicians,*h*
14 for they too will pray to the
Lord
that he should grant them success
in diagnosis *i*
and in healing, for the sake of
preserving life.
15 He who sins before his Maker,
may he fall into the care *j* of a
physician.

16 My son, let your tears fall for the
dead,
and as one who is suffering
grievously begin the lament.
Lay out his body with the honour
due him,

---

b Other authorities read *honour*   *c* Other authorities omit *with the honour due him*   *d* Or *its*
e Or *they*   *f* Or *peace*   *g* Heb: Vg omits *as much as you can afford;* Gk is obscure
h Gk *in their hands*   *i* Heb: Gk *rest*   *j* Gk *hands*

and do not neglect his burial.

17 Let your weeping be bitter and
your wailing fervent;
observe the mourning according
to his merit,
for one day, or two, to avoid
criticism;
then be comforted for your
sorrow.

18 For sorrow results in death,
and sorrow of heart saps one's
strength.

19 In calamity sorrow continues,
and the life of the poor man
weighs down his heart.

20 Do not give your heart to sorrow;
drive it away, remembering the
end of life.

21 Do not forget, there is no coming
back;
you do the dead *k* no good, and
you injure yourself.

22 "Remember my doom, for yours is
like it:
yesterday it was mine, and today it is yours."

23 When the dead is at rest, let his
remembrance cease,
and be comforted for him when
his spirit has departed.

24 The wisdom of the scribe depends
on the opportunity of leisure;
and he who has little business
may become wise.

25 How can he become wise who
handles the plough,
and who glories in the shaft of
a goad,
who drives oxen and is occupied
with their work,
and whose talk is about *l* bulls?

26 He sets his heart on ploughing
furrows,
and he is careful about fodder
for the heifers.

27 So too is every craftsman and
master workman
who labours by night as well as
by day;
those who cut the signets of seals,

each is diligent in making a
great variety;
he sets his heart on painting a
lifelike image,
and he is careful to finish his
work.

28 So too is the smith sitting by the
anvil,
intent upon his handiwork in
iron;
the breath of the fire melts his
flesh,
and he wastes away in *m* the heat
of the furnace;
he inclines his ear to the sound of
the hammer,*n*
and his eyes are on the pattern
of the object.
He sets his heart on finishing his
handiwork,
and he is careful to complete its
decoration.

29 So too is the potter sitting at his
work
and turning the wheel with his
feet;
he is always deeply concerned over
his work,
and all his output is by number.

30 He moulds the clay with his arm
and makes it pliable with his
feet;
he sets his heart to finish the
glazing,
and he is careful to clean the
furnace.

31 All these rely upon their hands,
and each is skilful in his own
work.

32 Without them a city cannot be
established,
and men can neither sojourn nor
live there.

33 Yet they are not sought out for
the council of the people,
nor do they attain eminence in
the public assembly.
They do not sit in the judge's seat,
nor do they understand the sentence of judgment;

k Gk *him*   *l* Or *among*   *m* Cn Compare Syr: Gk *contends with*
n Cn: Gk *the sound of the hammer renews his ear*

they cannot expound discipline or judgment,
and they are not found using proverbs.
34 But they keep stable the fabric of the world,
and their prayer is in the practice of their trade.

39 On the other hand he who devotes himself
to the study of the law of the Most High
will seek out the wisdom of all the ancients,
and will be concerned with prophecies;
2 he will preserve the discourse of notable men
and penetrate the subtleties of parables;
3 he will seek out the hidden meanings of proverbs
and be at home with the obscurities of parables.
4 He will serve among great men
and appear before rulers;
he will travel through the lands of foreign nations,
for he tests the good and the evil among men.
5 He will set his heart to rise early
to seek the Lord who made him,
and will make supplication before the Most High;
he will open his mouth in prayer
and make supplication for his sins.
6 If the great Lord is willing,
he will be filled with the spirit of understanding;
he will pour forth words *o* of wisdom
and give thanks to the Lord in prayer.
7 He will direct his counsel and knowledge aright,
and meditate on his secrets.
8 He will reveal instruction in his teaching,

and will glory in the law of the Lord's covenant.
9 Many will praise his understanding,
and it will never be blotted out;
his memory will not disappear,
and his name will live through all generations.
10 Nations will declare his wisdom,
and the congregation will proclaim his praise;
11 if he lives long, he will leave a name greater than a thousand,
and if he goes to rest, it is enough *p* for him.

12 I have yet more to say, which I have thought upon,
and I am filled, like the moon at the full.
13 Listen to me, O you holy sons,
and bud like a rose growing by a stream of water;
14 send forth fragrance like frankincense,
and put forth blossoms like a lily.
Scatter the fragrance, and sing a hymn of praise;
bless the Lord for all his works;
15 ascribe majesty to his name
and give thanks to him with praise,
with songs on your lips, and with lyres;
and this you shall say in thanksgiving:
16 "All things are the works of the Lord, for they are very good,
and whatever he commands will be done in his time."

17 No one can say, "What is this?" "Why is that?"
for in God's *q* time all things will be sought after.
At his word the waters stood in a heap,
and the reservoirs of water at the word of his mouth.
18 At his command whatever pleases him is done,

---

o Other authorities read *his words*   *p* Cn: the meaning of the Gk is uncertain   *q* Gk *his*

and none can limit his saving
power.

19 The works of all flesh are before
him,
and nothing can be hid from his
eyes.

20 From everlasting to everlasting he
beholds them,
and nothing is marvellous to him.

21 No one can say, "What is this?"
"Why is that?"
for everything has been created
for its use.

22 His blessing covers the dry land
like a river,
and drenches it like a flood.

23 The nations will incur his wrath,
just as he turns fresh water into
salt.

24 To the holy his ways are straight,
just as they are obstacles to the
wicked.

25 From the beginning good things
were created for good people,
just as evil things for sinners.

26 Basic to all the needs of man's life
are water and fire and iron and
salt
and wheat flour and milk and
honey,
the blood of the grape, and oil
and clothing.

27 All these are for good to the godly,
just as they turn into evils for
sinners.

28 There are winds that have been
created for vengeance,
and in their anger they scourge
heavily;
in the time of consummation they
will pour out their strength
and calm the anger of their
Maker.

29 Fire and hail and famine and pestilence,
all these have been created for
vengeance;

30 the teeth of wild beasts, and scor-
pions and vipers,

and the sword that punishes the
ungodly with destruction;

31 they will rejoice in his commands,
and be made ready on earth for
their service,
and when their times come they
will not transgress his word.

32 Therefore from the beginning I
have been convinced,
and have thought this out and
left it in writing:

33 The works of the Lord are all good,
and he will supply every need in
its hour.

34 And no one can say, "This is worse
than that,"
for all things will prove good in
their season.

35 So now sing praise with all your
heart and voice,
and bless the name of the Lord.

40 Much labour was created for
every man,
and a heavy yoke is upon the
sons of Adam,
from the day they come forth from
their mother's womb
till the day they return to *r* the
mother of all.

2 Their perplexities and fear of
heart—
their anxious thought is the day
of death,

3 from the man who sits on a splendid throne
to the one who is humbled in
dust and ashes,

4 from the man who wears purple
and a crown
to the one who is clothed in bur-
lap;

5 there is anger and envy and trouble and unrest,
and fear of death, and fury and
strife.
And when one rests upon his bed,
his sleep at night confuses his
mind.

6 He gets little or no rest,

r Other authorities read *are buried in*

and afterward in his sleep, as
though he were on watch,
he is troubled by the visions of his
mind
like one who has escaped from
the battle-front;

7 at the moment of his rescue he
wakes up,
and wonders that his fear came
to nothing.

8 With all flesh, both man and
beast,
and upon sinners seven times
more,

9 are death and bloodshed and strife
and sword,
calamities, famine and affliction
and plague.

10 All these were created for the
wicked,
and on their account the flood
came.

11 All things that are from the earth
turn back to the earth,
and what is from the waters returns to the sea.

12 All bribery and injustice will be
blotted out,
but good faith will stand for ever.

13 The wealth of the unjust will dry
up like a torrent,
and crash like a loud clap of
thunder in a rain.

14 A generous man will be made glad;
likewise transgressors will utterly fail.

15 The children of the ungodly will
not put forth many branches;
they are unhealthy roots upon
sheer rock.

16 The reeds by any water or river
bank
will be plucked up before any
grass.

17 Kindness is like a garden of blessings,
and almsgiving endures for ever.

18 Life is sweet for the self-reliant and
the worker,[s]

but he who finds treasure is better off than both.

19 Children and the building of a
city establish a man's name,
but a blameless wife is accounted
better than both.

20 Wine and music gladden the heart,
but the love of wisdom is better
than both.

21 The flute and the harp make pleasant melody,
but a pleasant voice is better
than both.

22 The eye desires grace and beauty,
but the green shoots of grain
more than both.

23 A friend or a companion never
meets one amiss,
but a wife with her husband is
better than both.

24 Brothers and help are for a time
of trouble,
but almsgiving rescues better
than both.

25 Gold and silver make the foot
stand sure,
but good counsel is esteemed
more than both.

26 Riches and strength lift up the
heart,
but the fear of the Lord is better than both.
There is no loss in the fear of the
Lord,
and with it there is no need to
seek for help.

27 The fear of the Lord is like a garden of blessing,
and covers a man[t] better than
any glory.

28 My son, do not lead the life of a
beggar;
it is better to die than to beg.

29 When a man looks to the table of
another,
his existence cannot be considered as life.
He pollutes himself with another
man's food,
but a man who is intelligent and

---

[s] Cn: Gk *self-reliant worker*   [t] Gk *him*

well-instructed guards against
that.

30 In the mouth of the shameless
begging is sweet,
but in his stomach a fire is kindled.

41

O death, how bitter is the
reminder of you
to one who lives at peace among
his possessions,
to a man without distractions, who
is prosperous in everything,
and who still has the vigour to
enjoy his food!

2 O death, how welcome is your sentence
to one who is in need and is
failing in strength,
very old and distracted over everything;
to one who is contrary, and has
lost his patience!

3 Do not fear the sentence of death;
remember your former days and
the end of life;
this is the decree from the Lord
for all flesh,

4 and how can you reject the good
pleasure of the Most High?
Whether life is for ten or a hundred or a thousand years,
there is no inquiry about it in
Hades.

5 The children of sinners are abominable children,
and they frequent the haunts of
the ungodly.

6 The inheritance of the children of
sinners will perish,
and on their posterity will be a
perpetual reproach.

7 Children will blame an ungodly
father,
for they suffer reproach because
of him.

8 Woe to you, ungodly men,
who have forsaken the law of the
Most High God!

9 When you are born, you are born
to a curse;

t Gk of fixing the elbow on the bread

and when you die, a curse is your
lot.

10 Whatever is from the dust returns
to dust;
so the ungodly go from curse to
destruction.

11 The mourning of men is about their
bodies,
but the evil name of sinners will
be blotted out.

12 Have regard for your name, since
it will remain for you
longer than a thousand great
stores of gold.

13 The days of a good life are numbered,
but a good name endures for ever.

14 My children, observe instruction
and be at peace;
hidden wisdom and unseen treasure,
what advantage is there in either
of them?

15 Better is the man who hides his
folly
than the man who hides his wisdom.

16 Therefore show respect for my
words:
For it is not good to retain every
kind of shame,
and not everything is confidently
esteemed by every one.

17 Be ashamed of immorality, before
your father or mother;
and of a lie, before a prince or a
ruler;

18 of a transgression, before a judge
or magistrate;
and of iniquity, before a congregation or the people;
of unjust dealing, before your partner or friend;

19 and of theft, in the place where
you live.
Be ashamed before the truth of
God and his covenant.
Be ashamed of selfish behaviour
at meals,*u*

of surliness in receiving and giving,
20 and of silence, before those who
         greet you;
of looking at a woman who is a
         harlot,
21 and of rejecting the appeal of a
         kinsman;
of taking away some one's portion
         or gift,
and of gazing at another man's
         wife;
22 of meddling with his maidserv-
         ant—
and do not approach her bed;
of abusive words, before friends—
         and do not upbraid after making
         a gift;
23 of repeating and telling what you
         hear,
and of revealing secrets.
Then you will show proper shame,
         and will find favour with every
         man.

42 Of the following things do
         not be ashamed,
         and do not let partiality lead
         you to sin:
2 of the law of the Most High and
         his covenant,
         and of rendering judgment to
         acquit the ungodly;
3 of keeping accounts with a partner
         or with travelling companions,
         and of dividing the inheritance
         of friends;
4 of accuracy with scales and weights,
         and of acquiring much or little;
5 of profit from dealing with mer-
         chants,
         and of much discipline of chil-
         dren,
         and of whipping a wicked serv-
         ant severely.v
6 Where there is an evil wife, a seal
         is a good thing;
         and where there are many hands,
         lock things up.
7 Whatever you deal out, let it be
         by number and weight,
         and make a record of all that you
         give out or take in.

8 Do not be ashamed to instruct the
         stupid or foolish
         or the aged man who quarrels
         with the young.
Then you will be truly instructed,
         and will be approved before all
         men.

9 A daughter keeps her father se-
         cretly wakeful,
         and worry over her robs him of
         sleep;
when she is young, lest she do not
         marry,
         or if married, lest she be hated;
10 while a virgin, lest she be defiled
         or become pregnant in her fa-
         ther's house;
         or having a husband, lest she prove
         unfaithful,
         or, though married, lest she be
         barren.
11 Keep strict watch over a headstrong
         daughter,
         lest she make you a laughing-
         stock to your enemies,
         a byword in the city and notori-
         ous w among the people,
         and put you to shame before the
         great multitude.

12 Do not look upon any one for
         beauty,
         and do not sit in the midst of
         women;
13 for from garments comes the moth,
         and from a woman comes wom-
         an's wickedness.
14 Better is the wickedness of a man
         than a woman who does good;
         and it is a woman who brings
         shame and disgrace.

15 I will now call to mind the works
         of the Lord,
         and will declare what I have seen.
By the words of the Lord his works
         are done.
16 The sun looks down on everything
         with its light,
         and the work of the Lord is full
         of his glory.

v Gk *making the side of a wicked servant bleed* w Gk *called out*

17 The Lord has not enabled his holy
ones
to recount all his marvellous
works,
which the Lord the Almighty has
established
that the universe may stand firm
in his glory.
18 He searches out the abyss, and the
hearts of men,*ˣ*
and considers their crafty devices.
For the Most High knows all that
may be known,
and he looks into the signs *ʸ* of
the age.
19 He declares what has been and
what is to be,
and he reveals the tracks of hidden things.
20 No thought escapes him,
and not one word is hidden from
him.
21 He has ordained the splendours of
his wisdom,
and he is from everlasting and to
everlasting.
Nothing can be added or taken
away,
and he needs no one to be his
counsellor.
22 How greatly to be desired are all
his works,
and how sparkling they are to
see! *ᶻ*
23 All these things live and remain
for ever
for every need, and are all obedient.
24 All things are twofold, one opposite the other,
and he has made nothing incom-
plete.
25 One confirms the good things of
the other,
and who can have enough of be-
holding his glory?

43 The pride of the heavenly
heights is the clear firmament,

the appearance of heaven in a
spectacle of glory.
2 The sun, when it appears, making
proclamation as it goes forth,
is a marvellous instrument, the
work of the Most High.
3 At noon it parches the land;
and who can withstand its burning heat?
4 A man tending *ᵃ* a furnace works
in burning heat,
but the sun burns the mountains three times as much;
it breathes out fiery vapours,
and with bright beams it blinds
the eyes.
5 Great is the Lord who made it;
and at his command it hastens
on its course.

6 He made the moon also, to serve
in its season *ᵇ*
to mark the times and to be an
everlasting sign.
7 From the moon comes the sign for
feast days,
a light that wanes when it has
reached the full.
8 The month is named for the moon,
increasing marvellously in its
phases,
an instrument of the hosts on high
shining forth in the firmament
of heaven.

9 The glory of the stars is the beauty
of heaven,
a gleaming array in the heights
of the Lord.
10 At the command of the Holy One
they stand as ordered,
they never relax in their watches.
11 Look upon the rainbow, and
praise him who made it,
exceedingly beautiful in its
brightness.
12 It encircles the heaven with its
glorious arc;
the hands of the Most High
have stretched it out.

ˣ Gk *and the heart* *ʸ* Gk *sign* *ᶻ* The Gk of this line is uncertain
ᵃ Other authorities read *blowing* *ᵇ* The Gk text of this line is uncertain

13 By his command he sends the driving snow
and speeds the lightnings of his judgment.
14 Therefore the storehouses are opened,
and the clouds fly forth like birds.
15 In his majesty he amasses the clouds,
and the hailstones are broken in pieces.
16 At his appearing the mountains are shaken;
at his will the south wind blows.
17 The voice of his thunder rebukes the earth;
so do the tempest from the north and the whirlwind.
He scatters the snow like birds flying down,
and its descent is like locusts alighting.
18 The eye marvels at the beauty of its whiteness,
and the mind is amazed at its falling.
19 He pours the hoarfrost upon the earth like salt,
and when it freezes, it becomes pointed thorns.
20 The cold north wind blows,
and ice freezes over the water;
it rests upon every pool of water,
and the water puts it on like a breastplate.
21 He consumes the mountains and burns up the wilderness,
and withers the tender grass like fire.
22 A mist quickly heals all things;
when the dew appears, it refreshes from the heat.

23 By his counsel he stilled the great deep
and planted islands in it.
24 Those who sail the sea tell of its dangers,
and we marvel at what we hear.

25 For in it are strange and marvellous works,
all kinds of living things, and huge creatures of the sea.
26 Because of him his messenger finds the way,
and by his word all things hold together.

27 Though we speak much we cannot reach the end,
and the sum of our words is: "He is the all."
28 Where shall we find strength to praise him?
For he is greater than all his works.
29 Terrible is the Lord and very great,
and marvellous is his power.
30 When you praise the Lord, exalt him as much as you can;
for he will surpass even that.
When you exalt him, put forth all your strength,
and do not grow weary, for you cannot praise him enough.
31 Who has seen him and can describe him?
Or who can extol him as he is?
32 Many things greater than these lie hidden,
for we have seen but few of his works.
33 For the Lord has made all things,
and to the godly he has granted wisdom.

44 Let us now praise famous men,
and our fathers in their generations.
2 The Lord apportioned to them *c* great glory,
his majesty from the beginning.
3 There were those who ruled in their kingdoms,
and were men renowned for their power,
giving counsel by their understanding,

c Heb: Gk *created*

and proclaiming prophecies;
4 leaders of the people in their de-
    liberations
    and in understanding of learn-
        ing for the people,
    wise in their words of instruc-
        tion;
5 those who composed musical tunes,
    and set forth verses in writing;
6 rich men furnished with resources,
    living peaceably in their habita-
        tions—
7 all these were honoured in their
    generations,
    and were the glory of their times.
8 There are some of them who have
    left a name,
    so that men declare their praise.
9 And there are some who have no
    memorial,
    who have perished as though
        they had not lived;
    they have become as though they
        had not been born,
    and so have their children after
        them.
10 But these were men of mercy,
    whose righteous deeds have not
        been forgotten;
11 their prosperity will remain with
    their descendants,
    and their inheritance to their
        children's children.*d*
12 Their descendants stand by the
    covenants;
    their children also, for their sake.
13 Their posterity will continue for
    ever,
    and their glory will not be
        blotted out.
14 Their bodies were buried in peace,
    and their name lives to all gen-
        erations.
15 Peoples will declare their wisdom,
    and the congregation proclaims
        their praise.
16 Enoch pleased the Lord, and was
    taken up;
    he was an example of repentance
        to all generations.

17 Noah was found perfect and right-
    eous;
    in the time of wrath he was
        taken in exchange;
    therefore a remnant was left to the
        earth
    when the flood came.
18 Everlasting covenants were made
    with him
    that all flesh should not be blot-
        ted out by a flood.

19 Abraham was the great father of
    a multitude of nations,
    and no one has been found like
        him in glory;
20 he kept the law of the Most High,
    and was taken into covenant
        with him;
    he established the covenant in his
        flesh,
    and when he was tested he was
        found faithful.
21 Therefore the Lord *e* assured him
    by an oath
    that the nations would be blessed
        through his posterity;
    that he would multiply him like
        the dust of the earth,
    and exalt his posterity like the
        stars,
    and cause them to inherit from
        sea to sea
    and from the River to the ends
        of the earth.

22 To Isaac also he gave the same as-
    surance
    for the sake of Abraham his fa-
        ther.
23 The blessing of all men and the
    covenant
    he made to rest upon the head
        of Jacob;
    he acknowledged him with his
        blessings,
    and gave him his inheritance;*f*
    he determined his portions,
    and distributed them among
        twelve tribes.

d Heb Compare Vg Syr: The Greek of this verse is uncertain *e* Gk *he* *f* Heb: Gk *by inheritance*

45

From his descendants the Lord *g* brought forth a man of mercy,

who found favour in the sight of all flesh

and was beloved by God and man, Moses, whose memory is blessed.

2 He made him equal in glory to the holy ones,

and made him great in the fears of his enemies.

3 By his words he caused signs to cease;

the Lord *g* glorified him in the presence of kings.

He gave him commands for his people,

and showed him part of his glory.

4 He sanctified him through faithfulness and meekness;

he chose him out of all mankind.

5 He made him hear his voice,

and led him into the thick darkness,

and gave him the commandments face to face,

the law of life and knowledge,

to teach Jacob the covenant,

and Israel his judgments.

6 He exalted Aaron, the brother of Moses,*h*

a holy man like him, of the tribe of Levi.

7 He made an everlasting covenant with him,

and gave him the priesthood of the people.

He blessed him with splendid vestments,

and put a glorious robe upon him.

8 He clothed him with superb perfection,

and strengthened him with the symbols of authority,

the linen breeches, the long robe, and the ephod.

9 And he encircled him with pomegranates,

with very many golden bells round about,

to send forth a sound as he walked,

to make their ringing heard in the temple

as a reminder to the sons of his people;

10 with a holy garment, of gold and blue and purple, the work of an embroiderer;

with the oracle of judgment, Urim and Thummim;

11 with twisted scarlet, the work of a craftsman;

with precious stones engraved like signets,

in a setting of gold, the work of a jeweller,

for a reminder, in engraved letters, according to the number of the tribes of Israel;

12 with a gold crown upon his turban, inscribed like a signet with "Holiness,"

a distinction to be prized, the work of an expert,

the delight of the eyes, richly adorned.

13 Before his time there never were such beautiful things.

No outsider ever put them on, but only his sons

and his descendants perpetually.

14 His sacrifices shall be wholly burned

twice every day continually.

15 Moses ordained him,

and anointed him with holy oil;

it was an everlasting covenant for him

and for his descendants all the days of heaven,

to minister to the Lord *i* and serve as priest

and bless his people in his name.

16 He chose him out of all the living to offer sacrifice to the Lord,

incense and a pleasing odour as a memorial portion,

to make atonement for the people.*j*

---

g Gk *he*   *h* Gk *him*   *i* Gk *him*   *j* Other authorities read *thy people*

17 In his commandments he gave him
authority in statutes and *k* judgments,
to teach Jacob the testimonies,
and to enlighten Israel with his
law.
18 Outsiders conspired against him,
and envied him in the wilderness,
Dathan and Abiram and their
men
and the company of Korah, in
wrath and anger.
19 The Lord saw it and was not
pleased,
and in the wrath of his anger
they were destroyed;
he wrought wonders against them
to consume them in flaming fire.
20 He added glory to Aaron
and gave him a heritage;
he allotted to him the first of the
first fruits,
he prepared bread of first fruits
in abundance;
21 for they eat the sacrifices to the
Lord,
which he gave to him and his descendants.
22 But in the land of the people he
has no inheritance,
and he has no portion among the
people;
for the Lord *l* himself is his *m*
portion and inheritance.

23 Phinehas the son of Eleazar is the
third in glory,
for he was zealous in the fear of
the Lord,
and stood fast, when the people
turned away,
in the ready goodness of his soul,
and made atonement for Israel.
24 Therefore a covenant of peace was
established with him,
that he should be leader of the
sanctuary and of his people,
that he and his descendants should
have

the dignity of the priesthood for
ever.
25 A covenant was also established
with David,
the son of Jesse, of the tribe of
Judah:
the heritage of the king is from
son to son only;
so the heritage of Aaron is for
his descendants.
26 May the Lord *n* grant you wisdom
in your heart
to judge his people in righteousness,
so that their prosperity may not
vanish,
and that their glory may endure
throughout their generations. *o*

46 Joshua the son of Nun was
mighty in war,
and was the successor of Moses
in prophesying.
He became, in accordance with his
name,
a great saviour of God's *p* elect,
to take vengeance on the enemies
that rose against them,
so that he might give Israel its
inheritance.
2 How glorious he was when he lifted
his hands
and stretched out his sword
against the cities!
3 Who before him ever stood so firm?
For he waged the wars of the
Lord.
4 Was not the sun held back by his
hand?
And did not one day become as
long as two?
5 He called upon the Most High,
the Mighty One,
when enemies pressed him on
every side,
6 and the great Lord answered him
with hailstones of mighty power.
He hurled down war upon that
nation,
and at the descent of Beth-

k Heb: Gk *in covenants of*   *l* Gk *he*   *m* Other authorities read *your*   *n* Gk *he*
o The Greek of this line is obscure   *p* Gk *his*

horon *q* he destroyed those
who resisted,
so that the nations might know
his armament,
that he was fighting in the sight
of the Lord;
for he wholly followed the
Mighty One.
7 And in the days of Moses he did
a loyal deed,
he and Caleb the son of Jephun-
neh:
they withstood the congregation,*r*
restrained the people from sin,
and stilled their wicked murmuring.
8 And these two alone were preserved
out of six hundred thousand people on foot,
to bring them into their inheritance,
into a land flowing with milk
and honey.
9 And the Lord gave Caleb strength,
which remained with him to
old age,
so that he went up to the hill
country,
and his children obtained it for
an inheritance;
10 so that all the sons of Israel might
see
that it is good to follow the Lord.

11 The judges also, with their respec-
tive names,
those whose hearts did not fall
into idolatry
and who did not turn away from
the Lord—
may their memory be blessed!
12 May their bones revive from where
they lie,
and may the name of those who
have been honoured
live again in their sons!

13 Samuel, beloved by his Lord,
a prophet of the Lord, established the kingdom
and anointed rulers over his people.

14 By the law of the Lord he judged
the congregation,
and the Lord watched over
Jacob.
15 By his faithfulness he was proved
to be a prophet,
and by his words he became
known as a trustworthy seer.
16 He called upon the Lord, the
Mighty One,
when his enemies pressed him on
every side,
and he offered in sacrifice a suck-
ing lamb.
17 Then the Lord thundered from
heaven,
and made his voice heard with
a mighty sound;
18 and he wiped out the leaders of the
people of Tyre
and all the rulers of the Philistines.
19 Before the time of his eternal
sleep,
Samuel *s* called men to witness
before the Lord and his
anointed:
"I have not taken any one's property,
not so much as a pair of shoes."
And no man accused him.
20 Even after he had fallen asleep he
prophesied
and revealed to the king his
death,
and lifted up his voice out of the
earth in prophecy,
to blot out the wickedness of
the people.

47 And after him Nathan rose
up
to prophesy in the days of David.
2 As the fat is selected from the
peace offering,
so David was selected from the
sons of Israel.
3 He played with lions as with
young goats,
and with bears as with lambs of
the flock.
4 In his youth did he not kill a giant,

---

q Compare Joshua 10.11: Gk lacks *of Beth-horon*   *r* Other authorities read *the enemy*   *s* Gk *he*

and take away reproach from
the people,
when he lifted his hand with a
stone in the sling
and struck down the boasting of
Goliath?
5 For he appealed to the Lord, the
Most High,
and he gave him strength in his
right hand
to slay a man mighty in war,
to exalt the power *t* of his people.
6 So they glorified him for his ten
thousands,
and praised him for the blessings of the Lord,
when the glorious diadem was
bestowed upon him.
7 For he wiped out his enemies on
every side,
and annihilated his adversaries
the Philistines;
he crushed their power *t* even
to this day.
8 In all that he did he gave thanks
to the Holy One, the Most High,
with ascriptions of glory;
he sang praise with all his heart,
and he loved his Maker.
9 He placed singers before the altar,
to make sweet melody with their
voices.
10 He gave beauty to the feasts,
and arranged their times
throughout the year,*u*
while they praised God's *v* holy
name,
and the sanctuary resounded
from early morning.
11 The Lord took away his sins,
and exalted his power *w* for ever;
he gave him the covenant of kings
and a throne of glory in Israel.

12 After him rose up a wise son
who fared amply*x* because of him;
13 Solomon reigned in days of peace,
and God gave him rest on every
side,
that he might build a house for his
name

and prepare a sanctuary to stand
for ever.
14 How wise you became in your youth!
You overflowed like a river with
understanding.
15 Your soul covered the earth,
and you filled it with parables
and riddles.
16 Your name reached to far-off islands,
and you were loved for your
peace.
17 For your songs and proverbs and
parables,
and for your interpretations, the
countries marvelled at you.
18 In the name of the Lord God,
who is called the God of Israel,
you gathered gold like tin
and amassed silver like lead.
19 But you laid your loins beside
women,
and through your body you were
brought into subjection.
20 You put a stain upon your honour,
and defiled your posterity,
so that you brought wrath upon
your children
and they were grieved *y* at your
folly,
21 so that the sovereignty was divided
and a disobedient kingdom arose
out of Ephraim.
22 But the Lord will never give up
his mercy,
nor cause any of his works to
perish;
he will never blot out the descendants of his chosen one,
nor destroy the posterity of him
who loved him;
so he gave a remnant to Jacob,
and to David a root of his stock.

23 Solomon rested with his fathers,
and left behind him one of his
sons,
ample in *z* folly and lacking in understanding,
Rehoboam, whose policy caused
the people to revolt.*a*

---

t Gk *horn* *u* Gk *to completion* *v* Gk *his* *w* Gk *horn* *x* Gk *lived in a broad place*
y Other authorities read *I was grieved*
a Heb (with a play on the name Rehoboam) Syr: Gk *the people's*

Also Jeroboam the son of Nebat,
  who caused Israel to sin
  and gave to Ephraim a sinful
    way.
24 Their sins became exceedingly
    many,
  so as to remove them from their
    land.
25 For they sought out every sort of
    wickedness,
  till vengeance came upon them.

48 Then the prophet Elijah
  arose like a fire,
  and his word burned like a torch.
2 He brought a famine upon them,
  and by his zeal he made them
    few in number.
3 By the word of the Lord he shut
    up the heavens,
  and also three times brought
    down fire.
4 How glorious you were, O Elijah,
    in your wondrous deeds!
  And who has the right to boast
    which you have?
5 You who raised a corpse from
    death
  and from Hades, by the word
    of the Most High;
6 who brought kings down to de-
    struction,
  and famous men from their
    beds;
7 who heard rebuke at Sinai
  and judgments of vengeance at
    Horeb;
8 who anointed kings to inflict retri-
    bution,
  and prophets to succeed you.*a*
9 You who were taken up by a whirl-
    wind of fire,
  in a chariot with horses of fire;
10 you who are ready *b* at the ap-
    pointed time, it is written,
  to calm the wrath of God before
    it breaks out in fury,
  to turn the heart of the father to
    the son,

and to restore the tribes of
    Jacob.
11 Blessed are those who saw you,
  and those who have been
    adorned *c* in love;
  for we also shall surely live.*d*

12 It was Elijah who was covered by
    the whirlwind,
  and Elisha was filled with his
    spirit;
  in all his days he did not tremble
    before any ruler,
  and no one brought him into
    subjection.
13 Nothing was too hard for him,
  and when he was dead his body
    prophesied.
14 As in his life he did wonders,
  so in death his deeds were
    marvellous.

15 For all this the people did not
    repent,
  and they did not forsake their
    sins,
  till they were carried away captive
    from their land
  and were scattered over all the
    earth;
  the people were left very few in
    number,
  but with rulers from the house
    of David.
16 Some of them did what was pleas-
    ing to God.*e*
  but others multiplied sins.

17 Hezekiah fortified his city,
  and brought water into the
    midst of it;
  he tunnelled the sheer rock with iron
    and built pools for water.
18 In his days Sennacherib came up,
    and sent the Rabshakeh;*f*
  he lifted up his hand against Zion
    and made great boasts in his
    arrogance.
19 Then their hearts were shaken and
    their hands trembled,

---

a Heb: Gk *him*   *b* Heb: Gk *are for reproofs*   *c* Other authorities read *who have died*
d The text and meaning of this verse are uncertain   *e* Gk lacks *to God*
f Other authorities add *and departed*

and they were in anguish, like
women in travail.
20 But they called upon the Lord who
is merciful,
spreading forth their hands toward him;
and the Holy One quickly heard
them from heaven,
and delivered them by the hand
of Isaiah.
21 The Lord *g* smote the camp of the
Assyrians,
and his angel wiped them out.
22 For Hezekiah did what was pleasing to the Lord,
and he held strongly to the ways
of David his father,
which Isaiah the prophet commanded,
who was great and faithful in
his vision.
23 In his days the sun went backward,
and he lengthened the life of
the king.
24 By the spirit of might he saw the
last things,
and comforted those who
mourned in Zion.
25 He revealed what was to occur to
the end of time,
and the hidden things before
they came to pass.

49 The memory of Josiah is like
a blending of incense
prepared by the art of the per-
fumer;
it is sweet as honey to every mouth,
and like music at a banquet of
wine.
2 He was led aright in converting
the people,
and took away the abominations
of iniquity.
3 He set his heart upon the Lord;
in the days of wicked men he
strengthened godliness.

4 Except David and Hezekiah and
Josiah
they all sinned greatly,

for they forsook the law of the
Most High;
the kings of Judah came to an end;
5 for they gave their power to others,
and their glory to a foreign nation,
6 who set fire to the chosen city of
the sanctuary,
and made her streets desolate,
according to the word *h* of Jeremiah.
7 For they had afflicted him;
yet he had been consecrated in
the womb as prophet,
to pluck up and afflict and destroy,
and likewise to build and to
plant.

8 It was Ezekiel who saw the vision
of glory
which God *i* showed him above
the chariot of the cherubim.
9 For God *i* remembered his enemies
with storm,
and did good to those who directed their ways aright.*j*

10 May the bones of the twelve
prophets
revive from where they lie,
for they comforted the people of
Jacob
and delivered them with confident hope.

11 How shall we magnify Zerubbabel?
He was like a signet on the right
hand,
12 and so was Jeshua the son of
Jozadak;
in their days they built the house
and raised a temple *k* holy to
the Lord,
prepared for everlasting glory.
13 The memory of Nehemiah also is
lasting;
he raised for us the walls that
had fallen,
and set up the gates and bars
and rebuilt our ruined houses.

g Gk *he*   *h* Gk *by the hand*   *i* Gk *he*   *j* The text and meaning of this verse are uncertain
k Other authorities read *people*

14 No one like Enoch has been created on earth,
for he was taken up from the
earth.
15 And no man like Joseph *l* has been
born,
and his bones are cared for.
16 Shem and Seth were honoured
among men,
and Adam above every living
being in the creation.

50 The leader of his brethren
and the pride of his
people *m*
was Simon the high priest, son
of Onias,
who in his life repaired the house,
and in his time fortified the
temple.
2 He laid the foundations for the
high double walls, *n*
the high retaining walls for the
temple enclosure.
3 In his days a cistern for water was
quarried out, *o*
a reservoir like the sea in circum-
ference.
4 He considered how to save his people from ruin,
and fortified the city to withstand a siege.
5 How glorious he was when the
people gathered round him
as he came out of the inner
sanctuary! *p*
6 Like the morning star among the
clouds,
like the moon when it is full;
7 like the sun shining upon the temple of the Most High,
and like the rainbow gleaming
in glorious clouds;
8 like roses in the days of the first
fruits,
like lilies by a spring of water,
like a green shoot on Lebanon *q*
on a summer day;
9 like fire and incense in the censer,
like a vessel of hammered gold

adorned with all kinds of precious stones;
10 like an olive tree putting forth its
fruit,
and like a cypress towering in
the clouds.
11 When he put on his glorious robe
and clothed himself with superb
perfection
and went up to the holy altar,
he made the court of the sanctuary glorious.
12 And when he received the portions
from the hands of the priests,
as he stood by the hearth of the
altar
with a garland of brethren around
him,
he was like a young cedar on
Lebanon;
and they surrounded him like the
trunks of palm trees,
13 all the sons of Aaron in their
splendour
with the Lord's offering in their
hands,
before the whole congregation
of Israel.
14 Finishing the service at the altars,
and arranging the offering to the
Most High, the Almighty,
15 he reached out his hand to the cup
and poured a libation of the
blood of the grape;
he poured it out at the foot of the
altar,
a pleasing odour to the Most
High, the King of all.
16 Then the sons of Aaron shouted,
they sounded the trumpets of
hammered work,
they made a great noise to be heard
for remembrance before the
Most High.
17 Then all the people together made
haste
and fell to the ground upon their
faces
to worship their Lord,
the Almighty, God Most High.

l Heb Syr: Gk adds *the leader of his brothers, the support of the people*
m Heb Syr: Gk lacks this line. Compare 49. 15 *n* The meaning of this phrase is obscure
o Cn Compare Heb: Gk *was diminished* *p* Gk *the house of the veil* *q* Or *a sprig of frankincense*

¹⁸ And the singers praised him with
their voices
in sweet and full-toned melody.^r
¹⁹ And the people besought the Lord
Most High
in prayer before him who is
merciful,
till the order of worship of the
Lord was ended;
so they completed his service.
²⁰ Then Simon^s came down, and
lifted up his hands
over the whole congregation of
the sons of Israel,
to pronounce the blessing of the
Lord with his lips,
and to glory in his name;
²¹ and they bowed down in worship
a second time,
to receive the blessing from the
Most High.

²² And now bless the God of all,
who in every way does great
things;
who exalts our days from birth,
and deals with us according to
his mercy.
²³ May he give us^t gladness of heart,
and grant that peace may be in
our days in Israel,
as in the days of old.
²⁴ May he entrust to us his mercy!
And let him deliver us in our^u
days!

²⁵ With two nations my soul is vexed,
and the third is no nation:
²⁶ Those who live on Mount Seir,^v
and the Philistines,
and the foolish people that dwell
in Shechem.

²⁷ Instruction in understanding and
knowledge
I have written in this book,
Jesus the son of Sirach, son of
Eleazar,^w of Jerusalem,

who out of his heart poured
forth wisdom.
²⁸ Blessed is he who concerns him-
self with these things,
and he who lays them to heart
will become wise.
²⁹ For if he does them, he will be
strong for all things,
for the light of the Lord is his
path.

51

I will give thanks to thee, O
Lord and King,
and will praise thee as God my
Saviour.
I give thanks to thy name,
² for thou hast been my protector
and helper
and hast delivered my body from
destruction
and from the snare of a slander-
ous tongue,
from lips that utter lies.
Before those who stood by
thou wast my helper, ³ and didst
deliver me,
in the greatness of thy mercy
and of thy name,
from the gnashings of teeth about
to devour me,^x
from the hand of those who
sought my life,
from the many afflictions that I
endured,
⁴ from choking fire on every side
and from the midst of fire which
I did not kindle,
⁵ from the depths of the belly of
Hades,
from an unclean tongue and
lying words—
⁶ the slander of an unrighteous
tongue to the king.
My soul drew near to death,
and my life was very near to
Hades beneath.
⁷ They surrounded me on every side,
and there was no one to help me;

---

^r Other authorities read *in sweet melody throughout the house*   ^s Gk *he*
^t Other authorities read *you*   ^u Other authorities read *his*
^v Heb Vg: Gk *on the mountain of Samaria*   ^w The text of this line is uncertain
^x Cn Compare Vg: Gk *when I was about to be devoured*

I looked for the assistance of men,
and there was none.
⁸ Then I remembered thy mercy, O
Lord,
and thy work from of old,
that thou dost deliver those who
wait for thee
and dost save them from the
hand of their enemies.
⁹ And I sent up my supplication
from the earth,
and prayed for deliverance from
death.
¹⁰ I appealed to the Lord, the Father
of my lord,
not to forsake me in the days
of affliction,
at the time when there is no
help against the proud.
¹¹ I will praise thy name continually,
and will sing praise with thanks-
giving.
My prayer was heard,
¹² for thou didst save me from de-
struction
and rescue me from an evil plight.
Therefore I will give thanks to
thee and praise thee,
and I will bless the name of the
Lord.
¹³ While I was still young, before I
went on my travels,
I sought wisdom openly in my
prayer.
¹⁴ Before the temple I asked for her,
and I will search for her to the
last.
¹⁵ From blossom to ^y ripening grape
my heart delighted in her;
my foot entered upon the straight
path;
from my youth I followed her
steps.
¹⁶ I inclined my ear a little and re-
ceived her,
and I found for myself much
instruction.
¹⁷ I made progress therein;
to him who gives me wisdom I
will give glory.

¹⁸ For I resolved to live according to
wisdom,^z
and I was zealous for the good;
and I shall never be put to
shame.
¹⁹ My soul grappled with wisdom,^z
and in my conduct I was strict; ^a
I spread out my hands to the
heavens,
and lamented my ignorance of
her.
²⁰ I directed my soul to her,
and through purification I
found her.
I gained understanding ^b with her
from the first,
therefore I will not be forsaken.
²¹ My heart was stirred to seek her,
therefore I have gained a good
possession.
²² The Lord gave me a tongue as my
reward,
and I will praise him with it.
²³ Draw near to me, you who are un-
taught,
and lodge in my school.
²⁴ Why do you say you are lacking
in these things,^c
and why are your souls very
thirsty?
²⁵ I opened my mouth and said,
Get these things ^d for yourselves
without money.
²⁶ Put your neck under the yoke,
and let your souls receive instruction;
it is to be found close by.
²⁷ See with your eyes that I have
laboured little
and found for myself much rest.
²⁸ Get instruction with a large sum
of silver,
and you will gain by it much gold.
²⁹ May your soul rejoice in his mercy,
and may you not be put to
shame when you praise him.
³⁰ Do your work before the appointed
time,
and in God's ^e time he will give
you your reward.

^y Other authorities read *As from*   ^z Gk *her*   ^a The Greek text of this line is uncertain   ^b Gk *heart*
^c Cn Compare Heb Syr: The Greek text of this line is uncertain   ^d Greek lacks *these things*
^e Gk *his*

BARUCH

1 These are the words of the book which Baruch the son of Neraiah, son of Mahseiah, son of Zedekiah, son of Hasadiah, son of Hilkiah, wrote in Babylon, ² in the fifth year, on the seventh day of the month, at the time when the Chaldeans took Jerusalem and burned it with fire. ³ And Baruch read the words of this book in the hearing of Jeconiah the son of Jehoiakim, king of Judah, and in the hearing of all the people who came to hear the book, ⁴ and in the hearing of the mighty men and the princes, and in the hearing of the elders, and in the hearing of all the people, small and great, all who dwelt in Babylon by the river Sud.

5 Then they wept, and fasted, and prayed before the Lord; ⁶ and they collected money, each giving what he could; ⁷ and they sent it to Jerusalem to Jehoiakim the high priest,ᵃ the son of Hilkiah, son of Shallum, and to the priests, and to all the people who were present with him in Jerusalem. ⁸ At the same time, on the tenth day of Sivan, Baruch ᵇ took the vessels of the house of the Lord, which had been carried away from the temple, to return them to the land of Judah—the silver vessels which Zedekiah the son of Josiah, king of Judah, had made, ⁹ after Nebuchadnezzar king of Babylon had carried away from Jerusalem Jeconiah and the princes and the prisoners and the mighty men and the people of the land, and brought them to Babylon.

10 And they said: "Herewith we send you money; so buy with the money burnt offerings and sin offerings and incense, and prepare a cereal offering, and offer them upon the altar of the Lord our God; ¹¹ and pray for the life of Nebuchadnezzar king of Babylon, and for the life of Belshazzar his son, that their days on earth may be like the days of heaven. ¹² And the Lord will give us strength, and he will give light to our eyes, and we shall live under the protection ᶜ of Nebuchadnezzar king of Babylon, and under the protection ᶜ of Belshazzar his son, and we shall serve them many days and find favour in their sight. ¹³ And pray for us to the Lord our God, for we have sinned against the Lord our God, and to this day the anger of the Lord and his wrath have not turned away from us. ¹⁴ And you shall read this book which we are sending you, to make your confession in the house of the Lord on the days of the feasts and at appointed seasons.

15 "And you shall say: 'Righteousness belongs to the Lord our God, but confusion of face, as at this day, to us, to the men of Judah, to the inhabitants of Jerusalem, ¹⁶ and to our kings and our princes and our priests and our prophets and our fathers, ¹⁷ because we have sinned before the Lord, ¹⁸ and have disobeyed him, and have not heeded the voice of the Lord our God, to walk in the statutes of the Lord which he set before us. ¹⁹ From the day when the Lord brought our fathers out of the land of Egypt until today, we have been disobedient to the Lord our God, and we have been negligent, in not heeding his voice. ²⁰ So to this day there have clung to us the calamities and the curse which the Lord declared through Moses his servant at the time when he brought our fathers out of the land of Egypt to give to us a land flowing with milk and honey. ²¹ We did not heed the voice of the Lord our God in all the words of the prophets whom he sent to us, but we each followed the intent of his own wicked heart by serving other gods and doing what is evil in the sight of the Lord our God.

ᵃ Gk *the priest* ᵇ Gk *he* ᶜ Gk *in the shadow*

172

2 " 'So the Lord confirmed his word, which he spoke against us, and against our judges who judged Israel, and against our kings and against our princes and against the men of Israel and Judah. ² Under the whole heaven there has not been done the like of what he has done in Jerusalem, in accordance with what is written in the law of Moses, ³ that we should eat, one the flesh of his son and another the flesh of his daughter. ⁴ And he gave them into subjection to all the kingdoms around us, to be a reproach and a desolation among all the surrounding peoples, where the Lord has scattered them. ⁵ They were brought low and not raised up, because we sinned against the Lord our God, in not heeding his voice.

6 " 'Righteousness belongs to the Lord our God, but confusion of face to us and our fathers, as at this day. ⁷ All those calamities with which the Lord threatened us have come upon us. ⁸ Yet we have not entreated the favour of the Lord by turning away, each of us, from the thoughts of his wicked heart. ⁹ And the Lord has kept the calamities ready, and the Lord has brought them upon us, for the Lord is righteous in all his works which he has commanded us to do. ¹⁰ Yet we have not obeyed his voice, to walk in the statutes of the Lord which he set before us.

11 " 'And now, O Lord God of Israel, who didst bring thy people out of the land of Egypt with a mighty hand and with signs and wonders and with great power and outstretched arm, and hast made thee a name, as at this day, ¹² we have sinned, we have been ungodly, we have done wrong, O Lord our God, against all thy ordinances. ¹³ Let thy anger turn away from us, for we are left, few in number, among the nations where thou hast scattered us. ¹⁴ Hear, O Lord, our prayer and our supplication, and for

thy own sake deliver us, and grant us favour in the sight of those who have carried us into exile; ¹⁵ that all the earth may know that thou art the Lord our God, for Israel and his descendants are called by thy name. ¹⁶ O Lord, look down from thy holy habitation, and consider us. Incline thy ear, O Lord, and hear; ¹⁷ open thy eyes, O Lord, and see; for the dead who are in Hades, whose spirit has been taken from their bodies, will not ascribe glory or justice to the Lord, ¹⁸ but the person that is greatly distressed,*ᵈ* that goes about bent over and feeble, and the eyes that are failing, and the person that hungers, will ascribe to thee glory and righteousness, O Lord. ¹⁹ For it is not because of any righteous deeds of our fathers or our kings that we bring before thee our prayer for mercy, O Lord our God. ²⁰ For thou hast sent thy anger and thy wrath upon us, as thou didst declare by thy servants the prophets, saying: ²¹ "Thus says the Lord: Bend your shoulders and serve the king of Babylon, and you will remain in the land which I gave to your fathers. ²² But if you will not obey the voice of the Lord and will not serve the king of Babylon, ²³ I will make to cease from the cities of Judah and from the region about Jerusalem the voice of mirth and the voice of gladness, the voice of the bridegroom and the voice of the bride, and the whole land will be a desolation without inhabitants."

24 " 'But we did not obey thy voice, to serve the king of Babylon; and thou hast confirmed thy words, which didst thou speak by thy servants the prophets, that the bones of our kings and the bones of our fathers would be brought out of their graves; *ᵉ* ²⁵ and behold, they have been cast out to the heat of day and the frost of night. They perished in great misery, by famine and sword and pestilence. ²⁶ And the house

ᵈ The meaning of the Greek is uncertain ᵉ Gk their place

173

which is called by thy name thou hast made as it is today, because of the wickedness of the house of Israel and the house of Judah.

27 " 'Yet thou hast dealt with us, O Lord our God, in all thy kindness and in all thy great compassion, 28 as thou didst speak by thy servant Moses on the day when thou didst command him to write thy law in the presence of the people of Israel, saying, 29 "If you will not obey my voice, this very great multitude will surely turn into a small number among the nations, where I will scatter them. 30 For I know that they will not obey me, for they are a stiff-necked people. But in the land of their exile they will come to themselves, 31 and they will know that I am the Lord their God. I will give them a heart that obeys and ears that hear; 32 and they will praise me in the land of their exile, and will remember my name, 33 and will turn from their stubbornness and their wicked deeds; for they will remember the ways of their fathers, who sinned before the Lord. 34 I will bring them again into the land which I swore to give to their fathers, to Abraham and to Isaac and to Jacob, and they will rule over it; and I will increase them, and they will not be diminished. 35 I will make an everlasting covenant with them to be their God and they shall be my people; and I will never again remove my people Israel from the land which I have given them."

3 " 'O Lord Almighty, God of Israel, the soul in anguish and the wearied spirit cry out to thee. 2 Hear, O Lord, and have mercy, for we have sinned before thee. 3 For thou art enthroned for ever, and we are perishing for ever. 4 O Lord Almighty, God of Israel, hear now the prayer of the dead of Israel and of the sons of those who sinned before thee, who did not heed the voice of the Lord their God, so that calamities have clung to us. 5 Remember

not the iniquities of our fathers, but in this crisis remember thy power and thy name. 6 For thou art the Lord our God, and thee, O Lord, will we praise. 7 For thou hast put the fear of thee in our hearts in order that we should call upon thy name; and we will praise thee in our exile, for we have put away from our hearts all the iniquity of our fathers who sinned before thee. 8 Behold, we are today in our exile where thou hast scattered us, to be reproached and cursed and punished for all the iniquities of our fathers who forsook the Lord our God.' "

9 Hear the commandments of life,
  O Israel;
  give ear, and learn wisdom!
10 Why is it, O Israel, why is it that
    you are in the land of your
    enemies,
    that you are growing old in a
    foreign country,
    that you are defiled with the dead,
11   that you are counted among
    those in Hades?
12 You have forsaken the fountain of
    wisdom.
13 If you had walked in the way of
    God,
    you would be dwelling in peace
    for ever.
14 Learn where there is wisdom,
    where there is strength,
    where there is understanding,
    that you may at the same time
    discern
    where there is length of days,
    and life,
    where there is light for the eyes,
    and peace.

15 Who has found her place?
    And who has entered her store-
    houses?
16 Where are the princes of the na-
    tions,
    and those who rule over the
    beasts on the earth;
17 those who have sport with the
    birds of the air,

and who hoard up silver and
　gold,
in which men trust,
　and there is no end to their get-
　　ting;
18 those who scheme to get silver,
　and are anxious,
whose labours are beyond meas-
　ure?
19 They have vanished and gone
　down to Hades,
and others have arisen in their
　place.
20 Young men have seen the light of
　day,
and have dwelt upon the earth;
but they have not learned the way
　to knowledge,
nor understood her paths,
　nor laid hold of her.
21 Their sons have strayed far from
　her *f* way.
22 She has not been heard of in
　Canaan,
nor seen in Teman;
23 the sons of Hagar, who seek for
　understanding on the earth,
the merchants of Merran and
　Teman,
the story-tellers and the seekers
　for understanding,
have not learned the way to wis-
　dom,
nor given thought to her paths.
24 O Israel, how great is the house
　of God!
And how vast the territory that
　he possesses!
25 It is great and has no bounds;
　it is high and immeasurable.
26 The giants were born there, who
　were famous of old,
great in stature, expert in war.
27 God did not choose them,
nor give them the way to knowl-
　edge;
28 so they perished because they had
　no wisdom,
they perished through their
　folly.

f Other authorities read their

29 Who has gone up into heaven,
　and taken her,
and brought her down from the
　clouds?
30 Who has gone over the sea, and
　found her,
and will buy her for pure gold?
31 No one knows the way to her,
　or is concerned about the path
　to her.
32 But he who knows all things knows
　her,
he found her by his under-
　standing.
He who prepared the earth for all
　time
filled it with four-footed crea-
　tures;
33 he who sends forth the light, and
　it goes,
called it, and it obeyed him in
　fear;
34 the stars shone in their watches,
　and were glad;
he called them, and they said,
　"Here we are!"
They shone with gladness for
　him who made them.
35 This is our God;
no other can be compared to
　him!
36 He found the whole way to knowl-
　edge,
and gave her to Jacob his servant
and to Israel whom he loved.
37 Afterward she appeared upon earth
　and lived among men.

4 She is the book of the com-
　mandments of God,
and the law that endures for
　ever.
All who hold her fast will live,
　and those who forsake her will
　die.
2 Turn, O Jacob, and take her;
walk toward the shining of her
　light.
3 Do not give your glory to another,
　or your advantages to an alien
　people.
4 Happy are we, O Israel,

for we know what is pleasing to
God.

5 Take courage, my people,
   O memorial of Israel!
6 It was not for destruction
      that you were sold to the na-
         tions,
   but you were handed over to your
      enemies
   because you angered God.
7 For you provoked him who made
      you,
      by sacrificing to demons and
         not to God.
8 You forgot the everlasting God,
      who brought you up,
   and you grieved Jerusalem, who
      reared you.
9 For she saw the wrath that came
      upon you from God,
   and she said:
   "Hearken, you neighbours of Zion,
      God has brought great sorrow
         upon me,
10 for I have seen the captivity of my
      sons and daughters,
      which the Everlasting brought
         upon them,
11 With joy I nurtured them,
      but I sent them away with weep-
         ing and sorrow.
12 Let no one rejoice over me, a
      widow
   and bereaved of many;
   I was left desolate because of the
      sins of my children,
      because they turned away from
         the law of God.
13 They had no regard for his statutes;
      they did not walk in the ways
         of God's commandments,
      nor tread the paths of discipline
         in his righteousness.
14 Let the neighbours of Zion come;
      remember the capture of my
         sons and daughters,
      which the Everlasting brought
         upon them.
15 For he brought against them a
      nation from afar,

a shameless nation, of a strange
   language,
who had no respect for an old
   man,
   and had no pity for a child.
16 They led away the widow's be-
      loved sons,
   and bereaved the lonely woman
      of her daughters.

17 "But I, how can I help you?
18 For he who brought these calami-
      ties upon you
   will deliver you from the hand
      of your enemies.
19 Go, my children, go;
   for I have been left desolate.
20 I have taken off the robe of peace
   and put on the sackcloth of my
      supplication;
   I will cry to the Everlasting all
      my days.

21 "Take courage, my children, cry
      to God,
   and he will deliver you from the
      power and hand of the enemy.
22 For I have put my hope in the
      Everlasting to save you,
   and joy has come to me from
      the Holy One,
   because of the mercy which soon
      will come to you
   from your everlasting Saviour.*9*
23 For I sent you out with sorrow and
      weeping,
      but God will give you back to
         me with joy and gladness for
         ever.
24 For as the neighbours of Zion have
      now seen your capture,
   so they soon will see your salva-
      tion by God,
   which will come to you with great
      glory
      and with the splendour of the
         Everlasting.
25 My children, endure with patience
      the wrath that has come upon
         you from God.
   Your enemy has overtaken you,

9 Or *from the Everlasting, your Saviour*

but you will soon see their destruction
and will tread upon their necks.
26 My tender sons have travelled rough roads;
they were taken away like a flock carried off by the enemy.

27 "Take courage, my children, and cry to God,
for you will be remembered by him who brought this upon you.
28 For just as you purposed to go astray from God,
return with tenfold zeal to seek him.
29 For he who brought these calamities upon you
will bring you everlasting joy with your salvation."

30 Take courage, O Jerusalem, for he who named you will comfort you.
31 Wretched will be those who afflicted you
and rejoiced at your fall.
32 Wretched will be the cities which your children served as slaves;
wretched will be the city which received your sons.
33 For just as she rejoiced at your fall and was glad for your ruin,
so she will be grieved at her own desolation.
34 And I will take away her pride in her great population,
and her insolence will be turned to grief.
35 For fire will come upon her from the Everlasting for many days,
and for a long time she will be inhabited by demons.

36 Look toward the east, O Jerusalem,
and see the joy that is coming to you from God!
37 Behold, your sons are coming, whom you sent away;

they are coming, gathered from east and west,
at the word of the Holy One,
rejoicing in the glory of God.

5 Take off the garment of your sorrow and affliction, O Jerusalem,
and put on for ever the beauty of the glory from God.
2 Put on the robe of the righteousness from God;
put on your head the diadem of the glory of the Everlasting.
3 For God will show your splendour everywhere under heaven.
4 For your name will for ever be called by God,
"Peace of righteousness and glory of godliness."

5 Arise, O Jerusalem, stand upon the height
and look toward the east,
and see your children gathered from west and east,
at the word of the Holy One,
rejoicing that God has remembered them.
6 For they went forth from you on foot,
led away by their enemies;
but God will bring them back to you,
carried in glory, as on a royal throne.
7 For God has ordered that every high mountain and the everlasting hills be made low
and the valleys filled up, to make level ground,
so that Israel may walk safely in the glory of God.
8 The woods and every fragrant tree have shaded Israel at God's command.
9 For God will lead Israel with joy, in the light of his glory,
with the mercy and righteousness that come from him.

THE LETTER OF JEREMIAH

6 [h] A copy of a letter which Jeremiah sent to those who were to be taken to Babylon as captives by the king of the Babylonians, to give them the message which God had commanded him.

2 Because of the sins which you have committed before God, you will be taken to Babylon as captives by Nebuchadnezzar, king of the Babylonians. [3] Therefore when you have come to Babylon you will remain there for many years, for a long time, up to seven generations; after that I will bring you away from there in peace. [4] Now in Babylon you will see gods made of silver and gold and wood, which are carried on men's shoulders and inspire fear in the heathen. [5] So take care not to become at all like the foreigners or to let fear for these gods [i] possess you, when you see the multitude before and behind them worshipping them. [6] But say in your heart, "It is thou, O Lord, whom we must worship." [7] For my angel is with you, and he is watching your lives.

8 Their tongues are smoothed by the craftsman, and they themselves are overlaid with gold and silver; but they are false and cannot speak. [9] People [j] take gold and make crowns for the heads of their gods, as they would for a girl who loves ornaments; [10] and sometimes the priests secretly take gold and silver from their gods and spend it upon themselves, [11] and even give some of it to the harlots in the brothel. They deck their gods [k] out with garments like men—these gods of silver and gold and wood, [12] which cannot save themselves from rust and corrosion. When they have been dressed in purple robes, [13] their faces are wiped because of the dust from the temple, which is thick upon them. [14] Like a local ruler the god [l]

holds a sceptre, though unable to destroy any one who offends it. [15] It has a dagger in its right hand, and has an axe; but it cannot save itself from war and robbers. [16] Therefore they evidently are not gods; so do not fear them.

17 For just as one's dish is useless when it is broken, so are the gods of the heathen, [m] when they have been set up in the temples. Their eyes are full of the dust raised by the feet of those who enter. [18] And just as the gates are shut on every side upon a man who has offended a king, as though he were sentenced to death, so the priests make their temples secure with doors and locks and bars, in order that they may not be plundered by robbers. [19] They light lamps, even more than they light for themselves, though their gods [n] can see none of them. [20] They are [o] just like a beam of the temple, but men say their hearts have melted, when worms from the earth devour them and their robes. They do not notice [21] when their faces have been blackened by the smoke of the temple. [22] Bats, swallows, and birds light on their bodies and heads; and so do cats. [23] From this you will know that they are not gods; so do not fear them.

24 As for the gold which they wear for beauty—they will not shine unless some one wipes off the rust; for even when they were being cast, they had no feeling. [25] They are bought at any cost, but there is no breath in them. [26] Having no feet, they are carried on men's shoulders, revealing to mankind their worthlessness. [27] And those who serve them are ashamed because through them these gods [n] are made to stand, lest they fall to the ground. If any one sets one of them upright, it cannot move of itself; and if it is tipped over, it can-

[h] The King James Version prints *The Epistle of Jeremy* as Chapter 6 of the book of Baruch, and the chapter and verse numbers are here retained [i] Gk *for them* [j] Gk *They* [k] Gk *them* [l] Gk *he* [m] Gk *of them* [n] Gk *they* [o] Gk *It is*

not straighten itself; but gifts are placed before them just as before the dead. 28 The priests sell the sacrifices that are offered to these gods *p* and use the money; and likewise their wives preserve some with salt, but give none to the poor or helpless. 29 Sacrifices to them may be touched by women in menstruation or at childbirth. Since you know by these things that they are not gods, do not fear them.

30 For why should they be called gods? Women serve meals for gods of silver and gold and wood; 31 and in their temples the priests sit with their clothes rent, their heads and beards shaved, and their heads uncovered. 32 They howl and shout before their gods as some do at a funeral feast for a man who has died. 33 The priests take some of the clothing of their gods *q* to clothe their wives and children. 34 Whether one does evil to them or good, they will not be able to repay it. They cannot set up a king or depose one. 35 Likewise they are not able to give either wealth or money; if one makes a vow to them and does not keep it, they will not require it. 36 They cannot save a man from death or rescue the weak from the strong. 37 They cannot restore sight to a blind man; they cannot rescue a man who is in distress. 38 They cannot take pity on a widow or do good to an orphan. 39 These things that are made of wood and overlaid with gold and silver are like stones from the mountain, and those who serve them will be put to shame. 40 Why then must any one think that they are gods, or call them gods?

Besides, even the Chaldeans themselves dishonour them; 41 for when they see a dumb man, who cannot speak, they bring him and pray Bel *r* that the man may speak, as though Bel *s* were able to understand. 42 Yet they themselves cannot perceive this and abandon them, for they have no sense. 43 And the women, with cords about them, sit along the passageways, burning bran for incense; and when one of them is led off by one of the passers-by and is lain with, she derides the woman next to her, because she was not as attractive as herself and her cord was not broken. 44 Whatever is done for them is false. Why then must any one think that they are gods, or call them gods?

45 They are made by carpenters and goldsmiths; they can be nothing but what the craftsmen wish them to be. 46 The men that make them will certainly not live very long themselves; how then can the things that are made by them be gods? 47 They have left only lies and reproach for those who come after. 48 For when war or calamity comes upon them, the priests consult together as to where they can hide themselves and their gods.*t* 49 How then can one fail to see that these are not gods, for they cannot save themselves from war or calamity? 50 Since they are made of wood and overlaid with gold and silver, it will afterward be known that they are false. 51 It will be manifest to all the nations and kings that they are not gods but the work of men's hands, and that there is no work of God in them. 52 Who then can fail to know that they are not gods? *u*

53 For they cannot set up a king over a country or give rain to men. 54 They cannot judge their own cause or deliver one who is wronged, for they have no power; they are like crows between heaven and earth. 55 When fire breaks out in a temple of wooden gods overlaid with gold or silver, their priests will flee and escape, but the gods *v* will be burnt in two like beams. 56 Besides, they can offer no resistance to a king or any enemies. Why then must any one admit or think that they are gods?

57 Gods made of wood and overlaid

p Gk *to them* *q* Gk *them* *r* Or *they bring Bel and pray* *s* Gk *he* *t* Gk *them*
u The Greek text of this verse is uncertain *v* Gk *they*

with silver and gold are not able to save themselves from thieves and robbers. [58] Strong men will strip them of their gold and silver and of the robes they wear, and go off with this booty, and they will not be able to help themselves. [59] So it is better to be a king who shows his courage, or a household utensil that serves its owner's need, than to be these false gods; better even the door of a house that protects its contents, than these false gods; better also a wooden pillar in a palace, than these false gods.

60 For sun and moon and stars, shining and sent forth for service, are obedient. [61] So also the lightning, when it flashes, is widely seen; and the wind likewise blows in every land. [62] When God commands the clouds to go over the whole world, they carry out his command. [63] And the fire sent from above to consume mountains and woods does what it is ordered. But these idols [w] are not to be compared with them in appearance or power. [64] Therefore one must not think that they are gods nor call them gods, for they are not

able either to decide a case or to do good to men. [65] Since you know then that they are not gods, do not fear them.

66 For they can neither curse nor bless kings; [67] they cannot show signs in the heavens and [x] among the nations, or shine like the sun or give light like the moon. [68] The wild beasts are better than they are, for they can flee to cover and help themselves. [69] So we have no evidence whatever that they are gods; therefore do not fear them.

70 Like a scarecrow in a cucumber bed, that guards nothing, so are their gods of wood, overlaid with gold and silver. [71] In the same way, their gods of wood, overlaid with gold and silver, are like a thorn bush in a garden, on which every bird sits; or like a dead body cast out in the darkness. [72] By the purple and linen [y] that rot upon them you will know that they are not gods; and they will finally themselves be consumed, and be a reproach in the land. [73] Better therefore is a just man who has no idols, for he will be far from reproach.

[w] Gk *these things*   [x] Other ancient authorities omit *and*   [y] Cn: Gk *marble,* Syr *silk*

THE PRAYER OF AZARIAH AND THE SONG OF THE THREE YOUNG MEN

Additions to Daniel, inserted between 3.23 and 3.24

And they walked about in the midst of the flames, singing hymns to God and blessing the Lord. ² Then Azariah stood and offered this prayer; in the midst of the fire he opened his mouth and said:

³ "Blessed art thou, O Lord, God of our fathers, and worthy of praise;
and thy name is glorified for ever.

⁴ For thou art just in all that thou hast done to us,
and all thy works are true and thy ways right,
and all thy judgments are truth.

⁵ Thou hast executed true judgments in all that thou hast brought upon us
and upon Jerusalem, the holy city of our fathers,
for in truth and justice thou hast brought all this upon us because of our sins.

⁶ For we have sinfully and lawlessly departed from thee,
and have sinned in all things and have not obeyed thy commandments;

⁷ we have not observed them or done them,
as thou hast commanded us that it might go well with us.

⁸ So all that thou hast brought upon us,
and all that thou hast done to us,
thou hast done in true judgment.

⁹ Thou hast given us into the hands of lawless enemies, most hateful rebels,
and to an unjust king, the most wicked in all the world.

¹⁰ And now we cannot open our mouths;

shame and disgrace have befallen thy servants and worshippers.

¹¹ For thy name's sake do not give us up utterly,
and do not break thy covenant,

¹² and do not withdraw thy mercy from us,
for the sake of Abraham thy beloved
and for the sake of Isaac thy servant
and Israel thy holy one,

¹³ to whom thou didst promise
to make their descendants as many as the stars of heaven
and as the sand on the shore of the sea.

¹⁴ For we, O Lord, have become fewer than any nation,
and are brought low this day in all the world because of our sins.

¹⁵ And at this time there is no prince, or prophet, or leader,
no burnt offering, or sacrifice, or oblation, or incense,
no place to make an offering before thee or to find mercy.

¹⁶ Yet with a contrite heart and a humble spirit may we be accepted,
as though it were with burnt offerings of rams and bulls,
and with tens of thousands of fat lambs;

¹⁷ such may our sacrifice be in thy sight this day,
and may we wholly follow thee,
for there will be no shame for those who trust in thee.

¹⁸ And now with all our heart we follow thee,
we fear thee and seek thy face.

¹⁹ Do not put us to shame,

but deal with us in thy forbearance
and in thy abundant mercy.
20 Deliver us in accordance with thy
marvellous works,
and give glory to thy name, O
Lord!
Let all who do harm to thy servants
be put to shame;
21 let them be disgraced and deprived of all power and dominion,
and let their strength be broken.
22 Let them know that thou art the
Lord, the only God,
glorious over the whole world."

23 Now the king's servants who
threw them in did not cease feeding
the furnace fires with naphtha, pitch,
tow, and brush. 24 And the flame
streamed out above the furnace forty-
nine cubits, 25 and it broke through
and burned those of the Chaldeans
whom it caught about the furnace.
26 But the angel of the Lord came
down into the furnace to be with
Azariah and his companions, and
drove the fiery flame out of the furnace, 27 and made the midst of the
furnace like a moist whistling wind,
so that the fire did not touch them at
all or hurt or trouble them.
28 Then the three, as with one
mouth, praised and glorified and
blessed God in the furnace, saying:
29 "Blessed art thou, O Lord, God of
our fathers,
and to be praised and highly
exalted for ever;
30 And blessed is thy glorious, holy
name
and to be highly praised and
highly exalted for ever;
31 Blessed art thou in the temple of
thy holy glory
and to be extolled and highly
glorified for ever.
32 Blessed art thou, who sittest upon
cherubim and lookest upon
the deeps,
and to be praised and highly
exalted for ever.

33 Blessed art thou upon the throne
of thy kingdom
and to be extolled and highly
exalted for ever.
34 Blessed art thou in the firmament
of heaven
and to be sung and glorified for
ever.

35 "Bless the Lord, all works of the
Lord,
sing praise to him and highly
exalt him for ever.
36 Bless the Lord, you heavens,
sing praise to him and highly
exalt him for ever.
37 Bless the Lord, you angels of the
Lord,
sing praise to him and highly
exalt him for ever.
38 Bless the Lord, all waters above
the heaven,
sing praise to him and highly
exalt him for ever.
39 Bless the Lord, all powers,
sing praise to him and highly
exalt him for ever.
40 Bless the Lord, sun and moon,
sing praise to him and highly
exalt him for ever.
41 Bless the Lord, stars of heaven,
sing praise to him and highly
exalt him for ever.
42 Bless the Lord, all rain and dew,
sing praise to him and highly
exalt him for ever.
43 Bless the Lord, all winds,
sing praise to him and highly
exalt him for ever.
44 Bless the Lord, fire and heat,
sing praise to him and highly
exalt him for ever.
45 Bless the Lord, winter cold and
summer heat,
sing praise to him and highly
exalt him for ever.
46 Bless the Lord, dews and snows,
sing praise to him and highly
exalt him for ever.
47 Bless the Lord, nights and days,
sing praise to him and highly
exalt him for ever.
48 Bless the Lord, light and darkness,

sing praise to him and highly
exalt him for ever.

⁴⁹ Bless the Lord, ice and cold,
sing praise to him and highly
exalt him for ever.

⁵⁰ Bless the Lord, frosts and snows,
sing praise to him and highly
exalt him for ever.

⁵¹ Bless the Lord, lightnings and
clouds,
sing praise to him and highly
exalt him for ever.

⁵² Let the earth bless the Lord;
let it sing praise to him and
highly exalt him for ever.

⁵³ Bless the Lord, mountains and hills,
sing praise to him and highly
exalt him for ever.

⁵⁴ Bless the Lord, all things that
grow on the earth,
sing praise to him and highly
exalt him for ever.

⁵⁵ Bless the Lord, you springs,
sing praise to him and highly
exalt him for ever.

⁵⁶ Bless the Lord, seas and rivers,
sing praise to him and highly
exalt him for ever.

⁵⁷ Bless the Lord, you whales and all
creatures that move in the
waters,
sing praise to him and highly
exalt him for ever.

⁵⁸ Bless the Lord, all birds of the air,
sing praise to him and highly
exalt him for ever.

⁵⁹ Bless the Lord, all beasts and cattle,
sing praise to him and highly
exalt him for ever.

⁶⁰ Bless the Lord, you sons of men,

sing praise to him and highly
exalt him for ever.

⁶¹ Bless the Lord, O Israel,
sing praise to him and highly
exalt him for ever.

⁶² Bless the Lord, you priests of the
Lord,
sing praise to him and highly
exalt him for ever.

⁶³ Bless the Lord, you servants of the
Lord,
sing praise to him and highly
exalt him for ever.

⁶⁴ Bless the Lord, spirits and souls of
the righteous,
sing praise to him and highly
exalt him for ever.

⁶⁵ Bless the Lord, you who are holy
and humble in heart,
sing praise to him and highly
exalt him for ever.

⁶⁶ Bless the Lord, Hananiah, **Azariah**,
and Mishael,
sing praise to him and highly
exalt him for ever;
for he has rescued us from Hades
and saved us from the hand
of death,
and delivered us from the midst
of the burning fiery furnace;
from the midst of the fire he has
delivered us.

⁶⁷ Give thanks to the Lord, for he is
good,
for his mercy endures for ever.

⁶⁸ Bless him, all who worship the
Lord, the God of gods,
sing praise to him and give
thanks to him,
for his mercy endures for ever."

SUSANNA

There was a man living in Babylon whose name was Joakim. ² And he took a wife named Susanna, the daughter of Hilkiah, a very beautiful woman and one who feared the Lord. ³ Her parents were righteous, and had taught their daughter according to the law of Moses. ⁴ Joakim was very rich, and had a spacious garden adjoining his house; and the Jews used to come to him because he was the most honoured of them all.

5 In that year two elders from the people were appointed as judges. Concerning them the Lord had said: "Iniquity came forth from Babylon, from elders who were judges, who were supposed to govern the people." ⁶ These men were frequently at Joakim's house, and all who had suits at law came to them.

7 When the people departed at noon, Susanna would go into her husband's garden to walk. ⁸ The two elders used to see her every day, going in and walking about, and they began to desire her. ⁹ And they perverted their minds and turned away their eyes from looking to Heaven or remembering righteous judgments. ¹⁰ Both were overwhelmed with passion for her, but they did not tell each other of their distress, ¹¹ for they were ashamed to disclose their lustful desire to possess her. ¹² And they watched eagerly, day after day, to see her.

13 They said to each other, "Let us go home, for it is mealtime." ¹⁴ And when they went out, they parted from each other. But turning back, they met again; and when each pressed the other for the reason, they confessed their lust. And then together they arranged for a time when they could find her alone.

15 Once, while they were watching for an opportune day, she went in as before with only two maids, and wished to bathe in the garden, for it was very hot. ¹⁶ And no one

was there except the two elders, who had hid themselves and were watching her. ¹⁷ She said to her maids, "Bring me oil and ointments, and shut the garden doors so that I may bathe." ¹⁸ They did as she said, shut the garden doors, and went out by the side doors to bring what they had been commanded; and they did not see the elders, because they were hidden.

19 When the maids had gone out, the two elders rose and ran to her, and said: ²⁰ "Look, the garden doors are shut, no one sees us, and we are in love with you; so give your consent, and lie with us. ²¹ If you refuse, we will testify against you that a young man was with you, and this was why you sent your maids away."

22 Susanna sighed deeply, and said, "I am hemmed in on every side. For if I do this thing, it is death for me; and if I do not, I shall not escape your hands. ²³ I choose not to do it and to fall into your hands, rather than to sin in the sight of the Lord."

24 Then Susanna cried out with a loud voice, and the two elders shouted against her. ²⁵ And one of them ran and opened the garden doors. ²⁶ When the household servants heard the shouting in the garden, they rushed in at the side door to see what had happened to her. ²⁷ And when the elders told their tale, the servants were greatly ashamed, for nothing like this had ever been said about Susanna.

28 The next day, when the people gathered at the house of her husband Joakim, the two elders came, full of their wicked plot to have Susanna put to death. ²⁹ They said before the people, "Send for Susanna, the daughter of Hilkiah, who is the wife of Joakim." ³⁰ So they sent for her. And she came, with her parents, her children, and all her kindred.

31 Now Susanna was a woman of

great refinement, and beautiful in appearance. 32 As she was veiled, the wicked men ordered her to be unveiled, that they might feast upon her beauty. 33 But her family and friends and all who saw her wept.

34 Then the two elders stood up in the midst of the people, and laid their hands upon her head. 35 And she, weeping, looked up toward heaven, for her heart trusted in the Lord. 36 The elders said, "As we were walking in the garden alone, this woman came in with two maids, shut the garden doors, and dismissed the maids. 37 Then a young man, who had been hidden, came to her and lay with her. 38 We were in a corner of the garden, and when we saw this wickedness we ran to them. 39 We saw them embracing, but we could not hold the man, for he was too strong for us, and he opened the doors and dashed out. 40 So we seized this woman and asked her who the young man was, but she would not tell us. These things we testify."

41 The assembly believed them, because they were elders of the people and judges; and they condemned her to death.

42 Then Susanna cried out with a loud voice, and said, "O eternal God, who dost discern what is secret, who art aware of all things before they come to be, 43 thou knowest that these men have borne false witness against me. And now I am to die! Yet I have done none of the things that they have wickedly invented against me!"

44 The Lord heard her cry. 45 And as she was being led away to be put to death, God aroused the holy spirit of a young lad named Daniel; 46 and he cried with a loud voice, "I am innocent of the blood of this woman."

47 All the people turned to him, and said, "What is this that you have said?" 48 Taking his stand in the midst of them, he said, "Are you

such fools, you sons of Israel? Have you condemned a daughter of Israel without examination and without learning the facts? 49 Return to the place of judgment. For these men have borne false witness against her."

50 Then all the people returned in haste. And the elders said to him, "Come, sit among us and inform us, for God has given you that right." 51 And Daniel said to them, "Separate them far from each other, and I will examine them."

52 When they were separated from each other, he summoned one of them and said to him, "You old relic of wicked days, your sins have now come home, which you have committed in the past, 53 pronouncing unjust judgments, condemning the innocent and letting the guilty go free, though the Lord said, 'Do not put to death an innocent and righteous person.' 54 Now then, if you really saw her, tell me this: Under what tree did you see them being intimate with each other?" He answered, "Under a mastic tree." *a* 55 And Daniel said, "Very well! You have lied against your own head, for the angel of God has received the sentence from God and will immediately cut *a* you in two."

56 Then he put him aside, and commanded them to bring the other. And he said to him, "You offspring of Canaan and not of Judah, beauty has deceived you and lust has perverted your heart. 57 This is how you both have been dealing with the daughters of Israel, and they were intimate with you through fear; but a daughter of Judah would not endure your wickedness. 58 Now then, tell me: Under what tree did you catch them being intimate with each other?" He answered, "Under an evergreen oak." *b* 59 And Daniel said to him, "Very well! You also have lied against your own head, for the angel of God is waiting with his

a The Greek words for *mastic tree* and *cut* are so similar that the use of *cut* is ironic wordplay
b The Greek words for *evergreen oak* and *saw* are so similar that the use of *saw* is ironic wordplay

sword to saw [b] you in two, that he may destroy you both."

60 Then all the assembly shouted loudly and blessed God, who saves those who hope in him. [61] And they rose against the two elders, for out of their own mouths Daniel had convicted them of bearing false witness; [62] and they did to them as they had wickedly planned to do to their neighbour; acting in accordance with

the law of Moses, they put them to death. Thus innocent blood was saved that day.

63 And Hilkiah and his wife praised God for their daughter Susanna, and so did Joakim her husband and all her kindred, because nothing shameful was found in her. [64] And from that day onward Daniel had a great reputation among the people.

[b] The Greek words for *evergreen oak* and *saw* are so similar that the use of *saw* is ironic wordplay

BEL AND THE DRAGON

When King Astyages was laid with his fathers, Cyrus the Persian received his kingdom. 2 And Daniel was a companion of the king, and was the most honoured of his friends.

3 Now the Babylonians had an idol called Bel, and every day they spent on it twelve bushels of fine flour and forty sheep and fifty gallons of wine. 4 The king revered it and went every day to worship it. But Daniel worshipped his own God.

5 And the king said to him, "Why do you not worship Bel?" He answered, "Because I do not revere man-made idols, but the living God, who created heaven and earth and has dominion over all flesh."

6 The king said to him, "Do you not think that Bel is a living God? Do you not see how much he eats and drinks every day?" 7 Then Daniel laughed, and said, "Do not be deceived, O king; for this is but clay inside and brass outside, and it never ate or drank anything."

8 Then the king was angry, and he called his priests and said to them, "If you do not tell me who is eating these provisions, you shall die. 9 But if you prove that Bel is eating them, Daniel shall die, because he blasphemed against Bel." And Daniel said to the king, "Let it be done as you have said."

10 Now there were seventy priests of Bel, besides their wives and children. And the king went with Daniel into the temple of Bel. 11 And the priests of Bel said, "Behold, we are going outside; you yourself, O king, shall set forth the food and mix and place the wine, and shut the door and seal it with your signet. 12 And when you return in the morning, if you do not find that Bel has eaten it all, we will die; or else Daniel will, who is telling lies about us." 13 They were unconcerned, for beneath the table they had made a hidden entrance, through which they used to go in

regularly and consume the provisions. 14 When they had gone out, the king set forth the food for Bel. Then Daniel ordered his servants to bring ashes and they sifted them throughout the whole temple in the presence of the king alone. Then they went out, shut the door and sealed it with the king's signet, and departed. 15 In the night the priests came with their wives and children, as they were accustomed to do, and ate and drank everything.

16 Early in the morning the king rose and came, and Daniel with him. 17 And the king said, "Are the seals unbroken, Daniel?" He answered, "They are unbroken, O king." 18 As soon as the doors were opened, the king looked at the table, and shouted in a loud voice, "You are great, O Bel; and with you there is no deceit, none at all."

19 Then Daniel laughed, and restrained the king from going in, and said, "Look at the floor, and notice whose footsteps these are." 20 The king said, "I see the footsteps of men and women and children."

21 Then the king was enraged, and he seized the priests and their wives and children; and they showed him the secret doors through which they were accustomed to enter and devour what was on the table. 22 Therefore the king put them to death, and gave Bel over to Daniel, who destroyed it and its temple.

23 There was also a great dragon, which the Babylonians revered. 24 And the king said to Daniel, "You cannot deny that this is a living god; so worship him." 25 Daniel said, "I will worship the Lord my God, for he is the living God. 26 But if you, O king, will give me permission, I will slay the dragon without sword or club." The king said, "I give you permission."

27 Then Daniel took pitch, fat,

and hair, and boiled them together and made cakes, which he fed to the dragon. The dragon ate them, and burst open. And Daniel said, "See what you have been worshipping!"

28 When the Babylonians heard it, they were very indignant and conspired against the king, saying, "The king has become a Jew; he has destroyed Bel, and slain the dragon, and slaughtered the priests." 29 Going to the king, they said, "Hand Daniel over to us, or else we will kill you and your household." 30 The king saw that they were pressing him hard, and under compulsion he handed Daniel over to them.

31 They threw Daniel into the lions' den, and he was there for six days. 32 There were seven lions in the den, and every day they had been given two human bodies and two sheep; but these were not given to them now, so that they might devour Daniel.

33 Now the prophet Habakkuk was in Judea. He had boiled pottage and had broken bread into a bowl, and was going into the field to take it to the reapers. 34 But the angel of the Lord said to Habakkuk, "Take the dinner which you have to Babylon, to Daniel, in the lions' den." 35 Habakkuk said, "Sir, I have never seen Babylon, and I know nothing about the den." 36 Then the angel of the Lord took him by the crown of his head, and lifted him by his hair and set him down in Babylon, right over the den, with the rushing sound of the wind itself.

37 Then Habakkuk shouted, "Daniel! Daniel! Take the dinner which God has sent you." 38 And Daniel said, "Thou hast remembered me, O God, and hast not forsaken those who love thee." 39 So Daniel arose and ate. And the angel of God immediately returned Habakkuk to his own place.

40 On the seventh day the king came to mourn for Daniel. When he came to the den he looked in, and there sat Daniel. 41 And the king shouted with a loud voice, "Thou art great, O Lord God of Daniel, and there is no other besides thee." 42 And he pulled Daniel [a] out, and threw into the den the men who had attempted his destruction, and they were devoured immediately before his eyes.

[a] Gk *him*

THE PRAYER OF MANASSEH

O Lord Almighty,
God of our fathers,
of Abraham and Isaac and Jacob
and of their righteous posterity;
2 thou who hast made heaven and
earth
with all their order;
3 who hast shackled the sea by thy
word of command,
who hast confined the deep
and sealed it with thy terrible
and glorious name;
4 at whom all things shudder,
and tremble before thy power,
5 for thy glorious splendour cannot
be borne,
and the wrath of thy threat to
sinners is irresistible;
6 yet immeasurable and unsearch-
able is thy promised mercy,
7 for thou art the Lord Most High,
of great compassion, long-suffer-
ing, and very merciful,
and repentest over the evils of
men.
Thou, O Lord, according to thy
great goodness
hast promised repentance and
forgiveness
to those who have sinned against
thee;
and in the multitude of thy mercies
thou hast appointed repentance
for sinners,
that they may be saved.
8 Therefore thou, O Lord, God of
the righteous,
hast not appointed repentance
for the righteous,
for Abraham and Isaac and Jacob,
who did not sin against thee,
but thou hast appointed repentance for me, who am a sinner.
9 For the sins I have committed are
more in number than the
sand of the sea;
my transgressions are multiplied,
O Lord, they are multiplied!
I am unworthy to look up and see
the height of heaven
because of the multitude of my
iniquities.
10 I am weighted down with many
an iron fetter,
so that I am rejected because of
my sins,
and I have no relief;
for I have provoked thy wrath
and have done what is evil in
thy sight,
setting up abominations and
multiplying offences.
11 And now I bend the knee of my
heart,
beseeching thee for thy kindness.
12 I have sinned, O Lord, I have
sinned,
and I know my transgressions.
13 I earnestly beseech thee,
forgive me, O Lord, forgive me!
Do not destroy me with my
transgressions!
Do not be angry with me for ever
or lay up evil for me;
do not condemn me to the
depths of the earth.
For thou, O Lord, art the God of
those who repent,
14 and in me thou wilt manifest
thy goodness;
for, unworthy as I am, thou wilt
save me in thy great mercy,
15 and I will praise thee continually all the days of my life.
For all the host of heaven sings
thy praise,
and thine is the glory for ever.
Amen.

THE FIRST BOOK OF THE

MACCABEES

1 After Alexander son of Philip, the Macedonian, who came from the land of Kittim, had defeated[a] Darius, king of the Persians and the Medes, he succeeded him as king. (He had previously become king of Greece.) [2] He fought many battles, conquered strongholds, and put to death the kings of the earth. [3] He advanced to the ends of the earth, and plundered many nations. When the earth became quiet before him, he was exalted, and his heart was lifted up. [4] He gathered a very strong army and ruled over countries, nations, and princes, and they became tributary to him.

[5] After this he fell sick and perceived that he was dying. [6] So he summoned his most honoured officers, who had been brought up with him from youth, and divided his kingdom among them while he was still alive. [7] And after Alexander had reigned twelve years, he died.

[8] Then his officers began to rule, each in his own place. [9] They all put on crowns after his death, and so did their sons after them for many years; and they caused many evils on the earth.

[10] From them came forth a sinful root, Antiochus Epiphanes, son of Antiochus the king; he had been a hostage in Rome. He began to reign in the one hundred and thirty-seventh year of the kingdom of the Greeks.[b]

[11] In those days lawless men came forth from Israel, and misled many, saying, "Let us go and make a covenant with the Gentiles round about us, for since we separated from them many evils have come upon us." [12] This proposal pleased them, [13] and some of the people eagerly went to the king. He authorized them to observe the ordinances of the Gentiles.

[14] So they built a gymnasium in Jerusalem, according to Gentile custom, [15] and removed the marks of circumcision, and abandoned the holy covenant. They joined with the Gentiles and sold themselves to do evil.

[16] When Antiochus saw that his kingdom was established, he determined to become king of the land of Egypt, that he might reign over both kingdoms. [17] So he invaded Egypt with a strong force, with chariots and elephants and cavalry and with a large fleet. [18] He engaged Ptolemy king of Egypt in battle, and Ptolemy turned and fled before him, and many were wounded and fell. [19] And they captured the fortified cities in the land of Egypt, and he plundered the land of Egypt.

[20] After subduing Egypt, Antiochus returned in the one hundred and forty-third year.[c] He went up against Israel and came to Jerusalem with a strong force. [21] He arrogantly entered the sanctuary and took the golden altar, the lampstand for the light, and all its utensils. [22] He took also the table for the bread of the Presence, the cups for drink offerings, the bowls, the golden censers, the curtain, the crowns, and the gold decoration on the front of the temple; he stripped it all off. [23] He took the silver and the gold, and the costly vessels; he took also the hidden treasures which he found. [24] Taking them all, he departed to his own land.

He committed deeds of murder,
    and spoke with great arrogance.
[25] Israel mourned deeply in every
    community,
[26]   rulers and elders groaned,
    maidens and young men became
        faint,

a Gk adds *and he defeated*   *b* 175 B.C.   *c* 169 B.C.

the beauty of the women faded.
27 Every bridegroom took up the
    lament;
  she who sat in the bridal cham-
    ber was mourning.
28 Even the land shook for its in-
    habitants,
  and all the house of Jacob was
    clothed with shame.

29 Two years later the king sent
to the cities of Judah a chief col-
lector of tribute, and he came to
Jerusalem with a large force. 30 Deceitfully he spoke peaceable words to
them, and they believed him; but he
suddenly fell upon the city, dealt it
a severe blow, and destroyed many
people of Israel. 31 He plundered the
city, burned it with fire, and tore
down its houses and its surrounding
walls. 32 And they took captive the
women and children, and seized the
cattle. 33 Then they fortified the city
of David with a great strong wall and
strong towers, and it became their
citadel. 34 And they stationed there
a sinful people, lawless men. These
strengthened their position; 35 they
stored up arms and food, and collecting the spoils of Jerusalem they
stored them there, and became a
great snare.
36 It became an ambush against the
    sanctuary,
  an evil adversary of Israel con-
    tinually.
37 On every side of the sanctuary
    they shed innocent blood;
  they even defiled the sanctuary.
38 Because of them the residents of
    Jerusalem fled;
  she became a dwelling of strang-
    ers;
  she became strange to her off-
    spring,
  and her children forsook her.
39 Her sanctuary became desolate as
    a desert;
  her feasts were turned into
    mourning,
  her sabbaths into a reproach,
  her honour into contempt.

40 Her dishonour now grew as great
    as her glory;
  her exaltation was turned into
    mourning.

41 Then the king wrote to his
whole kingdom that all should be
one people, 42 and that each should
give up his customs. 43 All the Gentiles accepted the command of the
king. Many even from Israel gladly
adopted his religion; they sacrificed
to idols and profaned the sabbath.
44 And the king sent letters by messengers to Jerusalem and the cities
of Judah; he directed them to follow
customs strange to the land, 45 to
forbid burnt offerings and sacrifices
and drink offerings in the sanctuary,
to profane sabbaths and feasts, 46 to
defile the sanctuary and the priests,
47 to build altars and sacred precincts
and shrines for idols, to sacrifice
swine and unclean animals, 48 and to
leave their sons uncircumcised. They
were to make themselves abominable
by everything unclean and profane,
49 so that they should forget the
law and change all the ordinances.
50 "And whoever does not obey the
command of the king shall die."

51 In such words he wrote to his
whole kingdom. And he appointed
inspectors over all the people and
commanded the cities of Judah to
offer sacrifice, city by city. 52 Many
of the people, every one who forsook
the law, joined them, and they did
evil in the land; 53 they drove Israel
into hiding in every place of refuge
they had.
54 Now on the fifteenth day of
Chislev, in the one hundred and
forty-fifth year,*d* they erected a deso-
lating sacrilege upon the altar of
burnt offering. They also built altars
in the surrounding cities of Judah,
55 and burned incense at the doors
of the houses and in the streets.
56 The books of the law which they
found they tore to pieces and burned
with fire. 57 Where the book of the
covenant was found in the possession

d 167 B.C.

of any one, or if any one adhered to the law, the decree of the king condemned him to death. 58 They kept using violence against Israel, against those found month after month in the cities. 59 And on the twenty-fifth day of the month they offered sacrifice on the altar which was upon the altar of burnt offering. 60 According to the decree, they put to death the women who had their children circumcised, 61 and their families and those who circumcised them; and they hung the infants from their mothers' necks.

62 But many in Israel stood firm and were resolved in their hearts not to eat unclean food. 63 They chose to die rather than to be defiled by food or to profane the holy covenant; and they did die. 64 And very great wrath came upon Israel.

2 In those days Mattathias the son of John, son of Simeon, a priest of the sons of Joarib, moved from Jerusalem and settled in Modein. 2 He had five sons, John surnamed Gaddi, 3 Simon called Thassi, 4 Judas called Maccabeus, 5 Eleazar called Avaran, and Jonathan called Apphus. 6 He saw the blasphemies being committed in Judah and Jerusalem, 7 and said,

"Alas! Why was I born to see this,
    the ruin of my people, the ruin
       of the holy city,
and to dwell there when it was
    given over to the enemy,
    the sanctuary given over to
       aliens?
8 Her temple has become like a man
    without honour; *e*
9   her glorious vessels have been
      carried into captivity.
Her babes have been killed in her
    streets,
    her youths by the sword of the
      foe.
10 What nation has not inherited her
    palaces *f*
and has not seized her spoils?

11 All her adornment has been taken
    away;
    no longer free, she has become
      a slave.
12 And behold, our holy place, our
    beauty,
    and our glory have been laid
      waste;
the Gentiles have profaned it.
13   Why should we live any longer?"

14 And Mattathias and his sons rent their clothes, put on sackcloth, and mourned greatly.

15 Then the king's officers who were enforcing the apostasy came to the city of Modein to make them offer sacrifice. 16 Many from Israel came to them; and Mattathias and his sons were assembled. 17 Then the king's officers spoke to Mattathias as follows: "You are a leader, honoured and great in this city, and supported by sons and brothers. 18 Now be the first to come and do what the king commands, as all the Gentiles and the men of Judah and those that are left in Jerusalem have done. Then you and your sons will be numbered among the friends of the king, and you and your sons will be honoured with silver and gold and many gifts."

19 But Mattathias answered and said in a loud voice: "Even if all the nations that live under the rule of the king obey him, and have chosen to do his commandments, departing each one from the religion of his fathers, 20 yet I and my sons and my brothers will live by the covenant of our fathers. 21 Far be it from us to desert the law and the ordinances. 22 We will not obey the king's words by turning aside from our religion to the right hand or to the left."

23 When he had finished speaking these words, a Jew came forward in the sight of all to offer sacrifice upon the altar in Modein, according to the king's command. 24 When Mattathias saw it, he burned with zeal and his heart was stirred. He gave vent to righteous anger; he ran and

---

e The text of this verse is uncertain   *f* Other authorities read *has not had a part in her kingdom*

killed him upon the altar. 25 At the same time he killed the king's officer who was forcing them to sacrifice, and he tore down the altar. 26 Thus he burned with zeal for the law, as Phinehas did against Zimri the son of Salu.

27 Then Mattathias cried out in the city with a loud voice, saying: "Let every one who is zealous for the law and supports the covenant come out with me!" 28 And he and his sons fled to the hills and left all that they had in the city.

29 Then many who were seeking righteousness and justice went down to the wilderness to dwell there, 30 they, their sons, their wives, and their cattle, because evils pressed heavily upon them. 31 And it was reported to the king's officers, and to the troops in Jerusalem the city of David, that men who had rejected the king's command had gone down to the hiding places in the wilderness. 32 Many pursued them, and overtook them; they encamped opposite them and prepared for battle against them on the sabbath day. 33 And they said to them, "Enough of this! Come out and do what the king commands, and you will live." 34 But they said, "We will not come out, nor will we do what the king commands and so profane the sabbath day." 35 Then the enemy *g* hastened to attack them. 36 But they did not answer them or hurl a stone at them or block up their hiding places, 37 for they said, "Let us all die in our innocence; heaven and earth testify for us that you are killing us unjustly." 38 So they attacked them on the sabbath, and they died, with their wives and children and cattle, to the number of a thousand persons.

39 When Mattathias and his friends learned of it, they mourned for them deeply. 40 And each said to his neighbour: "If we all do as our brethren have done and refuse to fight with the Gentiles for our lives

g Gk *they*

and our ordinances, they will quickly destroy us from the earth." 41 So they made this decision that day: "Let us fight against every man who comes to attack us on the sabbath day; let us not all die as our brethren died in their hiding places."

42 Then there united with them a company of Hasideans, mighty warriors of Israel, every one who offered himself willingly for the law. 43 And all who became fugitives to escape their troubles joined them and reinforced them. 44 They organized an army, and struck down sinners in their anger and lawless men in their wrath; the survivors fled to the Gentiles for safety. 45 And Mattathias and his friends went about and tore down the altars; 46 they forcibly circumcised all the uncircumcised boys that they found within the borders of Israel. 47 They hunted down the arrogant men, and the work prospered in their hands. 48 They rescued the law out of the hands of the Gentiles and kings, and they never let the sinner gain the upper hand.

49 Now the days drew near for Mattathias to die, and he said to his sons: "Arrogance and reproach have now become strong; it is a time of ruin and furious anger. 50 Now, my children, show zeal for the law, and give your lives for the covenant of our fathers.

51 "Remember the deeds of the fathers, which they did in their generations; and receive great honour and an everlasting name. 52 Was not Abraham found faithful when tested, and it was reckoned to him as righteousness? 53 Joseph in the time of his distress kept the commandment, and became lord of Egypt. 54 Phinehas our father, because he was deeply zealous, received the covenant of everlasting priesthood. 55 Joshua, because he fulfilled the command, became a judge in Israel. 56 Caleb, because he testified in the assembly, received an inheritance in the land.

⁵⁷ David, because he was merciful, inherited the throne of the kingdom for ever. ⁵⁸ Elijah because of great zeal for the law was taken up into heaven. ⁵⁹ Hananiah, Azariah, and Mishael believed and were saved from the flame. ⁶⁰ Daniel because of his innocence was delivered from the mouth of the lions.

61 "And so observe, from generation to generation, that none who put their trust in him will lack strength. ⁶² Do not fear the words of a sinner, for his splendour will turn into dung and worms. ⁶³ Today he will be exalted, but tomorrow he will not be found, because he has returned to the dust, and his plans will perish. ⁶⁴ My children, be courageous and grow strong in the law, for by it you will gain honour.

65 "Now behold, I know that Simeon your brother is wise in counsel; always listen to him; he shall be your father. ⁶⁶ Judas Maccabeus has been a mighty warrior from his youth; he shall command the army for you and fight the battle against the peoples.^h ⁶⁷ You shall rally about you all who observe the law, and avenge the wrong done to your people. ⁶⁸ Pay back the Gentiles in full, and heed what the law commands."

69 Then he blessed them, and was gathered to his fathers. ⁷⁰ He died in the one hundred and forty-sixth yearⁱ and was buried in the tomb of his fathers at Modein. And all Israel mourned for him with great lamentation.

3 Then Judas his son, who was called Maccabeus, took command in his place. ² All his brothers and all who had joined his father helped him; they gladly fought for Israel.

³ He extended the glory of his people.

Like a giant he put on his breastplate;

he girded on his armour of war and waged battles,

protecting the host by his sword.

⁴ He was like a lion in his deeds,

like a lion's cub roaring for prey.

⁵ He searched out and pursued the lawless;

he burned those who troubled his people.

⁶ Lawless men shrank back for fear of him;

all the evildoers were confounded;

and deliverance prospered by his hand.

⁷ He embittered many kings,

but he made Jacob glad by his deeds,

and his memory is blessed for ever.

⁸ He went through the cities of Judah;

he destroyed the ungodly out of the land;^j

thus he turned away wrath from Israel.

⁹ He was renowned to the ends of the earth;

he gathered in those who were perishing.

10 But Apollonius gathered together Gentiles and a large force from Samaria to fight against Israel. ¹¹ When Judas learned of it, he went out to meet him, and he defeated and killed him. Many were wounded and fell, and the rest fled. ¹² Then they seized their spoils; and Judas took the sword of Apollonius, and used it in battle the rest of his life.

13 Now when Seron, the commander of the Syrian army, heard that Judas had gathered a large company, including a body of faithful men who stayed with him and went out to battle, ¹⁴ he said, "I will make a name for myself and win honour in the kingdom. I will make war on Judas and his companions, who scorn the king's command." ¹⁵ And again a strong army of ungodly men went

^h Or *of the people*   ⁱ 166 B.C.   ^j Gk *it*

up with him to help him, to take vengeance on the sons of Israel.

16 When he approached the ascent of Beth-horon, Judas went out to meet him with a small company. 17 But when they saw the army coming to meet them, they said to Judas, "How can we, few as we are, fight against so great and strong a multitude? And we are faint, for we have eaten nothing today." 18 Judas replied, "It is easy for many to be hemmed in by few, for in the sight of Heaven there is no difference between saving by many or by few. 19 It is not on the size of the army that victory in battle depends, but strength comes from Heaven. 20 They come against us in great pride and lawlessness to destroy us and our wives and our children, and to despoil us; 21 but we fight for our lives and our laws. 22 He himself will crush them before us; as for you, do not be afraid of them."

23 When he finished speaking, he rushed suddenly against Seron and his army, and they were crushed before him. 24 They pursued them *k* down the descent of Beth-horon to the plain; eight hundred of them fell, and the rest fled into the land of the Philistines. 25 Then Judas and his brothers began to be feared, and terror fell upon the Gentiles round about them. 26 His fame reached the king, and the Gentiles talked of the battles of Judas.

27 When King Antiochus heard these reports, he was greatly angered; and he sent and gathered all the forces of his kingdom, a very strong army. 28 And he opened his coffers and gave a year's pay to his forces, and ordered them to be ready for any need. 29 Then he saw that the money in the treasury was exhausted, and that the revenues from the country were small because of the dissension and disaster which he had caused in the land by abolishing the laws that had existed from the earliest days. 30 He feared that he might

not have such funds as he had before for his expenses and for the gifts which he used to give more lavishly than preceding kings. 31 He was greatly perplexed in mind, and determined to go to Persia and collect the revenues from those regions and raise a large fund.

32 He left Lysias, a distinguished man of royal lineage, in charge of the king's affairs from the river Euphrates to the borders of Egypt. 33 Lysias was also to take care of Antiochus his son until he returned. 34 And he turned over to Lysias *l* half of his troops and the elephants, and gave him orders about all that he wanted done. As for the residents of Judea and Jerusalem, 35 Lysias was to send a force against them to wipe out and destroy the strength of Israel and the remnant of Jerusalem; he was to banish the memory of them from the place, 36 settle aliens in all their territory, and distribute their land. 37 Then the king took the remaining half of his troops and departed from Antioch his capital in the one hundred and forty-seventh year.*m* He crossed the Euphrates River and went through the upper provinces.

38 Lysias chose Ptolemy the son of Dorymenes, and Nicanor and Gorgias, mighty men among the friends of the king, 39 and sent with them forty thousand infantry and seven thousand cavalry to go into the land of Judah and destroy it, as the king had commanded. 40 So they departed with their entire force, and when they arrived they encamped near Emmaus in the plain. 41 When the traders of the region heard what was said of them, they took silver and gold in immense amounts, and fetters,*n* and went to the camp to get the sons of Israel for slaves. And forces from Syria and the land of the Philistines joined with them.

42 Now Judas and his brothers saw that misfortunes had increased and that the forces were encamped

k Other authorities read *him*   *l* Gk *him*   *m* 165 B.C.   *n* Syr: Gk *slaves*

in their territory. They also learned what the king had commanded to do to the people to cause their final destruction. ⁴³ But they said to one another, "Let us repair the destruction of our people, and fight for our people and the sanctuary." ⁴⁴ And the congregation assembled to be ready for battle, and to pray and ask for mercy and compassion.

⁴⁵ Jerusalem was uninhabited like a wilderness;
  not one of her children went in or out.
The sanctuary was trampled down,
  and the sons of aliens held the citadel;
  it was a lodging place for the Gentiles.
Joy was taken from Jacob;
  the flute and the harp ceased to play.

⁴⁶ So they assembled and went to Mizpah, opposite Jerusalem, because Israel formerly had a place of prayer in Mizpah. ⁴⁷ They fasted that day, put on sackcloth and sprinkled ashes on their heads, and rent their clothes. ⁴⁸ And they opened the book of the law to inquire into those matters about which the Gentiles were consulting the images of their idols. ⁴⁹ They also brought the garments of the priesthood and the first fruits and the tithes, and they stirred up the Nazirites who had completed their days; ⁵⁰ and they cried aloud to Heaven, saying,

"What shall we do with these?
  Where shall we take them?
⁵¹ Thy sanctuary is trampled down and profaned,
  and thy priests mourn in humiliation.
⁵² And behold, the Gentiles are assembled against us to destroy us;
  thou knowest what they plot against us.
⁵³ How will we be able to withstand them,
  if thou dost not help us?"

⁵⁴ Then they sounded the trumpets and gave a loud shout. ⁵⁵ After this Judas appointed leaders of the people, in charge of thousands and hundreds and fifties and tens. ⁵⁶ And he said to those who were building houses, or were betrothed, or were planting vineyards, or were fainthearted, that each should return to his home, according to the law. ⁵⁷ Then the army marched out and encamped to the south of Emmaus.

⁵⁸ And Judas said, "Gird yourselves and be valiant. Be ready early in the morning to fight with these Gentiles who have assembled against us to destroy us and our sanctuary. ⁵⁹ It is better for us to die in battle than to see the misfortunes of our nation and of the sanctuary. ⁶⁰ But as his will in heaven may be, so he will do."

4 Now Gorgias took five thousand infantry and a thousand picked cavalry, and this division moved out by night ² to fall upon the camp of the Jews and attack them suddenly. Men from the citadel were his guides. ³ But Judas heard of it, and he and his mighty men moved out to attack the king's force in Emmaus ⁴ while the division was still absent from the camp. ⁵ When Gorgias entered the camp of Judas by night, he found no one there, so he looked for them in the hills, because he said, "These men are fleeing from us."

⁶ At daybreak Judas appeared in the plain with three thousand men, but they did not have armour and swords such as they desired. ⁷ And they saw the camp of the Gentiles, strong and fortified, with cavalry round about it; and these men were trained in war. ⁸ But Judas said to the men who were with him, "Do not fear their numbers or be afraid when they charge. ⁹ Remember how our fathers were saved at the Red Sea, when Pharaoh with his forces pursued them. ¹⁰ And now let us cry to Heaven, to see whether he will favour us and remember his covenant with

our fathers and crush this army before us today. [11] Then all the Gentiles will know that there is one who redeems and saves Israel."

12 When the foreigners looked up and saw them coming against them, [13] they went forth from their camp to battle. Then the men with Judas blew their trumpets [14] and engaged in battle. The Gentiles were crushed and fled into the plain, [15] and all those in the rear fell by the sword. They pursued them to Gazara, and to the plains of Idumea, and to Azotus and Jamnia; and three thousand of them fell. [16] Then Judas and his force turned back from pursuing them, [17] and he said to the people, "Do not be greedy for plunder, for there is a battle before us; [18] Gorgias and his force are near us in the hills. But stand now against our enemies and fight them, and afterward seize the plunder boldly."

19 Just as Judas was finishing this speech, a detachment appeared, coming out of the hills. [20] They saw that their army *o* had been put to flight, and that the Jews *o* were burning the camp, for the smoke that was seen showed what had happened. [21] When they perceived this they were greatly frightened, and when they also saw the army of Judas drawn up in the plain for battle, [22] they all fled into the land of the Philistines. [23] Then Judas returned to plunder the camp, and they seized much gold and silver, and cloth dyed blue and sea purple, and great riches. [24] On their return they sang hymns and praises to Heaven, for he is good, for his mercy endures for ever. [25] Thus Israel had a great deliverance that day.

26 Those of the foreigners who escaped went and reported to Lysias all that had happened. [27] When he heard it, he was perplexed and discouraged, for things had not happened to Israel as he had intended, nor had they turned out as the king had commanded him. [28] But the next year he mustered sixty thousand picked infantrymen and five thousand cavalry to subdue them. [29] They came into Idumea and encamped at Beth-zur, and Judas met them with ten thousand men.

30 When he saw that the army was strong, he prayed, saying, "Blessed art thou, O Saviour of Israel, who didst crush the attack of the mighty warrior by the hand of thy servant David, and didst give the camp of the Philistines into the hands of Jonathan, the son of Saul, and of the man who carried his armour. [31] So do thou hem in this army by the hand of thy people Israel, and let them be ashamed of their troops and their cavalry. [32] Fill them with cowardice; melt the boldness of their strength; let them tremble in their destruction. [33] Strike them down with the sword of those who love thee, and let all who know thy name praise thee with hymns."

34 Then both sides attacked, and there fell of the army of Lysias five thousand men; they fell in action.*p* [35] And when Lysias saw the rout of his troops and observed the boldness which inspired those of Judas, and how ready they were either to live or to die nobly, he departed to Antioch and enlisted mercenaries, to invade Judea again with an even larger army.

36 Then said Judas and his brothers, "Behold, our enemies are crushed; let us go up to cleanse the sanctuary and dedicate it." [37] So all the army assembled and they went up to Mount Zion. [38] And they saw the sanctuary desolate, the altar profaned, and the gates burned. In the courts they saw bushes sprung up as in a thicket, or as on one of the mountains. They saw also the chambers of the priests in ruins. [39] Then they rent their clothes, and mourned with great lamentation, and sprinkled themselves with ashes. [40] They fell face down on the ground, and

o Gk *they*   *p* Or *and some fell on the opposite side*

sounded the signal on the trumpets, and cried out to Heaven. 41 Then Judas detailed men to fight against those in the citadel until he had cleansed the sanctuary.

42 He chose blameless priests devoted to the law, 43 and they cleansed the sanctuary and removed the defiled stones to an unclean place. 44 They deliberated what to do about the altar of burnt offering, which had been profaned 45 And they thought it best to tear it down, lest it bring reproach upon them, for the Gentiles had defiled it. So they tore down the altar, 46 and stored the stones in a convenient place on the temple hill until there should come a prophet to tell what to do with them. 47 Then they took unhewn q stones, as the law directs, and built a new altar like the former one. 48 They also rebuilt the sanctuary and the interior of the temple, and consecrated the courts. 49 They made new holy vessels, and brought the lampstand, the altar of incense, and the table into the temple. 50 Then they burned incense on the altar and lighted the lamps on the lampstand, and these gave light in the temple. 51 They placed the bread on the table and hung up the curtains. Thus they finished all the work they had undertaken.

52 Early in the morning on the twenty-fifth day of the ninth month, which is the month of Chislev, in the one hundred and forty-eighth year,r 53 they rose and offered sacrifice, as the law directs, on the new altar of burnt offering which they had built. 54 At the very season and on the very day that the Gentiles had profaned it, it was dedicated with songs and harps and lutes and cymbals. 55 All the people fell on their faces and worshipped and blessed Heaven, who had prospered them. 56 So they celebrated the dedication of the altar for eight days, and offered burnt offerings with gladness; they offered a sacrifice of deliverance and praise. 57 They decorated the front of the temple with golden crowns and small shields; they restored the gates and the chambers for the priests, and furnished them with doors. 58 There was very great gladness among the people, and the reproach of the Gentiles was removed.

59 Then Judas and his brothers and all the assembly of Israel determined that every year at that season the days of the dedication of the altar should be observed with gladness and joy for eight days, beginning with the twenty-fifth day of the month of Chislev.

60 At that time they fortified Mount Zion with high walls and strong towers round about, to keep the Gentiles from coming and trampling them down as they had done before. 61 And he stationed a garrison there to hold it. He also s fortified Beth-zur, so that the people might have a stronghold that faced Idumea.

5 When the Gentiles round about heard that the altar had been built and the sanctuary dedicated as it was before, they became very angry, 2 and they determined to destroy the descendants of Jacob who lived among them. So they began to kill and destroy among the people. 3 But Judas made war on the sons of Esau in Idumea, at Akrabattene, because they kept lying in wait for Israel. He dealt them a heavy blow and humbled them and despoiled them. 4 He also remembered the wickedness of the sons of Baean, who were a trap and a snare to the people and ambushed them on the highways. 5 They were shut up by him in their towers; and he encamped against them, vowed their complete destruction, and burned with fire their t towers and all who were in them. 6 Then he crossed over to attack the Ammonites, where he found a strong band and many people with Timothy as their leader.

q Gk whole   r 164 B.C.   s Gk adds to hold it   t Gk her

7 He engaged in many battles with them and they were crushed before him; he struck them down. 8 He also took Jazer and its villages; then he returned to Judea.

9 Now the Gentiles in Gilead gathered together against the Israelites who lived in their territory, and planned to destroy them. But they fled to the stronghold of Dathema, 10 and sent to Judas and his brothers a letter which said, "The Gentiles around us have gathered together against us to destroy us. 11 They are preparing to come and capture the stronghold to which we have fled, and Timothy is leading their forces. 12 Now then come and rescue us from their hands, for many of us have fallen, 13 and all our brethren who were in the land of Tob have been killed; the enemy *u* have captured their wives and children and goods, and have destroyed about a thousand men there."

14 While the letter was still being read, behold, other messengers, with their garments rent, came from Galilee and made a similar report; 15 they said that against them had gathered together men of Ptolemais and Tyre and Sidon, and all Galilee of the Gentiles,*v* "to annihilate us." 16 When Judas and the people heard these messages, a great assembly was called to determine what they should do for their brethren who were in distress and were being attacked by enemies.*w* 17 Then Judas said to Simon his brother, "Choose your men and go and rescue your brethren in Galilee; I and Jonathan my brother will go to Gilead." 18 But he left Joseph, the son of Zechariah, and Azariah, a leader of the people, with the rest of the forces, in Judea to guard it; 19 and he gave them this command, "Take charge of this people, but do not engage in battle with the Gentiles until we return." 20 Then three thousand men were assigned to Simon

to go to Galilee, and eight thousand to Judas for Gilead.

21 So Simon went to Galilee and fought many battles against the Gentiles, and the Gentiles were crushed before him. 22 He pursued them to the gate of Ptolemais, and as many as three thousand of the Gentiles fell, and he despoiled them. 23 Then he took the Jews *x* of Galilee and Arbatta, with their wives and children, and all they possessed, and led them to Judea with great rejoicing.

24 Judas Maccabeus and Jonathan his brother crossed the Jordan and went three days' journey into the wilderness. 25 They encountered the Nabateans, who met them peaceably and told them all that had happened to their brethren in Gilead: 26 "Many of them have been shut up in Bozrah and Bosor, in Alema and Chaspho, Maked and Carnaim"—all these cities were strong and large—27 "and some have been shut up in the other cities of Gilead; the enemy *y* are getting ready to attack the strongholds tomorrow and take and destroy all these men in one day."

28 Then Judas and his army quickly turned back by the wilderness road to Bozrah; and he took the city, and killed every male by the edge of the sword; then he seized all its spoils and burned it with fire. 29 He departed from there at night, and they went all the way to the stronghold of Dathema.*z* 30 At dawn they looked up, and behold, a large company, that could not be counted, carrying ladders and engines of war to capture the stronghold, and attacking the Jews within.*a* 31 So Judas saw that the battle had begun and that the cry of the city went up to Heaven with trumpets and loud shouts, 32 and he said to the men of his forces, "Fight today for your brethren!" 33 Then he came up behind them in three companies, who sounded their trumpets and cried aloud in prayer.

u Gk *they*　*v* Gk *aliens*　*w* Gk *them*　*x* Gk *those*　*y* Gk *they*　*z* Gk lacks of *Dathema.* See verse 9
a Gk *and they were attacking them*

199

34 And when the army of Timothy realized that it was Maccabeus, they fled before him, and he dealt them a heavy blow. As many as eight thousand of them fell that day.

35 Next he turned aside to Alema,[b] and fought against it and took it; and he killed every male in it, plundered it, and burned it with fire. 36 From there he marched on and took Chaspho, Maked, and Bosor, and the other cities of Gilead.

37 After these things Timothy gathered another army and encamped opposite Raphon, on the other side of the stream. 38 Judas sent men to spy out the camp, and they reported to him, "All the Gentiles around us have gathered to him; it is a very large force. 39 They also have hired Arabs to help them, and they are encamped across the stream, ready to come and fight against you." And Judas went to meet them.

40 Now as Judas and his army drew near to the stream of water, Timothy said to the officers of his forces, "If he crosses over to us first, we will not be able to resist him, for he will surely defeat us. 41 But if he shows fear and camps on the other side of the river, we will cross over to him and defeat him." 42 When Judas approached the stream of water, he stationed the scribes of the people at the stream and gave them this command, "Permit no man to encamp, but make them all enter the battle." 43 Then he crossed over against them first, and the whole army followed him. All the Gentiles were defeated before him, and they threw away their arms and fled into the sacred precincts at Carnaim. 44 But he took the city and burned the sacred precincts with fire, together with all who were in them. Thus Carnaim was conquered; they could stand before Judas no longer.

45 Then Judas gathered together all the Israelites in Gilead, the small and the great, with their wives and children and goods, a very large company, to go to the land of Judah. 46 So they came to Ephron. This was a large and very strong city on the road, and they could not go around it to the right or to the left; they had to go through it. 47 But the men of the city shut them out and blocked up the gates with stones. 48 And Judas sent them this friendly message, "Let us pass through your land to get to our land. No one will do you harm; we will simply pass by on foot." But they refused to open to him. 49 Then Judas ordered proclamation made to the army that each should encamp where he was. 50 So the men of the forces encamped, and he fought against the city all that day and all the night, and the city was delivered into his hands. 51 He destroyed every male by the edge of the sword, and razed and plundered the city. Then he passed through the city over the slain.

52 And they crossed the Jordan into the large plain before Bethshan. 53 And Judas kept rallying the laggards and encouraging the people all the way till he came to the land of Judah. 54 So they went up to Mount Zion with gladness and joy, and offered burnt offerings, because not one of them had fallen before they returned in safety.

55 Now while Judas and Jonathan were in Gilead and Simon his brother was in Galilee before Ptolemais, 56 Joseph, the son of Zechariah, and Azariah, the commanders of the forces, heard of their brave deeds and of the heroic war they had fought. 57 So they said, "Let us also make a name for ourselves; let us go and make war on the Gentiles around us." 58 And they issued orders to the men of the forces that were with them, and they marched against Jamnia. 59 And Gorgias and his men came out of the city to meet them in battle. 60 Then Joseph and Azariah were routed, and were pursued to the borders of Judea;

[b] The name is uncertain

as many as two thousand of the people of Israel fell that day. [61] Thus the people suffered a great rout because, thinking to do a brave deed, they did not listen to Judas and his brothers. [62] But they did not belong to the family of those men through whom deliverance was given to Israel.

63 The man Judas and his brothers were greatly honoured in all Israel and among all the Gentiles, wherever their name was heard. [64] Men gathered to them and praised them.

65 Then Judas and his brothers went forth and fought the sons of Esau in the land to the south. He struck Hebron and its villages and tore down its strongholds and burned its towers round about. Then he marched off to go into the land of the Philistines, and passed through Marisa.[c] [67] On that day some priests, who wished to do a brave deed, fell in battle, for they went out to battle unwisely. [68] But Judas turned aside to Azotus in the land of the Philistines; he tore down their altars, and the graven images of their gods he burned with fire; he plundered the cities and returned to the land of Judah.

6 King Antiochus was going through the upper provinces when he heard that Elymais in Persia was a city famed for its wealth in silver and gold. [2] Its temple was very rich, containing golden shields, breastplates, and weapons left there by Alexander, the son of Philip, the Macedonian king who first reigned over the Greeks. [3] So he came and tried to take the city and plunder it, but he could not, because his plan became known to the men of the city [4] and they withstood him in battle. So he fled and in great grief departed from there to return to Babylon.

5 Then some one came to him in Persia and reported that the armies which had gone into the land of Judah had been routed; [6] that Lysias had gone first with a strong force, but had turned and fled before the Jews;[d] that the Jews[e] had grown strong from the arms, supplies, and abundant spoils which they had taken from the armies they had cut down; [7] that they had torn down the abomination which he had erected upon the altar in Jerusalem; and that they had surrounded the sanctuary with high walls as before, and also Beth-zur, his city.

8 When the king heard this news, he was astounded and badly shaken. He took to his bed and became sick from grief, because things had not turned out for him as he had planned. [9] He lay there for many days, because deep grief continually gripped him, and he concluded that he was dying. [10] So he called all his friends and said to them, "Sleep departs from my eyes and I am downhearted with worry. [11] I said to myself, 'To what distress I have come! And into what a great flood I now am plunged! For I was kind and beloved in my power.' [12] But now I remember the evils I did in Jerusalem. I seized all her vessels of silver and gold; and I sent to destroy the inhabitants of Judah without good reason. [13] I know that it is because of this that these evils have come upon me; and behold, I am perishing of deep grief in a strange land."

14 Then he called for Philip, one of his friends, and made him ruler over all his kingdom. [15] He gave him the crown and his robe and the signet, that he might guide Antiochus his son and bring him up to be king. [16] Thus Antiochus the king died there in the one hundred and forty-ninth year.[f] [17] And when Lysias learned that the king was dead, he set up Antiochus the king's[g] son to reign. Lysias[h] had brought him up as a boy, and he named him Eupator.

18 Now the men in the citadel kept hemming Israel in around the sanctu-

---

c Other authorities read *Samaria*   *d* Gk *them*   *e* Gk *they*   *f* 163 B.C.   *g* Gk *his*   *h* Gk *he* ary. They were trying in every way to harm them and strengthen the Gentiles. [19] So Judas decided to destroy them, and assembled all the people to besiege them. [20] They gathered together and besieged the citadel [i] in the one hundred and fiftieth year; [j] and he built siege towers and other engines of war. [21] But some of the garrison escaped from the siege and some of the ungodly Israelites joined them. [22] They went to the king and said, "How long will you fail to do justice and to avenge our brethren? [23] We were happy to serve your father, to live by what he said and to follow his commands. [24] For this reason the sons of our people besieged the citadel [k] and became hostile to us; moreover, they have put to death as many of us as they have caught, and they have seized our inheritances. [25] And not against us alone have they stretched out their hands, but also against all the lands on their borders. [26] And behold, today they have encamped against the citadel in Jerusalem to take it; they have fortified both the sanctuary and Beth-zur; [27] and unless you quickly prevent them, they will do still greater things, and you will not be able to stop them."

28 The king was enraged when he heard this. He assembled all his friends, the commanders of his forces and those in authority. [l] [29] And mercenary forces came to him from other kingdoms and from islands of the seas. [30] The number of his forces was a hundred thousand foot soldiers, twenty thousand horsemen, and thirty-two elephants accustomed to war. [31] They came through Idumea and encamped against Beth-zur, and for many days they fought and built engines of war; but the Jews [m] sallied out and burned these with fire, and fought manfully.

32 Then Judas marched away from the citadel and encamped at Beth-zechariah, opposite the camp of the king. [33] Early in the morning the king rose and took his army by a forced march along the road to Beth-zechariah, and his troops made ready for battle and sounded their trumpets. [34] They showed the elephants the juice of grapes and mulberries, to arouse them for battle. [35] And they distributed the beasts among the phalanxes; with each elephant they stationed a thousand men armed with coats of mail, and with brass helmets on their heads; and five hundred picked horsemen were assigned to each beast. [36] These took their position beforehand wherever the beast was; wherever it went they went with it, and they never left it. [37] And upon the elephants [n] were wooden towers, strong and covered; they were fastened upon each beast by special harness, and upon each were four [o] armed men who fought from there, and also its Indian driver. [38] The rest of the horsemen were stationed on either side, on the two flanks of the army, to harass the enemy while being themselves protected by the phalanxes. [39] When the sun shone upon the shields of gold and brass, the hills were ablaze with them and gleamed like flaming torches.

40 Now a part of the king's army was spread out on the high hills, and some troops were on the plain, and they advanced steadily and in good order. [41] All who heard the noise made by their multitude, by the marching of the multitude and the clanking of their arms, trembled, for the army was very large and strong. [42] But Judas and his army advanced to the battle, and six hundred men of the king's army fell. [43] And Eleazar, called Avaran, saw that one of the beasts was equipped with royal armour. It was taller than all the others, and he supposed that the king was upon

---

[i] Gk *it*   [j] 162 B.C.   [k] The Gk text underlying *the sons . . . the citadel* is uncertain
[l] Gk *those over the reins*   [m] Gk *they*   [n] Gk *them*
[o] Cn: Some authorities read *thirty;* others *thirty-two*

it. ⁴⁴ So he gave his life to save his people and to win for himself an everlasting name. ⁴⁵ He courageously ran into the midst of the phalanx to reach it; he killed men right and left, and they parted before him on both sides. ⁴⁶ He got under the elephant, stabbed it from beneath, and killed it; but it fell to the ground upon him and there he died. ⁴⁷ And when the Jews *ᵖ* saw the royal might and the fierce attack of the forces, they turned away in flight.

48 The soldiers of the king's army went up to Jerusalem against them, and the king encamped in Judea and at Mount Zion. ⁴⁹ He made peace with the men of Beth-zur, and they evacuated the city, because they had no provisions there to withstand a siege, since it was a sabbatical year for the land. ⁵⁰ So the king took Beth-zur and stationed a guard there to hold it. ⁵¹ Then he encamped before the sanctuary for many days. He set up siege towers, engines of war to throw fire and stones, machines to shoot arrows, and catapults. ⁵² The Jews *q* also made engines of war to match theirs, and fought for many days. ⁵³ But they had no food in storage,*ʳ* because it was the seventh year; those who found safety in Judea from the Gentiles had consumed the last of the stores. ⁵⁴ Few men were left in the sanctuary, because famine had prevailed over the rest and they had been scattered, each to his own place.

55 Then Lysias heard that Philip, whom King Antiochus while still living had appointed to bring up Antiochus his son to be king, ⁵⁶ had returned from Persia and Media with the forces that had gone with the king, and that he was trying to seize control of the government. ⁵⁷ So he quickly gave orders to depart, and said to the king, to the commanders of the forces, and to the men. "We daily grow weaker, our food supply is scant, the place against which we are fighting is strong, and the affairs of the kingdom press urgently upon us. ⁵⁸ Now then let us come to terms with these men, and make peace with them and with all their nation, ⁵⁹ and agree to let them live by their laws as they did before; for it was on account of their laws which we abolished that they became angry and did all these things."

60 The speech pleased the king and the commanders, and he sent to the Jews *ˢ* an offer of peace, and they accepted it. ⁶¹ So the king and the commanders gave them their oath. On these conditions the Jews *t* evacuated the stronghold. ⁶² But when the king entered Mount Zion and saw what a strong fortress the place was, he broke the oath he had sworn and gave orders to tear down the wall all around. ⁶³ Then he departed with haste and returned to Antioch. He found Philip in control of the city, but he fought against him, and took the city by force.

7 In the one hundred and fifty-first *ᵘ* year Demetrius the son of Seleucus set forth from Rome, sailed with a few men to a city by the sea, and there began to reign. ² As he was entering the royal palace of his fathers, the army seized Antiochus and Lysias to bring them to him. ³ But when this act became known to him, he said, "Do not let me see their faces!" ⁴ So the army killed them, and Demetrius took his seat upon the throne of his kingdom.

5 Then there came to him all the lawless and ungodly men of Israel; they were led by Alcimus, who wanted to be high priest. ⁶ And they brought to the king this accusation against the people: "Judas and his brothers have destroyed all your friends, and have driven us out of our land. ⁷ Now then send a man whom you trust; let him go and see all

ᵖ Gk *they*   *q* Gk *they*   *ʳ* Other authorities read *in the sanctuary*   *ˢ* Gk *them*   *t* Gk *they*
ᵘ 161 B.C.

the ruin which Judas *v* has brought upon us and upon the land of the king, and let him punish them and all who help them."

8 So the king chose Bacchides, one of the king's friends, governor of the province Beyond the River; he was a great man in the kingdom and was faithful to the king. 9 And he sent him, and with him the ungodly Alcimus, whom he made high priest; and he commanded him to take vengeance on the sons of Israel. 10 So they marched away and came with a large force into the land of Judah; and he sent messengers to Judas and his brothers with peaceable but treacherous words. 11 But they paid no attention to their words, for they saw that they had come with a large force.

12 Then a group of scribes appeared in a body before Alcimus and Bacchides to ask for just terms. 13 The Hasideans were the first among the sons of Israel to seek peace from them, 14 for they said, "A priest of the line of Aaron has come with the army, and he will not harm us." 15 And he spoke peaceable words to them and swore this oath to them, "We will not seek to injure you or your friends." 16 So they trusted him; but he seized sixty of them and killed them in one day, in accordance with the word which was written,

17 "The flesh of thy saints and their blood
    they poured out round about Jerusalem,
    and there was none to bury them."

18 Then the fear and dread of them fell upon all the people, for they said, "There is no truth or justice in them, for they have violated the agreement and the oath which they swore."

19 Then Bacchides departed from Jerusalem and encamped in Bethzaith. And he sent and seized many of the men who had deserted to him,*w* and some of the people, and killed them and threw them into the great pit. 20 He placed Alcimus in charge of the country and left with him a force to help him; then Bacchides went back to the king.

21 Alcimus strove for the high priesthood, 22 and all who were troubling their people joined him. They gained control of the land of Judah and did great damage in Israel. 23 And Judas saw all the evil that Alcimus and those with him had done among the sons of Israel; it was more than the Gentiles had done. 24 So Judas *x* went out into all the surrounding parts of Judea, and took vengeance on the men who had deserted, and he prevented those in the city *y* from going out into the country. 25 When Alcimus saw that Judas and those with him had grown strong, and realized that he could not withstand them, he returned to the king and brought wicked charges against them.

26 Then the king sent Nicanor, one of his honoured princes, who hated and detested Israel, and he commanded him to destroy the people. 27 So Nicanor came to Jerusalem with a large force, and treacherously sent to Judas and his brothers this peaceable message, 28 "Let there be no fighting between me and you; I shall come with a few men to see you face to face in peace." 29 So he came to Judas, and they greeted one another peaceably. But the enemy were ready to seize Judas. 30 It became known to Judas that Nicanor *x* had come to him with treacherous intent, and he was afraid of him and would not meet him again. 31 When Nicanor learned that his plan had been disclosed, he went out to meet Judas in battle near Capharsalama. 32 About five hundred men of the army of Nicanor fell, and the rest *z* fled into the city of David.

33 After these events Nicanor went

v Gk *he*   *w* Or, *many of his men who had deserted*   *x* Gk *he*   *y* Gk *they were prevented*
z Gk *they*

up to Mount Zion. Some of the priests came out of the sanctuary, and some of the elders of the people, to greet him peaceably and to show him the burnt offering that was being offered for the king. ³⁴ But he mocked them and derided them and defiled them and spoke arrogantly, ³⁵ and in anger he swore this oath, "Unless Judas and his army are delivered into my hands this time, then if I return safely I will burn up this house." And he went out in great anger. ³⁶ Then the priests went in and stood before the altar and the temple, and they wept and said,

³⁷ "Thou didst choose this house to be called by thy name,
and to be for thy people a house of prayer and supplication.
³⁸ Take vengeance on this man and on his army,
and let them fall by the sword;
remember their blasphemies,
and let them live no longer."

39 Now Nicanor went out from Jerusalem and encamped in Bethhoron, and the Syrian army joined him. ⁴⁰ And Judas encamped in Adasa with three thousand men. Then Judas prayed and said, ⁴¹ "When the messengers from the king spoke blasphemy, thy angel went forth and struck down one hundred and eighty-five thousand of the Assyrians.ᵃ ⁴² So also crush this army before us today; let the rest learn that Nicanor ᵇ has spoken wickedly against thy sanctuary, and judge him according to this wickedness." ⁴³ So the armies met in battle on the thirteenth day of the month of Adar. The army of Nicanor was crushed, and he himself was the first to fall in the battle. ⁴⁴ When his army saw that Nicanor had fallen, they threw down their arms and fled. ⁴⁵ The Jews ᶜ pursued them a day's journey, from Adasa as far as Gazara, and as they followed kept sounding the battle call on the trumpets. ⁴⁶ And men came out of all the vil-

lages of Judea round about, and they outflanked the enemy ᵈ and drove them back to their pursuers,ᵉ so that they all fell by the sword; not even one of them was left. ⁴⁷ Then the Jews ᶠ seized the spoils and the plunder, and they cut off Nicanor's head and the right hand which he had so arrogantly stretched out, and brought them and displayed them just outside of Jerusalem. ⁴⁸ The people rejoiced greatly and celebrated that day as a day of great gladness. ⁴⁹ And they decreed that this day should be celebrated each year on the thirteenth day of Adar. ⁵⁰ So the land of Judah had rest for a few days.

8 Now Judas heard of the fame of the Romans, that they were very strong and were well-disposed toward all who made an alliance with them, that they pledged friendship to those who came to them, ² and that they were very strong. Men told him of their wars and of the brave deeds which they were doing among the Gauls, how they had defeated them and forced them to pay tribute, ³ and what they had done in the land of Spain to get control of the silver and gold mines there, ⁴ and how they had gained control of the whole region by their planning and patience, even though the place was far distant from them. They also subdued the kings who came against them from the ends of the earth, until they crushed them and inflicted great disaster upon them; the rest paid them tribute every year. ⁵ Philip, and Perseus king of the Macedonians,ᵍ and the others who rose up against them, they crushed in battle and conquered. ⁶ They also defeated Antiochus the Great, king of Asia, who went to fight against them with a hundred and twenty elephants and with cavalry and chariots and a very large army. He was crushed by them;

ᵃ Gk *of them*   ᵇ Gk *he*   ᶜ Gk *they*   ᵈ Gk *them*   ᵉ Gk *these*   ᶠ Gk *they*   ᵍ Or *Kittim*

⁷ they took him alive and decreed that he and those who should reign after him should pay a heavy tribute and give hostages and surrender some of their best provinces, ⁸ the country of India and Media and Lydia. These they took from him and gave to Eumenes the king. ⁹ The Greeks planned to come and destroy them, ¹⁰ but this became known to them, and they sent a general against the Greeks *ʰ* and attacked them. Many of them were wounded and fell, and the Romans *ⁱ* took captive their wives and children; they plundered them, conquered the land, tore down their strongholds, and enslaved them to this day. ¹¹ The remaining kingdoms and islands, as many as ever opposed them, they destroyed and enslaved; ¹² but with their friends and those who rely on them they have kept friendship. They have subdued kings far and near, and as many as have heard of their fame have feared them. ¹³ Those whom they wish to help and to make kings, they make kings, and those whom they wish they depose; and they have been greatly exalted. ¹⁴ Yet for all this not one of them has put on a crown or worn purple as a mark of pride, ¹⁵ but they have built for themselves a senate chamber, and every day three hundred and twenty senators constantly deliberate concerning the people, to govern them well. ¹⁶ They trust one man each year to rule over them and to control all their land; they all heed the one man, and there is no envy or jealousy among them.

17 So Judas chose Eupolemus the son of John, son of Accos, and Jason the son of Eleazar, and sent them to Rome to establish friendship and alliance, ¹⁸ and to free themselves from the yoke; for they saw that the kingdom of the Greeks was completely enslaving Israel. ¹⁹ They went to Rome, a very long journey; and they entered the senate chamber and

spoke as follows: ²⁰ "Judas, who is also called Maccabeus, and his brothers and the people of the Jews have sent us to you to establish alliance and peace with you, that we may be enrolled as your allies and friends." ²¹ The proposal pleased them, ²² and this is a copy of the letter which they wrote in reply, on bronze tablets, and sent to Jerusalem to remain with them there as a memorial of peace and alliance:

23 "May all go well with the Romans and with the nation of the Jews at sea and on land for ever, and may sword and enemy be far from them. ²⁴ If war comes first to Rome or to any of their allies in all their dominion, ²⁵ the nation of the Jews shall act as their allies wholeheartedly, as the occasion may indicate to them. ²⁶ And to the enemy who makes war they shall not give or supply grain, arms, money, or ships, as Rome has decided; and they shall keep their obligations without receiving any return. ²⁷ In the same way, if war comes first to the nation of the Jews, the Romans shall willingly act as their allies, as the occasion may indicate to them. ²⁸ And to the enemy allies shall be given no grain, arms, money, or ships, as Rome has decided; and they shall keep these obligations and do so without deceit. ²⁹ Thus on these terms the Romans make a treaty with the Jewish people. ³⁰ If after these terms are in effect both parties shall determine to add or delete anything, they shall do so at their discretion, and any addition or deletion that they may make shall be valid.

31 "And concerning the wrongs which King Demetrius is doing to them we have written to him as follows, 'Why have you made your yoke heavy upon our friends and allies the Jews? ³² If now they appeal again for help against you, we will defend their rights and fight you on sea and on land.'"

ʰ Gk *them*   *ⁱ* Gk *they*

9 When Demetrius heard that Nicanor and his army had fallen in battle, he sent Bacchides and Alcimus into the land of Judah a second time, and with them the right wing of the army. ² They went by the road which leads to Gilgal and encamped against Mesaloth in Arbela, and they took it and killed many people. ³ In the first month of the one hundred and fifty-second year *j* they encamped against Jerusalem; ⁴ then they marched off and went to Berea with twenty thousand foot soldiers and two thousand cavalry.

5 Now Judas was encamped in Elasa, and with him were three thousand picked men. ⁶ When they saw the huge number of the enemy forces, they were greatly frightened, and many slipped away from the camp, until no more than eight hundred of them were left.

7 When Judas saw that his army had slipped away and the battle was imminent, he was crushed in spirit, for he had no time to assemble them. ⁸ He became faint, but he said to those who were left, "Let us rise and go up against our enemies. We may be able to fight them." ⁹ But they tried to dissuade him, saying, "We are not able. Let us rather save our own lives now, and let us come back with our brethren and fight them; we are too few." ¹⁰ But Judas said, "Far be it from us to do such a thing as to flee from them. If our time has come, let us die bravely for our brethren, and leave no cause to question our honour."

11 Then the army of Bacchides *k* marched out from the camp and took its stand for the encounter. The cavalry was divided into two companies, and the slingers and the archers went ahead of the army, as did all the chief warriors. ¹² Bacchides was on the right wing. Flanked by the two companies, the phalanx advanced to the sound of the trumpets; and the men

with Judas also blew their trumpets. ¹³ The earth was shaken by the noise of the armies, and the battle raged from morning till evening.

14 Judas saw that Bacchides and the strength of his army were on the right; then all the stouthearted men went with him, ¹⁵ and they crushed the right wing, and he pursued them as far as Mount Azotus. ¹⁶ When those on the left wing saw that the right wing was crushed, they turned and followed close behind Judas and his men. ¹⁷ The battle became desperate, and many on both sides were wounded and fell. ¹⁸ Judas also fell, and the rest fled.

19 Then Jonathan and Simon took Judas their brother and buried him in the tomb of their fathers at Modein, ²⁰ and wept for him. And all Israel made great lamentation for him; they mourned many days and said,

²¹ "How is the mighty fallen,
    the saviour of Israel!"

²² Now the rest of the acts of Judas, and his wars and the brave deeds that he did, and his greatness, have not been recorded, for they were very many.

23 After the death of Judas, the lawless emerged in all parts of Israel; all the doers of injustice appeared. ²⁴ In those days a very great famine occurred, and the country deserted with them to the enemy. ²⁵ And Bacchides chose the ungodly and put them in charge of the country. ²⁶ They sought and searched for the friends of Judas, and brought them to Bacchides, and he took vengeance on them and made sport of them. ²⁷ Thus there was great distress in Israel, such as had not been since the time that prophets ceased to appear among them.

28 Then all the friends of Judas assembled and said to Jonathan, ²⁹ "Since the death of your brother Judas there has been no one like him to go against our enemies and

j 160 B.C.   *k* Gk *the army*

Bacchides, and to deal with those of our nation who hate us. [30] So now we have chosen you today to take his place as our ruler and leader, to fight our battle." [31] And Jonathan at that time accepted the leadership and took the place of Judas his brother.

[32] When Bacchides learned of this, he tried to kill him. [33] But Jonathan and Simon his brother and all who were with him heard of it, and they fled into the wilderness of Tekoa and camped by the water of the pool of Asphar. [34] Bacchides found this out on the sabbath day, and he with all his army crossed the Jordan.

[35] And Jonathan [l] sent his brother as leader of the multitude and begged the Nabateans, who were his friends, for permission to store with them the great amount of baggage which they had. [36] But the sons of Jambri from Medeba came out and seized John and all that he had, and departed with it.

[37] After these things it was reported to Jonathan and Simon his brother, "The sons of Jambri are celebrating a great wedding, and are conducting the bride, a daughter of one of the great nobles of Canaan, from Nadabath with a large escort." [38] And they remembered the blood of John their brother, and went up and hid under cover of the mountain. [39] They raised their eyes and looked, and saw a tumultuous procession with much baggage; and the bridegroom came out with his friends and his brothers to meet them with tambourines and musicians and many weapons. [40] Then they rushed upon them from the ambush and began killing them. Many were wounded and fell, and the rest fled to the mountain; and they took all their goods. [41] Thus the wedding was turned into mourning and the voice of their musicians into a funeral dirge. [42] And when they had fully avenged the blood of their brother,

they returned to the marshes of the Jordan.

[43] When Bacchides heard of this, he came with a large force on the sabbath day to the banks of the Jordan. [44] And Jonathan said to those with him, "Let us rise up now and fight for our lives, for today things are not as they were before. [45] For look! the battle is in front of us and behind us; the water of the Jordan is on this side and on that, with marsh and thicket; there is no place to turn. [46] Cry out now to Heaven that you may be delivered from the hands of our enemies." [47] So the battle began, and Jonathan stretched out his hand to strike Bacchides, but he eluded him and went to the rear. [48] Then Jonathan and the men with him leaped into the Jordan and swam across to the other side, and the enemy [m] did not cross the Jordan to attack them. [49] And about one thousand of Bacchides' men fell that day.

[50] Bacchides [n] then returned to Jerusalem and built strong cities in Judea: the fortress in Jericho, and Emmaus, and Beth-horon, and Bethel, and Timnath, and [o] Pharathon, and Tephon, with high walls and gates and bars. [51] And he placed garrisons in them to harass Israel. [52] He also fortified the city of Bethzur and Gazara, and the citadel, and in them he put troops and stores of food. [53] And he took the sons of the leading men of the land as hostages and put them under guard in the citadel at Jerusalem.

[54] In the one hundred and fifty-third year,[p] in the second month, Alcimus gave orders to tear down the wall of the inner court of the sanctuary. He tore down the work of the prophets! [55] But he only began to tear it down, for at that time Alcimus was stricken and his work was hindered; his mouth was stopped and he was paralyzed, so that he could no longer say a word or give commands concerning his house. [56] And Alcimus

[l] Gk *he*   [m] Gk *they*   [n] Gk *he*   [o] Some authorities omit *and*   [p] 159 B.C.

died at that time in great agony.
⁵⁷ When Bacchides saw that Alcimus was dead, he returned to the king, and the land of Judah had rest for two years.

58 Then all the lawless plotted and said, "See! Jonathan and his men are living in quiet and confidence. So now let us bring Bacchides back, and he will capture them all in one night." ⁵⁹ And they went and consulted with him. ⁶⁰ He started to come with a large force, and secretly sent letters to all his allies in Judea, telling them to seize Jonathan and his men; but they were unable to do it, because their plan became known. ⁶¹ And Jonathan's men *q* seized about fifty of the men of the country who were leaders in this treachery, and killed them.

62 Then Jonathan with his men, and Simon, withdrew to Bethbasi in the wilderness; he rebuilt the parts of it that had been demolished, and they fortified it. ⁶³ When Bacchides learned of this, he assembled all his forces, and sent orders to the men of Judea. ⁶⁴ Then he came and encamped against Bethbasi; he fought against it for many days and made machines of war.

65 But Jonathan left Simon his brother in the city, while he went out into the country; and he went with only a few men. ⁶⁶ He struck down Odomera and his brothers and the sons of Phasiron in their tents. ⁶⁷ Then he *r* began to attack and went into battle with his forces; and Simon and his men sallied out from the city and set fire to the machines of war. ⁶⁸ They fought with Bacchides, and he was crushed by them. They distressed him greatly, for his plan and his expedition had been in vain. ⁶⁹ So he was greatly enraged at the lawless men who had counselled him to come into the country, and he killed many of them. Then he decided to depart to his own land.

70 When Jonathan learned of this,

he sent ambassadors to him to make peace with him and obtain release of the captives. ⁷¹ He agreed, and did as he said; and he swore to Jonathan *s* that he would not try to harm him as long as he lived. ⁷² He restored to him the captives whom he had formerly taken from the land of Judah; then he turned and departed to his own land, and came no more into their territory. ⁷³ Thus the sword ceased from Israel. And Jonathan dwelt in Michmash. And Jonathan began to judge the people, and he destroyed the ungodly out of Israel.

10 In the one hundred and sixtieth year *t* Alexander Epiphanes, the son of Antiochus, landed and occupied Ptolemais. They welcomed him, and there he began to reign. ² When Demetrius the king heard of it, he assembled a very large army and marched out to meet him in battle. ³ And Demetrius sent Jonathan a letter in peaceable words to honour him; ⁴ for he said, "Let us act first to make peace with him *u* before he makes peace with Alexander against us, ⁵ for he will remember all the wrongs which we did to him and to his brothers and his nation." ⁶ So Demetrius *v* gave him authority to recruit troops, to equip them with arms, and to become his ally; and he commanded that the hostages in the citadel should be released to him.

7 Then Jonathan came to Jerusalem and read the letter in the hearing of all the people and of the men in the citadel. ⁸ They were greatly alarmed when they heard that the king had given him authority to recruit troops. ⁹ But the men in the citadel released the hostages to Jonathan, and he returned them to their parents.

10 And Jonathan dwelt in Jerusalem and began to rebuild and restore the city. ¹¹ He directed those who were doing the work to build the

q Gk *they*   *r* Other authorities read *they*   *s* Gk *him*   *t* 152 B.C.   *u* Gk *them*   *v* Gk *he*

walls and encircle Mount Zion with squared stones, for better fortification; and they did so.

12 Then the foreigners who were in the strongholds that Bacchides had built fled; 13 each left his place and departed to his own land. 14 Only in Beth-zur did some remain who had forsaken the law and the commandments, for it served as a place of refuge.

15 Now Alexander the king heard of all the promises which Demetrius had sent to Jonathan, and men told him of the battles that Jonathan *w* and his brothers had fought, of the brave deeds that they had done, and of the troubles that they had endured. 16 So he said, "Shall we find another such man? Come now, we will make him our friend and ally." 17 And he wrote a letter and sent it to him, in the following words:

18 "King Alexander to his brother Jonathan, greeting. 19 We have heard about you, that you are a mighty warrior and worthy to be our friend. 20 And so we have appointed you today to be the high priest of your nation; you are to be called the king's friend" (and he sent him a purple robe and a golden crown) "and you are to take our side and keep friendship with us."

21 So Jonathan put on the holy garments in the seventh month of the one hundred and sixtieth year,*x* at the feast of tabernacles, and he recruited troops and equipped them with arms in abundance. 22 When Demetrius heard of these things he was grieved and said, 23 "What is this that we have done? Alexander has gotten ahead of us in forming a friendship with the Jews to strengthen himself. 24 I also will write them words of encouragement and promise them honour and gifts, that I may have their help." 25 So he sent a message to them in the following words:

"King Demetrius to the nation of the Jews, greeting. 26 Since you have kept your agreement with us and have continued your friendship with us, and have not sided with our enemies, we have heard of it and rejoiced. 27 And now continue still to keep faith with us, and we will repay you with good for what you do for us. 28 We will grant you many immunities and give you gifts.

29 "And now I free you and exempt all the Jews from payment of tribute and salt tax and crown levies, 30 and instead of collecting the third of the grain and the half of the fruit of the trees that I should receive, I release them from this day and henceforth. I will not collect them from the land of Judah or from the three districts added to it from Samaria and Galilee, from this day and for all time. 31 And let Jerusalem and her environs, her tithes and her revenues, be holy and free from tax. 32 I release also my control of the citadel in Jerusalem and give it to the high priest, that he may station in it men of his own choice to guard it. 33 And every one of the Jews taken as a captive from the land of Judah into any part of my kingdom, I set free without payment; and let all officials cancel also the taxes on their cattle.

34 "And all the feasts and sabbaths and new moons and appointed days, and the three days before a feast and the three after a feast—let them all be days of immunity and release for all the Jews who are in my kingdom. 35 No one shall have authority to exact anything from them or annoy any of them about any matter.

36 "Let Jews be enrolled in the king's forces to the number of thirty thousand men, and let the maintenance be given them that is due to all the forces of the king. 37 Let some of them be stationed in the great strongholds of the king, and let some of them be put in positions of trust in the kingdom. Let their officers and

w Gk *he*   *x* 152 B.C.

leaders be of their own number, and
let them live by their own laws, just
as the king has commanded in the
land of Judah.

38 "As for the three districts that
have been added to Judea from the
country of Samaria, let them be so
annexed to Judea that they are considered to be under one ruler and
obey no other authority but the high
priest. 39 Ptolemais and the land adjoining it I have given as a gift to the
sanctuary in Jerusalem, to meet the
necessary expenses of the sanctuary.
40 I also grant fifteen thousand shekels of silver yearly out of the king's
revenues from appropriate places.
41 And all the additional funds which
the government officials have not
paid as they did in the first years,*y*
they shall give from now on for the
service of the temple.*z* 42 Moreover,
the five thousand shekels of silver
which my officials *a* have received
every year from the income of the
services of the temple, this too is
cancelled, because it belongs to the
priests who minister there. 43 And
whoever takes refuge at the temple
in Jerusalem, or in any of its precincts, because he owes money to the
king or has any debt, let him be released and receive back all his property in my kingdom.

44 "Let the cost of rebuilding and
restoring the structures of the sanctuary be paid from the revenues of
the king. 45 And let the cost of rebuilding the walls of Jerusalem and
fortifying it round about, and the
cost of rebuilding the walls in Judea,
also be paid from the revenues of the
king."

46 When Jonathan and the people
heard these words, they did not believe or accept them, because they
remembered the great wrongs which
Demetrius *b* had done in Israel and
how he had greatly oppressed them.
47 They favoured Alexander, because
he had been the first to speak peace-

able words to them, and they remained his allies all his days.

48 Now Alexander the king assembled large forces and encamped
opposite Demetrius. 49 The two
kings met in battle, and the army of
Demetrius fled, and Alexander *c* pursued him and defeated them. 50 He
pressed the battle strongly until the
sun set, and Demetrius fell on that
day.

51 Then Alexander sent ambassadors to Ptolemy king of Egypt with
the following message: 52 "Since I
have returned to my kingdom and
have taken my seat on the throne of
my fathers, and established my rule—
for I crushed Demetrius and gained
control of our country; 53 I met him
in battle, and he and his army were
crushed by us, and we have taken our
seat on the throne of his kingdom—
54 now therefore let us establish
friendship with one another; give me
now your daughter as my wife, and
I will become your son-in-law, and
will make gifts to you and to her in
keeping with your position."

55 Ptolemy the king replied and
said, "Happy was the day on which
you returned to the land of your
fathers and took your seat on the
throne of their kingdom. 56 And now
I will do for you as you wrote, but
meet me at Ptolemais, so that we
may see one another, and I will become your father-in-law, as you have
said."

57 So Ptolemy set out from Egypt,
he and Cleopatra his daughter, and
came to Ptolemais in the one hundred and sixty-second year.*d* 58 Alexander the king met him, and
Ptolemy *e* gave him Cleopatra his
daughter in marriage, and celebrated
her wedding at Ptolemais with great
pomp, as kings do.

59 Then Alexander the king wrote
Jonathan to come to meet him. 60 So
he went with pomp to Ptolemais
and met the two kings; he gave them

y The Gk text of this verse is uncertain.   z Gk house   a Gk they   b Gk he
c Other authorities read Alexander fled, and Demetrius   *d 150 B.C.   e Gk he*

211

and their friends silver and gold and many gifts, and found favour with them. 61 A group of pestilent men from Israel, lawless men, gathered together against him to accuse him; but the king paid no attention to them. 62 The king gave orders to take off Jonathan's garments and to clothe him in purple, and they did so. 63 The king also seated him at his side; and he said to his officers, "Go forth with him into the middle of the city and proclaim that no one is to bring charges against him about any matter, and let no one annoy him for any reason." 64 And when his accusers saw the honour that was paid him, in accordance with the proclamation, and saw him clothed in purple, they all fled. 65 Thus the king honoured him and enrolled him among his chief friends, and made him general and governor of the province. 66 And Jonathan returned to Jerusalem in peace and gladness.

67 In the one hundred and sixty-fifth year *f* Demetrius the son of Demetrius came from Crete to the land of his fathers. 68 When Alexander the king heard of it, he was greatly grieved and returned to Antioch. 69 And Demetrius appointed Apollonius the governor of Coelesyria, and he assembled a large force and encamped against Jamnia. Then he sent the following message to Jonathan the high priest:

70 "You are the only one to rise up against us, and I have become a laughingstock and reproach because of you. Why do you assume authority against us in the hill country? 71 If you now have confidence in your forces, come down to the plain to meet us, and let us match strength with each other there, for I have with me the power of the cities. 72 Ask and learn who I am and who the others are that are helping us. Men will tell you that you cannot stand before us, for your fathers were twice put to flight in their own land.

73 And now you will not be able to withstand my cavalry and such an army in the plain, where there is no stone or pebble, or place to flee."

74 When Jonathan heard the words of Apollonius, his spirit was aroused. He chose ten thousand men and set out from Jerusalem, and Simon his brother met him to help him. 75 He encamped before Joppa, but the men of the city closed its gates, for Apollonius had a garrison in Joppa. 76 So they fought against it, and the men of the city became afraid and opened the gates, and Jonathan gained possession of Joppa.

77 When Apollonius heard of it, he mustered three thousand cavalry and a large army, and went to Azotus as though he were going farther. At the same time he advanced into the plain, for he had a large troop of cavalry and put confidence in it. 78 Jonathan *g* pursued him to Azotus, and the armies engaged in battle. 79 Now Apollonius had secretly left a thousand cavalry behind them. 80 Jonathan learned that there was an ambush behind him, for they surrounded his army and shot arrows at his men from early morning till late afternoon. 81 But his men stood fast, as Jonathan commanded, and the enemy's *h* horses grew tired. 82 Then Simon brought forward his force and engaged the phalanx in battle (for the cavalry was exhausted); they were overwhelmed by him and fled, 83 and the cavalry was dispersed in the plain. They fled to Azotus and entered Beth-dagon, the temple of their idol, for safety. 84 But Jonathan burned Azotus and the surrounding towns and plundered them; and the temple of Dagon, and those who had taken refuge in it he burned with fire. 85 The number of those who fell by the sword, with those burned alive, came to eight thousand men.

86 Then Jonathan departed from there and encamped against Askalon,

f 147 B.C.   *g* Gk he   *h* Gk *their*

and the men of the city came out to meet him with great pomp. [87] And Jonathan and those with him returned to Jerusalem with much booty. [88] When Alexander the king heard of these things, he honoured Jonathan still more; [89] and he sent to him a golden buckle, such as it is the custom to give to the kinsmen of kings. He also gave him Ekron and all its environs as his possession.

11 Then the king of Egypt gathered great forces, like the sand by the seashore, and many ships; and he tried to get possession of Alexander's kingdom by trickery and add it to his own kingdom. [2] He set out for Syria with peaceable words, and the people of the cities opened their gates to him and went to meet him, for Alexander the king had commanded them to meet him, since he was Alexander's [i] father-in-law. [3] But when Ptolemy entered the cities he stationed forces as a garrison in each city.

[4] When he [j] approached Azotus, they showed him the temple of Dagon burned down, and Azotus and its suburbs destroyed, and the corpses lying about, and the charred bodies of those whom Jonathan [k] had burned in the war, for they had piled them in heaps along his route. [5] They also told the king what Jonathan had done, to throw blame on him; but the king kept silent. [6] Jonathan met the king at Joppa with pomp, and they greeted one another and spent the night there. [7] And Jonathan went with the king as far as the river called Eleutherus; then he returned to Jerusalem.

[8] So King Ptolemy gained control of the coastal cities as far as Seleucia by the sea, and he kept devising evil designs against Alexander. [9] He sent envoys to Demetrius the king, saying, "Come, let us make a covenant with each other, and I will give you in marriage my daughter who was Alexander's wife, and you shall reign over your father's kingdom. [10] For I now regret that I gave him my daughter, for he has tried to kill me." [11] He threw blame on Alexander [l] because he coveted his kingdom. [12] So he took his daughter away from him and gave her to Demetrius. He was estranged from Alexander, and their enmity became manifest.

[13] Then Ptolemy entered Antioch and put on the crown of Asia. Thus he put two crowns upon his head, the crown of Egypt and that of Asia. [14] Now Alexander the king was in Cilicia at that time, because the people of that region were in revolt. [15] And Alexander heard of it and came against him in battle. Ptolemy marched out and met him with a strong force, and put him to flight. [16] So Alexander fled into Arabia to find protection there, and King Ptolemy was exalted. [17] And Zabdiel the Arab cut off the head of Alexander and sent it to Ptolemy. [18] But King Ptolemy died three days later, and his troops in the strongholds were killed by the inhabitants of the strongholds. [19] So Demetrius became king in the one hundred and sixty-seventh year.[m]

[20] In those days Jonathan assembled the men of Judea to attack the citadel in Jerusalem, and he built many engines of war to use against it. [21] But certain lawless men who hated their nation went to the king and reported to him that Jonathan was besieging the citadel. [22] When he heard this he was angry, and as soon as he heard it he set out and came to Ptolemais; and he wrote Jonathan not to continue the siege, but to meet him for a conference at Ptolemais as quickly as possible.

[23] When Jonathan heard this, he gave orders to continue the siege; and he chose some of the elders of Israel and some of the priests, and put himself in danger, [24] for he went to the king at Ptolemais, taking silver and

[i] Gk *his*   [j] Other ancient authorities read *they*   [k] Gk *he*   [l] Gk *him*   [m] 145 B.C.

gold and clothing and numerous other gifts. And he won his favour. 25 Although certain lawless men of his nation kept making complaints against him, 26 the king treated him as his predecessors had treated him; he exalted him in the presence of all his friends. 27 He confirmed him in the high priesthood and in as many other honours as he had formerly had, and made him to be regarded as one of his chief friends. 28 Then Jonathan asked the king to free Judea and the three districts of Samaria [n] from tribute, and promised him three hundred talents. 29 The king consented, and wrote a letter to Jonathan about all these things; its contents were as follows:

30 "King Demetrius to Jonathan his brother and to the nation of the Jews, greeting. 31 This copy of the letter which we wrote concerning you to Lasthenes our kinsman we have written to you also, so that you may know what it says. 32 'King Demetrius to Lasthenes his father, greeting. 33 To the nation of the Jews, who are our friends and fulfil their obligations to us, we have determined to do good, because of the good will they show toward us. 34 We have confirmed as their possession both the territory of Judea and the three districts of Aphairema and Lydda and Rathamin; the latter, with all the region bordering them, were added to Judea from Samaria. To all those who offer sacrifice in Jerusalem, we have granted release from [o] the royal taxes which the king formerly received from them each year, from the crops of the land and the fruit of the trees. 35 And the other payments henceforth due to us of the tithes, and the taxes due to us, and the salt pits and the crown taxes due to us—from all these we shall grant them release. 36 And not one of these grants shall be cancelled from this time forth for ever. 37 Now therefore

take care to make a copy of this, and let it be given to Jonathan and put up in a conspicuous place on the holy mountain.'"

38 Now when Demetrius the king saw that the land was quiet before him and that there was no opposition to him, he dismissed all his troops, each man to his own place, except the foreign troops which he had recruited from the islands of the nations. So all the troops who had served his fathers hated him. 39 Now Trypho had formerly been one of Alexander's supporters. He saw that all the troops were murmuring against Demetrius. So he went to Imalkue the Arab, who was bringing up Antiochus, the young son of Alexander, 40 and insistently urged him to hand Antiochus [p] over to him, to become king in place of his father. He also reported to Imalkue [p] what Demetrius had done and told of the hatred which the troops of Demetrius [p] had for him; and he stayed there many days.

41 Now Jonathan sent to Demetrius the king the request that he remove the troops of the citadel from Jerusalem, and the troops in the strongholds; for they kept fighting against Israel. 42 And Demetrius sent this message to Jonathan, "Not only will I do these things for you and your nation, but I will confer great honour on you and your nation, if I find an opportunity. 43 Now then you will do well to send me men who will help me, for all my troops have revolted." 44 So Jonathan sent three thousand stalwart men to him at Antioch, and when they came to the king, the king rejoiced at their arrival.

45 Then the men of the city assembled within the city, to the number of a hundred and twenty thousand, and they wanted to kill the king. 46 But the king fled into the palace. Then the men of the city

[n] Cn: Gk *the three districts and Samaria*
[o] Or, *Samaria, for all those who offer sacrifice in Jerusalem, in place of*   [p] Gk *him*

214

seized the main streets of the city and began to fight. [47] So the king called the Jews to his aid, and they all rallied about him and then spread out through the city; and they killed on that day as many as a hundred thousand men. [48] They set fire to the city and seized much spoil on that day, and they saved the king. [49] When the men of the city saw that the Jews had gained control of the city as they pleased, their courage failed and they cried out to the king with this entreaty, [50] "Grant us peace, and make the Jews stop fighting against us and our city." [51] And they threw down their arms and made peace. So the Jews gained glory in the eyes of the king and of all the people in his kingdom, and they returned to Jerusalem with much spoil.

[52] So Demetrius the king sat on the throne of his kingdom, and the land was quiet before him. [53] But he broke his word about all that he had promised; and he became estranged from Jonathan and did not repay the favours which Jonathan *q* had done him, but oppressed him greatly.

[54] After this Trypho returned, and with him the young boy Antiochus, who began to reign and put on the crown. [55] All the troops that Demetrius had cast off gathered around him, and they fought against Demetrius,*r* and he fled and was routed. [56] And Trypho captured the elephants *s* and gained control of Antioch. [57] Then the young Antiochus wrote to Jonathan, saying, "I confirm you in the high priesthood and set you over the four districts and make you one of the friends of the king." [58] And he sent him gold plate and a table service, and granted him the right to drink from gold cups and dress in purple and wear a gold buckle. [59] Simon his brother he made governor from the Ladder of Tyre to the borders of Egypt.

[60] Then Jonathan set forth and travelled beyond the river and among the cities, and all the army of Syria gathered to him as allies. When he came to Askalon, the people of the city met him and paid him honour. [61] From there he departed to Gaza, but the men of Gaza shut him out. So he besieged it and burned its suburbs with fire and plundered them. [62] Then the people of Gaza pleaded with Jonathan, and he made peace with them, and took the sons of their rulers as hostages and sent them to Jerusalem. And he passed through the country as far as Damascus.

[63] Then Jonathan heard that the officers of Demetrius had come to Kadesh in Galilee with a large army, intending to remove him from office. [64] He went to meet them, but left his brother Simon in the country. [65] Simon encamped before Beth-zur and fought against it for many days and hemmed it in. [66] Then they asked him to grant them terms of peace, and he did so. He removed them from there, took possession of the city, and set a garrison over it.

[67] Jonathan and his army encamped by the waters of Gennesaret. Early in the morning they marched to the plain of Hazor, [68] and behold, the army of the foreigners met him in the plain; they had set an ambush against him in the mountains, but they themselves met him face to face. [69] Then the men in ambush emerged from their places and joined battle. [70] All the men with Jonathan fled; not one of them was left except Mattathias the son of Absalom, and Judas the son of Chalphi, commanders of the forces of the army. [71] Jonathan rent his garments and put dust on his head, and prayed. [72] Then he turned back to the battle against the enemy *t* and routed them, and they fled. [73] When his men who were fleeing saw this, they returned to him and joined him in the pursuit as far as Kadesh, to their camp, and there

q Gk *he*   *r* Gk *him*   *s* Gk *beasts*   *t* Gk *them*

they encamped. ⁷⁴ As many as three thousand of the foreigners fell that day. And Jonathan returned to Jerusalem.

12 Now when Jonathan saw that the time was favourable for him, he chose men and sent them to Rome to confirm and renew the friendship with them. ² He also sent letters to the same effect to the Spartans and to other places. ³ So they went to Rome and entered the senate chamber and said, "Jonathan the high priest and the Jewish nation have sent us to renew the former friendship and alliance with them." ⁴ And the Romans *ᵘ* gave them letters to the people in every place, asking them to provide for the envoys *ᵛ* safe conduct to the land of Judah.

5 This is a copy of the letter which Jonathan wrote to the Spartans: ⁶ "Jonathan the high priest, the senate of the nation, the priests, and the rest of the Jewish people to their brethren the Spartans, greeting. ⁷ Already in time past a letter was sent to Onias the high priest from Arius,*ᵂ* who was king among you, stating that you are our brethren, as the appended copy shows. ⁸ Onias welcomed the envoy with honour, and received the letter, which contained a clear declaration of alliance and friendship. ⁹ Therefore, though we have no need of these things, since we have as encouragement the holy books which are in our hands, ¹⁰ we have undertaken to send to renew our brotherhood and friendship with you, so that we may not become estranged from you, for considerable time has passed since you sent your letter to us. ¹¹ We therefore remember you constantly on every occasion, both in our feasts and on other appropriate days, at the sacrifices which we offer and in our prayers, as it is right and proper to remember brethren. ¹² And we rejoice in your glory. ¹³ But as for ourselves, many afflictions and many wars have encircled us; the kings round about us have waged war against us. ¹⁴ We were unwilling to annoy you and our other allies and friends with these wars, ¹⁵ for we have the help which comes from Heaven for our aid; and we were delivered from our enemies and our enemies were humbled. ¹⁶ We therefore have chosen Numenius the son of Antiochus and Antipater the son of Jason, and have sent them to Rome to renew our former friendship and alliance with them. ¹⁷ We have commanded them to go also to you and greet you and deliver to you this letter from us concerning the renewal of our brotherhood. ¹⁸ And now please send us a reply to this."

19 This is a copy of the letter which they sent to Onias: ²⁰ "Arius, king of the Spartans, to Onias the high priest, greeting. ²¹ It has been found in writing concerning the Spartans and the Jews that they are brethren and are of the family of Abraham. ²² And now that we have learned this, please write us concerning your welfare; ²³ we on our part write to you that your cattle and your property belong to us, and ours belong to you. We therefore command that our envoys *ˣ* report to you accordingly."

24 Now Jonathan heard that the commanders of Demetrius had returned, with a larger force than before, to wage war against him. ²⁵ So he marched away from Jerusalem and met them in the region of Hamath, for he gave them no opportunity to invade his own country. ²⁶ He sent spies to their camp, and they returned and reported to him that the enemy *ʸ* were being drawn up in formation to fall upon the Jews *ᶻ* by night. ²⁷ So when the sun set, Jonathan commanded his men to be alert and to keep their arms at hand so as to be ready all night for battle, and he stationed outposts around the camp. ²⁸ When the enemy heard that Jona-

---

ᵘ Gk *they*   *ᵛ* Gk *them*   *ᵂ* Vg Compare verse 20: Gk *Darius*   *ˣ* Gk *they*   *ʸ* Gk *they*   *ᶻ* Gk *them*

than and his men were prepared for battle, they were afraid and were terrified at heart; so they kindled fires in their camp and withdrew.ª ²⁹ But Jonathan and his men did not know it until morning, for they saw the fires burning. ³⁰ Then Jonathan pursued them, but he did not overtake them, for they had crossed the Eleutherus River. ³¹ So Jonathan turned aside against the Arabs who are called Zabadeans, and he crushed them and plundered them. ³² Then he broke camp and went to Damascus, and marched through all that region.

33 Simon also went forth and marched through the country as far as Askalon and the neighbouring strongholds. He turned aside to Joppa and took it by surprise, ³⁴ for he had heard that they were ready to hand over the stronghold to the men whom Demetrius had sent. And he stationed a garrison there to guard it.

35 When Jonathan returned he convened the elders of the people and planned with them to build strongholds in Judea, ³⁶ to build the walls of Jerusalem still higher, and to erect a high barrier between the citadel and the city to separate it from the city, in order to isolate it so that its garrison ᵇ could neither buy nor sell. ³⁷ So they gathered together to build up the city; part of the wall on the valley to the east had fallen, and he repaired the section called Chaphenatha. ³⁸ And Simon built Adida in the Shephelah; he fortified it and installed gates with bolts.

³⁹ Then Trypho attempted to become king of Asia and put on the crown, and to raise his hand against Antiochus the king. ⁴⁰ He feared that Jonathan might not permit him to do so, but might make war on him, so he kept seeking to seize and kill him, and he marched forth and came to Bethshan. ⁴¹ Jonathan went out to meet him with forty thousand picked fighting men, and he came to Beth-

shan. ⁴² When Trypho saw that he had come with a large army, he was afraid to raise his hand against him. ⁴³ So he received him with honour and commended him to all his friends, and he gave him gifts and commanded his friends and his troops to obey him as they would himself. ⁴⁴ Then he said to Jonathan, "Why have you wearied all these people when we are not at war? ⁴⁵ Dismiss them now to their homes and choose for yourself a few men to stay with you, and come with me to Ptolemais. I will hand it over to you as well as the other strongholds and the remaining troops and all the officials, and will turn around and go home. For that is why I am here."

46 Jonathan ᶜ trusted him and did as he said; he sent away the troops, and they returned to the land of Judah. ⁴⁷ He kept with himself three thousand men, two thousand of whom he left in Galilee, while a thousand accompanied him. ⁴⁸ But when Jonathan entered Ptolemais, the men of Ptolemais closed the gates and seized him, and all who had entered with him they killed with the sword.

49 Then Trypho sent troops and cavalry into Galilee and the Great Plain to destroy all of Jonathan's soldiers. ⁵⁰ But they realized that Jonathan ᶜ had been seized and had perished along with his men, and they encouraged one another and kept marching in close formation, ready for battle. ⁵¹ When their pursuers saw that they would fight for their lives, they turned back. ⁵² So they all reached the land of Judah safely, and they mourned for Jonathan and his companions and were in great fear; and all Israel mourned deeply. ⁵³ And all the nations round about them tried to destroy them, for they said, "They have no leader or helper. Now therefore let us make war on them and blot out the memory of them from among men."

ª Other ancient authorities omit *and withdrew*   ᵇ Gk *they*   ᶜ Gk *he*

13 Simon heard that Trypho had assembled a large army to invade the land of Judah and destroy it, ² and he saw that the people were trembling and fearful. So he went up to Jerusalem, and gathering the people together ³ he encouraged them, saying to them, "You yourselves know what great things I and my brothers and the house of my father have done for the laws and the sanctuary; you know also the wars and the difficulties which we have seen. ⁴ By reason of this all my brothers have perished for the sake of Israel, and I alone am left. ⁵ And now, far be it from me to spare my life in any time of distress, for I am not better than my brothers. ⁶ But I will avenge my nation and the sanctuary and your wives and children, for all the nations have gathered together out of hatred to destroy us."

7 The spirit of the people was rekindled when they heard these words, ⁸ and they answered in a loud voice, "You are our leader in place of Judas and Jonathan your brother. ⁹ Fight our battles, and all that you say to us we will do." ¹⁰ So he assembled all the warriors and hastened to complete the walls of Jerusalem, and he fortified it on every side. ¹¹ He sent Jonathan the son of Absalom to Joppa, and with him a considerable army; he drove out its occupants and remained there.

12 Then Trypho departed from Ptolemais with a large army to invade the land of Judah, and Jonathan was with him under guard. ¹³ And Simon encamped in Adida, facing the plain. ¹⁴ Trypho learned that Simon had risen up in place of Jonathan his brother, and that he was about to join battle with him, so he sent envoys to him and said, ¹⁵ "It is for the money that Jonathan your brother owed the royal treasury, in connection with the offices he held, that we are detaining him. ¹⁶ Send now a hundred talents of silver and

two of his sons as hostages, so that when released he will not revolt against us, and we will release him."

17 Simon knew that they were speaking deceitfully to him, but he sent to get the money and the sons, lest he arouse great hostility among the people, who might say, ¹⁸ "Because Simon *ᵈ* did not send him the money and the sons, he perished." ¹⁹ So he sent the sons and the hundred talents, but Trypho *ᵉ* broke his word and did not release Jonathan.

20 After this Trypho came to invade the country and destroy it, and he circled around by the way to Adora. But Simon and his army kept marching along opposite him to every place he went. ²¹ Now the men in the citadel kept sending envoys to Trypho urging him to come to them by way of the wilderness and to send them food. ²² So Trypho got all his cavalry ready to go, but that night a very heavy snow fell, and he did not go because of the snow. He marched off and went into the land of Gilead. ²³ When he approached Baskama, he killed Jonathan, and he was buried there. ²⁴ Then Trypho turned back and departed to his own land.

25 And Simon sent and took the bones of Jonathan his brother, and buried him in Modein, the city of his fathers. ²⁶ All Israel bewailed him with great lamentation, and mourned for him many days. ²⁷ And Simon built a monument over the tomb of his father and his brothers; he made it high that it might be seen, with polished stone in front and back. ²⁸ He also erected seven pyramids, opposite one another, for his father and mother and four brothers. ²⁹ And for the pyramids *ᶠ* he devised an elaborate setting, erecting about them great columns, and upon the columns he put suits of armour for a permanent memorial, and beside the suits of armour carved ships, so that they

ᵈ Gk I   ᵉ Gk he   ᶠ Gk for these

could be seen by all who sail the sea. ³⁰ This is the tomb which he built in Modein; it remains to this day.

31 Trypho dealt treacherously with the young king Antiochus; he killed him ³² and became king in his place, putting on the crown of Asia; and he brought great calamity upon the land. ³³ But Simon built up the strongholds of Judea and walled them all around, with high towers and great walls and gates and bolts, and he stored food in the strongholds. ³⁴ Simon also chose men and sent them to Demetrius the king with a request to grant relief to the country, for all that Trypho did was to plunder. ³⁵ Demetrius the king sent him a favourable reply to this request, and wrote him a letter as follows, ³⁶ "King Demetrius to Simon, the high priest and friend of kings, and to the elders and nation of the Jews, greeting. ³⁷ We have received the gold crown and the palm branch which you *g* sent, and we are ready to make a general peace with you and to write to our officials to grant you release from tribute. ³⁸ All the grants that we have made to you remain valid, and let the strongholds that you have built be your possession. ³⁹ We pardon any errors and offences committed to this day, and cancel the crown tax which you owe; and whatever other tax has been collected in Jerusalem shall be collected no longer. ⁴⁰ And if any of you are qualified to be enrolled in our bodyguard, *h* let them be enrolled, and let there be peace between us."

41 In the one hundred and seventieth year *i* the yoke of the Gentiles was removed from Israel, ⁴² and the people began to write in their documents and contracts, "In the first year of Simon the great high priest and commander and leader of the Jews."

43 In those days Simon *j* encamped against Gazara *k* and surrounded it

with troops. He made a siege engine, brought it up to the city, and battered and captured one tower. ⁴⁴ The men in the siege engine leaped out into the city, and a great tumult arose in the city. ⁴⁵ The men in the city, with their wives and children, went up on the wall with their clothes rent, and they cried out with a loud voice, asking Simon to make peace with them; ⁴⁶ they said, "Do not treat us according to our wicked acts but according to your mercy." ⁴⁷ So Simon reached an agreement with them and stopped fighting against them. But he expelled them from the city and cleansed the houses in which the idols were, and then entered it with hymns and praise. ⁴⁸ He cast out of it all uncleanness, and settled in it men who observed the law. He also strengthened its fortifications and built in it a house for himself.

49 The men in the citadel at Jerusalem were prevented from going out to the country and back to buy and sell. So they were very hungry, and many of them perished from famine. ⁵⁰ Then they cried to Simon to make peace with them, and he did so. But he expelled them from there and cleansed the citadel from its pollutions. ⁵¹ On the twenty-third day of the second month, in the one hundred and seventy-first year, *l* the Jews *m* entered it with praise and palm branches, and with harps and cymbals and stringed instruments, and with hymns and songs, because a great enemy had been crushed and removed from Israel. ⁵² And Simon *n* decreed that every year they should celebrate this day with rejoicing. He strengthened the fortifications of the temple hill alongside the citadel, and he and his men dwelt there. ⁵³ And Simon saw that John his son had reached manhood, so he made him commander of all the forces, and he dwelt in Gazara.

g The word *you* in verses 37–40 is plural. *h* Or *court* *i* 142 B.C. *j* Gk *he* *k* Cn: Gk *Gaza* *l* 141 B.C. *m* Gk *they* *n* Gk *he*

14 In the one hundred and seventy-second year[o] Demetrius the king assembled his forces and marched into Media to secure help, so that he could make war against Trypho. 2 When Arsaces the king of Persia and Media heard that Demetrius had invaded his territory, he sent one of his commanders to take him alive. 3 And he went and defeated the army of Demetrius, and seized him and took him to Arsaces, who put him under guard.

4 The land[p] had rest all the days of Simon.
He sought the good of his nation;
his rule was pleasing to them,
as was the honour shown him,
all his days.

5 To crown all his honours he took Joppa for a harbour,
and opened a way to the isles of the sea.

6 He extended the borders of his nation,
and gained full control of the country.

7 He gathered a host of captives;
he ruled over Gazara and Bethzur and the citadel,
and he removed its uncleanness from it;
and there was none to oppose him.

8 They tilled their land in peace;
the ground gave its increase,
and the trees of the plains their fruit.

9 Old men sat in the streets;
they all talked together of good things;
and the youths donned the glories and garments of war.

10 He supplied the cities with food,
and furnished them with the means of defence,
till his renown spread to the ends of the earth.

11 He established peace in the land,
and Israel rejoiced with great joy.

12 Each man sat under his vine and his fig tree,
and there was none to make them afraid.

13 No one was left in the land to fight them,
and the kings were crushed in those days.

14 He strengthened all the humble of his people;
he sought out the law,
and did away with every lawless and wicked man.

15 He made the sanctuary glorious,
and added to the vessels of the sanctuary.

16 It was heard in Rome, and as far away as Sparta, that Jonathan had died, and they were deeply grieved. 17 When they heard that Simon his brother had become high priest in his place, and that he was ruling over the country and the cities in it, 18 they wrote to him on bronze tablets to renew with him the friendship and alliance which they had established with Judas and Jonathan his brothers. 19 And these were read before the assembly in Jerusalem.

20 This is a copy of the letter which the Spartans sent: "The rulers and the city of the Spartans to Simon the high priest and to the elders and the priests and the rest of the Jewish people, our brethren, greeting. 21 The envoys who were sent to our people have told us about your glory and honour, and we rejoiced at their coming. 22 And what they said we have recorded in our public decrees, as follows, 'Numenius the son of Antiochus and Antipater the son of Jason, envoys of the Jews, have come to us to renew their friendship with us. 23 It has pleased our people to receive these men with honour and to put a copy of their words in the public archives, so that the people of the Spartans may have a record of them. And they have sent a copy of this to Simon the high priest.'"

---

[o] 140 B.C.   [p] Other authorities add *of Judah*

24 After this Simon sent Numenius to Rome with a large gold shield weighing a thousand minas, to confirm the alliance with the Romans.*q* 25 When the people heard these things they said, "How shall we thank Simon and his sons? 26 For he and his brothers and the house of his father have stood firm; they have fought and repulsed Israel's enemies and established its freedom." 27 So they made a record on bronze tablets and put it upon pillars on Mount Zion.

This is a copy of what they wrote: "On the eighteenth day of Elul, in the one hundred and seventy-second year,*r* which is the third year of Simon the great high priest, 28 in Asaramel,*s* in the great assembly of the priests and the people and the rulers of the nation and the elders of the country, the following was proclaimed to us: 29 "Since wars often occurred in the country, Simon the son of Mattathias, a priest of the sons *t* of Joarib, and his brothers, exposed themselves to danger and resisted the enemies of their nation, in order that their sanctuary and the law might be preserved; and they brought great glory to their nation. 30 Jonathan rallied the *u* nation, and became their high priest, and was gathered to his people. 31 And when their enemies decided to invade their country and lay hands on their sanctuary, 32 then Simon rose up and fought for his nation. He spent great sums of his own money; he armed the men of his nation's forces and paid them wages. 33 He fortified the cities of Judea, and Bethzur on the borders of Judea, where formerly the arms of the enemy had been stored, and he placed there a garrison of Jews. 34 He also fortified Joppa, which is by the sea, and Gazara, which is on the borders of Azotus, where the enemy formerly

dwelt. He settled Jews there, and provided in those cities *v* whatever was necessary for their restoration. 35 "The people saw Simon's faithfulness *w* and the glory which he had resolved to win for his nation, and they made him their leader and high priest, because he had done all these things and because of the justice and loyalty which he had maintained toward his nation. He sought in every way to exalt his people. 36 And in his days things prospered in his hands, so that the Gentiles were put out of the *x* country, as were also the men in the city of David in Jerusalem, who had built themselves a citadel from which they used to sally forth and defile the environs of the sanctuary and do great damage to its purity. 37 He settled Jews in it, and fortified it for the safety of the country and of the city, and built the walls of Jerusalem higher.

38 "In view of these things King Demetrius confirmed him in the high priesthood, 39 and he made him one of the king's *y* friends and paid him high honours. 40 For he had heard that the Jews were addressed by the Romans as friends and allies and brethren, and that the Romans *z* had received the envoys of Simon with honour.

41 "And *a* the Jews and their priests decided that Simon should be their leader and high priest for ever, until a trustworthy prophet should arise, 42 and that he should be governor over them and that he should take charge of the sanctuary and appoint men over its tasks and over the country and the weapons and the strongholds, and that he should take charge of the sanctuary, 43 and that he should be obeyed by all, and that all contracts in the country should be written in his name, and that he should be clothed in purple and wear gold.

---

q Gk *them*   *r* 140 B.C.
s This word resembles the Hebrew words for *the court of the people of God* or *the prince of the people of God*   *t* The Gk text of this phrase is uncertain   *u* Gk *their*   *v* Gk *them*
w Other authorities read *conduct*   *x* Gk *their*   *y* Gk *his*   *z* Gk *they*   *a* Gk *honour; and that*

44 "And none of the people or priests shall be permitted to nullify any of these decisions or to oppose what he says, or to convene an assembly in the country without his permission, or to be clothed in purple or put on a gold buckle. 45 Whoever acts contrary to these decisions or nullifies any of them shall be liable to punishment."

46 And all the people agreed to grant Simon the right to act in accord with these decisions. 47 So Simon accepted and agreed to be high priest, to be commander and ethnarch of the Jews and priests, and to be protector of them all.[b] 48 And they gave orders to inscribe this decree upon bronze tablets, to put them up in a conspicuous place in the precincts of the sanctuary, 49 and to deposit copies of them in the treasury, so that Simon and his sons might have them.

15 Antiochus, the son of Demetrius the king, sent a letter from the islands of the sea to Simon, the priest and ethnarch of the Jews, and to all the nation; 2 its contents were as follows: "King Antiochus to Simon the high priest and ethnarch and to the nation of the Jews, greeting. 3 Whereas certain pestilent men have gained control of the kingdom of our fathers, and I intend to lay claim to the kingdom so that I may restore it as it formerly was, and have recruited a host of mercenary troops and have equipped warships, 4 and intend to make a landing in the country so that I may proceed against those who have destroyed our country and those who have devastated many cities in my kingdom, 5 now therefore I confirm to you all the tax remissions that the kings before me have granted you, and release from all the other payments from which they have released you. 6 I permit you to mint your own coinage as money for your country, 7 and I grant freedom to

Jerusalem and the sanctuary. All the weapons which you have prepared and the strongholds which you have built and now hold shall remain yours. 8 Every debt you owe to the royal treasury and any such future debts shall be cancelled for you from henceforth and for all time. 9 When we gain control of our kingdom, we will bestow great honour upon you and your nation and the temple, so that your glory will become manifest in all the earth."

10 In the one hundred and seventy-fourth year[c] Antiochus set out and invaded the land of his fathers. All the troops rallied to him, so that there were few with Trypho. 11 Antiochus pursued him, and he came in his flight to Dor, which is by the sea; 12 for he knew that troubles had converged upon him, and his troops had deserted him. 13 So Antiochus encamped against Dor, and with him were a hundred and twenty thousand warriors and eight thousand cavalry. 14 He surrounded the city, and the ships joined battle from the sea; he pressed the city hard from land and sea, and permitted no one to leave or enter it.

15 Then Numenius and his companions arrived from Rome, with letters to the kings and countries, in which the following was written: 16 "Lucius, consul of the Romans, to King Ptolemy, greeting. 17 The envoys of the Jews have come to us as our friends and allies to renew our ancient friendship and alliance. They had been sent by Simon the high priest and by the people of the Jews, 18 and have brought a gold shield weighing a thousand minas. 19 We therefore have decided to write to the kings and countries that they should not seek their harm or make war against them and their cities and their country, or make alliance with those who war against them. 20 And it has seemed good to us to accept the shield from them. 21 Therefore if any

b Or, *to preside over them all* c 138 B.C.

pestilent men have fled to you from their country, hand them over to Simon the high priest, that he may punish them according to their law." 22 The consul*d* wrote the same thing to Demetrius the king and to Attalus and Ariarathes and Arsaces, 23 and to all the countries, and to Sampsames,*e* and to the Spartans, and to Delos, and to Myndos, and to Sicyon, and to Caria, and to Samos, and to Pamphylia, and to Lycia, and to Halicarnassus, and to Rhodes, and to Phaselis, and to Cos, and to Side, and to Aradus and Gortyna and Cnidus and Cyprus and Cyrene. 24 They also sent a copy of these things to Simon the high priest.

25 Antiochus the king besieged Dor anew,*f* continually throwing his forces against it and making engines of war; and he shut Trypho up and kept him from going out or in. 26 And Simon sent to Antiochus*g* two thousand picked men, to fight for him, and silver and gold and much military equipment. 27 But he refused to receive them, and he broke all the agreements he formerly had made with Simon,*g* and became estranged from him. 28 He sent to him Athenobius, one of his friends, to confer with him, saying, "You hold control of Joppa and Gazara and the citadel in Jerusalem; they are cities of my kingdom. 29 You have devastated their territory, you have done great damage in the land, and you have taken possession of many places in my kingdom. 30 Now then, hand over the cities which you have seized and the tribute money of the places which you have conquered outside the borders of Judea; 31 or else give me for them five hundred talents of silver, and for the destruction that you have caused and the tribute money of the cities, five hundred talents more. Otherwise we will come and conquer you."

32 So Athenobius the friend of the king came to Jerusalem, and when he saw the splendour of Simon, and the sideboard with its gold and silver plate, and his great magnificence, he was amazed. He reported to him the words of the king, 33 but Simon gave him this reply: "We have neither taken foreign land nor seized foreign property, but only the inheritance of our fathers, which at one time had been unjustly taken by our enemies. 34 Now that we have the opportunity, we are firmly holding the inheritance of our fathers. 35 As for Joppa and Gazara, which you demand, they were causing great damage among the people and to our land; for them we will give a hundred talents." Athenobius*h* did not answer him a word, 36 but returned in wrath to the king and reported to him these words and the splendour of Simon and all that he had seen. And the king was greatly angered.

37 Now Trypho embarked on a ship and escaped to Orthosia. 38 Then the king made Cendebeus commander-in-chief of the coastal country, and gave him troops of infantry and cavalry. 39 He commanded him to encamp against Judea, and commanded him to build up Kedron and fortify its gates, and to make war on the people; but the king pursued Trypho. 40 So Cendebeus came to Jamnia and began to provoke the people and invade Judea and take the people captive and kill them. 41 He built up Kedron and stationed there horsemen and troops, so that they might go out and make raids along the highways of Judea, as the king had ordered him.

16 John went up from Gazara and reported to Simon his father what Cendebeus had done. 2 And Simon called in his two older sons Judas and John, and said to them: "I and my brothers and the house of my father have fought the wars of Israel from our youth until this day, and things have prospered in our hands so that we have delivered

a Gk *He*   *e* The name is uncertain   *f* Or *on the second day*   *g* Gk *him*   *h* Gk *He*

Israel many times. ³ But now I have grown old, and you by His mercy are mature in years. Take my place and my brother's, and go out and fight for our nation, and may the help which comes from Heaven be with you."

4 So John *ᶦ* chose out of the country twenty thousand warriors and horsemen, and they marched against Cendebeus and camped for the night in Modein. ⁵ Early in the morning they arose and marched into the plain, and behold, a large force of infantry and horsemen was coming to meet them; and a stream lay between them. ⁶ Then he and his army lined up against them. And he saw that the soldiers were afraid to cross the stream, so he crossed over first; and when his men saw him, they crossed over after him. ⁷ Then he divided the army and placed the horsemen in the midst of the infantry, for the cavalry of the enemy were very numerous. ⁸ And they sounded the trumpets, and Cendebeus and his army were put to flight, and many of them were wounded and fell; the rest fled into the stronghold. ⁹ At that time Judas the brother of John was wounded, but John pursued them until Cendebeus *ʲ* reached Kedron, which he had built. ¹⁰ They also fled into the towers that were in the fields of Azotus, and John *ʲ* burned it with fire, and about two thousand of them fell. And he returned to Judea safely.

11 Now Ptolemy the son of Abubus had been appointed governor over the plain of Jericho, and he had much silver and gold, ¹² for he was son-in-law of the high priest. ¹³ His heart was lifted up; he determined to get control of the country, and made treacherous plans against Simon and his sons, to do away with them.

¹⁴ Now Simon was visiting the cities of the country and attending to their needs, and he went down to Jericho with Mattathias and Judas his sons, in the one hundred and seventy-seventh year, *ᵏ* in the eleventh month, which is the month of Shebat. ¹⁵ The son of Abubus received them treacherously in the little stronghold called Dok, which he had built; he gave them a great banquet, and hid men there. ¹⁶ When Simon and his sons were drunk, Ptolemy and his men rose up, took their weapons, and rushed in against Simon in the banquet hall, and they killed him and his two sons and some of his servants. ¹⁷ So he committed an act of great treachery and returned evil for good.

18 Then Ptolemy wrote a report about these things and sent it to the king, asking him to send troops to aid him and to turn over to him the cities and the country. ¹⁹ He sent other men to Gazara to do away with John; he sent letters to the captains asking them to come to him so that he might give them silver and gold and gifts; ²⁰ and he sent other men to take possession of Jerusalem and the temple hill. ²¹ But some one ran ahead and reported to John at Gazara that his father and brothers had perished, and that "he has sent men to kill you also." ²² When he heard this, he was greatly shocked; and he seized the men who came to destroy him and killed them, for he had found out that they were seeking to destroy him.

23 The rest of the acts of John and his wars and the brave deeds which he did, and the building of the walls which he built, and his achievements, ²⁴ behold, they are written in the chronicles of his high priesthood, from the time that he became high priest after his father.

ᶦ Other authorities read *he*   *ʲ* Gk *he*   *ᵏ* 134 B.C.

MACCABEES

1 The Jewish brethren in Jerusalem and those in the land of Judea,

To their Jewish brethren in Egypt, Greeting, and good peace.

2 May God do good to you, and may he remember his covenant with Abraham and Isaac and Jacob, his faithful servants. 3 May he give you all a heart to worship him and to do his will with a strong heart and a willing spirit. 4 May he open your heart to his law and his commandments, and may he bring peace. 5 May he hear your prayers and be reconciled to you, and may he not forsake you in time of evil. 6 We are now praying for you here.

7 In the reign of Demetrius, in the one hundred and sixty-ninth year,[a] we Jews wrote to you, in the critical distress which came upon us in those years after Jason and his company revolted from the holy land and the kingdom 8 and burned the gate and shed innocent blood. We besought the Lord and we were heard, and we offered sacrifice and cereal offering, and we lighted the lamps and we set out the loaves. 9 And now see that you keep the feast of booths in the month of Chislev, in the one hundred and eighty-eighth year.[b]

10 Those in Jerusalem and those in Judea and the senate and Judas,

To Aristobulus, who is of the family of the anointed priests, teacher of Ptolemy the king, and to the Jews in Egypt,

Greeting, and good health.

11 Having been saved by God out of grave dangers we thank him greatly for taking our side against the king.[c] 12 For he drove out those who fought against the holy city. 13 For when the leader reached Persia with a force that seemed irresistible, they were cut to pieces in the temple of Nanea by a deception employed by the priests of Nanea. 14 For under pretext of intending to marry her, Antiochus came to the place together with his friends, to secure most of its treasures as a dowry. 15 When the priests of the temple of Nanea had set out the treasures and Antiochus had come with a few men inside the wall of the sacred precinct, they closed the temple as soon as he entered it. 16 Opening the secret door in the ceiling, they threw stones and struck down the leader and his men, and dismembered them and cut off their heads and threw them to the people outside. 17 Blessed in every way be our God, who has brought judgment upon those who have behaved impiously.

18 Since on the twenty-fifth day of Chislev we shall celebrate the purification of the temple, we thought it necessary to notify you, in order that you also may celebrate the feast of booths and the feast of the fire given when Nehemiah, who built the temple and the altar, offered sacrifices. 19 For when our fathers were being led captive to Persia, the pious priests of that time took some of the fire of the altar and secretly hid it in the hollow of a dry cistern, where they took such precautions that the place was unknown to any one. 20 But after many years had passed, when it pleased God, Nehemiah, having been commissioned by the king of Persia, sent the descendants of the priests who had hidden the fire to get it. And when they reported to us that they had not found fire but thick liquid, he ordered them to dip it out and bring it. 21 And when the materials for the sacrifices were presented, Nehemiah ordered the priests to sprinkle the liquid on the

wood and what was laid upon it.
22 When this was done and some
time had passed and the sun, which
had been clouded over, shone out, a
great fire blazed up, so that all marvelled. 23 And while the sacrifice was
being consumed, the priests offered
prayer—the priests and every one.
Jonathan led, and the rest responded,
as did Nehemiah. 24 The prayer was
to this effect:

"O Lord, Lord God, Creator of all
things, who art awe-inspiring and
strong and just and merciful, who
alone art King and art kind, 25 who
alone art bountiful, who alone art
just and almighty and eternal, who
dost rescue Israel from every evil, who
didst choose the fathers and conse-
crate them, 26 accept this sacrifice on
behalf of all thy people Israel and
preserve thy portion and make it holy.
27 Gather together our scattered people, set free those who are slaves
among the Gentiles, look upon those
who are rejected and despised, and
let the Gentiles know that thou art
our God. 28 Afflict those who oppress
and are insolent with pride. 29 Plant
thy people in thy holy place, as Moses
said."

30 Then the priests sang the
hymns. 31 And when the materials of
the sacrifice were consumed, Nehemiah ordered that the liquid that was
left should be poured upon large
stones. 32 When this was done, a flame
blazed up; but when the light from
the altar shone back, it went out.
33 When this matter became known,
and it was reported to the king of the
Persians that, in the place where the
exiled priests had hidden the fire,
the liquid had appeared with which
Nehemiah and his associates had
burned the materials of the sacrifice,
34 the king investigated the matter,
and enclosed the place and made it
sacred. 35 And with those persons
whom the king favoured he exchanged
many excellent gifts. 36 Nehemiah
and his associates called this "neph-

thar," which means purification,
but by most people it is called
naphtha.*d*

2 One finds in the records that
Jeremiah the prophet ordered
those who were being deported to
take some of the fire, as has been
told, 2 and that the prophet after giving them the law instructed those
who were being deported not to forget the commandments of the Lord,
nor to be led astray in their thoughts
upon seeing the gold and silver statues
and their adornment. 3 And with
other similar words he exhorted them
that the law should not depart from
their hearts.

4 It was also in the writing that
the prophet, having received an oracle, ordered that the tent and the ark
should follow with him, and that he
went out to the mountain where
Moses had gone up and had seen the
inheritance of God. 5 And Jeremiah
came and found a cave, and he
brought there the tent and the ark
and the altar of incense, and he sealed
up the entrance. 6 Some of those who
followed him came up to mark the
way, but could not find it. 7 When
Jeremiah learned of it, he rebuked
them and declared: "The place shall
be unknown until God gathers his
people together again and shows his
mercy. 8 And then the Lord will disclose these things, and the glory of
the Lord and the cloud will appear,
as they were shown in the case of
Moses, and as Solomon asked that
the place should be specially consecrated."

9 It was also made clear that being
possessed of wisdom Solomon *e* offered sacrifice for the dedication and
completion of the temple. 10 Just as
Moses prayed to the Lord, and fire
came down from heaven and devoured the sacrifices, so also Solomon
prayed, and the fire came down and
consumed the whole burnt offerings.
11 And Moses said, "They were consumed because the sin offering had

---

d Gk *nephthai*   *e* Gk *he*

not been eaten." [12] Likewise Solomon also kept the eight days.

13 The same things are reported in the records and in the memoirs of Nehemiah, and also that he founded a library and collected the books about the kings and prophets, and the writings of David, and letters of kings about votive offerings. [14] In the same way Judas also collected all the books that had been lost on account of the war which had come upon us, and they are in our possession. [15] So if you have need of them, send people to get them for you.

16 Since, therefore, we are about to celebrate the purification, we write to you. Will you therefore please keep the days. [17] It is God who has saved all his people, and has returned the inheritance to all, and the kingship and priesthood and consecration, [18] as he promised through the law. For we have hope in God that he will soon have mercy upon us and will gather us from everywhere under heaven into his holy place, for he has rescued us from great evils and has purified the place.

19 The story of Judas Maccabeus and his brothers, and the purification of the great temple, and the dedication of the altar, [20] and further the wars against Antiochus Epiphanes and his son Eupator, [21] and the appearances which came from heaven to those who strove zealously on behalf of Judaism, so that though few in number they seized the whole land and pursued the barbarian hordes, [22] and recovered the temple famous throughout the world and freed the city and restored the laws that were about to be abolished, while the Lord with great kindness became gracious to them—[23] all this, which has been set forth by Jason of Cyrene in five volumes, we shall attempt to condense into a single book. [24] For considering the flood of numbers involved and the difficulty there is for those who wish to enter upon the narratives of history because of the mass of material, [25] we have aimed to please those who wish to read, to make it easy for those who are inclined to memorize, and to profit all readers. [26] For us who have undertaken the toil of abbreviating, it is no light matter but calls for sweat and loss of sleep, [27] just as it is not easy for one who prepares a banquet and seeks the benefit of others. However, to secure the gratitude of many we will gladly endure the uncomfortable toil, [28] leaving the responsibility for exact details to the compiler, while devoting our effort to arriving at the outlines of the condensation. [29] For as the master builder of a new house must be concerned with the whole construction, while the one who undertakes its painting and decoration has to consider only what is suitable for its adornment, such in my judgment is the case with us. [30] It is the duty of the original historian to occupy the ground and to discuss matters from every side and to take trouble with details, [31] but the one who recasts the narrative should be allowed to strive for brevity of expression and to forego exhaustive treatment. [32] At this point therefore let us begin our narrative, adding only so much to what has already been said; for it is foolish to lengthen the preface while cutting short the history itself.

3 While the holy city was inhabited in unbroken peace and the laws were very well observed because of the piety of the high priest Onias and his hatred of wickedness, [2] it came about that the kings themselves honoured the place and glorified the temple with the finest presents, [3] so that even Seleucus, the king of Asia, defrayed from his own revenues all the expenses connected with the service of the sacrifices. [4] But a man named Simon, of the tribe of Benjamin, who had been made captain of the temple, had a disagree-

ment with the high priest about the administration of the city market; 5 and when he could not prevail over Onias he went to Apollonius of Tarsus,*f* who at that time was governor of Coelesyria and Phoenicia. 6 He reported to him that the treasury in Jerusalem was full of untold sums of money, so that the amount of the funds could not be reckoned, and that they did not belong to the account of the sacrifices, but that it was possible for them to fall under the control of the king. 7 When Apollonius met the king, he told him of the money about which he had been informed. The king*g* chose Heliodorus, who was in charge of his affairs, and sent him with commands to effect the removal of the aforesaid money. 8 Heliodorus at once set out on his journey, ostensibly to make a tour of inspection of the cities of Coelesyria and Phoenicia, but in fact to carry out the king's purpose. 9 When he had arrived at Jerusalem and had been kindly welcomed by the high priest of*h* the city, he told about the disclosure that had been made and stated why he had come, and he inquired whether this really was the situation. 10 The high priest explained that there were some deposits belonging to widows and orphans, 11 and also some money of Hyrcanus, son of Tobias, a man of very prominent position, and that it totalled in all four hundred talents of silver and two hundred of gold. To such an extent the impious Simon had misrepresented the facts. 12 And he said that it was utterly impossible that wrong should be done to those people who had trusted in the holiness of the place and in the sanctity and inviolability of the temple which is honoured throughout the whole world. 13 But Heliodorus, because of the king's commands which he had, said that this money must in any case be confiscated for the king's treasury. 14 So he set a day and went in

to direct the inspection of these funds.

There was no little distress throughout the whole city. 15 The priests prostrated themselves before the altar in their priestly garments and called toward heaven upon him who had given the law about deposits, that he should keep them safe for those who had deposited them. 16 To see the appearance of the high priest was to be wounded at heart, for his face and the change in his colour disclosed the anguish of his soul. 17 For terror and bodily trembling had come over the man, which plainly showed to those who looked at him the pain lodged in his heart. 18 People also hurried out of their houses in crowds to make a general supplication because the holy place was about to be brought into contempt. 19 Women, girded with sackcloth under their breasts, thronged the streets. Some of the maidens who were kept indoors ran together to the gates, and some to the walls, while others peered out of the windows. 20 And holding up their hands to heaven, they all made entreaty. 21 There was something pitiable in the prostration of the whole populace and the anxiety of the high priest in his great anguish.

22 While they were calling upon the Almighty Lord that he would keep what had been entrusted safe and secure for those who had entrusted it, 23 Heliodorus went on with what had been decided. 24 But when he arrived at the treasury with his bodyguard, then and there the Sovereign of spirits and of all authority caused so great a manifestation that all who had been so bold as to accompany him were astounded by the power of God, and became faint with terror. 25 For there appeared to them a magnificently caparisoned horse, with a rider of frightening mien, and it rushed furiously at Heliodorus and struck at him with

f Gk *Apollonius son of Tharseas*   *g* Gk *He*   *h* Some authorities read *and*

its front hoofs. Its rider was seen to have armour and weapons of gold. 26 Two young men also appeared to him, remarkably strong, gloriously beautiful and splendidly dressed, who stood on each side of him and scourged him continuously, inflicting many blows on him. 27 When he suddenly fell to the ground and deep darkness came over him, his men took him up and put him on a stretcher 28 and carried him away, this man who had just entered the aforesaid treasury with a great retinue and all his bodyguard but was now unable to help himself; and they recognized clearly the sovereign power of God. 29 While he lay prostrate, speechless because of the divine intervention and deprived of any hope of recovery, 30 they praised the Lord who had acted marvellously for his own place. And the temple, which a little while before was full of fear and disturbance, was filled with joy and gladness, now that the Almighty Lord had appeared.

31 Quickly some of Heliodorus' friends asked Onias to call upon the Most High and to grant life to one who was lying quite at his last breath. 32 And the high priest, fearing that the king might get the notion that some foul play had been perpetrated by the Jews with regard to Heliodorus, offered sacrifice for the man's recovery. 33 While the high priest was making the offering of atonement, the same young men appeared again to Heliodorus, dressed in the same clothing, and they stood and said, "Be very grateful to Onias the high priest, since for his sake the Lord has granted you your life. 34 And see that you, who have been scourged by heaven, report to all men the majestic power of God." Having said this they vanished.

35 Then Heliodorus offered sacrifice to the Lord and made very great vows to the Saviour of his life, and having bidden Onias farewell, he marched off with his forces to the king. 36 And he bore testimony to all men of the deeds of the supreme God, which he had seen with his own eyes. 37 When the king asked Heliodorus what sort of person would be suitable to send on another mission to Jerusalem, he replied, 38 "If you have any enemy or plotter against your government, send him there, for you will get him back thoroughly scourged, if he escapes at all, for there certainly is about the place some power of God. 39 For he who has his dwelling in heaven watches over that place himself and brings it aid, and he strikes and destroys those who come to do it injury." 40 This was the outcome of the episode of Heliodorus and the protection of the treasury.

4 The previously mentioned Simon, who had informed about the money against *i* his own country, slandered Onias, saying that it was he who had incited Heliodorus and had been the real cause of the misfortune. 2 He dared to designate as a plotter against the government the man who was the benefactor of the city, the protector of his fellow countrymen, and a zealot for the laws. 3 When his hatred progressed to such a degree that even murders were committed by one of Simon's approved agents, 4 Onias recognized that the rivalry was serious and that Apollonius, the son of Menestheus *j* and governor of Coelesyria and Phoenicia, was intensifying the malice of Simon. 5 So he betook himself to the king, not accusing his fellow citizens but having in view the welfare, both public and private, of all the people. 6 For he saw that without the king's attention public affairs could not again reach a peaceful settlement, and that Simon would not stop his folly.

7 When Seleucus died and Antiochus who was called Epiphanes succeeded to the kingdom, Jason the brother of Onias obtained the high

i Gk *and* *j* Vg Compare verse 21: Gk uncertain

priesthood by corruption, [8] promising the king at an interview [k] three hundred and sixty talents of silver and, from another source of revenue, eighty talents. [9] In addition to this he promised to pay one hundred and fifty more if permission were given to establish by his authority a gymnasium and a body of youth for it, and to enrol the men of Jerusalem as citizens of Antioch. [10] When the king assented and Jason [l] came to office, he at once shifted his countrymen over to the Greek way of life. [11] He set aside the existing royal concessions to the Jews, secured through John the father of Eupolemus, who went on the mission to establish friendship and alliance with the Romans; and he destroyed the lawful ways of living and introduced new customs contrary to the law. [12] For with alacrity he founded a gymnasium right under the citadel, and he induced the noblest of the young men [m] to wear the Greek hat. [13] There was such an extreme of Hellenization and increase in the adoption of foreign ways because of the surpassing wickedness of Jason, who was ungodly and no high priest, [14] that the priests were no longer intent upon their service at the altar. Despising the sanctuary and neglecting the sacrifices, they hastened to take part in the unlawful proceedings in the wrestling arena after the call to the discus, [15] disdaining the honours prized by their fathers and putting the highest value upon Greek forms of prestige. [16] For this reason heavy disaster overtook them, and those whose ways of living they admired and wished to imitate completely became their enemies and punished them. [17] For it is no light thing to show irreverence to the divine laws—a fact which later events will make clear.

18 When the quadrennial games were being held at Tyre and the king was present, [19] the vile Jason sent envoys, chosen as being Antiochian citizens from Jerusalem, to carry three hundred silver drachmas for the sacrifice to Hercules. Those who carried the money, however, thought best not to use it for sacrifice, because that was inappropriate, but to expend it for another purpose. [20] So this money was intended by the sender for the sacrifice to Hercules, but by the decision of its carriers it was applied to the construction of triremes.

21 When Apollonius the son of Menestheus was sent to Egypt for the coronation [n] of Philometor as king, Antiochus learned that Philometor [o] had become hostile to his government, and he took measures for his own security. Therefore upon arriving at Joppa he proceeded to Jerusalem. [22] He was welcomed magnificently by Jason and the city, and ushered in with a blaze of torches and with shouts. Then he marched into Phoenicia.

23 After a period of three years Jason sent Menelaus, the brother of the previously mentioned Simon, to carry the money to the king and to complete the records of essential business. [24] But he, when presented to the king, extolled him with an air of authority, and secured the high priesthood for himself, outbidding Jason by three hundred talents of silver. [25] After receiving the king's orders he returned, possessing no qualification for the high priesthood, but having the hot temper of a cruel tyrant and the rage of a savage wild beast. [26] So Jason, who after supplanting his own brother was supplanted by another man, was driven as a fugitive into the land of Ammon. [27] And Menelaus held the office, but he did not pay regularly any of the money promised to the king. [28] When Sostratus the captain of the citadel kept requesting payment, for the col-

[k] Or *by a petition*   [l] Gk *he*   [m] Some authorities add *subjecting them*
[n] The exact meaning of the Greek word is uncertain   [o] Gk *he*

lection of the revenue was his responsibility, the two of them were summoned by the king on account of this issue. 29 Menelaus left his own brother Lysimachus as deputy in the high priesthood, while Sostratus left Crates, the commander of the Cyprian troops.

30 While such was the state of affairs, it happened that the people of Tarsus and of Mallus revolted because their cities had been given as a present to Antiochis, the king's concubine. 31 So the king went hastily to settle the trouble, leaving Andronicus, a man of high rank, to act as his deputy. 32 But Menelaus, thinking he had obtained a suitable opportunity, stole some of the gold vessels of the temple and gave them to Andronicus; other vessels, as it happened, he had sold to Tyre and the neighbouring cities. 33 When Onias became fully aware of these acts he publicly exposed them, having first withdrawn to a place of sanctuary at Daphne near Antioch. 34 Therefore Menelaus, taking Andronicus aside, urged him to kill Onias. Andronicus[p] came to Onias, and resorting to treachery offered him sworn pledges and gave him his right hand, and in spite of his suspicion persuaded Onias[q] to come out from the place of sanctuary; then, with no regard for justice, he immediately put him out of the way. 35 For this reason not only Jews, but many also of other nations, were grieved and displeased at the unjust murder of the man. 36 When the king returned from the region of Cilicia, the Jews in the city[r] appealed to him with regard to the unreasonable murder of Onias, and the Greeks shared their hatred of the crime. 37 Therefore Antiochus was grieved at heart and filled with pity, and wept because of the moderation and good conduct of the deceased; 38 and inflamed with anger, he immediately stripped off the purple robe from Andronicus, tore off his garments, and led him about the whole city to that very place where he had committed the outrage against Onias, and there he dispatched the bloodthirsty fellow. The Lord thus repaid him with the punishment he deserved.

39 When many acts of sacrilege had been committed in the city by Lysimachus with the connivance of Menelaus, and when report of them had spread abroad, the populace gathered against Lysimachus, because many of the gold vessels had already been stolen. 40 And since the crowds were becoming aroused and filled with anger, Lysimachus armed about three thousand men and launched an unjust attack, under the leadership of a certain Auranus, a man advanced in years and no less advanced in folly. 41 But when the Jews[s] became aware of Lysimachus' attack, some picked up stones, some blocks of wood, and others took handfuls of the ashes that were lying about, and threw them in wild confusion at Lysimachus and his men. 42 As a result, they wounded many of them, and killed some, and put them all to flight; and the temple robber himself they killed close by the treasury.

43 Charges were brought against Menelaus about this incident. 44 When the king came to Tyre, three men sent by the senate presented the case before him. 45 But Menelaus, already as good as beaten, promised a substantial bribe to Ptolemy son of Dorymenes to win over the king. 46 Therefore Ptolemy, taking the king aside into a colonnade as if for refreshment, induced the king to change his mind. 47 Menelaus, the cause of all the evil, he acquitted of the charges against him, while he sentenced to death those unfortunate men, who would have been freed uncondemned if they had pleaded even before Scythians. 48 And so those who had

[p] Gk *He* [q] Gk *him* [r] Or *in each city* [s] Gk *they*

spoken for the city and the villages [t] and the holy vessels quickly suffered the unjust penalty. [49] Therefore even the Tyrians, showing their hatred of the crime, provided magnificently for their funeral. [50] But Menelaus, because of the cupidity of those in power, remained in office, growing in wickedness, having become the chief plotter against his fellow citizens.

5 About this time Antiochus made his second invasion of Egypt. [2] And it happened that over all the city, for almost forty days, there appeared golden-clad horsemen charging through the air, in companies fully armed with lances and drawn swords—[3] troops of horsemen drawn up, attacks and counterattacks made on this side and on that, brandishing of shields, massing of spears, hurling of missiles, the flash of golden trappings, and armour of all sorts. [4] Therefore all men prayed that the apparition might prove to have been a good omen.

[5] When a false rumour arose that Antiochus was dead, Jason took no less than a thousand men and suddenly made an assault upon the city. When the troops upon the wall had been forced back and at last the city was being taken, Menelaus took refuge in the citadel. [6] But Jason kept relentlessly slaughtering his fellow citizens, not realizing that success at the cost of one's kindred is the greatest misfortune, but imagining that he was setting up trophies of victory over enemies and not over fellow countrymen. [7] He did not gain control of the government, however; and in the end got only disgrace from his conspiracy, and fled again into the country of the Ammonites. [8] Finally he met a miserable end. Accused [u] before Aretas the ruler of the Arabs, fleeing from city to city, pursued by all men, hated as a rebel against the laws, and abhorred as the executioner of his country and his fellow citizens,

he was cast ashore in Egypt; [9] and he who had driven many from their own country into exile died in exile, having embarked to go to the Lacedaemonians in hope of finding protection because of their kinship. [10] He who had cast out many to lie unburied had no one to mourn for him; he had no funeral of any sort and no place in the tomb of his fathers.

[11] When news of what had happened reached the king, he took it to mean that Judea was in revolt. So, raging inwardly, he left Egypt and took the city by storm. [12] And he commanded his soldiers to cut down relentlessly every one they met and to slay those who went into the houses. [13] Then there was killing of young and old, destruction of boys, women, and children, and slaughter of virgins and infants. [14] Within the total of three days eighty thousand were destroyed, forty thousand in hand-to-hand fighting; and as many were sold into slavery as were slain.

[15] Not content with this, Antiochus [v] dared to enter the most holy temple in all the world, guided by Menelaus, who had become a traitor both to the laws and to his country. [16] He took the holy vessels with his polluted hands, and swept away with profane hands the votive offerings which other kings had made to enhance the glory and honour of the place. [17] Antiochus was elated in spirit, and did not perceive that the Lord was angered for a little while because of the sins of those who dwelt in the city, and that therefore he was disregarding the holy place. [18] But if it had not happened that they were involved in many sins, this man would have been scourged and turned back from his rash act as soon as he came forward, just as Heliodorus was, whom Seleucus the king sent to inspect the treasury. [19] But the Lord did not choose the nation for the sake of the holy place, but the place for

[t] Other authorities read *the people* [u] Cn: Gk *Imprisoned* [v] Gk *he*

the sake of the nation. [20] Therefore the place itself shared in the misfortunes that befell the nation and afterward participated in its benefits; and what was forsaken in the wrath of the Almighty was restored again in all its glory when the great Lord became reconciled.

[21] So Antiochus carried off eighteen hundred talents from the temple, and hurried away to Antioch, thinking in his arrogance that he could sail on the land and walk on the sea, because his mind was elated. [22] And he left governors to afflict the people: at Jerusalem, Philip, by birth a Phrygian and in character more barbarous than the man who appointed him; [23] and at Gerizim, Andronicus; and besides these Menelaus, who lorded it over his fellow citizens worse than the others did. In his malice toward the Jewish citizens,[w] [24] Antiochus[x] sent Apollonius, the captain of the Mysians, with an army of twenty-two thousand, and commanded him to slay all the grown men and to sell the women and boys as slaves. [25] When this man arrived in Jerusalem, he pretended to be peaceably disposed and waited until the holy sabbath day; then, finding the Jews not at work, he ordered his men to parade under arms. [26] He put to the sword all those who came out to see them, then rushed into the city with his armed men and killed great numbers of people. [27] But Judas Maccabeus, with about nine others, got away to the wilderness, and kept himself and his companions alive in the mountains as wild animals do; they continued to live on what grew wild, so that they might not share in the defilement.

6 Not long after this, the king sent an Athenian[y] senator[z] to compel the Jews to forsake the laws of their fathers and cease to live by the laws of God, [2] and also to pollute the temple in Jerusalem and call it the temple of Olympian Zeus, and to call the one in Gerizim the temple of Zeus the Friend of Strangers, as did the people who dwelt in that place.

[3] Harsh and utterly grievous was the onslaught of evil. [4] For the temple was filled with debauchery and revelling by the Gentiles, who dallied with harlots and had intercourse with women within the sacred precincts, and besides brought in things for sacrifice that were unfit. [5] The altar was covered with abominable offerings which were forbidden by the laws. [6] A man could neither keep the sabbath, nor observe the feasts of his fathers, nor so much as confess himself to be a Jew.

[7] On the monthly celebration of the king's birthday, the Jews[a] were taken, under bitter constraint, to partake of the sacrifices; and when the feast of Dionysus came, they were compelled to walk in the procession in honour of Dionysus, wearing wreaths of ivy. [8] At the suggestion of Ptolemy a decree was issued to the neighbouring Greek cities, that they should adopt the same policy toward the Jews and make them partake of the sacrifices, [9] and should slay those who did not choose to change over to Greek customs. One could see, therefore, the misery that had come upon them. [10] For example, two women were brought in for having circumcised their children. These women they publicly paraded about the city, with their babies hung at their breasts, then hurled them down headlong from the wall. [11] Others who had assembled in the caves near by, to observe the seventh day secretly, were betrayed to Philip and were all burned together, because their piety kept them from defending themselves, in view of their regard for that most holy day.

---

[w] Or *worse than the others did in his malice toward the Jewish citizens.*   [x] Gk *he*
[y] Some authorities read *Antiochian*   [z] Or *Geron an Athenian*   [a] Gk *they*

12 Now I urge those who read this book not to be depressed by such calamities, but to recognize that these punishments were designed not to destroy but to discipline our people. 13 In fact, not to let the impious alone for long, but to punish them immediately, is a sign of great kindness. 14 For in the case of the other nations the Lord waits patiently to punish them until they have reached the full measure of their sins; but he does not deal in this way with us, 15 in order that he may not take vengeance on us afterward when our sins have reached their height. 16 Therefore he never withdraws his mercy from us. Though he disciplines us with calamities, he does not forsake his own people. 17 Let what we have said serve as a reminder; we must go on briefly with the story.

18 Eleazar, one of the scribes in high position, a man now advanced in age and of noble presence, was being forced to open his mouth to eat swine's flesh. 19 But he, welcoming death with honour rather than life with pollution, went up to the rack of his own accord, spitting out the flesh, 20 as men ought to go who have the courage to refuse things that it is not right to taste, even for the natural love of life.

21 Those who were in charge of that unlawful sacrifice took the man aside, because of their long acquaintance with him, and privately urged him to bring meat of his own providing, proper for him to use, and pretend that he was eating the flesh of the sacrificial meal which had been commanded by the king, 22 so that by doing this he might be saved from death, and be treated kindly on account of his old friendship with them. 23 But making a high resolve, worthy of his years and the dignity of his old age and the grey hairs which he had reached with distinction and his excellent life even from childhood, and moreover according

to the holy God-given law, he declared himself quickly, telling them to send him to Hades.

24 "Such pretence is not worthy of our time of life," he said, "lest many of the young should suppose that Eleazar in his ninetieth year has gone over to an alien religion, 25 and through my pretence, for the sake of living a brief moment longer, they should be led astray because of me, while I defile and disgrace my old age. 26 For even if for the present I should avoid the punishment of men, yet whether I live or die I shall not escape the hands of the Almighty. 27 Therefore, by manfully giving up my life now, I will show myself worthy of my old age 28 and leave to the young a noble example of how to die a good death willingly and nobly for the revered and holy laws."

When he had said this, he went *b* at once to the rack. 29 And those who a little before had acted toward him with good will now changed to ill will, because the words he had uttered were in their opinion sheer madness.*c* 30 When he was about to die under the blows, he groaned aloud and said: "It is clear to the Lord in his holy knowledge that, though I might have been saved from death, I am enduring terrible sufferings in my body under this beating, but in my soul I am glad to suffer these things because I fear him."

31 So in this way he died, leaving in his death an example of nobility and a memorial of courage, not only to the young but to the great body of his nation.

7 It happened also that seven brothers and their mother were arrested and were being compelled by the king, under torture with whips and cords, to partake of unlawful swine's flesh. 2 One of them, acting as their spokesman, said, "What do you intend to ask and learn from us?

b Other authorities read *was dragged* *c* The Gk text of this verse is uncertain

For we are ready to die rather than transgress the laws of our fathers." 3 The king fell into a rage, and gave orders that pans and cauldrons be heated. 4 These were heated immediately, and he commanded that the tongue of their spokesman be cut out and that they scalp him and cut off his hands and feet, while the rest of the brothers and the mother looked on. 5 When he was utterly helpless, the king *d* ordered them to take him to the fire, still breathing, and to fry him in a pan. The smoke from the pan spread widely, but the brothers *e* and their mother encouraged one another to die nobly, saying, 6 "The Lord God is watching over us and in truth has compassion on us, as Moses declared in his song which bore witness against the people to their faces, when he said, 'And he will have compassion on his servants.' "

7 After the first brother had died in this way, they brought forward the second for their sport. They tore off the skin of his head with the hair, and asked him, "Will you eat rather than have your body punished limb by limb?" 8 He replied in the language of his fathers, and said to them, "No." Therefore he in turn underwent tortures as the first brother had done. 9 And when he was at his last breath, he said, "You accursed wretch, you dismiss us from this present life, but the King of the universe will raise us up to an everlasting renewal of life, because we have died for his laws."

10 After him, the third was the victim of their sport. When it was demanded, he quickly put out his tongue and courageously stretched forth his hands, 11 and said nobly, "I got these from Heaven, and because of his laws I disdain them, and from him I hope to get them back again." 12 As a result the king himself and those with him were astonished at the young man's spirit, for he regarded his sufferings as nothing.

13 When he too had died, they maltreated and tortured the fourth in the same way. 14 And when he was near death, he said, "One cannot but choose to die at the hands of men and to cherish the hope that God gives of being raised again by him. But for you there will be no resurrection to life!"

15 Next they brought forward the fifth and maltreated him. 16 But he looked at the king, *f* and said, "Because you have authority among men, mortal though you are, you do what you please. But do not think that God has forsaken our people. 17 Keep on, and see how his mighty power will torture you and your descendants!"

18 After him they brought forward the sixth. And when he was about to die, he said, "Do not deceive yourself in vain. For we are suffering these things on our own account, because of our sins against our own God. Therefore *g* astounding things have happened. 19 But do not think that you will go unpunished for having tried to fight against God!"

20 The mother was especially admirable and worthy of honourable memory. Though she saw her seven sons perish within a single day, she bore it with good courage because of her hope in the Lord. 21 She encouraged each of them in the language of their fathers. Filled with a noble spirit, she fired her woman's reasoning with a man's courage, and said to them, 22 "I do not know how you came into being in my womb. It was not I who gave you life and breath, nor I who set in order the elements within each of you. 23 Therefore the Creator of the world, who shaped the beginning of man and devised the origin of all things, will in his mercy give life and breath back to you again, since you now forget yourselves for the sake of his laws."

24 Antiochus felt that he was be-

d Gk *he*   *e* Gk *they*   *f* Gk *him*   *g* Lat: other authorities omit *Therefore*

ing treated with contempt, and he was suspicious of her reproachful tone. The youngest brother being still alive, Antiochus [h] not only appealed to him in words, but promised with oaths that he would make him rich and enviable if he would turn from the ways of his fathers, and that he would take him for his friend and entrust him with public affairs. [25] Since the young man would not listen to him at all, the king called the mother to him and urged her to advise the youth to save himself. [26] After much urging on his part, she undertook to persuade her son. [27] But, leaning close to him, she spoke in their native tongue as follows, deriding the cruel tyrant: "My son, have pity on me. I carried you nine months in my womb, and nursed you for three years, and have reared you and brought you up to this point in your life, and have taken care of you. [i] [28] I beseech you, my child, to look at the heaven and the earth and see everything that is in them, and recognize that God did not make them out of things that existed. [j] Thus also mankind comes into being. [29] Do not fear this butcher, but prove worthy of your brothers. Accept death, so that in God's mercy I may get you back again with your brothers."

[30] While she was still speaking, the young man said, "What are you [k] waiting for? I will not obey the king's command, but I obey the command of the law that was given to our fathers through Moses. [31] But you, [l] who have contrived all sorts of evil against the Hebrews, will certainly not escape the hands of God. [32] For we are suffering because of our own sins. [33] And if our living Lord is angry for a little while, to rebuke and discipline us, he will again be reconciled with his own servants. [34] But you, unholy wretch, you most defiled

of all men, do not be elated in vain and puffed up by uncertain hopes, when you raise your hand against the children of heaven. [35] You have not yet escaped the judgment of the almighty, all-seeing God. [36] For our brothers after enduring a brief suffering have drunk [m] of everflowing life under God's covenant; but you, by the judgment of God, will receive just punishment for your arrogance. [37] I, like my brothers, give up body and life for the laws of our fathers, appealing to God to show mercy soon to our nation and by afflictions and plagues to make you confess that he alone is God, [38] and through me and my brothers to bring to an end the wrath of the Almighty which has justly fallen on our whole nation."

[39] The king fell into a rage, and handled him worse than the others, being exasperated at his scorn. [40] So he died in his integrity, putting his whole trust in the Lord.

[41] Last of all, the mother died, after her sons.

[42] Let this be enough, then, about the eating of sacrifices and the extreme tortures.

8 But Judas, who was also called Maccabeus, and his companions secretly entered the villages and summoned their kinsmen and enlisted those who had continued in the Jewish faith, and so they gathered about six thousand men. [2] They besought the Lord to look upon the people who were oppressed by all, and to have pity on the temple which had been profaned by ungodly men, [3] and to have mercy on the city which was being destroyed and about to be levelled to the ground, and to hearken to the blood that cried out to him, [4] and to remember also the lawless destruction of the innocent babies and the blasphemies com-

---

[h] Gk *he*   [i] Or *have borne the burden of your education*
[j] Or *God made them out of things that did not exist*   [k] The Greek here for *you* is plural
[l] The Greek word here for *you* is singular   [m] Cn: Gk *fallen*

mitted against his name, and to show his hatred of evil.

5 As soon as Maccabeus got his army organized, the Gentiles could not withstand him, for the wrath of the Lord had turned to mercy. [6] Coming without warning, he would set fire to towns and villages. He captured strategic positions and put to flight not a few of the enemy. [7] He found the nights most advantageous for such attacks. And talk of his valour spread everywhere.

8 When Philip saw that the man was gaining ground little by little, and that he was pushing ahead with more frequent successes, he wrote to Ptolemy, the governor of Coelesyria and Phoenicia, for aid to the king's government. [9] And Ptolemy[n] promptly appointed Nicanor the son of Patroclus, one of the king's chief friends, and sent him, in command of no fewer than twenty thousand Gentiles of all nations, to wipe out the whole race of Judea. He associated with him Gorgias, a general and a man of experience in military service. [10] Nicanor determined to make up for the king the tribute due to the Romans, two thousand talents, by selling the captured Jews into slavery. [11] And he immediately sent to the cities on the sea coast, inviting them to buy Jewish slaves and promising to hand over ninety slaves for a talent, not expecting the judgment from the Almighty that was about to overtake him.

12 Word came to Judas concerning Nicanor's invasion; and when he told his companions of the arrival of the army, [13] those who were cowardly and distrustful of God's justice ran off and got away. [14] Others sold all their remaining property, and at the same time besought the Lord to rescue those who had been sold by the ungodly Nicanor before he ever met them, [15] if not for their own sake, yet for the sake of the covenants made with their fathers, and because

he had called them by his holy and glorious name. [16] But Maccabeus gathered his men together, to the number of six thousand, and exhorted them not to be frightened by the enemy and not to fear the great multitude of Gentiles who were wickedly coming against them, but to fight nobly, [17] keeping before their eyes the lawless outrage which the Gentiles[o] had committed against the holy place, and the torture of the derided city, and besides, the overthrow of their ancestral way of life. [18] "For they trust to arms and acts of daring," he said, "but we trust in the Almighty God, who is able with a single nod to strike down those who are coming against us and even the whole world."

19 Moreover he told them of the times when help came to their ancestors; both the time of Sennacherib, when one hundred and eighty-five thousand perished, [20] and the time of the battle with the Galatians that took place in Babylonia, when eight thousand in all went into the affair, with four thousand Macedonians; and when the Macedonians were hard pressed, the eight thousand, by the help that came to them from heaven, destroyed one hundred and twenty thousand and took much booty.

21 With these words he filled them with good courage and made them ready to die for their laws and their country; then he divided his army into four parts. [22] He appointed his brothers also, Simon and Joseph and Jonathan, each to command a division, putting fifteen hundred men under each. [23] Besides, he appointed Eleazar to read aloud[p] from the holy book, and gave the watchword, "God's Help"; then, leading the first division himself, he joined battle with Nicanor.

24 With the Almighty as their ally, they slew more than nine thousand of the enemy, and wounded and

[n] Gk *he*   [o] Gk *they*   [p] The Gk text of this clause is uncertain

disabled most of Nicanor's army, and forced them all to flee. [25] They captured the money of those who had come to buy them as slaves. After pursuing them for some distance, they were obliged to return because the hour was late. [26] For it was the day before the sabbath, and for that reason they did not continue their pursuit. [27] And when they had collected the arms of the enemy and stripped them of their spoils, they kept the sabbath, giving great praise and thanks to the Lord, who had preserved them for that day and allotted it to them as the beginning of mercy. [28] After the sabbath they gave some of the spoils to those who had been tortured and to the widows and orphans, and distributed the rest among themselves and their children. [29] When they had done this, they made common supplication and besought the merciful Lord to be wholly reconciled with his servants.

30 In encounters with the forces of Timothy and Bacchides they killed more than twenty thousand of them and got possession of some exceedingly high strongholds, and they divided very much plunder, giving to those who had been tortured and to the orphans and widows, and also to the aged, shares equal to their own. [31] Collecting the arms of the enemy,[q] they stored them all carefully in strategic places, and carried the rest of the spoils to Jerusalem. [32] They killed the commander of Timothy's forces, a most unholy man, and one who had greatly troubled the Jews. [33] While they were celebrating the victory in the city of their fathers, they burned those who had set fire to the sacred gates, Callisthenes and some others, who had fled into one little house; so these received the proper recompense for their impiety.[r]

34 The thrice-accursed Nicanor, who had brought the thousand merchants to buy the Jews, [35] having been humbled with the help of the Lord by opponents whom he regarded as of the least account, took off his splendid uniform and made his way alone like a runaway slave across the country till he reached Antioch, having succeeded chiefly in the destruction of his own army! [36] Thus he who had undertaken to secure tribute for the Romans by the capture of the people of Jerusalem proclaimed that the Jews had a Defender, and that therefore the Jews were invulnerable, because they followed the laws ordained by him.

9 About that time, as it happened, Antiochus had retreated in disorder from the region of Persia. [2] For he had entered the city called Persepolis, and attempted to rob the temples and control the city. Therefore the people rushed to the rescue with arms, and Antiochus and his men were defeated,[s] with the result that Antiochus was put to flight by the inhabitants and beat a shameful retreat. [3] While he was in Ecbatana, news came to him of what had happened to Nicanor and the forces of Timothy. [4] Transported with rage, he conceived the idea of turning upon the Jews the injury done by those who had put him to flight; so he ordered his charioteer to drive without stopping until he completed the journey. But the judgment of heaven rode with him! For in his arrogance he said, "When I get there I will make Jerusalem a cemetery of Jews."

5 But the all-seeing Lord, the God of Israel, struck him an incurable and unseen blow. As soon as he ceased speaking he was seized with a pain in his bowels for which there was no relief and with sharp internal tortures —[6] and that very justly, for he had tortured the bowels of others with many and strange inflictions. [7] Yet he did not in any way stop his insolence, but was even more filled with arrogance, breathing fire in his rage

against the Jews, and giving orders to hasten the journey. And so it came about that he fell out of his chariot as it was rushing along, and the fall was so hard as to torture every limb of his body. ⁸ Thus he who had just been thinking that he could command the waves of the sea, in his superhuman arrogance, and imagining that he could weigh the high mountains in a balance, was brought down to earth and carried in a litter, making the power of God manifest to all. ⁹ And so the ungodly man's body swarmed with worms, and while he was still living in anguish and pain, his flesh rotted away, and because of his stench the whole army felt revulsion at his decay. ¹⁰ Because of his intolerable stench no one was able to carry the man who a little while before had thought that he could touch the stars of heaven. ¹¹ Then it was that, broken in spirit, he began to lose much of his arrogance and to come to his senses under the scourge of God, for he was tortured with pain every moment. ¹² And when he could not endure his own stench, he uttered these words: "It is right to be subject to God, and no mortal should think that he is equal to God." *t*

13 Then the abominable fellow made a vow to the Lord, who would no longer have mercy on him, stating ¹⁴ that the holy city, which he was hastening to level to the ground and to make a cemetery, he was now declaring to be free; ¹⁵ and the Jews, whom he had not considered worth burying but had planned to throw out with their children to the beasts, for the birds to pick, he would make, all of them, equal to citizens of Athens; ¹⁶ and the holy sanctuary, which he had formerly plundered, he would adorn with the finest offerings; and the holy vessels he would give back, all of them, many times over; and the expenses incurred for the sacrifices he would provide from his

own revenues; ¹⁷ and in addition to all this he also would become a Jew and would visit every inhabited place to proclaim the power of God. ¹⁸ But when his sufferings did not in any way abate, for the judgment of God had justly come upon him, he gave up all hope for himself and wrote to the Jews the following letter, in the form of a supplication. This was its content:

19 "To his worthy Jewish citizens, Antiochus their king and general sends hearty greetings and good wishes for their health and prosperity. ²⁰ If you and your children are well and your affairs are as you wish, I am glad. As my hope is in heaven, ²¹ I remember with affection your esteem and good will. On my way back from the region of Persia I suffered an annoying illness, and I have deemed it necessary to take thought for the general security of all. ²² I do not despair of my condition, for I have good hope of recovering from my illness, ²³ but I observed that my father, on the occasions when he made expeditions into the upper country, appointed his successor, ²⁴ so that, if anything unexpected happened or any unwelcome news came, the people throughout the realm would not be troubled, for they would know to whom the government was left. ²⁵ Moreover, I understand how the princes along the borders and the neighbours to my kingdom keep watching for opportunities and waiting to see what will happen. So I have appointed my son Antiochus to be king, whom I have often entrusted and commended to most of you when I hastened off to the upper provinces; and I have written to him what is written here. ²⁶ I therefore urge and beseech you to remember the public and private services rendered to you and to maintain your present good will, each of you, toward me and my son. ²⁷ For I am sure that he will follow my policy and will

t Or *think thoughts proper only to God*

treat you with moderation and kindness."

28 So the murderer and blasphemer, having endured the most intense suffering, such as he had inflicted on others, came to the end of his life by a most pitiable fate, among the mountains in a strange land. ²⁹ And Philip, one of his courtiers, took his body home; then, fearing the son of Antiochus, he betook himself to Ptolemy Philometor in Egypt.

10 Now Maccabeus and his followers, the Lord leading them on, recovered the temple and the city; ² and they tore down the altars which had been built in the public square by the foreigners, and also destroyed the sacred precincts. ³ They purified the sanctuary, and made another altar of sacrifice; then, striking fire out of flint, they offered sacrifices, after a lapse of two years, and they burned incense and lighted lamps and set out the bread of the Presence. ⁴ And when they had done this, they fell prostrate and besought the Lord that they might never again fall into such misfortunes, but that, if they should ever sin, they might be disciplined by him with forbearance and not be handed over to blasphemous and barbarous nations. ⁵ It happened that on the same day on which the sanctuary had been profaned by the foreigners, the purification of the sanctuary took place, that is, on the twenty-fifth day of the same month, which was Chislev. ⁶ And they celebrated it for eight days with rejoicing, in the manner of the feast of booths, remembering how not long before, during the feast of booths, they had been wandering in the mountains and caves like wild animals. ⁷ Therefore bearing ivy-wreathed wands and beautiful branches and also fronds of palm, they offered hymns of thanksgiving to him who had given success to the purifying of his own holy place.

⁸ They decreed by public ordinance and vote that the whole nation of the Jews should observe these days every year.

9 Such then was the end of Antiochus, who was called Epiphanes.

10 Now we will tell what took place under Antiochus Eupator, who was the son of that ungodly man, and will give a brief summary of the principal calamities of the wars. ¹¹ This man, when he succeeded to the kingdom, appointed one Lysias to have charge of the government and to be chief governor of Coelesyria and Phoenicia. ¹² Ptolemy, who was called Macron, took the lead in showing justice to the Jews because of the wrong that had been done to them, and attempted to maintain peaceful relations with them. ¹³ As a result he was accused before Eupator by the king's friends. He heard himself called a traitor at every turn, because he had abandoned Cyprus, which Philometor had entrusted to him, and had gone over to Antiochus Epiphanes. Unable to command the respect due his office,ᵘ he took poison and ended his life.

14 When Gorgias became governor of the region, he maintained a force of mercenaries, and at every turn kept on warring against the Jews. ¹⁵ Besides this, the Idumeans, who had control of important strongholds, were harassing the Jews; they received those who were banished from Jerusalem, and endeavoured to keep up the war. ¹⁶ But Maccabeus and his men, after making solemn supplication and beseeching God to fight on their side, rushed to the strongholds of the Idumeans. ¹⁷ Attacking them vigorously, they gained possession of the places, and beat off all who fought upon the wall, and slew those whom they encountered, killing no fewer than twenty thousand.

ᵘ Cn: the Gk text here is uncertain

18 When no less than nine thousand took refuge in two very strong towers well equipped to withstand a siege, 19 Maccabeus left Simon and Joseph, and also Zacchaeus and his men, a force sufficient to besiege them; and he himself set off for places where he was more urgently needed. 20 But the men with Simon, who were money-hungry, were bribed by some of those who were in the towers, and on receiving seventy thousand drachmas let some of them slip away. 21 When word of what had happened came to Maccabeus, he gathered the leaders of the people, and accused these men of having sold their brethren for money by setting their enemies free to fight against them. 22 Then he slew these men who had turned traitor, and immediately captured the two towers. 23 Having success at arms in everything he undertook, he destroyed more than twenty thousand in the two strongholds.

24 Now Timothy, who had been defeated by the Jews before, gathered a tremendous force of mercenaries and collected the cavalry from Asia in no small number. He came on, intending to take Judea by storm. 25 As he drew near, Maccabeus and his men sprinkled dust upon their heads and girded their loins with sackcloth, in supplication to God. 26 Falling upon the steps before the altar, they besought him to be gracious to them and to be an enemy to their enemies and an adversary to their adversaries, as the law declares. 27 And rising from their prayer they took up their arms and advanced a considerable distance from the city; and when they came near to the enemy they halted. 28 Just as dawn was breaking, the two armies joined battle, the one having as pledge of success and victory not only their valour but their reliance upon the Lord, while the other made rage their leader in the fight.

29 When the battle became fierce, there appeared to the enemy from heaven five resplendent men on horses with golden bridles, and they were leading the Jews. 30 Surrounding Maccabeus and protecting him with their own armour and weapons, they kept him from being wounded. And they showered arrows and thunderbolts upon the enemy, so that, confused and blinded, they were thrown into disorder and cut to pieces. 31 Twenty thousand five hundred were slaughtered, besides six hundred horsemen.

32 Timothy himself fled to a stronghold called Gazara, especially well garrisoned, where Chaereas was commander. 33 Then Maccabeus and his men were glad, and they besieged the fort for four days. 34 The men within, relying on the strength of the place, blasphemed terribly and hurled out wicked words. 35 But at dawn of the fifth day, twenty young men in the army of Maccabeus, fired with anger because of the blasphemies, bravely stormed the wall and with savage fury cut down every one they met. 36 Others who came up in the same way wheeled around against the defenders and set fire to the towers; they kindled fires and burned the blasphemers alive. Others broke open the gates and let in the rest of the force, and they occupied the city. 37 They killed Timothy, who was hidden in a cistern, and his brother Chaereas, and Apollophanes. 38 When they had accomplished these things, with hymns and thanksgivings they blessed the Lord who shows great kindness to Israel and gives them the victory.

11 Very soon after this, Lysias, the king's guardian and kinsman, who was in charge of the government, being vexed at what had happened, 2 gathered about eighty thousand men and all his cavalry and came against the Jews. He intended to make the city a home for Greeks, 3 and to levy tribute on the temple as he did on the sacred places of the

other nations, and to put up the high priesthood for sale every year. ⁴ He took no account whatever of the power of God, but was elated with his ten thousands of infantry, and his thousands of cavalry, and his eighty elephants. ⁵ Invading Judea, he approached Beth-zur, which was a fortified place about five leagues ᵛ from Jerusalem, and pressed it hard.

⁶ When Maccabeus and his men got word that Lysias ʷ was besieging the strongholds, they and all the people, with lamentations and tears, besought the Lord to send a good angel to save Israel. ⁷ Maccabeus himself was the first to take up arms, and he urged the others to risk their lives with him to aid their brethren. Then they eagerly rushed off together. ⁸ And there, while they were still near Jerusalem, a horseman appeared at their head, clothed in white and brandishing weapons of gold. ⁹ And they all together praised the merciful God, and were strengthened in heart, ready to assail not only men but the wildest beasts or walls of iron. ¹⁰ They advanced in battle order, having their heavenly ally, for the Lord had mercy on them. ¹¹ They hurled themselves like lions against the enemy, and slew eleven thousand of them and sixteen hundred horsemen, and forced all the rest to flee. ¹² Most of them got away stripped and wounded, and Lysias himself escaped by disgraceful flight. ¹³ And as he was not without intelligence, he pondered over the defeat which had befallen him, and realized that the Hebrews were invincible because the mighty God fought on their side. So he sent to them ¹⁴ and persuaded them to settle everything on just terms, promising that he would persuade the king, constraining him to be their friend.ˣ ¹⁵ Maccabeus, having regard for the common good, agreed to all that Lysias urged. For the king granted every request in behalf of the Jews which Maccabeus delivered to Lysias in writing.

¹⁶ The letter written to the Jews by Lysias was to this effect:

"Lysias to the people of the Jews, greeting. ¹⁷ John and Absalom, who were sent by you, have delivered your signed communication and have asked about the matters indicated therein. ¹⁸ I have informed the king of everything that needed to be brought before him, and he has agreed to what was possible. ¹⁹ If you will maintain your good will toward the government, I will endeavour for the future to help promote your welfare. ²⁰ And concerning these matters and their details, I have ordered these men and my representatives to confer with you. ²¹ Farewell. The one hundred and forty-eighth year,ʸ Dioscorinthius twenty-fourth."

²² The king's letter ran thus:

"King Antiochus to his brother Lysias, greeting. ²³ Now that our father has gone on to the gods, we desire that the subjects of the kingdom be undisturbed in caring for their own affairs. ²⁴ We have heard that the Jews do not consent to our father's change to Greek customs but prefer their own way of living and ask that their own customs be allowed them. ²⁵ Accordingly, since we choose that this nation also be free from disturbance, our decision is that their temple be restored to them and that they live according to the customs of their ancestors. ²⁶ You will do well, therefore, to send word to them and give them pledges of friendship, so that they may know our policy and be of good cheer and go on happily in the conduct of their own affairs."

²⁷ To the nation the king's letter was as follows:

"King Antiochus to the senate of the Jews and to the other Jews, greeting. ²⁸ If you are well, it is as we desire. We also are in good health.

ᵛ About twenty miles. The text is uncertain here.   ʷ Gk *he*
ˣ The Gk text here is corrupt.   ʸ 164 B.C.

29 Menelaus has informed us that you wish to return home and look after your own affairs. 30 Therefore those who go home by the thirtieth day of Xanthicus will have our pledge of friendship and full permission 31 for the Jews to enjoy their own food and laws, just as formerly, and none of them shall be molested in any way for what he may have done in ignorance. 32 And I have also sent Menelaus to encourage you. 33 Farewell. The one hundred and forty-eighth year,ᵍ Xanthicus fifteenth."

34 The Romans also sent them a letter, which read thus:

"Quintus Memmius and Titus Manius, envoys of the Romans, to the people of the Jews, greeting. 35 With regard to what Lysias the kinsman of the king has granted you, we also give consent. 36 But as to the matters which he decided are to be referred to the king, as soon as you have considered them, send some one promptly, so that we may make proposals appropriate for you. For we are on our way to Antioch. 37 Therefore make haste and send some men, so that we may have your judgment. 38 Farewell. The one hundred and forty-eighth year,ᵃ Xanthicus fifteenth."

12 When this agreement had been reached, Lysias returned to the king, and the Jews went about their farming.

2 But some of the governors in various places, Timothy and Apollonius the son of Gennaeus, as well as Hieronymus and Demophon, and in addition to these Nicanor the governor of Cyprus, would not let them live quietly and in peace. 3 And some men of Joppa did so ungodly a deed as this: they invited the Jews who lived among them to embark, with their wives and children, on boats which they had provided, as though there were no ill will to the Jews; ᵇ

4 and this was done by public vote of the city. And when they accepted, because they wished to live peaceably and suspected nothing, the men of Joppa ᶜ took them out to sea and drowned them, not less than two hundred. 5 When Judas heard of the cruelty visited on his countrymen, he gave orders to his men 6 and, calling upon God the righteous Judge, attacked the murderers of his brethren. He set fire to the harbour by night, and burned the boats, and massacred those who had taken refuge there. 7 Then, because the city's gates were closed, he withdrew, intending to come again and root out the whole community of Joppa. 8 But learning that the men in Jamnia meant in the same way to wipe out the Jews who were living among them, 9 he attacked the people of Jamnia by night and set fire to the harbour and the fleet, so that the glow of the light was seen in Jerusalem, thirty miles ᵈ distant.

10 When they had gone more than a mile ᵉ from there, on their march against Timothy, not less than five thousand Arabs with five hundred horsemen attacked them. 11 After a hard fight Judas and his men won the victory, by the help of God. The defeated nomads besought Judas to grant them pledges of friendship, promising to give him cattle and to help his people ᶠ in all other ways. 12 Judas, thinking that they might really be useful in many ways, agreed to make peace with them; and after receiving his pledges they departed to their tents.

13 He also attacked a certain city which was strongly fortified with earthworks ᵍ and walls, and inhabited by all sorts of Gentiles. Its name was Caspin. 14 And those who were within, relying on the strength of the walls and on their supply of provisions, behaved most insolently toward Judas and his men, railing at them

᙮ 164 B.C.   ᵃ 164 B.C.   ᵇ Gk *them*   ᶜ Gk *they*   ᵈ Gk *two hundred and forty stadia*
ᵉ Gk *nine stadia*   ᶠ Gk *them*   ᵍ The Gk text here is uncertain

and even blaspheming and saying un-holy things. [15] But Judas and his men, calling upon the great Sovereign of the world, who without battering-rams or engines of war overthrew Jericho in the days of Joshua, rushed furiously upon the walls. [16] They took the city by the will of God, and slaughtered untold numbers, so that the adjoining lake, a quarter of a mile *h* wide, appeared to be running over with blood.

[17] When they had gone ninety-five miles *i* from there, they came to Charax, to the Jews who are called Toubiani. [18] They did not find Timothy in that region, for he had by then departed from the region with-out accomplishing anything, though in one place he had left a very strong garrison. [19] Dositheus and Sosipater, who were captains under Maccabeus, marched out and destroyed those whom Timothy had left in the strong-hold, more than ten thousand men. [20] But Maccabeus arranged his army in divisions, set men *j* in command of the divisions, and hastened after Timothy, who had with him a hun-dred and twenty thousand infantry and two thousand five hundred cav-alry. [21] When Timothy learned of the approach of Judas, he sent off the women and the children and also the baggage to a place called Carnaim; for that place was hard to besiege and difficult of access because of the nar-rowness of all the approaches. [22] But when Judas' first division appeared, terror and fear came over the enemy at the manifestation to them of him who sees all things; and they rushed off in flight and were swept on, this way and that, so that often they were injured by their own men and pierced by the points of their swords. [23] And Judas pressed the pursuit with the ut-most vigour, putting the sinners to the sword, and destroyed as many as thirty thousand men.

[24] Timothy himself fell into the hands of Dositheus and Sosipater and their men. With great guile he besought them to let him go in safety, because he held the parents of most of them and the brothers of some and no consideration would be shown them. [25] And when with many words he had confirmed his solemn promise to restore them unharmed, they let him go, for the sake of saving their brethren.

[26] Then Judas *k* marched against Carnaim and the temple of Atargatis, and slaughtered twenty-five thousand people. [27] After the rout and destruc-tion of these, he marched also against Ephron, a fortified city where Lysias dwelt with multitudes of people of all nationalities.*l* Stalwart young men took their stand before the walls and made a vigorous defence; and great stores of war engines and missiles were there. [28] But the Jews *m* called upon the Sovereign who with power shat-ters the might of his enemies, and they got the city into their hands, and killed as many as twenty-five thousand of those who were within it.

[29] Setting out from there, they hastened to Scythopolis, which is seventy-five miles *n* from Jerusalem. [30] But when the Jews who dwelt there bore witness to the good will which the people of Scythopolis had shown them and their kind treatment of them in times of misfortune, [31] they thanked them and exhorted them to be well disposed to their race in the future also. Then they went up to Jerusalem, as the feast of weeks was close at hand.

[32] After the feast called Pentecost, they hastened against Gorgias, the governor of Idumea. [33] And he came out with three thousand infantry and four hundred cavalry. [34] When they joined battle, it happened that a few of the Jews fell. [35] But a certain Dositheus, one of Bacenor's men, who was on horseback and was a

---

h Gk *two stadia*   *i* Gk *seven hundred and fifty stadia*   *j* Gk *them*   *k* Gk *he*
l The Gk text of this sentence is uncertain   *m* Gk *they*   *n* Gk *six hundred stadia*

strong man, caught hold of Gorgias, and grasping his cloak was dragging him off by main strength, wishing to take the accursed man alive, when one of the Thracian horsemen bore down upon him and cut off his arm; so Gorgias escaped and reached Marisa.

36 As Esdris and his men had been fighting for a long time and were weary, Judas called upon the Lord to show himself their ally and leader in the battle. ³⁷ In the language of their fathers he raised the battle cry, with hymns; then he charged against Gorgias' men when they were not expecting it, and put them to flight.

38 Then Judas assembled his army and went to the city of Adullam. As the seventh day was coming on, they purified themselves according to the custom, and they kept the sabbath there.

39 On the next day, as by that time it had become necessary, Judas and his men went to take up the bodies of the fallen and to bring them back to lie with their kinsmen in the sepulchres of their fathers. ⁴⁰ Then under the tunic of every one of the dead they found sacred tokens of the idols of Jamnia, which the law forbids the Jews to wear. And it became clear to all that this was why these men had fallen. ⁴¹ So they all blessed the ways of the Lord, the righteous Judge, who reveals the things that are hidden; ⁴² and they turned to prayer, beseeching that the sin which had been committed might be wholly blotted out. And the noble Judas exhorted the people to keep themselves free from sin, for they had seen with their own eyes what had happened because of the sin of those who had fallen. ⁴³ He also took up a collection, man by man, to the amount of two thousand drachmas of silver, and sent it to Jerusalem to provide for a sin offering. In doing this he acted very well and honourably, taking account of the resurrection. ⁴⁴ For if he

were not expecting that those who had fallen would rise again, it would have been superfluous and foolish to pray for the dead. ⁴⁵ But if he was looking to the splendid reward that is laid up for those who fall asleep in godliness, it was a holy and pious thought. Therefore he made atonement for the dead, that they might be delivered from their sin.

13 In the one hundred and forty-ninth year ⁰ word came to Judas and his men that Antiochus Eupator was coming with a great army against Judea, ² and with him Lysias, his guardian, who had charge of the government. Each of them had a Greek force of one hundred and ten thousand infantry, five thousand three hundred cavalry, twenty-two elephants, and three hundred chariots armed with scythes.

3 Menelaus also joined them and with utter hypocrisy urged Antiochus on, not for the sake of his country's welfare, but because he thought that he would be established in office. ⁴ But the King of kings aroused the anger of Antiochus against the scoundrel; and when Lysias informed him that this man was to blame for all the trouble, he ordered them to take him to Beroea and to put him to death by the method which is the custom in that place. ⁵ For there is a tower in that place, fifty cubits high, full of ashes, and it has a rim running around it which on all sides inclines precipitously into the ashes. ⁶ There they all push to destruction any man guilty of sacrilege or notorious for other crimes. ⁷ By such a fate it came about that Menelaus the lawbreaker died, without even burial in the earth. ⁸ And this was eminently just; because he had committed many sins against the altar whose fire and ashes were holy, he met his death in ashes.

9 The king with barbarous arrogance was coming to show to the Jews things far worse than those that

⁰ 163 B.C.

had been done *p* in his father's time.
¹⁰ But when Judas heard of this, he
ordered the people to call upon the
Lord day and night, now if ever to
help those who were on the point of
being deprived of the law and their
country and the holy temple, ¹¹ and
not to let the people who had just
begun to revive fall into the hands of
the blasphemous Gentiles. ¹² When
they had all joined in the same petition and had besought the merciful
Lord with weeping and fasting and
lying prostrate for three days without
ceasing, Judas exhorted them and
ordered them to stand ready.

13 After consulting privately with
the elders, he determined to march
out and decide the matter by the
help of God before the king's army
could enter Judea and get possession
of the city. ¹⁴ So, committing the decision to the Creator of the world
and exhorting his men to fight nobly
to the death for the laws, temple,
city, country, and commonwealth,
he pitched his camp near Modein.
¹⁵ He gave his men the watchword,
"God's victory," and with a picked
force of the bravest young men, he
attacked the king's pavilion at night
and slew as many as two thousand
men in the camp. He stabbed *q* the
leading elephant and its rider. ¹⁶ In
the end they filled the camp with terror and confusion and withdrew in
triumph. ¹⁷ This happened, just as
day was dawning, because the Lord's
help protected him.

18 The king, having had a taste
of the daring of the Jews, tried strategy in attacking their positions. ¹⁹ He
advanced against Beth-zur, a strong
fortress of the Jews, was turned back,
attacked again,*r* and was defeated.
²⁰ Judas sent in to the garrison whatever was necessary. ²¹ But Rhodocus,
a man from the ranks of the Jews,
gave secret information to the enemy; he was sought for, caught, and
put in prison. ²² The king negotiated

a second time with the people in
Beth-zur, gave pledges, received
theirs, withdrew, attacked Judas and
his men, was defeated; ²³ he got word
that Philip, who had been left in
charge of the government, had revolted in Antioch; he was dismayed,
called in the Jews, yielded and swore
to observe all their rights, settled with
them and offered sacrifice, honoured
the sanctuary and showed generosity
to the holy place. ²⁴ He received
Maccabeus, left Hegemonides as governor from Ptolemais to Gerar, ²⁵ and
went to Ptolemais. The people of
Ptolemais were indignant over the
treaty; in fact they were so angry
that they wanted to annul its terms.*s*
²⁶ Lysias took the public platform,
made the best possible defence, convinced them, appeased them, gained
their good will, and set out for Antioch. This is how the king's attack
and withdrawal turned out.

14 Three years later, word
came to Judas and his men
that Demetrius, the son of Seleucus,
had sailed into the harbour of Tripolis
with a strong army and a fleet, ² and
had taken possession of the country,
having made away with Antiochus
and his guardian Lysias.

3 Now a certain Alcimus, who had
formerly been high priest but had
wilfully defiled himself in the times
of separation, realized that there was
no way for him to be safe or to have
access again to the holy altar, ⁴ and
went to King Demetrius in about the
one hundred and fifty-first year,*t* pre-
senting to him a crown of gold and a
palm, and besides these some of the
customary olive branches from the
temple. During that day he kept
quiet. ⁵ But he found an opportunity
that furthered his mad purpose when
he was invited by Demetrius to a
meeting of the council and was
asked about the disposition and in-
tentions of the Jews. He answered:

---

p Or *the worst of the things that had been done*   *q* The Gk text here is uncertain   *r* Or *faltered*
s The Gk text of this clause is uncertain   *t* 161 B.C.

6 "Those of the Jews who are called Hasidaeans, whose leader is Judas Maccabeus, are keeping up war and stirring up sedition, and will not let the kingdom attain tranquillity. 7 Therefore I have laid aside my ancestral glory—I mean the high priesthood—and have now come here, 8 first because I am genuinely concerned for the interests of the king, and second because I have regard also for my fellow citizens. For through the folly of those whom I have mentioned our whole nation is now in no small misfortune. 9 Since you are acquainted, O king, with the details of this matter, deign to take thought for our country and our hard-pressed nation with the gracious kindness which you show to all. 10 For as long as Judas lives, it is impossible for the government to find peace."

11 When he had said this, the rest of the king's friends, who were hostile to Judas, quickly inflamed Demetrius still more. 12 And he immediately chose Nicanor, who had been in command of the elephants, appointed him governor of Judea, and sent him off 13 with orders to kill Judas and scatter his men, and to set up Alcimus as high priest of the greatest temple. 14 And the Gentiles throughout Judea, who had fled before *u* Judas, flocked to join Nicanor, thinking that the misfortunes and calamities of the Jews would mean prosperity for themselves. 15 When the Jews *v* heard of Nicanor's coming and the gathering of the Gentiles, they sprinkled dust upon their heads and prayed to him who established his own people for ever and always upholds his own heritage by manifesting himself. 16 At the command of the leader, they *w* set out from there immediately and engaged them in battle at a village called Dessau. *x* 17 Simon, the brother of Judas, had encountered Nicanor, but had been temporarily *y* checked

because of the sudden consternation created by the enemy. 18 Nevertheless Nicanor, hearing of the valour of Judas and his men and their courage in battle for their country, shrank from deciding the issue by bloodshed. 19 Therefore he sent Posidonius and Theodotus and Mattathias to give and receive pledges of friendship. 20 When the terms had been fully considered, and the leader had informed the people, and it appeared that they were of one mind, they agreed to the covenant. 21 And the leaders *z* set a day on which to meet by themselves. A chariot came forward from each army; seats of honour were set in place; 22 Judas posted armed men in readiness at key places to prevent sudden treachery on the part of the enemy; they held the proper conference.

23 Nicanor stayed on in Jerusalem and did nothing out of the way, but dismissed the flocks of people that had gathered. 24 And he kept Judas always in his presence; he was warmly attached to the man. 25 And he urged him to marry and have children; so he married, settled down, and shared the common life.

26 But when Alcimus noticed their good will for one another, he took the covenant that had been made and went to Demetrius. He told him that Nicanor was disloyal to the government, for he had appointed that conspirator against the kingdom, Judas, to be his successor. 27 The king became excited and, provoked by the false accusations of that depraved man, wrote to Nicanor, stating that he was displeased with the covenant and commanding him to send Maccabeus to Antioch as a prisoner without delay.

28 When this message came to Nicanor, he was troubled and grieved that he had to annul their agreement when the man had done no wrong. 29 Since it was not possible to op-

---

u The Gk text is uncertain   *v* Gk *they*   *w* Gk *he*   *x* The name is uncertain
y Other authorities read *slowly*   *z* Gk *they*

247

pose the king, he watched for an opportunity to accomplish this by a stratagem. [30] But Maccabeus, noticing that Nicanor was more austere in his dealings with him and was meeting him more rudely than had been his custom, concluded that this austerity did not spring from the best motives. So he gathered not a few of his men, and went into hiding from Nicanor.

[31] When the latter became aware that he had been cleverly outwitted by the man, he went to the great[a] and holy temple while the priests were offering the customary sacrifices, and commanded them to hand the man over. [32] And when they declared on oath that they did not know where the man was whom he sought, [33] he stretched out his right hand toward the sanctuary, and swore this oath: "If you do not hand Judas over to me as a prisoner, I will level this precinct of God to the ground and tear down the altar, and I will build here a splendid temple to Dionysus."

[34] Having said this, he went away. Then the priests stretched forth their hands toward heaven and called upon the constant Defender of our nation, in these words: [35] "O Lord of all, who hast need of nothing, thou wast pleased that there be a temple for thy habitation among us; [36] so now, O holy One, Lord of all holiness, keep undefiled for ever this house that has been so recently purified."

[37] A certain Razis, one of the elders of Jerusalem, was denounced to Nicanor as a man who loved his fellow citizens and was very well thought of and for his good will was called father of the Jews. [38] For in former times, when there was no mingling with the Gentiles, he had been accused of Judaism, and for Judaism he had with all zeal risked body and life. [39] Nicanor, wishing to exhibit the enmity which he had for the Jews, sent more than five hundred soldiers to arrest him; [40] for he thought that by arresting[b] him he would do them an injury. [41] When the troops were about to capture the tower and were forcing the door of the courtyard, they ordered that fire be brought and the doors burned. Being surrounded, Razis[c] fell upon his own sword, [42] preferring to die nobly rather than to fall into the hands of sinners and suffer outrages unworthy of his noble birth. [43] But in the heat of the struggle he did not hit exactly, and the crowd was now rushing in through the doors. He bravely ran up on the wall, and manfully threw himself down into the crowd. [44] But as they quickly drew back, a space opened and he fell in the middle of the empty space. [45] Still alive and aflame with anger, he rose, and though his blood gushed forth and his wounds were severe he ran through the crowd; and standing upon a steep rock, [46] with his blood now completely drained from him, he tore out his entrails, took them with both hands and hurled them at the crowd, calling upon the Lord of life and spirit to give them back to him again. This was the manner of his death.

15 When Nicanor heard that Judas and his men were in the region of Samaria, he made plans to attack them with complete safety on the day of rest. [2] And when the Jews who were compelled to follow him said, "Do not destroy so savagely and barbarously, but show respect for the day which he who sees all things has honoured and hallowed above other days," [3] the thrice-accursed wretch asked if there were a sovereign in heaven who had commanded the keeping of the sabbath day. [4] And when they declared, "It is the living Lord himself, the Sovereign in heaven, who ordered us to observe the seventh day," [5] he replied, "And I am a sovereign also, on earth, and I command you to take up arms and

---

a Gk *greatest*   *b* The Gk text here is uncertain   *c* Gk *he*

finish the king's business." Nevertheless, he did not succeed in carrying out his abominable design.

6 This Nicanor in his utter boastfulness and arrogance had determined to erect a public monument of victory over Judas and his men. 7 But Maccabeus did not cease to trust with all confidence that he would get help from the Lord. 8 And he exhorted his men not to fear the attack of the Gentiles, but to keep in mind the former times when help had come to them from heaven, and now to look for the victory which the Almighty would give them. 9 Encouraging them from the law and the prophets, and reminding them also of the struggles they had won, he made them the more eager. 10 And when he had aroused their courage, he gave his orders, at the same time pointing out the perfidy of the Gentiles and their violation of oaths. 11 He armed each of them not so much with confidence in shields and spears as with the inspiration of brave words, and he cheered them all by relating a dream, a sort of vision,*d* which was worthy of belief.

12 What he saw was this: Onias, who had been high priest, a noble and good man, of modest bearing and gentle manner, one who spoke fittingly and had been trained from childhood in all that belongs to excellence, was praying with outstretched hands for the whole body of the Jews. 13 Then likewise a man appeared, distinguished by his grey hair and dignity, and of marvellous majesty and authority. 14 And Onias spoke, saying, "This is a man who loves the brethren and prays much for the people and the holy city, Jeremiah, the prophet of God." 15 Jeremiah stretched out his right hand and gave to Judas a golden sword, and as he gave it he addressed him thus: 16 "Take this holy sword, a gift from God, with which you will strike down your adversaries."

17 Encouraged by the words of Judas, so noble and so effective in arousing valour and awaking manliness in the souls of the young, they determined not to carry on a campaign but to attack bravely, and to decide the matter, by fighting hand to hand with all courage, because the city and the sanctuary and the temple were in danger. 18 Their concern for wives and children, and also for brethren and relatives, lay upon them less heavily; their greatest and first fear was for the consecrated sanctuary. 19 And those who had to remain in the city were in no little distress, being anxious over the encounter in the open country.

20 When all were now looking forward to the coming decision, and the enemy was already close at hand with their army drawn up for battle, the elephants *e* strategically stationed and the cavalry deployed on the flanks, 21 Maccabeus, perceiving the hosts that were before him and the varied supply of arms and the savagery of the elephants,*e* stretched out his hands toward heaven and called upon the Lord who works wonders; for he knew that it is not by arms, but as the Lord *f* decides, that he gains the victory for those who deserve it. 22 And he called upon him in these words: "O Lord, thou didst send thy angel in the time of Hezekiah king of Judea, and he slew fully a hundred and eighty-five thousand in the camp of Sennacherib. 23 So now, O Sovereign of the heavens, send a good angel to carry terror and trembling before us. 24 By the might of thy arm may these blasphemers who come against thy holy people be struck down." With these words he ended his prayer.

25 Nicanor and his men advanced with trumpets and battle songs; 26 and Judas and his men met the enemy in battle with invocation to God and prayers. 27 So, fighting with their hands and praying to God in

d The Gk text here is uncertain   *e* Gk *beasts*   *f* Gk *he*

249

their hearts, they laid low no less than thirty-five thousand men, and were greatly gladdened by God's manifestation.

28 When the action was over and they were returning with joy, they recognized Nicanor, lying dead, in full armour. 29 Then there was shouting and tumult, and they blessed the Sovereign Lord in the language of their fathers. 30 And the man who was ever in body and soul the defender of his fellow citizens, the man who maintained his youthful good will toward his countrymen, ordered them to cut off Nicanor's head and arm and carry them to Jerusalem. 31 And when he arrived there and had called his countrymen together and stationed the priests before the altar, he sent for those who were in the citadel. 32 He showed them the vile Nicanor's head and that profane man's arm, which had been boastfully stretched out against the holy house of the Almighty; 33 and he cut out the tongue of the ungodly Nicanor and said that he would give it piecemeal to the birds and hang up these rewards of his folly opposite the sanctuary. 34 And they all, looking to heaven, blessed the Lord who had manifested himself, saying, "Blessed is he who has kept his own place undefiled." 35 And he hung Nicanor's head from the citadel, a clear and conspicuous sign to every one of the help of the Lord. 36 And they all decreed by public vote never to let this day go unobserved, but to celebrate the thirteenth day of the twelfth month—which is called Adar in the Syrian language— the day before Mordecai's day.

37 This, then, is how matters turned out with Nicanor. And from that time the city has been in the possession of the Hebrews. So I too will here end my story. 38 If it is well told and to the point, that is what I myself desired; if it is poorly done and mediocre, that was the best I could do. 39 For just as it is harmful to drink wine alone, or, again, to drink water alone, while wine mixed with water is sweet and delicious and enhances one's enjoyment, so also the style of the story delights the ears of those who read the work. And here will be the end.